Applications, Challenges, and the Future of ChatGPT

Priyanka Sharma
Swami Keshvanand Institute of Technology, Management, and Gramothan, Jaipur, India

Monika Jyotiyana
Manipal University Jaipur, India

A.V. Senthil Kumar
Hindusthan College of Arts and Sciences, India

A volume in the Advances in Computational
Intelligence and Robotics (ACIR) Book Series

Published in the United States of America by
IGI Global
Engineering Science Reference (an imprint of IGI Global)
701 E. Chocolate Avenue
Hershey PA, USA 17033
Tel: 717-533-8845
Fax: 717-533-8661
E-mail: cust@igi-global.com
Web site: http://www.igi-global.com

Library of Congress Cataloging-in-Publication Data

CIP DATA PROCESSING

2024 Engineering Science Reference
ISBN(hc) 9798369368244 | ISBN(sc) 9798369368251 | eISBN 9798369368268

This book is published in the IGI Global book series Advances in Computational Intelligence and Robotics (ACIR) (ISSN: 2327-0411; eISSN: 2327-042X)

British Cataloguing in Publication Data
A Cataloguing in Publication record for this book is available from the British Library.

All work contributed to this book is new, previously-unpublished material. The views expressed in this book are those of the authors, but not necessarily of the publisher.

For electronic access to this publication, please contact: eresources@igi-global.com.

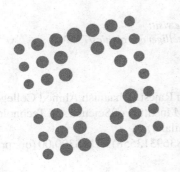

Advances in Computational Intelligence and Robotics (ACIR) Book Series

Ivan Giannoccaro
University of Salento, Italy

ISSN:2327-0411
EISSN:2327-042X

MISSION

While intelligence is traditionally a term applied to humans and human cognition, technology has progressed in such a way to allow for the development of intelligent systems able to simulate many human traits. With this new era of simulated and artificial intelligence, much research is needed in order to continue to advance the field and also to evaluate the ethical and societal concerns of the existence of artificial life and machine learning.

The **Advances in Computational Intelligence and Robotics (ACIR) Book Series** encourages scholarly discourse on all topics pertaining to evolutionary computing, artificial life, computational intelligence, machine learning, and robotics. ACIR presents the latest research being conducted on diverse topics in intelligence technologies with the goal of advancing knowledge and applications in this rapidly evolving field.

COVERAGE

- Natural Language Processing
- Computational Intelligence
- Neural Networks
- Fuzzy Systems
- Pattern Recognition
- Computer Vision
- Synthetic Emotions
- Adaptive and Complex Systems
- Evolutionary Computing
- Artificial Life

IGI Global is currently accepting manuscripts for publication within this series. To submit a proposal for a volume in this series, please contact our Acquisition Editors at Acquisitions@igi-global.com or visit: http://www.igi-global.com/publish/.

Titles in this Series

For a list of additional titles in this series, please visit:
http://www.igi-global.com/book-series/advances-computational-intelligence-robotics/73674

Explainable AI Applications for Human Behavior Analysis
P. Paramasivan (Dhaanish Ahmed College of Engineering, India) S. Suman Rajest (Dhaanish Ahmed College of Engineering, India) Karthikeyan Chinnusamy (Veritas, USA) R. Regin (SRM Institute of Science and Technology, India) and Ferdin Joe John Joseph (Thai-Nichi Institute of Technology, Thailand)
Engineering Science Reference • copyright 2024 • 369pp • H/C (ISBN: 9798369313558) • US $300.00 (our price)

Bio-Inspired Intelligence for Smart Decision-Making
Ramkumar Jaganathan (Sri Krishna Arts and Science College, India) Shilpa Mehta (Auckland University of Technology, New Zealand) and Ram Krishan (Mata Sundri University Girls College, Mansa, India)
Information Science Reference • copyright 2024 • 334pp • H/C (ISBN: 9798369352762) • US $385.00 (our price)

AI and IoT for Proactive Disaster Management
Mariyam Ouaissa (Chouaib Doukkali University, Morocco) Mariya Ouaissa (Cadi Ayyad University, Morocco) Zakaria Boulouard (Hassan II University, Casablanca, Morocco) Celestine Iwendi (University of Bolton, UK) and Moez Krichen (Al-Baha University, Saudi Arabia)
Engineering Science Reference • copyright 2024 • 299pp • H/C (ISBN: 9798369338964) • US $355.00 (our price)

Utilizing AI and Machine Learning for Natural Disaster Management
D. Satishkumar (Nehru Institute of Technology, India) and M. Sivaraja (Nehru Institute of Technology, India)
Engineering Science Reference • copyright 2024 • 340pp • H/C (ISBN: 9798369333624) • US $315.00 (our price)

Shaping the Future of Automation With Cloud-Enhanced Robotics
Rathishchandra Ramachandra Gatti (Sahyadri College of Engineering and Management, India) and Chandra Singh (Sahyadri College of Engineering and Management, India)
Engineering Science Reference • copyright 2024 • 431pp • H/C (ISBN: 9798369319147) • US $345.00 (our price)

Bio-inspired Swarm Robotics and Control Algorithms, Mechanisms, and Strategies
Parijat Bhowmick (Indian Institute of Technology, Guwahati, India) Sima Das (Bengal College of Engineering and Technology, India) and Farshad Arvin (Durham University, UK)
Engineering Science Reference • copyright 2024 • 261pp • H/C (ISBN: 9798369312773) • US $315.00 (our price)

Comparative Analysis of Digital Consciousness and Human Consciousness Bridging the Divide in AI Discourse
Remya Lathabhavan (Indian Institute of Management, Bodh Gaya, India) and Nidhi Mishra (Indian Institute of Management, Bodh Gaya, India)
Engineering Science Reference • copyright 2024 • 355pp • H/C (ISBN: 9798369320150) • US $315.00 (our price)

701 East Chocolate Avenue, Hershey, PA 17033, USA
Tel: 717-533-8845 x100 • Fax: 717-533-8661
E-Mail: cust@igi-global.com • www.igi-global.com

Table of Contents

Detailed Table of Contents

Chapter 1

Riaz Kurbanali Israni, RK University, India

This study delves into contemporary research trends in the dynamic field of artificial intelligence (AI), particularly focusing on ChatGPT and its synergies with other AI tools. The research investigates the evolving landscape of AI applications, emphasizing collaborative potentials and emerging paradigms. The exploration encompasses diverse domains such as natural language processing, machine learning, and human-computer interaction. Through a comprehensive analysis of recent literature, this abstract sheds light on the interplay between ChatGPT and other AI tools, examining their combined efficacy in addressing complex challenges. The study also explores the ethical implications and societal impacts associated with the integration of these technologies. By identifying current research gaps and potential future directions, this work contributes to the ongoing discourse surrounding AI advancements, fostering a deeper understanding of the synergistic possibilities in the realm of intelligent systems.

Chapter 2

V. Karthikeyan, Mepco Schlenk Engineering College, India
G. Kirubakaran, Mepco Schlenk Engineering College, India
R. Varun Prakash, Mepco Schlenk Engineering College, India
Y. Palin Visu, St. Mother Theresa Engineering College, India

The utilization of ChatGPT and other AI technologies has led to the emergence of novel and stimulating research avenues across various disciplines. Researchers are currently focusing on developing Conversational AI systems that can understand natural language and provide context-aware responses. An increasing number of individuals are choosing multimodal integration, enabling them to participate in more comprehensive conversations by combining text, pictures, and music. Investigating methods to mitigate bias and enhance response equity in language models like ChatGPT is a crucial field of research. This enables the provision of replies that are highly customized to the specific requirements of industries such as healthcare and finance. Enhancing the comprehensibility of AI judgments continues to be a primary focus, promoting openness and user confidence. The practical utilization of AI technologies emphasizes the user experience and usefulness by showcasing their real-world applications, which span from virtual assistance to customer care.

Large language model (LLM) ChatGPT has made tremendous progress in natural language processing (NLP), especially in human-quality text production, multilingual translation, and content creation. However, because of its extensive use, algorithmic issues, challenges, and theoretical queries come up. Fairness, bias, explainability, generalization, originality, inventiveness, and safety are the main topics of this study's examination of ChatGPT's intricate theoretical and algorithmic components. It looks into the possibility of explainability, transferability, generalization, bias in the data, and the model's capacity to provide original and imaginative content. It also covers possible issues including harmful use, disseminating incorrect information, and offensive or misleading content. These limitations can be addressed so that ChatGPT can be improved to provide LLMs that are more dependable, accountable, and long-lasting while posing no needless risks.

AI developments have led to the creation of complex language models like ChatGPT, which can produce text that appears human. Although ChatGPT has limitations, it can be helpful in elucidating concepts and offering basic guidance. It cannot access original medical databases or offer the most recent scientific knowledge. Public opinion in a number of areas, including healthcare, education, manufacturing, artificial intelligence (AI), machine revolution, science, industry, and cyber security, has been scrutinizing ChatGPT. However, there hasn't been as much research done on the analysis of ChatGPT studies in these settings. The present chapter looks at the various potential applications, difficulties, and upcoming projects for ChatGPT. A synopsis of studies on ChatGPT in the literature on applications is given by this review. The authors also offer a thorough and original assessment of ChatGPT's future concerns in Diff applications, including their promise and limitations.

Using regenerative artificial intelligence (AI) models, ChatGPT and its variations have quickly gained attention in scientific and public debate about the possible advantages and disadvantages they may have in economics, a republic, the community, and the environment. It is unclear if these advancements will create new jobs or eliminate existing ones, or if they redistribute human labour by producing additional knowledge and choices that may be insignificant or functionally unimportant. In light of the swift progress in productive neural networks (AI) as well as their arising consequences for job procedures worldwide and HR management in especially, this HRMJ argument writing generates jointly a variety of opinions concerning how we may improve HRM academic discourse. Giving a synopsis of the most recent advances in the discipline and creating a collection of possibilities for study are the main goals of this approach. By assuming tangible proof, we hope to advance the comprehension of artificial intelligence and push beyond the borders of what is currently known as science.

Chapter 6

Ajay Bhardwaj, Swami Keshvanand Institute of Technology, Management, and Gramothan, Jaipur, India
Sarfaraz Nawaz, Swami Keshvanand Institute of Technology, Management, and Gramothan, Jaipur, India

The successful implementation of the electricity market model has challenged the conventional way of operating the power system. In the electricity market model, power system is restructured to promote private companies to participate in a market structure where companies can sign a binding contract with large customers or can participate into pool market structure. Generation companies (GENCOs) and customers submit their bids in blocks in a pool market structure. GENCOs can achieve profit through strategic bidding due to the competitive nature of market structure. For this objective to realize, historical data of bidding of other participants should be modeled. This chapter addresses the application of dynamic programming, game theory and various AI based tools to form strategic bidding in the real time electricity market. To extend the analysis, a comparison of methods of designing bidding strategies has been presented. Based on this comparison, a critical review has been carried out to investigate the leading methods of strategic bidding.

Chapter 7

Soumya P. S., Karpagam Academy of Higher Education, India
S. Mythili, Karpagam Academy of Higher Education, India

The way that education is taught has changed dramatically since ChatGPT, a cutting-edge conversational AI model, was integrated into classrooms. This study looks into ChatGPT's wide-ranging implications on teaching strategies and outcomes. ChatGPT is an adaptation of technology that allows both teachers and students to create personalized, in-demand learning experiences. The major portion of technological changes in education are caused by the integration of chat GPT. This chapter analyses how chat GPT is involved in the way of teaching learning process and how it affects the revolution of education.

The goal of the proposed chapter is to give readers a thorough understanding of the complex effects of ChatGPT on higher education. It will cover the short- and long-term benefits that ChatGPT offers, as well as limitations that may affect both educators and learners. The chapter will also highlight a wide range of ethical issues and challenges that arise while using ChatGPT. Research in this area is very limited and the literature review reveals that there are benefits as well as limitations of using ChatGPT in the domain of higher education but the fact is that it is going to grow further which makes it an urgent need for the policymakers and stakeholders to explore and understand how ChatGPT should be integrated into higher education to deliver more value to the educators and learners. The proposed chapter will cover the evolution of ChatGPT, its growing popularity and impact, benefits it offers, the associated disadvantages and the road ahead.

This research investigates the transformative impact of integrating ChatGPT, an advanced language model, in education. Exploring its natural language processing and chatbot capabilities, the study analyzes its influence on personalized learning, student engagement, instructional support, and administrative efficiency. Through case studies, user feedback, and literature, it unveils ChatGPT's paradigm-shifting potential in shaping the future of education. This contributes valuable insights for educators, administrators, and policymakers navigating the digital era, highlighting AI's role in revolutionizing teaching and learning approaches. In the context of University 4.0, the emergence of ChatGPT sparks interest in its capacity to reshape higher education through AI-enabled chatbots, fostering personalized and interactive learning experiences.

In smart cities, generative artificial intelligence (AI) models such as ChatGPT have become revolutionary tools in many respects, chiefly due to their ability to process and communicate natural language. These artificial intelligence (AI) systems have greatly enhanced communication and problem-solving skills, leading to increased productivity and efficiency in a variety of fields, including healthcare, education, environmental monitoring, public health, smart grid management, traffic management, citizen engagement, environmental monitoring, and environmental monitoring. This study looks at ChatGPT's and similar Generative AI's changing role in smartcity contexts. It highlights the need for ethical frameworks and regulatory rules by examining the difficulties in putting them into practice. Concurrently, it highlights the enormous potential these technologies provide, from promoting inclusivity to igniting innovation, forming a future in which artificial intelligence augments human capabilities and fosters peaceful coexistence between sentient machines and people.

Chapter 11

Sachin Lalar, Kurukshetra University, India
Tajinder Kumar, Jai Parkash Mukand lal Innovative Engineering and Technology Institute, India
Rajinder Kumar, Punjab University, India
Shubham Kumar, IIMT University, India

The increasing popularity of large-scale language models, such as ChatGPT, has led to growing worries about their safety, potential security threats, and ethical implications. This chapter thoroughly examines ChatGPT, an AI-powered chatbot that utilizes topic modeling and reinforcement learning to generate natural and coherent answers. Even though ChatGPT has enormous promise in a variety of fields, it is crucial to critically assess its security, privacy, and ethical implications. By analyzing possible security flaws in ChatGPT deployment across several scenarios, the chapter begins a thorough investigation. The authors thoroughly examine the security concerns that come with the extensive use of this powerful language model, including exploiting its flaws via adversarial attacks and the unexpected ramifications in real-world applications. Finally, the authors examine the unresolved issues in these domains, encouraging collaborative endeavors to guarantee the advancement of safe and ethically extensive language models.

Chapter 12

Ayushi Agarwal, Swami Keshvanand Institute of Technology, Management, and Gramothan, Jaipur, India
Aaditya Trivedi, Swami Keshvanand Institute of Technology, Management, and Gramothan, Jaipur, India
Priyanka Sharma, Swami Keshvanand Institute of Technology, Management, and Gramothan, Jaipur, India
Ajay Bhardwaj, Swami Keshvanand Institute of Technology, Management, and Gramothan, Jaipur, India

The text explores the impact of large language models (LLMs), such as ChatGPT, on various industries, emphasizing their accessibility and efficiency. However, it highlights the limitations of LLMs, including token constraints, and the unexpected threat posed to creative jobs as AI models like DALL-E replicate art styles. Companies face a choice between AI-driven solutions and human consultants, with the importance of crafting effective prompts for LLMs emphasized. To adapt, startups and established companies must consider utilizing LLMs, even if lacking in-house expertise, to navigate the evolving landscape effectively, as AI continues to reshape industries and professional roles.

Chapter 13

Riaz Kurbanali Israni, RK University, India

ChatGPT, a cutting-edge language model, exemplifies the evolving capabilities of natural language processing. ChatGPT facilitates more nuanced and context-aware interactions, fostering seamless human-machine collaboration. Moreover, in education, the model's ability to generate informative and engaging content enhances personalized learning experiences. The integration of AI tools, driven by advancements in ChatGPT, revolutionizes industries by streamlining processes, automating tasks, and optimizing decision-making. Ethical considerations and responsible AI development remain integral to harnessing this potential. As society embraces these innovations, the future holds promise for increased efficiency, creativity, and connectivity. However, challenges related to privacy, bias, and the ethical use of AI necessitate ongoing scrutiny and regulation. The potential future with ChatGPT technology and AI tools is marked by both unprecedented opportunities and the imperative for responsible implementation.

In November 2022, OpenAI introduced ChatGPT, an AI chatbot tool built upon the generative pre-trained transformer (GPT) architecture. ChatGPT swiftly gained prominence on the internet, providing users with a platform to engage in conversations with an AI system, leveraging OpenAI's sophisticated language model. While ChatGPT exhibits remarkable capabilities, generating content spanning from tales, poetry, songs, and essays, it does have inherent limitations. Users can pose queries to the chatbot, which responds with relevant and persuasive information. The tool has garnered significant attention in academic circles, leading institutions to establish task forces and host widespread discussions on its adoption. This chapter offers an overview of ChatGPT and its significance, presenting a visual representation of Progressive Workflow Processes associated with the tool.

Preface

In the rapidly evolving landscape of artificial intelligence, few innovations have captured the imagination quite like ChatGPT. Born out of the quest to create AI systems that can understand and generate human-like text, ChatGPT has emerged as a versatile tool with a myriad of applications across various domains. This book is a testament to the journey of ChatGPT – from its inception to its current state, exploring its diverse applications, confronting the challenges it encounters, and envisioning its future trajectory. As we delve into the pages ahead, we invite you to embark on a journey of discovery, where we unravel the potential of ChatGPT and contemplate its implications for the world we inhabit.

The authors of the book *Applications, Challenges, and the Future of ChatGPT* discuss the promising applications, challenges and future aspects of ChatGPT. The book is organized into fourteen chapters, through a collection of insightful chapters authored by experts in the field, we aim to provide a comprehensive overview of the applications of ChatGPT across domains such as: medical, education, manufacturing, generative AI, machine revolution, science, industry, smart cities, intelligence approaches on human resource administration, real-time intelligent bidding in electricity markets, and more. Beginning with research trends and potentials of ChatGPT/other AI tools, algorithmic issues, challenges and theoretical concerns. The remaining chapters discuss the applications areas, possibilities and limitations, privacy, security and ethical concerns and potential future of ChatGPT. From conversational agents guiding users through complex tasks to creative collaborators sparking inspiration, ChatGPT has already begun to reshape how we interact with technology and each other.

However, amidst its remarkable capabilities, ChatGPT also faces its fair share of challenges. Ethical considerations, biases in training data, and the potential for misuse are just some of the hurdles that must be addressed as we navigate the ethical and societal implications of AI technology. Through candid discussions and critical reflections, we aim to confront these challenges head-on, fostering a deeper understanding of the responsibilities that come with the power of AI.

Chapter 1. Exploring Research Trends and Potentials in Conjunction with ChatGPT and Other AI Tools

The intersection of research trends and artificial intelligence tools, particularly ChatGPT, presents a captivating landscape for exploration and innovation. In recent years, AI has become an integral part of various fields, transforming the way we approach research and problem-solving. ChatGPT, a cutting-edge language model developed by OpenAI, stands out as a versatile tool that can be harnessed to enhance communication and generate human-like text. Its ability to understand context, respond contextually, and generate coherent and contextually relevant content opens up new possibilities for researchers seeking efficient ways to process and analyze vast amounts of information.

This book chapter demonstrates the notable aspect of this evolving landscape i.e. the symbiotic relationship between researchers and AI tools. ChatGPT, along with other advanced AI tools, acts as a facilitator in research endeavors by providing valuable insights, aiding in data analysis, and assisting in the formulation of hypotheses. As researchers increasingly integrate AI into their methodologies, the potential for uncovering patterns, predicting outcomes, and gaining deeper insights into complex phenomena grows exponentially. The synergy between human expertise and AI capabilities creates a dynamic environment where researchers can push the boundaries of their disciplines and make breakthroughs that were once thought unattainable.

Chapter 2. Trends and Research Potentials with the use of ChatGPT and Other AI Tools: Application and Challenges of Generative AI Tools

This chapter describes a revolutionary force, the incorporation of AI tools into the communication sphere that is changing the way people, companies, and communities interact with data. In this age of rapid technological development, artificial intelligence provides a set of potent tools that improve adaptability, understanding, and effectiveness throughout numerous forms of communication. The utilization of ChatGPT and other AI technologies has led to the emergence of novel and stimulating research avenues across various disciplines. Researchers are currently focusing on developing Conversational AI systems that can understand natural language and provide context-aware responses.

An increasing number of individuals are choosing multimodal integration, enabling them to participate in more comprehensive conversations by combining text, pictures, and music. Investigating methods to mitigate bias and enhance response equity in language models like ChatGPT is a crucial field of research. This enables the provision of replies that are highly customized to the specific requirements of industries such as healthcare and finance. Enhancing the comprehensibility of AI judgments continues to be a primary focus, promoting openness and user confidence. The practical utilization of AI technologies emphasizes the user experience and usefulness by showcasing their real-world applications, which span from virtual assistance to customer care.

Chapter 3. Algorithmic Issues, Challenges, and Theoretical Concerns of ChatGPT

Recent years have witnessed a notable improvement in the field of Natural Language Processing (NLP), with ChatGPT pushing the frontiers of conversational AI. However, alongside these advancements come algorithmic issues, challenges, and theoretical concerns that demand careful consideration and investigation. This chapter delves into the critical aspects surrounding ChatGPT, exploring the motivations behind addressing these issues, outlining proposed solutions, and providing an overview of the chapter's contents.

The motivation behind studying algorithmic issues, challenges, and theoretical concerns in ChatGPT stems from the dual objectives of advancing the capabilities of conversational AI while ensuring ethical and responsible deployment. Biases, fairness, interpretability, and performance optimization are among the key motivations driving this exploration, aiming to enhance the robustness, inclusivity, and reliability of AI-generated conversations.

The proposed work in this chapter encompasses a comprehensive analysis of algorithmic issues such as bias amplification, stereotypical responses, lack of diversity, contextual bias, data source bias, fairness, and equity within ChatGPT. Additionally, solutions and mitigation strategies, including bias detection techniques, fairness-aware training algorithms, data augmentation approaches, and contextual calibration methods, will be discussed and evaluated.

Chapter 4. Applications areas, Possibilities and Limitations of ChatGPT

This chapter examines the history, uses, main obstacles, and potential future developments of ChatGPT, a prominent artificial intelligence language model developed by Open AI. ChatGPT is a conversational Chabot that uses neural network architecture to process and comprehend natural language, making it applicable in various fields such as customer service, healthcare, and education. It marks a new era in AI's widespread use and application. AI developments have led to the creation of complex language models like ChatGPT, which can produce text that appears human. Although ChatGPT has limitations, it can be helpful in elucidating concepts and offering basic guidance. It cannot access original medical databases or offer the most recent scientific knowledge.

Public opinion in a number of areas, including healthcare, education, manufacturing, artificial intelligence (AI), machine revolution, science, industry, and cyber security, has been scrutinizing ChatGPT. However, there hasn't been as much research done on the analysis of ChatGPT studies in these settings. The present chapter looks at the various potential applications, difficulties, and upcoming projects for ChatGPT. A synopsis of studies on ChatGPT in the literature on applications is given by our review. We also offer a thorough and original assessment of ChatGPT's future concerns in Diff applications, including their promise and limitations.

Chapter 5. Insights and Future Prospects for ChatGPT: A Productive Computational Intelligence Approach on Administration of Human Resources

Over the past ten years, artificial intelligence (AI) tools and digital platforms—or at least devices and networks that assert "intelligent status" have established a necessary component of commercial organizations and civilization. This results from AI algorithms' greater cognitive and mathematical powers compared to humans, their capacity to simplify corporate operations, harvest information from huge data, and to make forecasts and suggestions. It is contradictory due to the fact it generates fresh data as well as judgments that must be taken in areas that may be of tremendous significance or mere insignificance, taking stuff out from people's hands while giving people additional duties to do.

This chapter involves a number of contemporary technical developments, that may be challenging to separate myth form reality, and AI has shown to be more effective in certain domains that some (e.g., producing written material that appears believable on the surface) (e.g., creating robotics with true agility). It is still unclear if artificial intelligence that regenerates devalue or kills, provides employment or generates new ones.

The different kinds of AI, including automated robotic procedures (such as autonomous machines in warehouses), techniques involving computer vision, recognizing words, deep-learning and machine-learning computations, and machine learning, have opened up a wide range possibilities and distinctive advantages for organizations to rethink company operations and procedures, develop ways to operate and customer experiences (like based on information flexible and target choices, handling projects, and other areas) and more.

Chapter 6. Bibliographical Survey of Extensive Uses of AI Based Tools in Real-Time Intelligent Bidding in Electricity Markets

Conventional power systems, consisting of vertical integrated utility suffer from rigidity, organizational complexity, management difficulties and risk of failure. The regulations which were followed earlier in these systems are not much relevant at the present time. Advanced technologies, research, integration of renewable sources and enhancement in security of power system and revenues demanded deregulation of power system. Deregulation or restructuring of power system required leniency in government policies and encouragement of private firms to participate in the operation of power system. This led to inception of market structure where public and/or private firms participate to sell produced power in blocks.

This chapter addresses the application of dynamic programming, game theory and various AI based tools to form strategic bidding in the real time electricity market. To extend the analysis, a comparison of methods of designing bidding strategies has been presented. Based on this comparison, a critical review has been carried out to investigate the leading methods of strategic bidding. Customer participation is of great significance here to improve energy efficiency and reliability. Large customers can play a vital role in the market structure as they can bid to purchase electricity. In a pool market structure, the market operator records the bid submitted by market participants and determines Market Clearing Price (MCP). MCP is an equilibrium price determined from the supply and demand curve and it is the maximum price at which energy can be sold or purchased. Prices remain close or moving towards MCP in a competitive market structure. But due to the oligopolistic nature of electricity markets, large companies can exercise market power and influence MCP.

Chapter 7. The Impact of ChatGPT on the Revolution of Educational Trends

The way that education is taught has changed dramatically since ChatGPT, a cutting-edge conversational AI model, was integrated into classrooms. This study looks into ChatGPT's wide-ranging implications on teaching strategies and outcomes. ChatGPT is an adaptation of technology that allows both teachers and students to create personalized, in-demand learning experiences. The major portion of technological changes in education is caused by the integration of chat GPT. This chapter analyses, how chat GPT is involved in the way of teaching learning process and how it effect in the revolution of education.

Modern machine learning model ChatGPT is well known for its ability to comprehend natural language. With incredible fluency and coherence, ChatGPT can comprehend, produce, and react to human language because to its transformer architecture, which it was trained on a massive quantity of text data. It is a flexible tool for a range of applications, including customer service, education, and entertainment, because to its capacity to have conversations, respond to inquiries, and deliver contextually relevant information. More natural interactions between humans and machines are made possible by ChatGPT, a notable development in the field of artificial intelligence because to its versatility and ability to comprehend complex linguistic patterns.

Chapter 8. Beyond Boundaries - Role of Artificial Intelligence and ChatGPT in Transforming Higher Education

Artificial intelligence (AI) is proving to be a disruptive force across several industries, catalysing innovative breakthroughs that are reshaping the manner that we live and work. One domain where AI's impact is particularly profound is education, an essential component of societal evolution and individual development. The amalgamation of AI tools into educational systems aims to redefine the learning experience for students, the teaching methods for educators, and the overall functioning of institutions. By tailoring learning and development experiences to individual needs, automating administrative tasks, and facilitating instantaneous feedback, AI is dramatically changing the educational landscape, enhancing its inclusivity and effectiveness. However, as AI advances, it has become imperative that we consider its ramifications and adopt safeguards to ensure its responsible use.

The goal of this chapter is to give readers a thorough understanding of the complex effects of ChatGPT on higher education. It will cover the short- and long-term benefits that ChatGPT offers, as well as limitations that may affect both educators and learners. The chapter will also highlight a wide range of ethical issues and challenges that arise while using ChatGPT. Research in this area is very limited and the literature review reveals that there are benefits as well as limitations of using ChatGPT in the domain of higher education but the fact is that it is going to grow further which makes it an urgent need for the policymakers and stakeholders to explore and understand how ChatGPT should be integrated into higher education to deliver more value to the educators and learners. The proposed chapter will cover the evolution of ChatGPT, its growing popularity and impact, benefits it offers, the associated disadvantages and the road ahead.

One prominent application of AI in the field of education is natural language processing (NLP), exemplified by intelligent chatbots that have transformed customer service across various industries. In education, the application of chatbots is continuously on the rise, with studies revealing their potential to enhance students' learning experiences. In November 2022, the launch of ChatGPT marked a pivotal moment in adopting AI in education. Its exceptional comprehension and responding abilities captured the attention of a diverse audience and sparked debates within the entire educational community including basic level and higher level of education. A more conversational and natural method of computer interaction is made possible by the language model known as ChatGPT. The term GPT, "Generative Pre-trained Transformer," refers to a group of natural language models created via open artificial intelligence (AI). Because of its capacity to generate unique outcomes, this is often referred to as generative AI.

Chapter 9. Examining the Paradigm Shifting Potential of ChatGPT with AI-enabled Chatbots in Teaching and Learning: Shaping University 4.0 System

Universities are continually looking for new ideas to enhance the teaching and learning expertise for their students in the ever-changing educational landscape. Artificial intelligence technology advancements have created new opportunities for modernizing static educational systems into dynamic and individualized learning environment. The development of chatbots, intelligent conversational agents that can interact with students in a natural and effective way, is one area where AI has shown enormous potential. With an emphasis on their effects on teaching and learning, this study states to explore the paradigm-shifting capabilities of AI-enabled chatbots in defining the university 4.0 system.

This chapter investigates the transformative impact of integrating ChatGPT, an advanced language model, in education. Exploring its natural language processing and chatbot capabilities, the study analyzes its influence on personalized learning, student engagement, instructional support, and administrative efficiency. Through case studies, user feedback, and literature, it unveils ChatGPT's paradigm-shifting potential in shaping the future of education. This contributes valuable insights for educators, administrators, and policymakers navigating the digital era, highlighting AI's role in revolutionizing teaching and learning approaches. In the context of university 4.0, the emergence of ChatGPT sparks interest in its capacity to reshape higher education through AI-enabled chatbots, fostering personalized and interactive learning experiences.

The term "University 4.0" alludes to the fourth industrial revolution, in which various facets of higher education are automated and digital technologies are integrated. Chatbots powered by AI have the potential to transform the environment of educational sector delivering individualized help, encouraging active interaction, and reducing administrative procedures.

Numerous opportunities arise from the incorporation of AI-enabled Chatbots in learning and teaching contexts. These Chatbots can serve as online instructors, directing learners along personalized learning pathways, giving immediate feedback, and addressing specific learning needs. By using AI algorithms and the processing of natural language abilities, chatbots can adapt to the choices, methods of learning, and pace of students, enhancing the efficacy of the educational process.

Chapter 10. Role of ChatGPT in Smart Cities

A smart city, at its foundation, is an urban area that uses the Internet of Things (IoT) and data-driven technology to enhance many facets of city life. These communities hope to give their residents a smooth and sustainable living environment by incorporating state-of-the-art technology into their infrastructure.

Natural language inquiries can be understood and answered using ChatGPT, an artificial intelligence program that is language-based. It has the ability to comprehend intricate instructions and queries and to respond with precision and speed. Because it helps cities to manage their operations more effectively and respond to citizen requests promptly, it is a crucial tool for smart city initiatives.

This study looks at ChatGPT's and similar Generative AI's changing role in smartcity contexts. It highlights the need for ethical frameworks and regulatory rules by examining the difficulties in putting them into practice. Concurrently, it highlights the enormous potential these technologies provide, from promoting inclusivity to igniting innovation, forming a future in which artificial intelligence augments human capabilities and fosters peaceful coexistence between sentient machines and people.

Chapter 11. Unveiling Privacy, Security and Ethical Concerns of ChatGPT

Large language Models (LLMs) demonstrate notable performance improvements compared to smaller models when their parameters reach a certain scale. They excel in producing language outputs that are more accurate and cohesive. LLMs demonstrate superior proficiency in language comprehension and creating activities. They are adept at handling complicated linguistic situations because they have the ability to decipher subtle human language as described by grammatical rules. They have advanced language comprehension and generation skills, which enable them to perceive complex human emotions and adhere to grammatical intricacies with remarkable grace.

The ability of models such as ChatGPT to engage in coherent and engaging conversations has garnered attention, representing a significant advancement in the field of dialogue systems driven by artificial intelligence. In addition to being highly beautiful, these models are capable of comprehensive representation of the complexity of human language because to their ability to recognize patterns and subtleties seen in large-scale corpora. This learning potential pushes the boundaries of what is possible in the field of natural language generation and interpretation, positioning wide language models as essential tools for language modelling and analysis tasks.

This chapter thoroughly examines ChatGPT, an AI-powered chatbot that utilizes topic modeling and reinforcement learning to generate natural and coherent answers. Even though ChatGPT has enormous promise in a variety of fields, it is crucial to critically assess its security, privacy, and ethical implications. By analyzing possible security flaws in ChatGPT deployment across several scenarios, the chapter begins a thorough investigation. We thoroughly examine the security concerns that come with the extensive use of this powerful language model, including exploiting its flaws via adversarial attacks and the unexpected ramifications in real-world applications. Finally, the unresolved issues in these domains are examined, encouraging collaborative endeavors to guarantee the advancement of safe and ethically extensive language models.

Chapter 12. Use-Cases of ChatGPT and Other AI Tools With Security Concerns

As the industry has made progress toward Artificial Intelligence and has in turn invested in training Large Language Models (LLM) to understand our language and act as a tool that can under such language. The processing that these LLMs are using is called the Natural Language Process (NLP) which is basically a branch in Artificial Intelligence that aims to make machines capable of understanding as well as generating human language in such a way that it is meaningful. The organization that is taking the world by storm in the LLM market is currently OpenAI, which has developed ChatGPT 3.5 as well as the new rendition of the family, ChatGPT 4. Although the company has been working on these LLMs for quite a while now as the GPT 3 model was a marvel of technology and Generative Pre-trained Transformer (GPT in ChatGPT) was fine-tuned with the number of tokens, the correctness of the information, and a better understanding of the human language.

The chapter explores the impact of Large Language Model ChatGPT, on various industries, emphasizing their accessibility and efficiency. However, it highlights the limitations of LLMs, including token constraints, and the unexpected threat posed to creative jobs as AI models like DALL-E replicate art styles. Companies face a choice between AI-driven solutions and human consultants, with the importance of crafting effective prompts for LLMs emphasized. To adapt, startups and established companies must consider utilizing LLMs, even if lacking in-house expertise, to navigate the evolving landscape effectively, as AI continues to reshape industries and professional roles.

Chapter 13. The Potential Future with ChatGPT Technology and AI Tools

The potential future with ChatGPT technology and AI tools holds tremendous promise across various aspects of human life. As we continue to advance in the area of Artificial Intelligence (AI), an impact of these technologies is likely to be profound, influencing how we work, communicate, learn, and solve complex problems. ChatGPT and similar AI tools are at the forefront of revolutionizing communication (Rathore, 2023). NLP (Natural Language Processing) capabilities allow these organisms to realize

& generate human-like text, facilitating more seamless and effective interactions. In the future, we can expect improved language models to enhance communication across languages and cultures, making global collaboration more accessible.

AI tools, containing ChatGPT, enclose the capacity to afford modified and efficient assistance in various domains. From customer support to educational tutoring, these systems can understand individual needs and deliver targeted information or solutions. The future may see further developments in creating AI companions that offer emotional support and personalized guidance. The combination of AI tools in teaching & learning is likely to transform a learning experience. Intelligent tutoring systems are able to acclimatize to personal education techniques, providing tailored lessons and response. The ChatGPT could play a role in enhancing virtual classrooms, supporting students with instant answers to questions and fostering interactive learning environments.

This chapter demonstrates the transformative changes across diverse domains. ChatGPT, a cutting-edge language model, exemplifies the evolving capabilities of natural language processing. ChatGPT facilitates more nuanced and context-aware interactions, fostering seamless human-machine collaboration. Moreover, in education, the model's ability to generate informative and engaging content enhances personalized learning experiences. The integration of AI tools, driven by advancements in ChatGPT, revolutionizes industries by streamlining processes, automating tasks, and optimizing decision-making. Ethical considerations and responsible AI development remain integral to harnessing this potential. As society embraces these innovations, the future holds promise for increased efficiency, creativity, and connectivity. However, challenges related to privacy, bias, and the ethical use of AI necessitate ongoing scrutiny and regulation. The potential future with ChatGPT technology and AI tools is marked by both unprecedented opportunities & the imperative for responsible implementation.

Chapter 14. The Future of ChatGPT: Exploring Features, Capabilities, and Challenges as a Leading Support Tool

The swift advancement in natural language processing (NLP) and artificial intelligence (AI) has led to the creation of increasingly complex and adaptable language models, such as ChatGPT. A branch of AI known as "generative AI" deals with models that can produce new data from preexisting data in a variety of domains, including text, images, and music, by using learnt patterns and structures. These generative AI models, like ChatGPT, use deep learning techniques and neural networks to evaluate, understand, and produce material that appears to be human-generated. It delves into the specific features and capabilities of the ChatGPT Support System. Finally, explore and discuss the pivotal roles played by ChatGPT in the contemporary landscape. The neural language models underpinning character AI have been meticulously designed to understand and generate human-like text. This technology processes and creates text using DL methods, utilizing vast internet databases to understand the subtleties of natural language.

ChatGPT swiftly gained prominence on the internet, providing users with a platform to engage in conversations with an AI system, leveraging OpenAI's sophisticated language model. While ChatGPT exhibits remarkable capabilities, generating content spanning from tales, poetry, songs, to essays, it does have inherent limitations. Users can pose queries to the chatbot, which responds with relevant and persuasive information. The tool has garnered significant attention in academic circles, leading institutions to establish task forces and host widespread discussions on its adoption. This chapter offers an overview of ChatGPT and its significance, presenting a visual representation of Progressive Workflow Processes associated with the tool.

As we embark on this journey together, we invite you to join the conversation, to challenge assumptions, and to envision the possibilities that lie ahead. Whether you are a seasoned researcher, a curious enthusiast, or simply intrigued by the potential of AI, we hope that this book will serve as a valuable resource and inspire further exploration into the world of ChatGPT.

Happy reading!

Priyanka Sharma
Swami Keshvanand Institute of Technology, Management, and Gramothan, Jaipur, India

Monika Jyotiyana
Manipal University Jaipur, India

A V Senthil Kumar
Hindusthan College of Arts and Sciences, India

Acknowledgment

The book *Applications, Challenges, and the Future of ChatGPT* is based on trends, research potentials, features, capabilities, algorithmic issues, challenges, and theoretical concerns of ChatGPT along with applications areas, possibilities, limitations, insights, future prospects and extensive uses of AI based tools. This book very effectively demonstrates the impact of ChatGPT on the revolution of educational trends, paradigm-shifting potential of ChatGPT, role of ChatGPT in smart cities, privacy, security and ethical concerns, use-cases and the potential the future of ChatGPT.

Planning and designing a book outline to introduce to readers across the globe is the passion and noble goal of the editor. Editors tried to be able to make ideas to a reality and the success of this book where the biggest reward is efforts, knowledge, skills, expertise, experiences, enthusiasm, collaboration, and trust of the contributors. We express our deepest thanks to all the contributors who have submitted their chapters from which 14 quality chapters have been selected post review for the publication in the book. We acknowledge the tremendous support and valuable comments of the esteemed advisory members and reviewers throughout the globe for their valuable suggestions to improve and enhance the quality of the book, with whom we have had the opportunity to collaborate and monitor their hard work remotely, not only for this book but also for future book projects. We also express our deep gratitude for all the pieces of discussion, advice, support, motivation, sharing, collaboration, and inspiration we received from our faculty, contributors, educators, professors, scientists, scholars, engineers, and academic colleagues. At last, but not least, we are really grateful to our publisher IGI Global for the wonderful support in making sure the timely processing of the manuscript and bringing out this book to the readers soonest.

Priyanka Sharma would dedicate this book to her parents Shri Atmaram Sharma and Smt. Geeta Sharma who have always been a backbone to her, for allowing and foregoing the quality time dedicated to this book. A special acknowledgement of all the near and dear ones. Last but not the least special thanks to book co-editors Dr. Monika Jyotiyana and Dr. A. V. Senthil Kumar who have been constantly the driving force behind this project.

Dr. Monika Jyotiyana would like to dedicate this book to her parents, husband and her best friend Mrs. Sonali Jain who have always been good supporters in managing and editing the book. Special thanks to editor Ms. Priyanka Sharma, without her support and vision, the book can't be a good success.

Thank you, everyone.

Priyanka Sharma
Swami Keshvanand Institute of Technology, Management, and Gramothan, Jaipur, India

Monika Jyotiyana
Manipal University Jaipur, India

A V Senthil Kumar
Hindusthan College of Arts and Sciences, India

Chapter 1
Exploring Research Trends and Potential in Conjunction With ChatGPT and Other AI Tools

Riaz Kurbanali Israni
iD https://orcid.org/0000-0001-7185-4132
RK University, India

ABSTRACT

This study delves into contemporary research trends in the dynamic field of artificial intelligence (AI), particularly focusing on ChatGPT and its synergies with other AI tools. The research investigates the evolving landscape of AI applications, emphasizing collaborative potentials and emerging paradigms. The exploration encompasses diverse domains such as natural language processing, machine learning, and human-computer interaction. Through a comprehensive analysis of recent literature, this abstract sheds light on the interplay between ChatGPT and other AI tools, examining their combined efficacy in addressing complex challenges. The study also explores the ethical implications and societal impacts associated with the integration of these technologies. By identifying current research gaps and potential future directions, this work contributes to the ongoing discourse surrounding AI advancements, fostering a deeper understanding of the synergistic possibilities in the realm of intelligent systems.

INTRODUCTION

The intersection of research trends and artificial intelligence tools, particularly ChatGPT, presents a captivating landscape for exploration and innovation. In recent years, AI has become an integral part of various fields, transforming the way we approach research and problem-solving. ChatGPT, a cutting-edge language model developed by OpenAI, stands out as a versatile tool that can be harnessed to enhance communication and generate human-like text. Its ability to understand context, respond contextually, and generate coherent and contextually relevant content opens up new possibilities for researchers seeking efficient ways to process and analyze vast amounts of information.

DOI: 10.4018/979-8-3693-6824-4.ch001

Figure 1. Research trends and potentials in the market with ChatGPT / AI tools

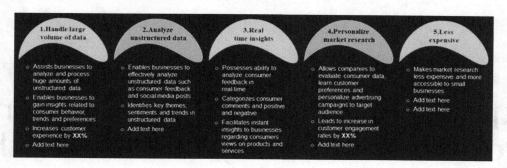

One notable aspect of this evolving landscape is the symbiotic relationship between researchers and AI tools. ChatGPT, along with other advanced AI tools, acts as a facilitator in research endeavors by providing valuable insights, aiding in data analysis, and assisting in the formulation of hypotheses (Lancaster, 2023). As researchers increasingly integrate AI into their methodologies, the potential for uncovering patterns, predicting outcomes, and gaining deeper insights into complex phenomena grows exponentially. The synergy between human expertise and AI capabilities creates a dynamic environment where researchers can push the boundaries of their disciplines and make breakthroughs that were once thought unattainable. ChatGPT and AI tool is changing market research and potential like handle large volume of database as per below figure.

The implications of leveraging ChatGPT and other AI tools in research extend beyond specific domains, reaching into areas such as natural language processing, data interpretation, and even interdisciplinary collaboration. As we navigate this frontier, ethical considerations, responsible AI usage, and transparent communication about the limitations and biases of AI models become paramount (Ronanki *et al.,* 2022). By understanding and harnessing the potentials of AI tools like ChatGPT, researchers can pave the way for a future where human-machine collaboration propels scientific discovery and innovation to unprecedented heights (Ronanki *et al.,* 2022).

LITERATURE REVIEW

The research on ChatGPT encompasses a wide array of studies that delve into its various research, potentials and applications. These studies have been classified into five distinct categories based on their context and focus. These categories are,

A. Healthcare: Within this domain, studies investigate how ChatGPT can be utilized to enhance healthcare services, including patient support, mental health counseling, medical data analysis, and assisting healthcare professionals in decision-making processes.

ChatGPT holds the promise of transforming the healthcare sector through enhancements in patient outcomes, cost reduction, and the streamlining of diagnosis and treatment processes, leading to greater efficiency and precision. (Table 1)

B. Natural Language Processing: Research in this category explores the capabilities of ChatGPT in understanding and generating human-like text, advancing techniques in language understanding,

Table 1. Literature review for research and potentials in healthcare sector

Reference	Main Contributions	Significant Strengths	Shortcomings
(Rajest *et al.,* 2023)	Transforming the landscape: AI-enhanced medical education	ChatGPT boasts a heightened potential as a more precise and expedient AI model, engaging in critical discussions surrounding the ethical implications entailed by its implementation	Limited sample size and Absence of compelling evidence demonstrating the superiority of AI-assisted medical education over traditional methods
(Reyes *et al.,* 2020)	ChatGPT offers precise and tailored ophthalmological guidance at an affordable rate	Precise diagnoses and treatment options, Equips doctors with a variety of approaches for patient care	Does not fully explore the potential of ChatGPT in various medical specialties and does not provide comparisons with similar systems
(Mandapuram *et al.,* 2018)	ChatGPT was tasked with summarizing research on environmental health	ChatGPT enhances scholarly exploration by making research more accessible, while its summaries facilitate effective communication	Fails to offer enhancement suggestions and Disregards ethical considerations
(Kumar *et al.,* 2023)	ChatGPT-powered NLP systems demonstrate exceptional precision in streamlining radiology reports	Simplify radiology reports for enhanced comprehension and present a case study detailing current methodologies and their constraints	Limited sample size, absence of accuracy evaluation, and insufficient data on potential consequences

generation, and dialogue systems. ChatGPT's advancements in NLP have the potential to transform human-machine interaction and language data processing.

This chapter assesses ChatGPT's dialogue quality against human experts, using a comparison corpus and three evaluation metrics. They also devise a model to distinguish human and ChatGPT dialogues. Results show ChatGPT performs comparably to humans. Yet, the chapter lacks comprehensive evaluation, focusing narrowly on metrics and neglecting aspects like accuracy, fluency, and scalability. Summarized analysis for NLP is described in Table 2.

C. Education: Research in this area examines the potential of ChatGPT in educational settings, such as personalized tutoring, language learning, automated grading, and educational content generation. ChatGPT possesses the capability to revolutionize education by delivering tailored, student-centric learning opportunities, thereby bolstering academic achievements and fostering student triumph. (Table 3)

D. Industry: Studies focusing on the industrial applications of ChatGPT explore its use cases in customer service, marketing, content creation, automation of repetitive tasks, and improving overall operational efficiency in various sectors. ChatGPT revolutionizes industries, enhancing customer service, marketing, and operations, yielding insights across sectors for heightened satisfaction and efficiency. (Table 4)

E. Ethics: This category addresses the ethical considerations surrounding the development and deployment of ChatGPT, including issues related to bias, privacy, fairness, transparency, and responsible AI usage. ChatGPT has sparked extensive discourse within the realm of ethics, primarily concerning its potential societal ramifications. (Table 5)

Table 2. Literature review for research and potentials in NLP area

Reference	Main Contributions	Significant Strengths	Shortcomings
(Roumeliotis et al., 2023)	Explored the intricacies of linguistic ambiguity within ChatGPT and its implications for Natural Language Processing (NLP)	Enhancing disambiguation tasks via context-based analysis and extracting invaluable insights for leveraging transformer-based language models within NLP systems	Failed to acknowledge linguistic characteristics or resource constraints, nor did it offer innovative approaches to resolve linguistic ambiguity
(Yan et al., 2023)	Examines the machine translation proficiency of ChatGPT	Explores insights, methodologies, and constraints in assessing ChatGPT's translation proficiency	Insufficient test data coverage and a lack of comprehensive analysis of translation performance
(Cooper, 2023)	Comparison of ChatGPT's zero-shot learning performance with GPT-3.5 across diverse NLP tasks	Empirical research, Qualitative analyses, and Zero-shot evaluation comparisons	Absence of scrutiny regarding fine-tuning nuances and ethical implications
(Rosselló-Geli, 2022)	Assessing conversation quality between ChatGPT and humans utilizing a dataset and three metrics	Evaluated ChatGPT's performance against that of human experts and proposed a method for identifying chatbot impersonation	The assessment of ChatGPT's performance remains unfinished, as it primarily concentrates on a restricted set of metrics
(Mandapuram et al., 2018)	Assessed and scrutinized the performance of ChatGPT across three tasks, pinpointing areas ripe for enhancement and exploring potential applications	Updating the line: Introducing a pioneering evaluation framework for conversational agents	Inadequate support for the proposed evaluation methods. Absence of specifics regarding the training data and evaluation metrics

Table 3. Literature review for research and potentials in education

Reference	Main Contributions	Significant Strengths	Shortcomings
(Kumar et al., 2023)	Revolutionize Education with ChatGPT	Exploring ChatGPT's role in education	Insufficient sample size and Restricted ethical analysis
(Geis et al., 2019)	In addressing mathematical inquiries and resolving mathematical challenges, ChatGPT outperforms other models	ChatGPT for advanced tutoring systems	Theoretical approach devoid of empirical evidence and deficient in metrics or results demonstrating effectiveness
(Kumar et al., 2023)	Enhance and revolutionize library reference services	Impact analysis of ChatGPT and its implications for society and stakeholders	Needs elaboration regarding the benefits, implementation, and ethical considerations of ChatGPT

Table 4. Literature review for research and potentials in industry

Reference	Main Contributions	Significant Strengths	Shortcomings
(Faggiano et al., 2021)	Construction project scheduling for ChatGPT's project	Mining data solutions and Time-saving techniques	Insufficient details regarding implementation of ChatGPT and Absence of dependable data
(Wang et al., 2022)	Exploring ChatGPT's capabilities and constraints in the design process	Exploring advantages and constraints within the design process	Limitations in transferability and Objective Assessments
(Fui-Hoon et al., 2023)	Enhanced financial research with ChatGPT	NLP's innovative approach	Constricted focus, Limited financial information and Inadequate exploration of implications

Table 5. Literature review for research and potentials in ethics

Reference	Main Contributions	Significant Strengths	Shortcomings
(Imran *et al.*, 2023)	Improving plagiarism detection beyond current methods, achieving an accuracy rate of 88.3%.	Referring to ChatGPT as a tool for identifying plagiarism	Lack of substantiated evidence and a dearth of thorough ethical discourse pertaining to ChatGPT's plagiarism detection
(Rawat *et al.*, 2023)	ChatGPT for societal advancement and public welfare	Explores the latest advancements in chatbots and Provides insight into the rationale behind intricate decision-making processes	Insufficient consideration of the repercussions on privacy, security, and ethics
(Sharma *et al.*, 2023)	Evaluates ChatGPT for biases, reliability, robustness, and toxicity	Identifies emerging ethical hazards and Bridges deficiencies in prior investigations	Insufficient quantitative analysis and Restricted exploration of alternative LLMs

THE RISE OF AI IN RESEARCH

The integration of AI tools into the research process has become a cornerstone of contemporary scientific exploration. AI technologies, including natural language processing (NLP) models like ChatGPT, have empowered researchers to analyze vast amounts of data, extract meaningful insights, and accelerate the pace of discovery. As a result, the scientific community is witnessing a paradigm shift in how research is conducted, with AI playing a pivotal role in various stages of the research lifecycle.

AI technologies, particularly machine learning (ML) and deep learning, have significantly enhanced the efficiency, speed, and capabilities of research processes. Here are some key areas where AI has made a notable impact (Mandapuram *et al.*, 2018).

Data Analysis and Pattern Recognition

Data Analysis and Pattern Recognition are crucial components of Artificial Intelligence (AI) in research, driving insights and innovation across diverse domains. In the realm of data analysis, researchers leverage AI algorithms to sift through vast datasets, identifying trends, correlations, and anomalies (Mandapuram *et al.*, 2018). Techniques such as machine learning and statistical analysis enable the extraction of meaningful information, offering a deeper understanding of complex phenomena.

Pattern recognition, an integral aspect of AI, involves the identification of recurring structures or behaviors within data. In research, this aids in recognizing subtle patterns that may elude human observation. AI-powered pattern recognition facilitates the detection of trends over time, contributing to predictive modeling and forecasting. Researchers harness the power of AI for data classification, clustering, and regression analysis, streamlining the interpretation of complex information. Machine learning models, such as neural networks, excel in recognizing intricate patterns, allowing for more accurate predictions and informed decision-making.

AI-driven data analysis enhances efficiency by automating repetitive tasks, enabling researchers to focus on higher-level thinking and hypothesis formulation. This synergy between AI and data analysis accelerates the pace of research, fostering breakthroughs in fields like medicine, finance, and environmental science.

Figure 2. Various categories of data analysis

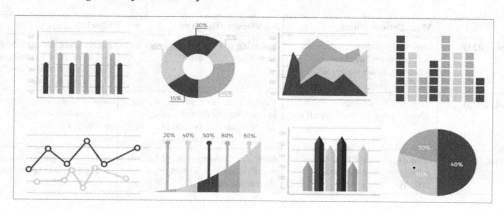

Figure 3. Different techniques for pattern recognition

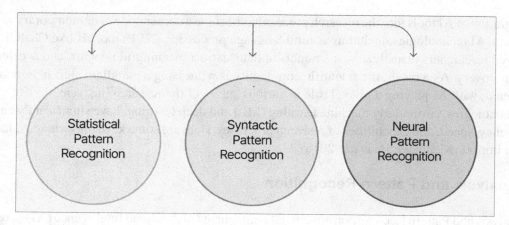

Data Analysis and Pattern Recognition with AI in research marks a transformative era, unlocking new possibilities and revolutionizing the way we extract knowledge from data. This symbiotic relationship propels scientific inquiry, paving the way for advancements that shape the future of research across diverse disciplines.

Drug Discovery and Healthcare

The integration of artificial intelligence (AI) in drug discovery has ushered in a transformative era for healthcare research. AI algorithms are adept at analyzing vast datasets, identifying patterns, and predicting potential drug candidates with unprecedented speed and accuracy. This has significantly accelerated the drug discovery process, reducing the time and resources required to bring new therapies to market. Machine learning models can analyze biological data, including genomics and proteomics, to uncover potential drug targets and predict the efficacy of different compounds. Additionally, AI enables the exploration of complex interactions within biological systems, leading to a more comprehensive understanding of diseases and their underlying mechanisms (Kumar *et al.*, 2023). The rise of AI in drug

Figure 4. AI based healthcare organism

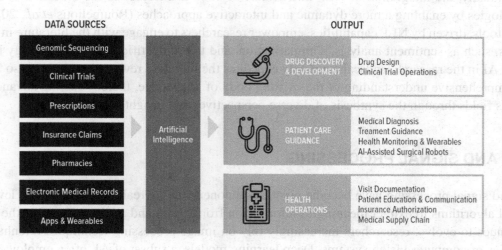

Figure 5. Rise of AI in NLP

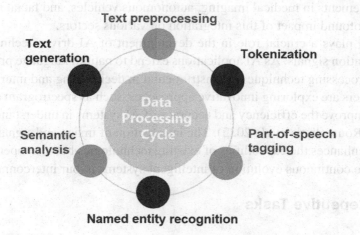

discovery not only expedites the development of novel treatments but also enhances the precision and personalization of healthcare interventions.

In healthcare, AI is revolutionizing various aspects of patient care and management. Advanced AI algorithms can analyze medical records, diagnostic images, and patient data to aid in disease diagnosis and treatment planning. This allows for more accurate and timely diagnoses, leading to improved patient outcomes. AI-driven technologies also contribute to the optimization of hospital operations, resource allocation, and patient management. With the integration of AI, healthcare professionals can leverage predictive analytics to anticipate disease trends, customize treatment plans, and enhance preventive care strategies. The synergy between AI and healthcare is creating a more efficient, personalized, and data-driven approach to medicine, ultimately improving the quality of patient care on a global scale.

Additionally, the integration of NLP in literature reviews contributes to the evolution of research methodologies by enabling a more dynamic and interactive approaches (Roumeliotis *et al.,* 2023). AI-powered tools, driven by NLP capabilities, empower researchers to engage with the literature in innovative ways, such as sentiment analysis, summarization, and trend identification. This synergy between NLP and AI in the research landscape not only expedites the literature review process but also fosters a more comprehensive understanding of the existing body of knowledge, thereby fueling advancements in various fields through the synthesis of diverse perspectives and insights.

IMAGE AND SIGNAL PROCESSING

Image and signal processing have become pivotal components in the realm of AI research, leveraging advanced algorithms to extract meaningful information from visual and auditory data. As the field of AI continues to evolve, researchers increasingly rely on image processing techniques to enhance the capabilities of computer vision systems. Deep learning models, a subset of AI, often employ convolution neural networks (CNNs) for image recognition tasks, utilizing intricate signal processing methods to identify patterns and features within vast datasets. The synergy between AI and image processing has propelled advancements in medical imaging, autonomous vehicles, and facial recognition systems, demonstrating the profound impact of this integration on various sectors.

Signal processing plays a crucial role in the development of AI-driven technologies that rely on audio and communication signals. As AI applications extend to natural language processing and speech recognition, signal processing techniques are instrumental in deciphering and interpreting complex auditory data. Researchers are exploring innovative approaches, such as spectrogram analysis and wavelet transformations, to improve the efficiency and accuracy of AI systems in understanding and responding to spoken language (Roumeliotis *et al.,* 2023). The intersection of image and signal processing with AI in research not only enhances the capabilities of existing technologies but also opens doors to novel applications, driving the continuous evolution of intelligent systems in our interconnected world.

Automation of Repetitive Tasks

The rise of artificial intelligence (AI) has significantly influenced the automation of repetitive tasks in research, revolutionizing the way scientific investigations are conducted. AI-driven automation has

Figure 6. AI based automation for the repetitive task

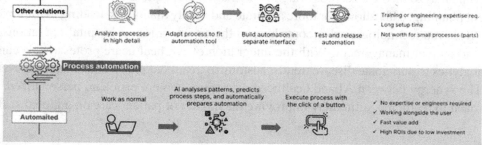

the potential to accelerate research processes by taking over monotonous and repetitive tasks, allowing researchers to focus on more complex and creative aspects of their work. Here's how solutions like "automated" are bridging these gaps with AI-powered automation.

Tasks such as data collection, analysis, and literature reviews can be efficiently handled by AI algorithms, saving researchers valuable time and resources.

RISE OF AI IN NATURAL LANGUAGE PROCESSING (NLP)

Natural Language Processing (NLP) has emerged as a pivotal component in the realm of AI-driven research, marking a significant paradigm shift in how information is processed and analyzed in the context of literature reviews. As the rise of AI in research gains momentum, NLP plays a crucial role in automating the extraction, organization, and synthesis of information from vast amounts of textual data. Researchers can leverage NLP algorithms to sift through extensive literary databases, identify relevant themes, and extract valuable insights from scholarly articles, books, and other textual sources. This not only accelerates the literature review process but also enhances the precision and depth of analysis, allowing researchers to uncover patterns and connections that might be challenging to discern through traditional manual methods. NLP covers a wide range of activities, including text summarization, named entity recognition, text generation, sentiment analysis, language translation, and sentiment analysis.

COLLABORATIVE RESEARCH

Collaborative research in the realm of artificial intelligence (AI) has become increasingly essential as the field continues to advance at a rapid pace. The interdisciplinary nature of AI research, which incorporates elements of computer science, mathematics, neuroscience, and more, necessitates the collaboration of experts from various domains. As AI technologies evolve and find applications in diverse fields such as healthcare, finance, and autonomous systems, researchers from different disciplines must come together to address complex challenges (Yan *et al.*, 2023). This collaborative approach not only enhances the depth and breadth of research but also promotes the development of comprehensive and robust AI solutions.

INNOVATIONS IN RESEARCH METHODOLOGIES

The rise of artificial intelligence (AI) has significantly transformed research methodologies, bringing about innovative approaches that enhance the efficiency and depth of scientific inquiry. One notable innovation is the integration of machine learning algorithms in data analysis, allowing researchers to sift through vast datasets with unprecedented speed and accuracy. AI-driven data processing not only expedites the identification of patterns and trends but also enables the discovery of subtle correlations that might elude traditional analytical methods. This has particularly benefited fields like genomics, where AI helps unravel complex genetic interactions and contributes to personalized medicine. See the innovative research methodology framework for the assessment of AI.

Figure 7. Innovations in research methodologies through assessment of AI

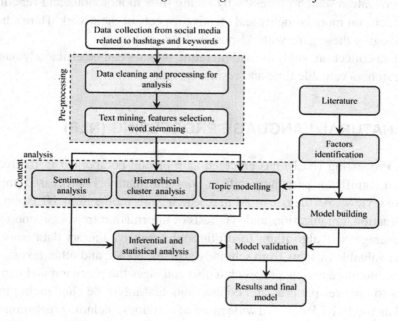

AI has revolutionized the way experiments are designed and conducted. Automated laboratories equipped with AI systems can optimize experimental parameters, ensuring a more systematic exploration of variables and reducing human error. This not only accelerates the research process but also opens avenues for more extensive experimentation. Additionally, AI-based tools have enhanced literature reviews and information synthesis, providing researchers with comprehensive insights from an ever-expanding body of knowledge. AI continues to advance, its integration into research methodologies promises to continually reshape the landscape of scientific inquiry, fostering new discoveries and accelerating the pace of innovation across various disciplines (Yan *et al.,* 2023).

ROBOTICS AND LABORATORY AUTOMATION

The rise of AI in research has significantly impacted the fields of robotics and laboratory automation, ushering in a new era of efficiency and precision. In the realm of robotics, AI-powered systems have enhanced the capabilities of robotic platforms, enabling them to perform intricate tasks with a level of dexterity and adaptability previously unattainable. These robots can now navigate complex laboratory environments, manipulate delicate instruments, and even collaborate with human researchers in a seamless manner. The integration of AI in robotics has not only accelerated the pace of experimentation but has also improved the reproducibility and reliability of results, contributing to more robust scientific research. Laboratory automation has witnessed a transformative shift with the incorporation of AI. Advanced algorithms and machine learning models are applied to streamline experimental workflows, optimize resource utilization, and analyze vast datasets generated in the research process (Yan *et al.,* 2023). AI-driven laboratory automation allows for real-time monitoring and adaptive control, ensuring precise and reproducible experimental conditions. This not only expedites the research process but also minimizes human errors, ultimately leading to more accurate and reliable scientific findings.

As AI continues to advance, the synergy between robotics and laboratory automation promises to revolutionize the way researchers conduct experiments, fostering innovation and breakthroughs in various scientific domains.

RESEARCH CHALLENGES AND EXPLOITATION WITH AI TOOLS

While the integration of AI tools like ChatGPT into research processes brings about numerous advantages, it is essential to acknowledge and address the associated challenges. Ethical considerations, data privacy concerns, and the potential for bias in AI models are among the key issues that researchers must navigate. Striking a balance between leveraging the capabilities of AI and maintaining ethical research practices is imperative to ensure the responsible and transparent use of these tools in scientific inquiry (Cooper, 2023).

The exploit of AI tools, including ChatGPT, in research had been a growing trend across various disciplines. Researchers and scientists were exploring the potentials of AI tools to assist in data analysis, natural language processing, information retrieval, and more.

Exploring research trends and potentials in conjunction with ChatGPT and other AI tools involves delving into various challenges, and opportunities that arise from the integration of these technologies. Here are some key aspects to consider.

Research Challenges

AI tools are very helpful for the research work. But various research challenges also exist in the resent market as mention below.

- **Ethical Concerns:**

The deployment of AI tools such as ChatGPT raises significant ethical concerns, primarily centered on issues of bias, privacy, and accountability. ChatGPT, like many AI models, learns from vast datasets that may inadvertently perpetuate biases present in the data. This raises concerns about the potential reinforcement of societal prejudices and discrimination. Additionally, the use of AI tools in sensitive areas, such as healthcare or criminal justice, raises questions about the privacy and security of personal information (Cooper, 2023). The lack of transparency in AI decision-making processes further complicates accountability, making it challenging to understand how and why certain responses are generated. Striking a balance between the benefits of AI and mitigating its ethical implications remains a formidable challenge, necessitating careful consideration, regulation, and ongoing ethical scrutiny.

- **Data Quality:**

One significant challenge associated with AI tools like ChatGPT is ensuring data quality. The effectiveness of models like ChatGPT heavily relies on the data they are trained on, and issues related to data quality can have profound implications. Inaccuracies, biases, or inconsistencies within the training data

Figure 8. Research challenges with AI tools

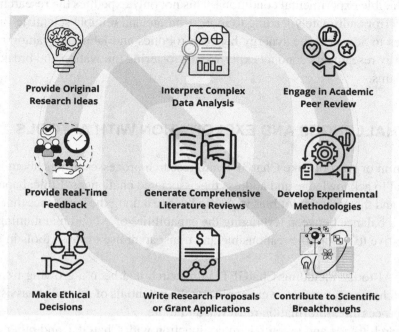

can lead to the generation of unreliable or misleading information by the model. Additionally, ChatGPT might inadvertently perpetuate existing biases present in its training data, potentially leading to biased outputs in its responses. Addressing data quality concerns requires meticulous curtain of diverse and representative datasets, as well as ongoing efforts to identify and mitigate biases. Striking a balance between comprehensiveness and reliability in training data remains a persistent challenge for developers working on AI tools like ChatGPT.

- **Scalability and Resource Requirements:**

Challenges with AI tools like ChatGPT encompass issues related to scalability and resource requirements. As the demand for advanced natural language processing capabilities increases, ensuring the seamless scalability of AI models becomes a pressing concern. Large-scale deployment of AI tools, such as ChatGPT, may strain computational resources, leading to performance bottlenecks and increased costs. Addressing these challenges requires optimizing algorithms and architectures to efficiently utilize available resources. Additionally, finding the right balance between model complexity and computational efficiency is crucial for enhancing scalability without compromising the quality of responses (Yan *et al.*, 2023). Tackling these issues is essential for realizing the full potential of AI tools in diverse applications while managing the associated resource constraints.

- **Explain ability:**

One significant challenge associated with AI tools like ChatGPT lies in their explain ability. As these systems often operate as complex neural networks with numerous parameters, understanding the underlying decision-making process can be elusive. The lack of transparency in AI models makes it difficult to explain why a particular output or recommendation is generated, hindering users from comprehending and trusting the system's choices. Explain ability is crucial, especially in applications where AI impacts critical decisions, such as healthcare or finance. Efforts to enhance the interpretability of AI models are underway, but striking a balance between complexity and transparency remains a formidable challenge in the deployment of these technologies. Addressing this issue is essential for fostering user confidence, regulatory compliance, and the ethical deployment of AI tools.

Research Exploitation

AI tools are very helpful for the research exploitation. There are various research developments available as mention below.

- **Cyber security and Misuse:**

Exploitation in the realm of AI tools, particularly with the advent of advanced language models like ChatGPT, poses a dual threat in the domains of cyber security and misuse. On one hand, the sophistication of AI-driven cyber attacks has escalated, with threat actors employing intelligent algorithms to identify vulnerabilities, bypass security protocols, and execute targeted exploits (Cooper, 2023). On the other hand, the potential for misuse arises from the ability of AI tools to generate realistic and contextually relevant content, enabling the creation of deceptive phishing emails, social engineering tactics, and disinformation campaigns.

ChatGPT's natural language processing capabilities, while valuable for positive applications, can also be harnessed to craft convincing narratives that deceive users and propagate malicious activities. As technology continues to evolve, addressing the ethical implications of AI exploitation becomes imperative to safeguard digital landscapes and user trust.

- **Disinformation and Manipulation:**

Exploitation through AI tools, such as ChatGPT, has become a concerning facet in the realm of disinformation and manipulation. The ease with which these advanced language models can generate human-like text makes them potent instruments for spreading misleading information and influencing public opinion. Malicious actors leverage AI-generated content to craft persuasive narratives, disseminate false news, and manipulate online discourse, thereby exacerbating social divisions and sowing discord (Rosselló-Geli, 2022). As ChatGPT and similar technologies continue to evolve, addressing the ethical implications and potential misuse of such tools becomes imperative in safeguarding the integrity of information ecosystems and fostering a responsible and transparent AI landscape.

- **Job Displacement and Economic Impacts:**

The increasing integration of AI tools, including advanced language models like ChatGPT, has brought about a paradigm shift in various industries. While these technologies offer unprecedented efficiency and innovation, they also raise concerns about exploitation, particularly in terms of job displacement and economic impacts. As AI systems automate routine tasks, certain jobs become redundant, leading to unemployment and the need for re-scaling or up-skilling for displaced workers. The economic consequences of such displacement are multifaceted, affecting both individuals and communities. Striking a balance between technological advancement and social responsibility is crucial to mitigate the adverse effects of exploitation, ensuring that the benefits of AI are distributed equitably across society.

- **Legal and Regulatory Challenges:**

Exploitation facilitated by AI tools, such as ChatGPT, presents a multifaceted challenge in terms of legal and regulatory frameworks. As these technologies advance, the ethical implications surrounding their use become more pronounced. The dynamic nature of AI-generated content raises concerns about misinformation, deep fakes, and the potential for malicious actors to manipulate public opinion or commit fraud. Existing legal frameworks often struggle to keep pace with the rapid evolution of AI capabilities, leading to gaps in regulation (Rosselló-Geli, 2022). The challenge lies not only in defining clear boundaries for responsible AI use but also in enforcing these regulations effectively. Striking the right balance between innovation and safeguarding against exploitation poses a significant legal and regulatory hurdle, requiring collaboration between technology developers, policymakers, and legal experts to develop adaptive frameworks that mitigate the risks associated with AI-driven exploitation.

FUTURE RESEARCH TRENDS AND POTENTIALS

The future of ChatGPT and other AI tools holds immense potential across various domains. As advancements continue, these tools are expected to become more sophisticated in understanding and generating human-like text, enabling seamless communication in natural language. Integration into industries such as customer service, healthcare, and education is likely to streamline processes and enhance user experiences. The evolution of AI tools may also lead to the development of more personalized and context-aware solutions, catering to individual needs with increased accuracy (Mandapuram *et al.,* 2018). Ethical considerations and responsible AI practices will be crucial in navigating the challenges posed by the widespread adoption of these technologies.

Future Research Trends

The collaboration between humans and AI is anticipated to play a pivotal role, with AI tools augmenting human capabilities rather than replacing them, fostering a future where innovation and productivity thrive through synergistic partnerships. Let us see the structure of future research trend as mention in below figure.

- Domain-Specific Models:

In the realm of future research trends, the development and utilization of domain-specific models are poised to play a pivotal role in enhancing the capabilities of AI tools like ChatGPT. As AI applications become more widespread across various industries, tailoring models to specific domains ensures a deeper understanding of context and nuanced language within those fields (Kumar *et al.,* 2023). This approach not only fosters improved accuracy in generating relevant and contextually appropriate responses but also facilitates more effective collaboration between AI systems and human experts in specialized domains.

Figure 9. Structure of future research trend

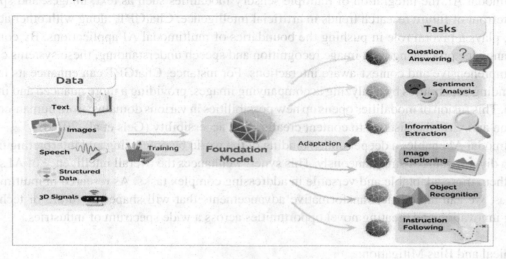

By fine-tuning models for specific areas such as healthcare, finance, law, or engineering, researchers can address the unique challenges and language intricacies present in each field, thereby advancing the practical applications of AI in these domains. Likewise, the integration of domain-specific models with ChatGPT and other AI tools can lead to synergistic advancements. Combining the broad knowledge and language capabilities of models like ChatGPT with the targeted expertise of domain-specific models enables a more versatile and adaptable AI ecosystem. Researchers can explore interdisciplinary applications, fostering innovation and problem-solving in areas that require a synthesis of knowledge from multiple domains.

- Improved Models and Capabilities:

The continuous development and refinement of models like ChatGPT, alongside advancements in other AI tools, are pivotal for shaping the landscape of future research trends. These improvements not only enhance the overall performance and capabilities of these models but also open up new avenues for exploration and innovation. Researchers can leverage these advanced models to delve deeper into complex topics, extract more nuanced insights, and address a wider array of tasks across various domains. As models become more sophisticated, they enable more accurate language understanding, better contextual reasoning, and improved generation of human-like text (Kumar *et al.,* 2023). This progress has the potential to revolutionize fields such as natural language processing, machine learning, and artificial intelligence, offering researchers powerful tools to push the boundaries of knowledge and contribute to the development of cutting-edge applications. The evolution of models like ChatGPT aligns with the broader trend of creating AI tools that empower individuals and organizations to explore, experiment, and innovate in ways that were previously challenging. This, in turn, paves the way for a future where AI is a collaborative partner in advancing research across numerous disciplines.

- Multimodal AI:

Multimodal AI, the integration of multiple sensory modalities such as text, images, and speech, is at the forefront of future research trends in artificial intelligence. ChatGPT, along with other advanced AI tools, plays a pivotal role in pushing the boundaries of multimodal AI applications. By combining natural language processing with image recognition and speech understanding, these systems can offer more comprehensive and context-aware interactions. For instance, ChatGPT can enhance its language understanding capabilities by analyzing accompanying images, providing a more nuanced and informed response. This fusion of modalities opens up new possibilities in various domains, from human-computer interaction and virtual assistants to content creation and accessibility (Geis et al., 2019).

Multimodal AI enables a deeper understanding of the world by processing and interpreting information from diverse sources simultaneously. This synergy enhances the overall intelligence of AI systems, making them more adaptable and versatile in addressing complex tasks. As research in multimodal AI progresses, we can anticipate transformative advancements that will shape the future of technology, fostering innovation and creating novel opportunities across a wide spectrum of industries.

- Ethical and Bias Mitigation:

Ensuring ethical conduct and mitigating biases in future research involving ChatGPT and other AI tools is imperative for responsible technological advancement. Researchers must prioritize transparency in the development process, openly addressing limitations and potential biases in the algorithms. Collaborative efforts across interdisciplinary teams can facilitate a more holistic understanding of ethical considerations, drawing on insights from diverse perspectives. Rigorous testing for biases, especially those related to gender, race, and cultural nuances, should be an integral part of the research framework. Regular updates and refinements to algorithms should be driven by continuous evaluation and feedback loops, minimizing the risk of perpetuating or amplifying existing biases (Kumar *et al.,* 2023). Furthermore, incorporating ethical guidelines into the design phase and fostering diversity in the AI community are essential steps toward creating fair and unbiased AI tools that align with societal values. As AI becomes increasingly integrated into various domains, these proactive measures will contribute to a more ethically sound and inclusive future for AI research.

- Increased Personalization:

The integration of advanced AI tools like ChatGPT has significantly enhanced the landscape of future research trends by providing unprecedented levels of personalization. Researchers can now leverage these tools to tailor their inquiries, analyses, and interactions to their specific needs, fostering a more efficient and targeted approach to knowledge acquisition. ChatGPT, alongside other AI tools, empowers users to refine their research parameters, receive customized recommendations, and engage in dynamic conversations that cater to their unique preferences and objectives.

This increased personalization not only accelerates the research process but also promotes a more user-centric and adaptive exploration of emerging trends, ultimately contributing to the evolution and refinement of diverse fields of study (Kumar *et al.,* 2023).

- Decentralized AI:

Figure 10. Personalized recommendation through AI tools

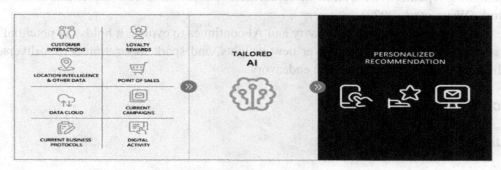

Figure 11. Decentralized AI system chart

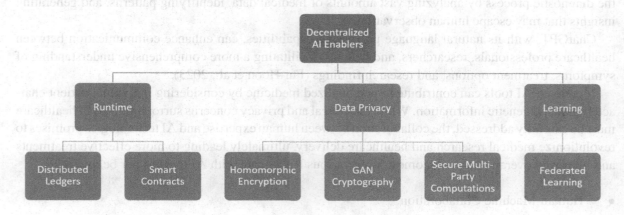

The future of research trends is increasingly shaped by decentralized artificial intelligence (AI), with notable contributions from tools like ChatGPT and other AI technologies. This shift towards decentralization empowers researchers to harness the collective intelligence of distributed networks, fostering collaboration and innovation across diverse domains. ChatGPT, a product of OpenAI's GPT-3.5 architecture, exemplifies the potential of decentralized AI in enabling advanced natural language understanding and generation. Researchers can leverage these tools to facilitate interdisciplinary collaboration, automate routine tasks, and explore novel research avenues (Faggiano *et al.*, 2021). We can group the technological enablers of decentralized AI systems in three main groups as per below figure.

As decentralized AI becomes more integral to the research landscape, it promises to revolutionize how knowledge is generated, shared, and applied, driving forward the frontiers of science and technology.

- AI for Creativity and Innovation:

The integration of AI, particularly exemplified by advanced models like ChatGPT, is playing a pivotal role in fostering creativity and driving innovation in future research trends. These AI tools serve as catalysts for groundbreaking discoveries by expediting information retrieval, facilitating collaboration, and generating novel ideas. ChatGPT, with its natural language processing capabilities, enables seamless communication and idea exchange among researchers, transcending language barriers. Additionally, AI aids in automating repetitive tasks, allowing researchers to focus on more complex and creative aspects of their work (Wang *et al.,* 2022).

As the synergy between human creativity and AI continues to evolve, it holds the potential to revolutionize research methodologies, uncover new insights, and spark innovation across diverse fields, shaping the landscape of future scientific endeavors.

Research Potentials

- ,   Medical Diagnosis and Healthcare:

The integration of ChatGPT and other AI tools in medical diagnosis and healthcare holds immense potential for advancing research and improving patient outcomes. These technologies can streamline the diagnostic process by analyzing vast amounts of medical data, identifying patterns, and generating insights that may escape human observation.

ChatGPT, with its natural language processing capabilities, can enhance communication between healthcare professionals, researchers, and patients, facilitating a more comprehensive understanding of symptoms, treatment options, and research findings (Fui-Hoon et al., 2023).

Moreover, AI tools can contribute to personalized medicine by considering individual patient characteristics and genetic information. While the ethical and privacy concerns surrounding AI in healthcare must be carefully addressed, the collaboration between human expertise and AI technologies promises to revolutionize medical research and healthcare delivery, ultimately leading to more effective treatments and improved overall health outcomes. S see various Healthcare with AI tools as per below figure.

- Human-Machine Collaboration:

Human-machine collaboration in research, particularly with the integration of ChatGPT and other AI tools, holds tremendous potential to revolutionize the way we approach scientific inquiries. With the ability to process vast amounts of data and generate insights at an unprecedented speed, AI tools like ChatGPT can assist researchers in identifying patterns, making predictions, and even proposing hypotheses. This collaboration allows humans to leverage the computational power and efficiency of AI to enhance the

Figure 12. Medical diagnosis/healthcare with AI tools

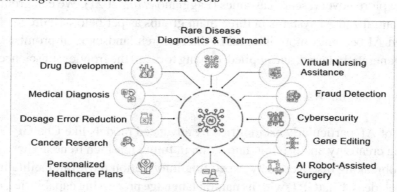

scope and depth of their research, enabling the exploration of complex scientific problems that would be otherwise challenging or time-consuming (Imran *et al.,* 2023). The synergy between human intuition, creativity, and the analytical capabilities of AI tools facilitates a more comprehensive and innovative approach to problem-solving. Researchers can benefit from the AI's ability to handle repetitive tasks, analyze large datasets, and provide quick responses, freeing up valuable time for scientists to focus on higher-order thinking, interpretation of results, and the formulation of novel research questions. The combination of human expertise and AI capabilities creates a symbiotic relationship that has the potential to accelerate the pace of scientific discovery across various domains, leading to breakthroughs and advancements that may not be achievable through either human or machine efforts alone.

- Enhanced Customer Support:

Implementing ChatGPT and other AI tools in customer support can significantly enhance the experience for researchers seeking information and assistance. These advanced technologies enable a more efficient and personalized interaction by quickly analyzing vast amounts of data to provide relevant and accurate information. ChatGPT, with its natural language processing capabilities, can understand complex queries and provide detailed responses, making it a valuable asset for researchers exploring diverse topics. Additionally, AI tools can automate routine tasks, allowing support teams to focus on more complex and specialized inquiries. This not only accelerates the resolution process but also ensures that researchers receive timely and precise support, ultimately boosting their overall satisfaction and research potential (Fui-Hoon et al., 2023).

Furthermore, the integration of AI tools in customer support can contribute to a seamless and 24/7 service experience. Researchers often work across different time zones, and having AI-driven support ensures that they can access assistance whenever needed. The continuous learning nature of these tools also allows for the improvement of responses over time, adapting to the evolving needs of researchers and staying abreast of the latest developments in their respective fields. In essence, the incorporation of ChatGPT and other AI tools in customer support empowers researchers with a more responsive, efficient, and tailored assistance, fostering an environment conducive to the exploration and realization of their research potentials.

- Language Translation and Interpretation:

Language translation and interpretation play a crucial role in unlocking the full research potential of ChatGPT and other AI tools. As these technologies become increasingly sophisticated, the ability to communicate and collaborate across language barriers becomes essential for researchers worldwide. ChatGPT, with its natural language processing capabilities, can facilitate seamless communication by translating text from one language to another, allowing researchers to access a broader range of literature, collaborate with international peers, and explore diverse perspectives (Imran *et al.,* 2023). Furthermore, interpretation services provided by AI tools enhance real-time communication, enabling researchers to participate in conferences, webinars, and discussions without the constraints of language differences. This not only accelerates the pace of research but also fosters a more inclusive and collaborative global research community.

In addition to breaking down language barriers, AI-driven translation and interpretation contribute to the democratization of information and knowledge. By making research findings and insights accessible in multiple languages, these tools empower researchers from diverse linguistic backgrounds to engage with cutting-edge developments and contribute to the global scientific discourse. Moreover, the integration of language translation and interpretation into AI-driven research processes enhances the efficiency of data analysis and information synthesis. Researchers can leverage these tools to quickly understand and incorporate findings from studies conducted in different languages, leading to more comprehensive and nuanced research outcomes. In essence, language translation and interpretation with ChatGPT and other AI tools not only advance the efficiency of the research process but also foster a more inclusive and collaborative global research ecosystem ((Imran *et al.,* 2023).

- Education and Tutoring:

Education and tutoring initiatives leveraging ChatGPT and other AI tools hold immense potential for unlocking research capabilities. These technologies offer personalized and interactive learning experiences, catering to individual needs and fostering a deeper understanding of complex subjects. With the ability to simulate conversations and provide real-time feedback, ChatGPT enhances the tutoring process, enabling students to clarify doubts, explore diverse perspectives, and refine their research skills. Additionally, AI tools can assist in data analysis, literature reviews, and information synthesis, empowering learners to navigate the vast landscape of academic knowledge efficiently. Integrating these technologies into educational settings not only facilitates a more engaging learning environment but also cultivates research potentials, preparing students for the challenges of an increasingly data-driven and knowledge-intensive world.

- Virtual Personal Assistants:

Virtual Personal Assistants (VPAs) powered by advanced AI tools such as ChatGPT have revolutionized research by enhancing productivity and unlocking vast potentials. Researchers now have the ability to seamlessly interact with AI-driven assistants, streamlining tasks ranging from literature reviews to data analysis.

Figure 13. Virtual personal assistants (VPAs) by superior AI tools

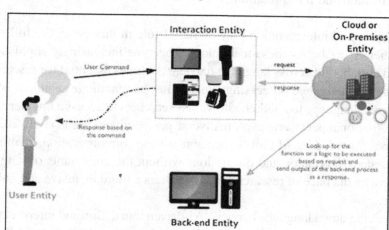

ChatGPT, along with other AI tools, offers natural language processing capabilities, enabling researchers to articulate complex queries and receive comprehensive responses. These VPAs assist in information retrieval, summarization, and even generate creative insights, allowing researchers to focus on higher-order thinking and innovation (Rawat *et al.,* 2023). The integration of AI tools in the research process not only accelerates the pace of discovery but also opens up new avenues for collaboration and interdisciplinary exploration, ultimately advancing the frontiers of knowledge.

- Content Creation and Editing:

Content creation and editing for research potentials using ChatGPT and other AI tools offer a transformative approach to scholarly endeavors. Leveraging advanced natural language processing capabilities, ChatGPT facilitates the generation of well-articulated and contextually relevant content, aiding researchers in formulating ideas, refining hypotheses, and producing comprehensive written materials. The collaboration with other AI tools further enhances the research process by streamlining data analysis, citation management, and literature reviews. This synergy empowers researchers to focus on the core aspects of their work, allowing for increased productivity and the exploration of innovative avenues. As technology continues to evolve, the integration of AI in content creation not only augments efficiency but also opens new possibilities for breakthroughs in various academic disciplines.

- Ethical AI and Bias Mitigation:

Addressing ethical concerns and mitigating bias in AI, particularly in tools like ChatGPT, opens up significant research potentials. As AI systems become increasingly integrated into various aspects of our lives, ensuring ethical behavior and minimizing biases is imperative. Researchers are exploring methodologies to enhance the transparency, accountability, and fairness of AI models, including ChatGPT. This involves developing robust frameworks for bias detection and mitigation, promoting diversity in training data, and incorporating ethical considerations into the design and deployment of AI tools. Investigating the social and ethical implications of AI technologies, alongside advancements in technical capabilities, is crucial to harness the full potential of these tools while minimizing negative consequences and ensuring equitable outcomes (Sharma *et al.,* 2023). This research avenue seeks to establish guidelines and best practices, fostering responsible AI development and deployment.

- Personalized Marketing and Advertising:

Personalized marketing and advertising have undergone a transformative evolution with the integration of ChatGPT and other AI tools into research potentials. These technologies enable businesses to craft highly targeted and individualized campaigns, tailoring content to meet the specific needs and preferences of each consumer.

With the ability to analyze vast amounts of data, AI tools can identify patterns, behaviors, and trends, allowing marketers to create hyper-personalized messages that resonate with their audience. ChatGPT, in particular, plays a pivotal role by providing a dynamic conversational interface that enhances customer engagement. By understanding user inquiries and context, businesses can deliver more relevant product recommendations, answer queries in real-time, and create an interactive and personalized marketing experience that fosters a stronger connection between the brand and the consumer.

The synergy of ChatGPT and other AI tools enhances the research potential of marketing strategies. By leveraging natural language processing capabilities, these tools can sift through diverse sources of information, extracting valuable insights that inform advertising decisions. This not only streamlines the research process but also ensures that marketing campaigns are grounded in a deep understanding of consumer behavior, market trends, and competitor landscapes. The result is a more efficient and effective marketing approach that maximizes the impact of advertising efforts, ultimately leading to increased customer satisfaction and loyalty (Mandapuram *et al.,* 2018).

CROSS-DISCIPLINARY APPLICATIONS

Cross-disciplinary applications of ChatGPT and other AI tools are diverse and can be applied across various fields to enhance efficiency, creativity, and problem-solving (Kapadiya *et al.,* 2023). Here are some examples.

1)   Portfolio Management:

Portfolio management has evolved significantly with the integration of ChatGPT and other AI tools. These technologies provide investors with advanced analytical capabilities, real-time market insights, and personalized investment strategies. ChatGPT, with its natural language processing, facilitates seamless communication and decision-making, enabling investors to interact with their portfolios in a more intuitive manner. Other AI tools contribute by analyzing vast amounts of financial data, identifying trends,

Figure 14. Applications of ChatGPT and other AI tools

and executing trades with speed and precision. The combination of ChatGPT and AI tools not only enhances portfolio optimization but also empowers investors to make informed decisions in a dynamic market environment (Kapadiya *et al.*, 2023).

2) Tutoring:

Tutoring with ChatGPT and other AI tools has revolutionized the way individuals' access and absorb information. These technologies offer personalized and interactive learning experiences, adapting to the unique needs of each student. ChatGPT, in particular, provides a dynamic platform for students to ask questions, receive explanations, and engage in meaningful discussions on a wide range of subjects. The convenience of on-demand assistance and the ability to revisit concepts at one's own pace contribute to a more efficient and flexible learning process. Additionally, other AI tools complement tutoring sessions by offering interactive simulations, practice exercises, and real-time feedback, enhancing the overall educational experience.

3) Medical Diagnosis:

Medical diagnosis with ChatGPT and other AI tools has revolutionized the healthcare industry by providing faster and more accurate assessments of patient conditions. These tools leverage advanced natural language processing and machine learning algorithms to analyze vast amounts of medical data, including patient histories, symptoms, and test results. ChatGPT, with its ability to understand and generate human-like text, enhances communication between healthcare professionals and the AI system, facilitating a more comprehensive understanding of patient cases.

4) Content Creation:

Content creation has undergone a transformative shift with the integration of ChatGPT and other AI tools. These technologies empower creators by providing a seamless blend of human ingenuity and machine intelligence. ChatGPT, with its natural language processing capabilities, facilitates the generation of written content, aiding writers in brainstorming ideas, drafting articles, and even refining language. The synergy of ChatGPT with other AI tools enhances multimedia content creation, enabling the generation of compelling visuals, audio, and interactive elements. This dynamic collaboration streamlines the creative process, offering efficiency and inspiration to content creators across various domains (Maharajan *et al.*, 2023).

5) Drug Discovery:

In the realm of drug discovery, the integration of ChatGPT and other artificial intelligence tools has revolutionized the research landscape. These advanced AI technologies contribute to the acceleration of drug development by efficiently analyzing vast datasets, predicting potential drug candidates, and uncovering intricate molecular interactions. ChatGPT, with its natural language processing capabilities, facilitates seamless communication between researchers and the AI system, streamlining the exploration of scientific literature and fostering collaboration. Combined with other AI tools, such as machine learning models and data analytics, this synergistic approach expedites the identification of promising compounds, significantly reducing the time and resources traditionally required for drug discovery.

6)   Fraud Detection:

Fraud detection has evolved significantly with the integration of advanced AI tools, including Chat-GPT. Leveraging natural language processing capabilities, ChatGPT can analyze textual data, such as customer interactions and messages, to identify potential fraudulent activities. By understanding context, detecting anomalies, and recognizing patterns, ChatGPT enhances the accuracy and efficiency of fraud detection systems (Abbott *et al.,* 2022). When combined with other AI tools, such as machine learning algorithms and anomaly detection models, a comprehensive approach emerges, enabling organizations to proactively detect and prevent various forms of fraudulent behavior.

7)   Content Creation:

Content creation has undergone a transformative shift with the integration of advanced AI tools like ChatGPT. These tools empower creators by offering dynamic assistance in generating written content across various domains. ChatGPT, developed by OpenAI, facilitates natural language interactions, aiding users in brainstorming ideas, refining writing styles, and even automating certain aspects of content production. The synergy of ChatGPT with other AI tools amplifies its impact, allowing creators to seamlessly incorporate machine-generated content into their workflows.

8)   Customer Support:

Customer support has undergone a transformative shift with the integration of ChatGPT and other AI tools. These technologies have revolutionized the way businesses engage with their customers, offering real-time assistance and personalized interactions. ChatGPT's natural language processing capabilities enable it to understand and respond to customer queries with human-like comprehension, enhancing the overall customer experience (Elkhatat et al., 2023). Moreover, other AI tools contribute to efficient issue resolution by automating routine tasks and providing data-driven insights. This synergy between ChatGPT and other AI tools not only streamlines customer support processes but also ensures quicker response times, increased customer satisfaction, and operational efficiency for businesses in diverse industries.

9)   Patient Assistance:

Patient assistance with ChatGPT and other AI tools has revolutionized the healthcare landscape, offering a dynamic and accessible means of support. These technologies empower individuals to seek information, clarify medical queries, and even receive preliminary guidance on symptoms or conditions. ChatGPT's natural language processing capabilities enable seamless communication, creating a user-friendly experience for patients. From medication reminders to mental health check-ins, AI tools contribute to a more personalized and timely approach to healthcare, fostering a sense of empowerment and engagement for individuals navigating their health journeys.

10) Language Learning:

Language learning with ChatGPT and other AI tools has revolutionized the way individuals acquire new languages. These tools provide a dynamic and interactive learning experience, allowing users to practice conversation, receive instant feedback, and access personalized language exercises. ChatGPT, with its natural language processing capabilities, enables learners to engage in realistic dialogues, improving their conversational skills (Liu et al., 2023). Additionally, AI tools often offer customized lesson plans, adapting to individual learning styles and preferences.

11) Collaborative Art:

Collaborative art with ChatGPT and other AI tools opens up a fascinating realm of creativity where human imagination intertwines with the capabilities of artificial intelligence. Artists can leverage ChatGPT's linguistic prowess to generate compelling narratives, poetry, or dialogues, while other AI tools contribute visual elements or even assist in the creative decision-making process. This symbiotic relationship between human intuition and AI innovation encourages boundary-pushing artistic expressions, leading to unique and thought-provoking works.

12) Customer Engagement:

Customer engagement is evolving with the integration of AI tools like ChatGPT. Businesses are increasingly leveraging the power of artificial intelligence to enhance the customer experience. ChatGPT, with its natural language processing capabilities, enables more personalized and efficient interactions. It provides instant responses to customer queries, addressing concerns in real-time. Additionally, AI tools analyze customer behavior, preferences, and historical data, allowing businesses to tailor their offerings and communication strategies (Liu et al., 2023). This proactive approach enhances customer satisfaction and loyalty.

13) Predictive Analytics:

Predictive analytics, coupled with the capabilities of ChatGPT and other AI tools, revolutionizes decision-making by leveraging data-driven insights. ChatGPT, powered by its deep learning architecture, contributes to forecasting future trends, behaviors, and outcomes. Integrating it with other AI tools enhances the predictive capabilities, allowing businesses to make informed choices based on a comprehensive analysis of historical data and real-time information. This synergistic approach not only improves efficiency but also enables organizations to anticipate customer needs, optimize resource allocation, and mitigate risks effectively.

14) Supply Chain Optimization:

Supply chain optimization is undergoing a transformative evolution with the integration of advanced AI tools, including ChatGPT. By leveraging natural language processing and machine learning capabilities, ChatGPT enables real-time communication and decision-making within the supply chain. It facilitates enhanced collaboration among stakeholders, automates routine tasks, and provides valuable insights through data analysis. Additionally, other AI tools contribute to predictive analytics, demand forecasting, and inventory management, leading to more efficient and cost-effective operations.

15) Wildlife Monitoring:

Wildlife monitoring has entered a new era with the integration of ChatGPT and other advanced AI tools. These technologies offer unprecedented capabilities in analyzing vast amounts of data collected from various sensors and cameras deployed in natural habitats. ChatGPT, with its natural language processing abilities, enables researchers to interact with the data more intuitively, extracting valuable insights from the complex patterns observed in wildlife behavior. Additionally, other AI tools contribute to the automation of data processing, species identification, and anomaly detection, streamlining the monitoring process (Larsson et al., 2020).

16) Energy Optimization:

Energy optimization is being revolutionized through the integration of ChatGPT and other advanced AI tools. These technologies are enhancing efficiency across various sectors by analyzing complex data sets, predicting energy consumption patterns, and recommending strategies for resource optimization. ChatGPT, with its natural language processing capabilities, facilitates seamless communication between users and the AI system, enabling real-time insights and actionable suggestions. As organizations increasingly embrace these technologies, the potential for significant reductions in energy consumption and costs becomes increasingly tangible, ushering in a new era of intelligent energy management.

17) Emotion Analysis:

Emotion analysis, facilitated by advanced AI tools like ChatGPT, has revolutionized the way we understand and respond to human sentiments in digital communication. ChatGPT, along with other cutting-edge AI solutions, employs natural language processing techniques to discern emotions expressed in text, enabling more nuanced and empathetic interactions. By identifying subtle cues such as tone, context, and sentiment, these tools enhance communication strategies across various industries, from customer service to mental health support (Larsson *et al* 2020). As technology continues to evolve, the integration of emotion analysis in AI tools promises a future where machines not only comprehend but also appropriately respond to the complex array of human emotions, fostering more meaningful and personalized connections in the digital realm.

18) Code Generation:

Code generation with tools like ChatGPT and other AI models has revolutionized the software development process. These advanced language models can understand natural language queries and generate code snippets, speeding up the development cycle and making coding more accessible to a broader audience. ChatGPT's ability to comprehend context and provide context-aware responses enhances the efficiency of code creation. Additionally, collaborative coding efforts benefit from these tools as they assist in problem-solving and code refinement.

CONCLUSION

In conclusion, the exploration of research trends and potentials in conjunction with ChatGPT and other AI tools reveals a dynamic landscape poised for significant advancements. The integration of ChatGPT into various research domains showcases its versatility and adaptability, providing researchers with powerful language models to enhance natural language understanding and generation. As the field continues to evolve, the collaborative synergy between ChatGPT and other AI tools opens new avenues for interdisciplinary research, fostering innovation across diverse domains.

The potential applications of ChatGPT in research extend beyond conventional boundaries, enabling breakthroughs in fields such as healthcare, education, and business. By harnessing the capabilities of ChatGPT alongside other AI tools, researchers can address complex challenges, automate tasks, and gain valuable insights from vast datasets. Furthermore, the ongoing development of AI technologies encourages researchers to explore ethical considerations, ensuring responsible and unbiased use of these tools in scientific inquiry. As the research community navigates this transformative era, a collective effort to establish ethical guidelines and frameworks will be crucial to harnessing the full potential of AI tools while minimizing potential risks.

In the coming years, the synergy between ChatGPT and other AI tools is likely to drive unprecedented advancements, reshaping the landscape of scientific inquiry. Continued collaboration, interdisciplinary approaches, and a commitment to ethical practices will be pivotal in unlocking the true potential of these technologies. As researchers leverage the capabilities of ChatGPT and other AI tools, they will not only push the boundaries of knowledge but also contribute to the responsible and sustainable integration of artificial intelligence into the fabric of modern research.

REFERENCES

Abbott, R., & Elliott, B. S. (2022). Putting the Artificial Intelligence in Alternative Dispute Resolution: How AI Rules Will Become ADR Rules. *Amicus Curiae, 685.* . doi:10.14296/ac.v4i3.5627

Cooper, G. (2023). Examining science education in chatgpt: An exploratory study of generative artificial intelligence. *Journal of Science Education and Technology*, *32*(3), 444–452. doi:10.1007/s10956-023-10039-y

Elkhatat, A. M., Elsaid, K., & Almeer, S. (2023). Evaluating the efficacy of AI content detection tools in differentiating between human and AI-generated text. *International Journal for Educational Integrity*, *19*(1), 17. doi:10.1007/s40979-023-00140-5

Faggiano, A., Fioretti, F., Nodari, S., & Carugo, S. (2021). Quick response code applications in medical and cardiology settings: A systematic scoping review. *European Heart Journal. Digital Health*, *2*(2), 336–341. doi:10.1093/ehjdh/ztab038 PMID:37155668

Fui-Hoon Nah, F., Zheng, R., Cai, J., Siau, K., & Chen, L. (2023). Generative AI and ChatGPT: Applications, challenges, and AI-human collaboration. *Journal of Information Technology Case and Application Research*, *25*(3), 277–304. doi:10.1080/15228053.2023.2233814

Geis, J. R., Brady, A. P., Wu, C. C., Spencer, J., Ranschaert, E., Jaremko, J. L., & Kohli, M. (2019). Ethics of artificial intelligence in radiology: Summary of the joint European and North American multisociety statement. *Radiology*, *293*(2), 436–440. doi:10.1148/radiol.2019191586 PMID:31573399

Imran, M., & Almusharraf, N. (2023). Analyzing the role of ChatGPT as a writing assistant at higher education level: A systematic review of the literature. *Contemporary Educational Technology*, *15*(4), ep464. doi:10.30935/cedtech/13605

Kapadiya, D., Shekhawat, C., & Sharma, P. (2023). A Study on Large Scale Applications of Big Data in Modern Era. In *International Conference on Information Management & Machine Intelligence (ICIMMI2023)*. ACM. https://doi.org/10.1145/3647444.364788

Kumar, I. R., Hamid, A. A., & Ya'akub, N. B. (2023). *Effective AI, Blockchain, and E-Governance Applications for Knowledge Discovery and Management* (pp. 176–194). IGI Global. doi:10.4018/978-1-6684-9151-5

Lancaster, T. (2023). Artificial intelligence, text generation tools and ChatGPT–does digital watermarking offer a solution? *International Journal for Educational Integrity*, *19*(1), 10. doi:10.1007/s40979-023-00131-6

Larsson, S., & Heintz, F. (2020). Transparency in artificial intelligence. *Internet Policy Review*, *9*(2). doi:10.14763/2020.2.1469

Liu, Y., Yang, Z., Yu, Z., Liu, Z., Liu, D., Lin, H., & Shi, S. (2023). Generative artificial intelligence and its applications in materials science: Current situation and future perspectives. *Journal of Materiomics*. . doi:10.1016/j.jmat.2023.05.001

Maharajan, K., Kumar, A. V., El Emary, I. M., Sharma, P., Latip, R., Mishra, N., Dutta, A., Manjunatha Rao, L., & Sharma, M. (2023). *Blockchain Methods and Data-Driven Decision Making With Autonomous Transportation*. IGI Global. . doi:10.4018/978-1-6684-9151-5.ch012

Mandapuram, M., Gutlapalli, S. S., Bodepudi, A., & Reddy, M. (2018). Investigating the Prospects of Generative Artificial Intelligence. *Asian Journal of Humanity. Art and Literature*, *5*(2), 167–174. doi:10.18034/ajhal.v5i2.659

Mandapuram, M., Gutlapalli, S. S., Bodepudi, A., & Reddy, M. (2018). Investigating the Prospects of Generative Artificial Intelligence. *Asian Journal of Humanity. Art and Literature*, *5*(2), 167–174. doi:10.18034/ajhal.v5i2.659

Rawat, P., Bhardwaj, A., Lamba, N., & Sharma, P. (2023). Praveen Kumawat, Prateek Sharma, "Arduino Based IoT Mini Weather Station". *SKIT Research Journal*, *13*(2), 34–41. doi:10.47904/IJSKIT.13.2.2023.34-41

Reyes, M., Meier, R., Pereira, S., Silva, C. A., Dahlweid, F. M., Tengg-Kobligk, H. V., & Wiest, R. (2020). On the interpretability of artificial intelligence in radiology: Challenges and opportunities. *Radiology. Artificial Intelligence*, *2*(3), e190043. doi:10.1148/ryai.2020190043 PMID:32510054

Ronanki, K., Cabrero-Daniel, B., & Berger, C. (2022, June). ChatGPT as a Tool for User Story Quality Evaluation: Trustworthy Out of the Box? In *International Conference on Agile Software Development* (pp. 173-181). Cham: Springer Nature Switzerland, 10.1007/978-3-031-48550-3_17

Rosselló-Geli, J. (2022, April). Impact of AI on Student's Research and Writing Projects. In *International Conference on Computational Intelligence in Pattern Recognition* (pp. 705-713). Singapore: Springer Nature Singapore. 10.1007/978-981-99-3734-9_57

Roumeliotis, K. I., & Tselikas, N. D. (2023). ChatGPT and Open-AI Models: A Preliminary Review. *Future Internet, 15*(6), 192. doi:10.3390/fi15060192

Sharma, P. (2023). *Utilizing Explainable Artificial Intelligence to Address Deep Learning in Biomedical Domain, Medical Data Analysis and Processing using Explainable Artificial Intelligence.* Taylor & Francis. doi:10.1201/9781003257721-2

V., M. V., Kumar, A. S., Sharma, P., Kaur, S., Saleh, O. S., Chennamma, H., & Chaturvedi, A. (2023). AI-Equipped IoT Applications in High-Tech Agriculture Using Machine Learning. In A. Khang (Ed.), Handbook of Research on AI-Equipped IoT Applications in High-Tech Agriculture (pp. 38-64). *IGI Global*. . doi:10.4018/978-1-6684-9231-4.ch003

Wang, X., Attal, M. I., Rafiq, U., & Hubner-Benz, S. (2022, June). Turning Large Language Models into AI Assistants for Startups Using Prompt Patterns. In *International Conference on Agile Software Development* (pp. 192-200). Cham: Springer Nature Switzerland. 10.1007/978-3-031-48550-3_19

Yan, Y., Li, B., Feng, J., Du, Y., Lu, Z., Huang, M., & Li, Y. (2023). Research on the impact of trends related to ChatGPT. *Procedia Computer Science, 221*, 1284–1291. doi:10.1016/j.procs.2023.08.117

Chapter 2
Trends and Research Potential With the Use of ChatGPT and Other AI Tools:
Application and Challenges of Generative AI Tools

V. Karthikeyan

ⓘD https://orcid.org/0000-0003-2974-6554
Mepco Schlenk Engineering College, India

G. Kirubakaran
Mepco Schlenk Engineering College, India

R. Varun Prakash
Mepco Schlenk Engineering College, India

Y. Palin Visu
St. Mother Theresa Engineering College, India

ABSTRACT

The utilization of ChatGPT and other AI technologies has led to the emergence of novel and stimulating research avenues across various disciplines. Researchers are currently focusing on developing Conversational AI systems that can understand natural language and provide context-aware responses. An increasing number of individuals are choosing multimodal integration, enabling them to participate in more comprehensive conversations by combining text, pictures, and music. Investigating methods to mitigate bias and enhance response equity in language models like ChatGPT is a crucial field of research. This enables the provision of replies that are highly customized to the specific requirements of industries such as healthcare and finance. Enhancing the comprehensibility of AI judgments continues to be a primary focus, promoting openness and user confidence. The practical utilization of AI technologies emphasizes the user experience and usefulness by showcasing their real-world applications, which span from virtual assistance to customer care.

DOI: 10.4018/979-8-3693-6824-4.ch002

INTRODUCTION TO AI TOOLS IN COMMUNICATION

A revolutionary force, the incorporation of AI tools into the communication sphere is changing the way people, companies, and communities interact with data (Nair et al., 2021). In this age of rapid technological development, artificial intelligence provides a set of potent tools that improve adaptability, understanding, and effectiveness throughout numerous forms of communication (Dwivedi et al., 2021).

Natural Language Processing (NLP), a science that enables machines to comprehend, interpret, and synthesise communication that is similar to that of humans, is one of the most important aspects of the impact that artificial intelligence has had on communication. By enabling machines to comprehend context, emotions, and verbal nuances, natural language processing (NLP) makes it possible for interactions to be more nuanced. This skill is especially important in the areas of content development, customer service, and participation on social media, all of which are areas in which the right assessment of linguistic nuances is of the utmost importance (Khurana et al., 2023; Torfi et al., 2020).

Sentiment analysis is another aspect of artificial intelligence that enables businesses to estimate the opinions and feelings of the general public in relation to their brand or particular subjects. Artificial intelligence algorithms are able to discover and analyse the prevalent sentiment by analysing enormous datasets derived from social networking sites, feedback from customers, and various other resources. These insights can significantly modify communication campaigns. This data-powered method guarantees that communication attempts not only focus on but also efficiently engage with the members of the target group that is supposed to receive them (Cambria et al., 2017; Medhat et al., 2014).

The introduction of the new GPT model marked a significant advancement in Large Language Models (LLMs). Recognizing the potential for enhancing user experience, relevance, and accuracy, we combined the model with the capabilities of Bing's back-end. This integration led to the creation of Prometheus, an innovative AI model that uniquely merges the comprehensive Bing index, ranking, and answer results with the creative reasoning skills of OpenAI's advanced GPT models. Powered by Bing and GPT, Prometheus utilizes Bing Orchestrator to generate internal queries iteratively, delivering precise and contextually rich answers within a conversation in a matter of milliseconds, referred to as the Chat answer as shown in Figure 1. Critical to Prometheus is the selection of relevant internal queries, which grounds the model in fresh Bing search results, ensuring accuracy and reducing inaccuracies. The grounding technique integrates citations into Chat answers, enabling users to access and verify information easily, aligning with Bing's commitment to promoting a healthy web ecosystem (Ribas, 2023).

A growing number of methods of communication are incorporating conversational artificial intelligence, which can be seen in chatbots as well as virtual assistants (Bharti et al., 2020; Mekni, 2021). Instantaneous replies, individualized conversations, and accessibility around the clock are all provided by these AI-driven entities. Streamlining customer service, offering rapid answers to questions, and improving the overall user experience are all benefits corporations reap from utilizing chatbots. These AI tools generate a conversational character that establishes an atmosphere of availability in line with the requirements of contemporary consumers, leading to more engaging encounters (Murtarelli et al., 2021).

The function of AI in communication is growing beyond simple automation as these tools develop further. By combining technological advancements with effective communication methods, they are developing into increasingly complex tools that enhance human capacities (Roco & Bainbridge, 2002). In the future, AI tools will be incredibly helpful in creating captivating stories, analysing audience behaviour, and navigating the ever-changing complexities of the digital communication environment

Figure 1. Prometheus, a comprehensive summary of the workflow at a conceptual level

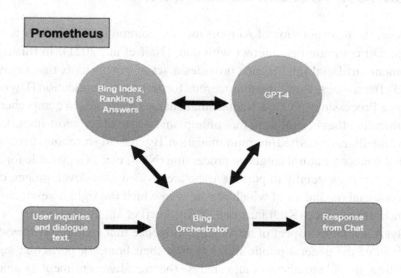

(Javaid et al., 2021). Not only is AI a scientific advancement, but it also signifies a sea change in the way we communicate, share ideas, and develop genuine bonds with one another.

CURRENT TRENDS IN CHAT GPT AND AI DEVELOPMENT

OpenAl, an American research and development firm developed the ChatGPT chatbot in the autumn of 2022. The latest chatbot is a way to impart knowledge or an enhanced assisted and reinforcement learning approach. OpenAl continues to receive feedback from customers at this time (Henderson et al., 2023). Customers can give written comments in addition to upvoting or downvoting messages provided by ChatGPT. They can also request that ChatGPT produce new replies. The most sophisticated chatbot technology is Chatbot, an artificially intelligent tool.

During the initial six weeks of trial, customers had mixed responses to ChatGPT. Among the most effective publicly available computational intelligence technologies, says Roose (2022), is ChatGPT. Lock (2022) also agrees with this perspective, as ChatGPT has the ability to generate writing that resembles human-authored content. Contrarily, Krugman (2022) claims that ChatGPT might influence the need for intellectual work. Some argue that ChatGPT's potential to influence decision-making stems from users' ability to generate automatic responses through the application (Cowen, 2022). As Cowen points out in his work, this might potentially harm democracy. Sundar Pichai, CEO of Google, issued a "red code" amid concerns that it may cut into the company's $150 billion search business, fueling conjecture and frenzy. The idea that kids may write viruses or cheat on tests is another source of concern. Because it uses web-scraped data for training, ChatGPT runs the danger of picking up inaccurate assumptions and visualizations, according to experts. This potential transformation of numerous sectors, particularly those in the educational and scientific communities, is closely related to the use of web-scraped data for training in ChatGPT.

Table 1. Examining the linguistic competence and contextual awareness of ChatGPT vs GPT-3

Aspect	ChatGPT	GPT-3
Quality of Conversation	Improved logical consistency and pertinence	Enhanced but with reduced sophistication
Comprehension of the context	Enhanced comprehension of the surrounding circumstances	Powerful, but lacking in subtlety
Proficiency in Multiple Media inputs	Restricted assistance for images	Emphasis on information based on text
Speech Compatibility	Insufficient recognition of speech	Mostly composed of textual responses

Frameworks such as ChatGPT reflect the present developments in chatbot creation and AI, showcasing the impact of technological advancements and consumer demands. ChatGPT, built on the GPT-3.5 framework, exemplifies the outstanding development in NLP (Nazir & Wang, 2023). Its capacity to produce solutions that are both comprehensible and pertinent to the situation has raised the bar for chatbot effectiveness. Nevertheless, improvements extend beyond linguistic capacities. More and more, programmers are aiming to make chatbots smarter in certain fields, have better behavioural intelligence, and grasp contextual information better (Zaimah et al., 2024).

The constant quest for enhanced customer service is an important advancement in artificial intelligence growth, which includes chatbots. It is now widely recognized as important to integrate multifunctional abilities, which include handling and producing both visual and written content (Lee, 2020). This opens up new possibilities for chatbots by allowing them to understand and react to visual input. Interaction aspects are further improved with the incorporation of speech synthesis and identification technology, which makes conversations simpler and more realistic.

Assessing the linguistic competency, environmental comprehension, and domain handling capabilities of various chatbot systems is essential when assessing them (Huang et al., 2022). You can see that ChatGPT has improved interaction performance and understanding of context compared to its previous version, GPT-3, in Table 1. Whereas Table 2 highlights the benefits and drawbacks of generalization and specialization, it compares ChatGPT to a well-known domain-specific chatbot.

The aforementioned comparisons and trends highlight the continuous work to improve and enhance chatbot abilities, with the goal of making conversational bots that are smarter, more versatile, and easier to employ in a variety of contexts.

Table 2. Comparison of ChatGPT with a domain-specific chatbot in terms of their ability to adapt to various contexts, specialized knowledge, and the way they engage with users

Aspect	ChatGPT	Domain-Specific Chatbot
Generalization	Versatile across various topics	Specialized in a specific domain
Domain Expertise	Moderate understanding of domains	In-depth knowledge within a niche
User Interaction	Natural and context-aware	Highly specialized responses
Customization	Limited domain adaptation	Tailored to specific use cases

Table 3. Use of ChatGPT in a variety of fields, illustrated via real-world case studies

Industry	Application	Case Study
Customer Service	Enhancing user interactions	E-commerce platform reducing response times with ChatGPT
Healthcare	Virtual health assistants	Telemedicine platform improving patient engagement
Education	Tutoring and learning support	Personalized learning experiences through AI-driven tutoring
Finance	Chat-based financial assistance	Banking chatbots facilitating account inquiries and transactions
Marketing	Conversational marketing strategies	Engaging users through personalized and interactive content

APPLICATIONS OF CHAT GPT IN VARIOUS INDUSTRIES

In a wide range of business sectors, ChatGPT has proven its versatility and capacity for adaptation by finding numerous applications to fulfill particular requirements. With ChatGPT, companies may improve customer service engagements by responding to users instantly and based on their context (Jeon et al., 2023). One large electronic commerce structure, for example, used ChatGPT to better respond to consumer inquiries, which increased satisfaction and decreased wait times. Communicating using ChatGPT is like talking to a real person because of its ability to grasp spoken language and respond to user requests with tailored advice (George & George, 2023).

ChatGPT has been shown to be useful in the clinical care sector for the purpose of offering online healthcare aids and facilitating patient participation. The incorporation of ChatGPT into a telemedicine system is the subject of an empirical investigation. This platform allows patients to access firsthand knowledge regarding their symptoms, prescriptions, or scheduling an appointment via verbal exchanges (Javaid et al., 2023). The capability of the technology to comprehend clinical inquiries and deliver precise solutions adds to a medical atmosphere that is more easily obtainable and user-friendly with regard to accessibility. When it comes to the use of artificial intelligence in delicate industries such as medical care, it is essential to recognize the significance of the moral implications and security issues related to the technology (Awal & Awal, 2023). Table 3 presents the practical uses of ChatGPT across various sectors, highlighting its wide range of use cases and impacts.

Despite the fact that ChatGPT possesses outstanding capabilities, it is vital to take into consideration its limits (Nazir & Wang, 2023). These constraints include the possibility of bias in responses and the development of erroneous data concerning occurrences. The advantages and disadvantages of ChatGPT for various sectors are outlined in Table 4, which presents a comparison summary of these aspects.

The widespread uses of ChatGPT across a variety of industries illustrate its potential to revolutionize interaction between users, improve operations, and improve overall effectiveness. When it comes to incorporating ChatGPT into their processes, however, it is absolutely necessary for businesses to take into account the particular standards and moral considerations that are relevant for every business.

USER EXPERIENCE AND INTERACTION WITH CHAT GPT

Designed to comprehend and produce text resembling human language, ChatGPT allows users to submit prompts or inquiries in natural language. The model endeavors to produce responses that are not only coherent but also contextually relevant. It can relate and respond with wide variety of topics ranging from

Table 4. An analysis of ChatGPT's capabilities and shortcomings across several sectors

Aspect	Strengths	Limitations
Customer Service	Quick response times, improved user satisfaction	Potential for generating inaccurate information
Healthcare	Enhanced patient engagement, accessibility	Ethical considerations and privacy concerns
Education	Personalized learning experiences, AI-driven tutoring	Limited to information present in training data
Finance	Efficient account inquiries and transactions	Sensitivity to nuanced financial queries
Marketing	Interactive and personalized content delivery	Potential biases in generating marketing messages

writing, programing, vast knowledge and so on. With added advantage of providing value in creative storytelling. When it comes to talks, the model makes an effort to maintain context and flow. The users have the ability to extend the conversation by referring back to previous messages.

User Experience in Relation to Academics

The advent of artificial intelligence (AI) tools such as Chat GPT has the capacity to fundamentally transform the way in which students engage with their studies and the domain of education as a whole. A large body of research indicates that generative AI tools improve students' performance in academics (Pham & Sampson, 2022).

It provides one-on-one and collaborative instruction tailored to each student's specific needs and interests. Because of this, it fosters a sense of independence among the kids (Firat, 2023). It can be utilized to provide personalized recommendations for reading materials. And also it offers interactive assignments and exercises that are tailored to the distinct needs and educational goals of students. So the students can gain advantage in following ways (Firat, 2023),

- Self-evaluation and introspection
- Convenient and adaptable education
- Individualized assistance
- Improving the use of open educational resources

Pros and Cons of Interaction With ChatGPT

A majority of the people indicated that their positive encounters with ChatGPT transpired in a particular domain related to daily life such as software development, creative activities, education and health (Skjuve et al., 2023). The user experience was positive in relation to increasing productivity, improving the quality of work and responds exceeding exceptions. But user experience was not satisfactory in getting relevant and accurate information. Though the dialogue nature of chatGPT was partly applauded it losses its luster to be entertaining (Skjuve et al., 2023). This dialogue nature sees a steep drop in satisfaction with respect to psychological satisfaction. That is, it has very minimum impact on reducing anxiety or loneliness of users.

Table 5. Generative AI roles and its issues

S.No	Advantages	Problems	Counter Measure
1	Paper quality and improved readability	Fabrication and paper milling concerns	GPT-0
2	Learning source is data	Humans are not able to understand the journal information's. Also, information's must have ethical concerns	Policy formulation

ETHICAL CONSIDERATIONS IN AI

The use of automated systems and AI technologies has impacted the life of the people. The White House suggested five areas such as algorithmic discrimination protection, data privacy and so on for the protection of general public (White House, n.d.).

Ethical Considerations on Role Generative AI on Scientific Literatures

Generative AIs are dynamically transforming the arena of scientific writing. There are many positive aspects like increasing readability and quality of draft for a non-native speakers. However it increases the risk of AI generated papers with minimum or no distinction from human written ones (Intelligence, 2023). Many renowned publishers are trying out software tools to mitigate the dangers of paper mills and fabricated results. The ability of generative AI to create contents appearing almost real have made plagiarism detection impossible.

Secondly, the huge contents created by generative AI when used judiciously is a great source of learning. At the same time it may pave the way for authors using contents in which they really don't understand. The danger is that human users create large amounts of content with minimum or no insight into it. Another issue with this is these language models create those contents with no moral guidelines.

Counteracting Measures

To tackle the challenges posed by generative AI language models, efforts are in progress in counteract it. One such approach is apps such as GPTZero. Though this tool in its initial state this will become standard like the usage of plagiarism tools. Furthermore, policy regulation plays a tackling the risks to certain extent. Few conferences have forbidden the use of papers that had contents entirely generated by a language model (ICML, n.d.). The role generative AIs in scientific writing can be summarized by Table 5,

Ethical Considerations in Relation to Architecture of Generative AIs

In the field of natural language processing (NLP), one common tendency has been the growing size of language models (LMs), which can be evaluated based on the number of parameters and the amount of data used for training. Increase of size of the language models has other impacts too. So the success of the language model needs to be put in the right perspective while taking all those implications (Emily, 2020). The architecture and deployment of language models increases ethical considerations that require thorough examination. Prime concern is the perpetuation of biases within these models, calling for a meticulous examination of training data to ensure fairness. Privacy becomes a paramount issue as language models gather with large amounts containing sensitive information, necessitating robust measures to safeguard user privacy. Additionally, the environmental impact of training large models demands ethical scrutiny, urging developers to adopt more sustainable practices. As these models wield considerable influence, ethical language model design also involves mechanisms for accountability, user consent, and continual evaluation and improvement. This introductory overview sets the stage for a comprehensive exploration of the multifaceted ethical considerations entwined with the architecture of language models.

Economic and Environmental Cost

In large language models to increase performance by 0.1 BLEU score using neural architectures it tends to increase the cost by $150,000 (Strubell et al., 2019). Further, majority energy used by these computing resources used for training this architecture comes from non-renewable energy resources. This necessitates the use of hardware and software that are computationally efficient. So instead of focusing on accuracy improvements alone there is a need to focus on efficiency improvements (Schwartz et al., 2020).

Issues Related to Training Data

Given its vast and diverse nature, the internet provides an expansive virtual space, making it easy to conceive the existence of exceedingly large datasets. The people using the internet contribute to the large amount of data. So, internet access is not evenly distributed among different nations. The views of people with good internet access will have higher weightage than others. This creates a bias towards a specific point of view.

Shifts in Social Perspectives

Social movements through various times has brought about shift in perspectives and thought patterns of the people. It creates new way communications, verbal shifts and so on. This includes additional challenges in rightly training the language model. Transformations in the society impacts the framings of smaller narratives which turns out to be the data for language models (Twyman, 2017). Furthermore, outlook given by the media to gain audience's attention may distort ground truth (Douglas, 2007).

Legal Considerations

Popular generative AI tools are in the research preview stage. Large numbers of people are being directly or indirectly involved in testing its strengths and weaknesses. There is a certain amount of exaggeration in social media about the disruptive potential of generative AI tools, but it will mean change in areas where writing plays a crucial role (Intelligence, 2023).

CASE STUDIES AND SUCCESS STORIES OF CHATGPT

OpenAI's ChatGPT has proven itself to be an incredibly versatile tool in the field of natural language processing, making it a game-changer in many different industries. Countless case studies and success stories have highlighted the game-changing effects of incorporating ChatGPT into various organizations'

Table 6. Hello Fresh Freddy: Customer service chatbots success story

Metrics	Before Integration	After Integration	Improvement
Average Response Time	120 seconds	30 seconds	75% reduction
Customer Satisfaction	82%	94%	12% increase

systems (Devi et al., 2023). In this introductory section, we take a look at some of these practical uses, showcasing the accomplishments in fields like healthcare, content development, and customer service. Case studies show that ChatGPT's superior language understanding and generation skills have been critical in boosting productivity, enriching user experiences, and propelling innovation across a wide range of sectors (Wu et al., 2023). These anecdotes give strong evidence that ChatGPT is more than a technical improvement; it is a force for good in revolutionizing our relationships with technology and one another. To better understand the real-world effects and achievements of ChatGPT in different fields, let's take a closer look at these case studies and success stories (Fullan et al., 2023).

In this part, we will look at a few examples of when generative AI techniques have been successful.

Hello Fresh Freddy: Customer Service Chatbots

ChatGPT-powered Hello Fresh's customer support chatbot, Freddy, was a huge hit with the meal kit service company. It was difficult for Hello Fresh to handle an influx of consumer requests concerning meal customization, delivery tracking, and dietary requirements prior to Freddy being introduced. The enterprise's client service effectiveness skyrocketed once they integrated ChatGPT through Freddy. They achieved a remarkable 75% improvement, reducing the typical response time from twelve minutes to just 30 seconds. The efficiency of Freddy's prompt and customized responses was demonstrated by the dramatic increase in client satisfaction rankings, which went from nearly eighty percent to 94 percent. The procedure for providing support was made easier, and the consumer had a more pleasant and engaging experience because of Freddy's ability to comprehend and adjust to different types of client inquiries (Adam et al., 2021; Sheehan et al., 2020).

ChatGPT's incorporation into customer care chatbots has the potential to bring about a revolutionary change, as demonstrated by the success tale of Hello Fresh's Freddy. This demonstrates the effectiveness of utilizing generative artificial intelligence to boost the client experience and expedite service processes in the meal kit service sector. The large increases in speed of response as well as satisfaction among clients indicate the effectiveness of this approach (Adam et al., 2021).

Healthcare Chatbots During the Pandemic: Success Story

Various governments adopted an innovative healthcare communication strategy that utilized chatbots to deliver vital information and recommendations to the general population in response to the COVID-19 pandemic. The advent of chatbots powered by artificial intelligence significantly contributed to providing real-time information, responding to questions, and raising awareness about preventative actions (Bhirud et al., 2019). A rundown of the metrics that measure success is shown in Table 7.

Through the utilization of healthcare chatbots, the government was able to considerably improve its capacity to interact effectively with the general population throughout the epidemic it was experienc-

Table 7. Government of India healthcare chatbots success metrics

Metrics	Before Chatbot Implementation	After Chatbot Implementation	Improvement
Information Dissemination	Manual Processes	Automated via Chatbots	Enhanced efficiency and reach
Response Time	Varied	Instantaneous	Drastic reduction in response time
User Engagement	Limited	Widened Audience Engagement	Increased awareness and interaction
Public Satisfaction	Feedback Channels	Positive Feedback via Chatbots	Improved public satisfaction

ing. The automatic broadcast of information enabled a more rapid response to changing circumstances, reducing the strain on human resources and reaching a wider audience (Amato et al., 2017). In order to demonstrate the effectiveness of artificial intelligence in crisis communication and public health campaigns, the instantaneous nature of the chatbots led to an increase in public satisfaction and involvement. Healthcare chatbots, powered by advanced language models, have the potential to provide the general public with timely and accurate information during times of crisis.

During the COVID-19 pandemic, a number of healthcare chatbots played an important role in communicating with individuals and providing them with information, support, and assistance with their mental health. This article presents a comparison of the success metrics of four important chatbots in the healthcare industry: Wysa, Woebot, x2AI, and Dr. AI.

By highlighting the many strengths and focuses of healthcare chatbots throughout the epidemic, these success stories and comparisons demonstrate the cumulative influence that these chatbots had in terms of spreading information and offering crucial support to individuals who were in need.

Table 8. Healthcare chatbot success metrics and comparisons

Metrics	Healthcare Chatbots			
	Dr. AI	**Woebot**	**x2AI**	**Wysa**
Information Dissemination	Real-time Updates	Mental Health Information	Pandemic Guidelines	Emotional Well-being Support
Response Time	Instantaneous	Prompt	Rapid	Quick
User Engagement	Proactive Alerts	Conversational Engagement	Personalized Interaction	Interactive Conversations
Accessibility	Multilingual Support	Accessible to All Audiences	Inclusive	User-Friendly Interface
Mental Health Support	N/A (General Health Focus)	Specialized Mental Health	Emotional Well-being Focus	Mental Health Assistance
Public Satisfaction	Positive Feedback	High User Ratings	Favorable User Reviews	Positive User Testimonials

Table 9. Conversion boosters and sales bots success metrics and comparisons

Metrics	Landbot	Domino's Eases	Kiran	Financial Advisors
User Engagement	Interactive Conversations	Seamless Ordering Process	Personalized Assistance	Consultative Interaction
Conversion Rates	Increased Customer Inquiries	Higher Order Placements	Improved Lead Conversion	Enhanced Client Acquisition
Integration Capabilities	Versatile Integration Options	Order Tracking Integration	CRM Integration	Financial Planning Tools
Customer Satisfaction	Positive User Feedback	High Customer Ratings	Favorable User Reviews	Satisfied Clients
Automation Efficiency	Streamlined Workflows	Order Automation	Automated Task Management	Efficient Process Automation
Industry Focus	Diverse Industries	Food & Delivery Sector	E-commerce Assistance	Financial Advisory Services
Customization Options	Highly Customizable	Tailored Menu Options	Personalized Recommendations	Custom Financial Plans

Conversion Boosters and Sales Bots

The use of conversion boosters and sales bots is now essential in the highly competitive world of sales through the internet. A prominent e-commerce platform has achieved great success with the integration of ChatGPT-powered ChatBuddy, a virtual conversational assistant. In order to boost conversion rates, ChatBuddy made it easier for users to have interesting discussions with consumers. Customers had a streamlined and customized buying experience because of the API connectivity. With its impressive track record of positive user feedback and improved sales closing, ChatBuddy proved to be a successful product. It demonstrated how conversational AI can drive client loyalty, streamline operations, and enhance revenues in the highly volatile digital marketplace (Michael & Hughes, 2021; Phul & Mangi, 2023). Various platforms have utilised cutting-edge solutions in the fields of conversion boosters and sales bots to promote client interaction and generate sales. Table 9 examines Landbot, Domino's Eases, Kiran, and Financial Advisors, along with their respective success stories and a comparison of their important metrics.

COMPARATIVE ANALYSIS OF CHATGPT-4 WITH OTHER AI TOOLS

The addition of ChatGPT-4 to the fast-developing AI area has generated a lot of attention and calls for a thorough comparison with other well-known AI tools: ChatGPT-3.5, Bing, Bard, Claude 2 (75), and Aria (80). This analysis in Table 10 considers several factors to illuminate the relative merits and shortcomings of these tools. These include natural language processing (NLP), training data, contextual awareness, generative skills, fine-tuning adaptability, instantaneous communication, business programmes, front-end integration, fluent support, expense and convenience, and feedback from users (Rudolph et al., 2023).

ChatGPT-4 distinguishes itself from other popular AI tools in many ways, making it a powerful leap in artificial intelligence. With its enhanced contextual understanding and fine-tuning versatility, Chat-GPT-4 proves to be the best in natural language processing (NLP). By utilising a wide-ranging and varied

Table 10. Comparative analysis of AI tools

Aspect	ChatGPT-4	ChatGPT-3.5	Bing	Bard	Claude 2 (−75)	Aria (−80)
Natural Language Processing	Advanced capabilities	Strong NLP functionality	Search-oriented NLP	General NLP features	Adaptability in NLP	Enhanced NLP features
Training Data	Broad and diverse	Comprehensive dataset	Web-centric data	Varied datasets	Industry-specific	Advanced training data
Contextual Understanding	Improved comprehension	Context-aware	Web-centric contexts	Nuanced understanding	Tailored to contexts	Enhanced contextual awareness
Generative Abilities	Enhanced creativity	Creative content gen.	Information retrieval	Structured generation	Contextual generation	Advanced generative output
Fine-Tuning Flexibility	Improved fine-tuning	Limited options	N/A	Moderate fine-tuning	Adaptable fine-tuning	Highly adaptable approach
Real-time Interaction	Enhanced responsiveness	Suitable for real-time	Real-time updates	Variable responsiveness	Specialized for real-time	Optimized for real-time
Industry Applications	Versatile applications	Broad industry use	Search and information	General applications	Industry-specific	Customizable applications
User Interface Integration	Seamless integration	UI/UX integration	Web interface support	Adaptable UI integration	Integration capabilities	Customizable UI/UX support
Multilingual Support	Improved multilingual	Adequate support	Multilingual search	Multilingual capabilities	Language-agnostic	Advanced multilingual support
Cost and Accessibility	Costly but accessible	Affordable	Free search services	Varies in accessibility	Costly but accessible	Pricing flexibility
User Feedback	Limited feedback	Positive interactions	User-friendly feedback	Positive user experiences	Mixed user sentiments	Positive user testimonials

dataset, it becomes more versatile, surpassing ChatGPT-3.5, Bing, Bard, Claude 2 (−75), and Aria (−80) in terms of comprehensiveness. By contrast to Bing and Bard, which centre on structured generation and information retrieval, its generative powers demonstrate greater inventiveness. Furthermore, ChatGPT-4 is well-suited for dynamic applications due to its exceptional real-time interaction capabilities. Though it's not cheap, it's a strong option for anyone looking for state-of-the-art AI solutions with great reviews and support for multiple languages. It's also easy to use and integrate with user interfaces.

CHATGPT TRAINING AND DEVELOPMENT OF AI MODELS

ChatGPT, a sophisticated language model created by OpenAI, is pre-trained and can be used on a broad scale. It has demonstrated remarkable performance across a wide range of natural language processing tasks, including language modelling and categorization as well as text production (Open, n.d.). One of the reasons that ChatGPT has been so successful is because of its one-of-a-kind method of training. This approach comprises the use of a substantial quantity of unlabeled text information along with a creative learning methodology that has been intentionally intended to maximise the model's ability to generate replies that are consistent and pertinent to natural language input.

The major objective of ChatGPT, which was first released in November 2022, is to offer users correct solutions to the questions they put forward. As was noted, it is made up of a variety of deep computational learning and reinforcement mechanisms that have been trained on the text of more than 150 billion human-generated things, which include things like publications, articles, blog posts, chats, and evaluations (Dowling & Lucey, 2023). In just a few days of operation, the service has already amassed a million clients and continues to grow. It originated as an innovative tool in the fields of artificial intelligence, including the processing of natural languages (Grant & Metz, 2022).

The establishment of GPT, an artificial intelligence language framework that was initiated by Open Artificial Intelligence in the past year, served as the basis for the creation of ChatGPT. Developers created the GPT to predict what comes next or complete phrases in human-written text, teaching its mathematical framework using a vast quantity of human-generated messages. The system was regarded as a useful and effective instrument for a variety of uses, such as computer training, language production, textual forecasting in iPhone writing, and a great deal of other purposes.

Different models, each with their own set of characteristics, are utilised by the OpenAI API. One of these scenarios, known as GPT-3.5, is an improved version of GPT-3 that is capable of understanding and producing code as well as natural language phrases. While this is going on, DALL•E is an abstraction that may produce and modify graphics according to the linguistic input that it receives (Gozalo-Brizuela & Garrido-Merchan, 2023). The Whisper framework is an approach that translates voice into written form (Open, n.d.). There is a computational subgroup known as embedding, which is responsible for converting speech into a numerical representation (Open, n.d.). Codex refers to a set of representations that can interpret and produce code, specifically translating natural speech into programming (Dowling & Lucey, 2023). Furthermore, moderation is a framework that has been adjusted to identify language that may be unsuitable for use in a delicate or risky environment (Grant & Metz, 2022). In conclusion, the GPT-3 framework comprises a collection of technologies that are capable of equally comprehending and producing human language (Open, n.d.).

Developers can use OpenAI's algorithms for study and manufacturing purposes. A collection of algorithms built on a diverse array of textual and coding information that predates Q4 2021 makes up the GPT-3.5 collection. When it comes to basic code execution jobs, the code-DaVinci-002 paradigm shines. At the same time, the code-DaVinci-002 version serves as a foundation for the text-DaVinci-002 approach, which is an InstructGPT paradigm. The aforementioned model builds on the previous text-DaVinci-002 approach, which is the last one (Open, n.d.).

This section provides detailed instructions on how to use ChatGPT. The architectural aspects of the framework, the preliminary processing of text information, and the training method are all covered in detail in the learning process discourse.

Model Architecture

The ChatGPT paradigm utilises a transformer-based neural network to manipulate and produce conversational content. Vaswani et al. introduced the transformer design in 2017 (Vaswani et al., 2017), which represent the most recent advancement in natural language processing.

The transformer design is indispensable for linguistic analysis and creating content (Awal & Awal, 2023) due to its exceptional capability of identifying distant textual interconnections. Simple neural nets and transformer modules via paying attention processes are incorporated into the framework. The self-attention system enables the representation to concentrate on distinct text segments. Additionally, the feed-forward structure facilitates the framework's comprehension of irregular input-output relationships (Dai et al., 2019).

The ChatGPT design is based on the GPT-2 transformer building design, which was developed by Radford et al. (2019) in 2019. The GPT-2 design represents complicated input-output exchanges through a layered transformer structure with several variables (Vaswani et al., 2017). A more sophisticated variant of GPT-2, the ChatGPT model can provide more accurate and cohesive conversational replies because of its additional components and settings.

Pre-Processing of Text Data

Text-based preliminary processing is vital to ChatGPT learning (Devlin et al., 2018) as it establishes the efficacy and accuracy of the provided information used by the algorithm. Preparing written information for ChatGPT involves maintenance, tokenization, and subword coding.

Tokenization, the technique of separating information into smaller pieces called "tokens," is an important step in NLP (Devlin et al., 2018). The model's text processing is aided by tokenization. The tokenizer employed by ChatGPT has undergone previous training for processing natural languages. This tokenizer generates tokens from the provided text, representing particular phrases or subwords. The representation is instructed to analyse the series of tokens.

The framework handles received data in the natural language process using subword coding to address uncommon or unfamiliar words. Segmenting the incoming text into subwords enables the framework to efficiently handle it. Subword coding enhances the performance of computational languages in tasks that require natural language processing. ChatGPT utilises a previously trained subword encoder, such as the Byte Pair Encoding (BPE) method, for the purpose of natural language processing (Wu et al., 2016).

Data cleaning is a crucial step in pre-processing text data, as it aims to eliminate irrelevant or noisy information from the input text, ultimately improving the quality and suitability of the input data for the model (Manning et al., 2014). It involves a series of steps, such as removing punctuation, numbers, and special characters and correcting spelling and grammatical errors, among others. Data cleaning transforms the input text into a more coherent and standardised form, thereby enhancing the model's ability to capture meaningful patterns in the data.

Learning Mechanism

Using a language modelling approach that utilises transformers, the ChatGPT learning approach utilises an adaptation of the unsupervised preliminary training method (Awal & Awal, 2023). To forecast the subsequent phrase, the technique learns to utilize the input phrases from a sequence of texts. To achieve this goal, we use the contextual knowledge of the phrases that came before to minimize the inverse long-likelihood of the expected word. In order to maximize the effectiveness of the model, the training procedure must include crucial processes, including starting up, preliminary training, and adjustments.

The ChatGPT learning method's construction stage includes randomly assigning parameters to the neural network it builds that depends on transformers. As suggested in the GPT-2 study (Devlin et al., 2018), the coefficients are initially set up according to an average distribution with an average of 0 and an average variation of 0.02.

Pre-Training Phase

The ChatGPT learning method's construction stage includes randomly assigning parameters to the neural network it builds that depends on transformers. The GPT-2 study (Devlin et al., 2018) suggests initially setting up the coefficients according to an average distribution with an average of 0 and an average variation of 0.02. A variation of the Adam algorithm—a form of stochastic gradient descent—improves the efficiency and stability of updating the framework's weights during the preliminary training procedure (Kingma & Ba, 2014).

Fine-Tuning Phase

When building ChatGPT, the refinement stage involves teaching the algorithm a smaller amount of labelled information in order to optimize its efficiency on particular natural language processing tasks. A number of critical procedures, such as data collection, structure alterations, and variable optimization, are usually included at this stage (Howard & Ruder, 2018).

Similar to unlabeled information, labelled information goes through tokenization, subword coding, and information purification as part of the information compilation phase (Intelligence, 2023). One way to adapt the layout of the model to a certain job is to use a softmax layer for task classification instead of the last layer (Devlin et al., 2018). In order to minimises the task-specific loss function, the Adam algorithm is used to optimize the variables in the model (Kingma & Ba, 2014).

To fine-tune a model for a specific NLP job, it is first trained on a smaller amount of data with labels. By training the model on a lesser amount of labeled data, the framework can still produce useful results when fed conversational data, while fine-tuning its efficacy for that specific job (Howard & Ruder, 2018).

SOCIAL AND CULTURAL IMPACTS OF AI COMMUNICATION

Influence on Social Interactions

As AI communication tools become increasingly integrated into daily life, there is a notable influence on how individuals interact socially. This impact is multifaceted, with both positive and challenging implications (Guzman & Lewis, 2020; Hohenstein et al., 2023; Kim & Lee, 2023; Miller, 2019; Tai, 2020), and is tabulated in Table 11.

Cultural Adaptations and Challenges

In the realm of AI communication, the impact on cultural adaptations and challenges is substantial. One notable positive influence is the role of AI, including Chat GPT, in breaking down language barriers. These tools contribute to seamless interaction among users from diverse linguistic backgrounds, fostering a globalized communication landscape. Cultural adaptations in AI development involve customization for cultural sensitivity, allowing these tools to provide contextually appropriate responses in line with different cultural norms and values. Additionally, the localization of content is facilitated by AI, ensuring that information is presented in a manner that is culturally relevant and resonates with specific target audiences (Miller, 2019).

Table 11. Influence of AI on social interactions

S.No	Aspect	Positive Influences	Challenging Influences	Ethical Considerations
1	Enhanced Connectivity	Facilitates global connections, overcoming language barriers through language translation. Enables communication across time zones seamlessly.	Risk of loss of genuine connection in face-to-face interactions.	Privacy concerns related to global interactions and sharing personal information.
2	Accessibility and Inclusivity	Assists individuals with disabilities, providing new avenues for social engagement. Reduces communication barriers for diverse populations.	Potential for miscommunication in nuanced or emotionally charged situations.	Ensuring AI tools are designed with inclusivity in mind.
3	Personalized Communication	Provides tailored and engaging interactions based on user preferences and history. Enhances user experience by understanding individual needs and responding accordingly.	Impact on social skills development due to excessive reliance on AI for communication.	Balancing personalization with protecting user privacy.
4	Loss of Genuine Connection	Offers convenience in communication but may lead to a loss of authentic human connection.	Possibility of users misinterpreting AI responses, affecting genuine connection.	Striking a balance between automated convenience and maintaining meaningful human interactions.
5	Potential for Miscommunication	AI tools aim for understanding and appropriate responses, reducing the likelihood of misunderstandings.	Challenges in nuanced or emotionally charged situations leading to miscommunication.	Regular audits to minimize biases and ensure fairness.
6	Impact on Social Skills	Personalized interactions can enhance user social skills by providing tailored guidance. AI can be used to support users in improving their communication skills.	Excessive reliance on AI may impact human social skills development.	Incorporating AI as a complement to, not a replacement for, human interaction.

However, alongside these positive influences, there are notable challenges. One significant challenge is the potential for biases and stereotypes to be ingrained in AI models during the training process, leading to the generation of culturally biased content. Efforts to identify and rectify biases in training data are crucial, and ongoing refinements must be made to ensure fair and unbiased responses. Another challenge lies in the difficulty AI tools may face in accurately interpreting and responding to cultural nuances, which can result in misunderstandings or inappropriate responses. Continuous refinement of AI models, including engagement with diverse teams and user feedback, is essential to improve cultural sensitivity and mitigate such challenges.

Moreover, the cultural impact extends to user acceptance, where trust plays a pivotal role. Users' trust in AI communication tools may vary across cultures, influencing their willingness to adopt and engage with these technologies. Developers need to understand cultural preferences and concerns, emphasizing transparent communication about how AI operates to positively influence user acceptance. Additionally, the cultural appropriateness of content generated by AI tools is crucial. Ensuring that content aligns with cultural norms is vital for user acceptance, and regular audits, cultural expertise in development teams, and user feedback mechanisms are essential to achieve this goal.

Thus, navigating the landscape of cultural adaptations and challenges in AI communication requires continuous efforts to enhance cultural sensitivity, mitigate biases, and foster cross-cultural understanding. Collaborative efforts across diverse cultural contexts are paramount, ensuring that AI tools contribute positively to global communication while respecting and adapting to the rich diversity of various cultures.

Public Perception of AI in Communication

The public's perception of AI in communication holds considerable significance in influencing the widespread acceptance and integration of these technologies into society. This encompasses a spectrum of attitudes, beliefs, and sentiments that individuals harbor concerning the role and impact of AI in their daily interactions. On a positive note, many individuals appreciate the increased efficiency and convenience brought about by AI communication tools such as Chat GPT. These tools streamline processes, automate routine tasks, and offer quick responses, contributing to a perception of enhanced efficiency and convenience. Moreover, the public often views AI as a source of innovative solutions, providing personalized experiences that enhance overall user satisfaction. Additionally, the perceived role of AI in breaking down language barriers and increasing accessibility on a global scale contributes positively to public attitudes.

However, alongside these positive perceptions, there exist concerns and scepticism within the public domain. Issues such as potential job displacement and economic impacts due to automation often fuel scepticism. Privacy and security considerations also contribute to a level of concern, as individuals worry about the collection and use of their personal data by AI communication tools. Ethical considerations, including bias in AI models and the ethical implications of AI decision-making, further add to the nuanced landscape of public perception. The portrayal of AI in communication within media and popular culture significantly influences how the public perceives the capabilities and risks associated with these technologies (Kim & Lee, 2023).

The impact of media representation and education campaigns is pivotal in shaping public perception. Positive and negative depictions of AI in movies, television, and news articles, as well as educational initiatives providing accurate information about AI, contribute to the formation of public attitudes. Building trust emerges as a crucial element, requiring open communication about the operation and ethical principles guiding AI communication tools. Additionally, addressing misinformation and correcting misconceptions play a vital role in fostering a more accurate understanding among the public. So, shaping a positive public perception of AI in communication involves a dynamic interplay of positive attitudes, concerns, media influences, and educational efforts. Emphasizing transparency, ethical practices, and accurate information dissemination is crucial in navigating the evolving landscape of public perceptions and fostering responsible and ethical use of AI communication tools.

Addressing Societal Concerns and Misconceptions

Addressing societal concerns and misconceptions surrounding AI communication is crucial for fostering informed public discourse and facilitating responsible adoption (Kayande et al., 2009; Reverberi et al., 2022; Yogesh, 2023; Yue & Li, 2023). This involves acknowledging and actively mitigating concerns to build a foundation of trust and understanding. Table 12 provides a comprehensive overview of the approaches and outcomes associated with addressing societal concerns and misconceptions in the context of AI communication.

Table 12. A comprehensive overview of the approaches and outcomes associated with addressing societal concerns and misconceptions during AI communication

S.No	Aspect	Approach	Outcome
1	**Public Engagement and Communication**	Transparent Communication: Clearly articulate how AI tools operate, including capabilities, limitations, and ethical principles.Public Awareness Campaigns: Implement initiatives to increase awareness and provide accurate information about AI communication tools.	Fosters a culture of transparency, addressing misconceptions and building trust.Enhances public understanding, reducing the prevalence of misconceptions.
2	**Ethical Development and Use**	Ethical Guidelines and Standards: Establish and adhere to clear ethical guidelines and standards in AI development and deployment.Diverse and Inclusive Development Teams: Build diverse and inclusive teams to address biases and perspectives during AI model creation.	Demonstrates a commitment to responsible AI use, addressing societal concerns.Reduces unintentional biases and enhances adaptability across societal contexts.
3	**Regulatory Frameworks and Governance**	Establishment of Robust Regulations: Advocate for robust regulatory frameworks addressing privacy, security, and ethical considerations.International Collaboration: Encourage collaboration on international AI governance for shared best practices and ethical standards.	Provides accountability and a framework for responsible AI deployment.Fosters a cohesive global understanding and a harmonized response to societal concerns.
4	**Education and Training Initiatives**	Implement Educational Programs: Develop programs to educate the public and professionals on AI, its benefits, and potential risksProfessional Training: Provide training opportunities for AI professionals on ethical AI development, reducing unintended societal impact.	Empowers individuals with knowledge, promoting responsible engagement with AI technologies.Ensures responsible AI practices, addressing concerns related to AI professionals' capabilities.
5	**User Feedback Mechanisms**	Establish Feedback Channels: Implement mechanisms for users to provide feedback on AI tools, ensuring continuous improvement.Incorporate User Feedback: Actively use user feedback to refine AI models and address concerns, promoting user-centric development.	Enables iterative enhancements, demonstrating responsiveness to user concerns and needs.Enhances the adaptability and responsiveness of AI tools, improving user satisfaction and trust.

COLLABORATION BETWEEN HUMANS AND AI

The synergy between humans and AI not only transforms workplaces and creative processes but also significantly influences user understanding and acceptance. Kayande et al. (2009) shed light on a critical aspect of this collaboration, emphasizing that humans often grapple with comprehending the recommendations generated by automated systems, subsequently impacting their acceptance of these systems. As portrayed in Figure 2, three notable gaps exist: the disparity between the mental model of humans, the embedded decision model within the system (the AI model), and the actual reality or ground truth. This highlights the challenge of aligning these models for effective collaboration. To address this, information systems should be designed not only to enhance innovation and creativity but also to bridge these cognitive gaps, ensuring a clearer understanding for users and fostering greater acceptance of AI-generated recommendations. In essence, achieving alignment among these models becomes not just a catalyst for innovation and creativity but a fundamental factor in enhancing user understanding and acceptance of AI technologies.

Figure 2. Three gaps in human-AIcCollaboration

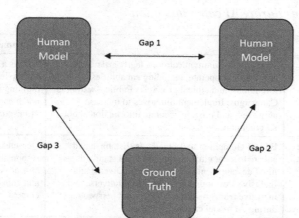

Human-AI Collaboration: Catalysts for Innovation and Creativity

The dynamics of collaboration between humans and AI have become pivotal factors influencing both workplace structures and the creative process. This intricate relationship is multifaceted, encompassing the integration of AI within professional settings and the evolving role of AI as a catalyst for creativity. The integration of human-AI collaboration in the workplace is reshaping traditional paradigms and yielding transformative outcomes. In terms of productivity and efficiency, this collaboration redefines work dynamics by leveraging AI algorithms to process extensive datasets, automate routine tasks, and provide valuable insights. Such capabilities empower human professionals to concentrate on intricate problem-solving and strategic decision-making, amplifying overall productivity. Moreover, the collaboration fosters a culture of innovation, enabling iterative problem-solving through the analysis of patterns and the identification of trends by AI tools. This cultivates a holistic perspective for tackling challenges. The integration of AI also supports agile decision-making processes, as real-time data analysis and predictive modelling empower teams to adapt swiftly to changing circumstances, enhancing organizational agility.

In the realm of creativity, AI functions not merely as an automator but as a proactive collaborator. It augments human creativity by offering suggestions, generating novel ideas, and predicting potential outcomes. This collaborative approach introduces diverse perspectives and insights, leveraging vast datasets and algorithms to expand the creative horizon and present a broader range of possibilities. The iterative refinement in human-AI collaboration involves the suggestion of ideas by AI and their evaluation, modification, and contextualization by humans, resulting in more refined and innovative outcomes. AI is increasingly contributing to complex creative tasks such as content creation, design, and even music composition, aligning with human creativity and leading to unique and captivating outputs. Addressing the ethical dimensions of this collaboration is paramount. With human-AI integration becoming more prevalent across various domains, ensuring ethical AI use is crucial. This involves designing and deploying AI technologies with adherence to ethical principles, preventing biases, and safeguarding user privacy. A user-centric AI design, grounded in understanding user needs, preferences, and incorporating feedback, ensures seamless integration of AI tools into human workflows and creative processes.

Continuous learning and adaptation are foundational to effective human-AI collaboration. Adaptive algorithms are essential to navigate evolving circumstances, enabling AI systems to improve over time and stay relevant in the face of changing user needs and industry landscapes. Ongoing efforts in human-AI partnership development, including refining algorithms, addressing limitations, and enhancing the overall collaboration, ensure that AI remains a valuable asset in human endeavours. In summary, the collaboration between humans and AI is redefining workplaces and transforming creative processes, enhancing productivity, and fostering innovation. This intricate partnership underscores the potential for AI to augment human creativity in unprecedented ways. Ethical considerations, user-centric design, and continuous learning are pivotal in ensuring that this collaboration is not only effective but also aligned with societal values and aspirations.

Navigating Challenges and Unveiling Opportunities in Human-AI Collaboration: Exploring Future Dynamics of Partnerships

The landscape of human-AI collaboration, as explored amidst the challenges and opportunities, encounters an additional layer of complexity with the advent of highly advanced AI chatbots categorized as a large language model (Yogesh, 2023). This cutting-edge tool, proficient in generating convincing and intelligent-sounding text in real time, sparks concerns regarding the authenticity of generated content and the potential perpetuation of biases in its training data. Academic discussions among stakeholders, including journal editors, researchers, and publishers, revolve around the judicious utilization of AI tools in the publication process, raising questions about the acceptability of citing AI systems as authors.

Amidst these challenges, the potential transformative impact of AI tools in education, business, and research comes to the forefront. In the educational realm, conversational AI platforms like ChatGPT hold the promise to revolutionize traditional faculty-centric approaches. These platforms, exemplified by ChatGPT and Amelia, could provide 24/7 access to virtual instructors with globally validated knowledge, transcending language barriers and device constraints. This shift towards a student-centric educational paradigm has the potential to be highly beneficial, transforming the role of faculty into facilitators of learning and implementation.

In the business sector, conversational AI emerges as a potent force in enhancing creativity by facilitating fast, effective, and human-like customer interactions. The potential for businesses to engage in new and innovative customer interactions, automate routine tasks, and gain valuable insights into customer behavior and preferences is significant (Kietzmann et al., 2018; Ma & Sun, 2020). Notable companies, including H&M, Airbnb, Capital One, Oracle, Bank of America, and Google, are already leveraging conversational AI for various applications, ranging from personalized recommendations to customer service automation. However, these advancements are not without challenges. The use of ChatGPT introduces concerns related to the generation of deep fake text, misinformation propagation, lack of awareness of local rules and regulations, and the potential for inaccuracies due to the model's training on vast internet information. Ongoing research is essential to develop methods for detecting deep fake text, mitigating biases in training data, and addressing the ethical implications of AI-generated content.

In light of these challenges, the focus should extend to ongoing research that addresses potential risks while realizing the benefits of this technology. Key areas of concentration include developing methods to detect and mitigate bias, improving deep fake text detection, exploring applications in education and accessibility, leveraging ChatGPT in industry, and advancing our understanding of language and human communication. Thus, the increasing prevalence of generative AI systems like ChatGPT necessitates that future employees and managers acquire a diverse set of human skills to effectively and responsibly collaborate with these systems. The challenges extend beyond educational paradigms to reshape curricula in business schools, emphasizing critical thinking, digital literacy, creative problem-solving, and ethical decision-making. These skills, essential for navigating the evolving AI landscape, empower individuals to make informed and ethical decisions while working with these powerful systems.

CONCLUSION AND RECOMMENDATIONS

In concluding our exploration of AI communication and its evolving landscape, several key findings emerge. The intricate interplay between humans and AI brings forth a spectrum of opportunities, from enhancing productivity to transforming creative processes. Simultaneously, challenges such as interpretability, biases, and ethical concerns underscore the need for a careful and deliberate approach. The emergence of advanced AI tools like ChatGPT further amplifies these dynamics, prompting considerations about authenticity, biases, and the transformative potential of AI across various sectors.

To enhance AI communication, a multifaceted approach is crucial. Firstly, investing in research and development to improve the interpretability of AI systems is imperative, narrowing the gap between machine-generated decisions and human understanding. Addressing biases in training data demands ongoing efforts, ensuring that AI systems reflect diverse perspectives without perpetuating stereotypes. User education is equally vital, fostering an understanding of AI capabilities and limitations, which can contribute to more informed and responsible interactions. Ethics must remain at the forefront of AI development. Continuous scrutiny and refinement of algorithms are necessary to mitigate biases and avoid unintended consequences. Emphasizing transparency in AI processes, including the disclosure of training data sources, helps build trust. Collaboration among stakeholders, including researchers, developers, policymakers, and ethicists, can contribute to establishing robust ethical guidelines. Additionally, incorporating diverse voices in AI development teams promotes inclusivity and reduces the risk of unintentional biases.

Looking ahead, the future of AI communication holds promise and challenges. Advancements in explainable AI, privacy-preserving technologies, and ethical frameworks will shape a more trustworthy and user-friendly AI landscape. The integration of AI into diverse industries is inevitable, requiring a proactive approach in preparing individuals for the changing nature of work and collaboration. As AI continues to evolve, a commitment to responsible development, ethical use, and ongoing research will be instrumental in unlocking its full potential for the benefit of society. In conclusion, the journey through AI communication unveils a complex tapestry of opportunities and challenges. By embracing ethical practices, fostering transparency, and prioritizing user education, we can navigate the evolving landscape with resilience and responsibility. The future of AI communication rests not just on technological advancements but on the collective commitment to shaping an AI ecosystem that aligns with human values, diversity, and ethical considerations.

REFERENCES

Adam, M., Wessel, M., & Benlian, A. (2021). AI-based chatbots in customer service and their effects on user compliance. *Electronic Markets*, *31*(2), 427–445. doi:10.1007/s12525-020-00414-7

AlAfnan, M. A., Dishari, S., Jovic, M., & Lomidze, K. (2023). Chatgpt as an educational tool: Opportunities, challenges, and recommendations for communication, business writing, and composition courses. *Journal of Artificial Intelligence and Technology, 3*(2), 60–68. doi:10.37965/jait.2023.0184

Amato, F., Marrone, S., Moscato, V., Piantadosi, G., Picariello, A., & Sansone, C. (2017, November). Chatbots Meet eHealth: Automatizing Healthcare. In WAIAH@ AI* IA (pp. 40-49). Research Gate.

Awal, S. S., & Awal, S. S. (2023). ChatGPT and the healthcare industry: A comprehensive analysis of its impact on medical writing. *Journal of Public Health (Berlin)*, 1–4. doi:10.1007/s10389-023-02170-2

Bharti, U., Bajaj, D., Batra, H., Lalit, S., Lalit, S., & Gangwani, A. (2020, June). Medbot: Conversational artificial intelligence powered chatbot for delivering tele-health after covid-19. In *2020 5th international conference on communication and electronics systems (ICCES)* (pp. 870-875). IEEE.

Bhirud, N., Tataale, S., Randive, S., & Nahar, S. (2019). A literature review on chatbots in healthcare domain. *International Journal of Scientific & Technology Research, 8*(7), 225-231.

Cambria, E., Das, D., Bandyopadhyay, S., & Feraco, A. (Eds.). (2017). *A practical guide to sentiment analysis* (Vol. 5). Springer International Publishing. doi:10.1007/978-3-319-55394-8_1

Cowen, T. (2022). *ChatGPT Could Make Democracy Even More Messy*. Bloomberg.

Dai, Z., Yang, Z., Yang, Y., Carbonell, J., Le, Q. V., & Salakhutdinov, R. (2019). *Transformer-xl: Attentive language models beyond a fixed-length context*. arXiv preprint arXiv:1901.02860. doi:10.18653/v1/P19-1285

Devi, K. V., Manjula, V., & Pattewar, T. (2023). *ChatGPT: Comprehensive Study on Generative AI Tool*. Academic Guru Publishing House.

Devlin, J., Chang, M. W., Lee, K., & Toutanova, K. (2018). *Bert: Pre-training of deep bidirectional transformers for language understanding*. arXiv preprint arXiv:1810.04805.

Douglas, M. (2007). News coverage and social protest: How the media's protect paradigm exacerbates social conflict. *Journal of Dispute Resolution*, 185.

Dowling, M., & Lucey, B. (2023). ChatGPT for (finance) research: The Bananarama conjecture. *Finance Research Letters, 53*, 103662. doi:10.1016/j.frl.2023.103662

Dwivedi, Y. K., Hughes, L., Ismagilova, E., Aarts, G., Coombs, C., Crick, T., Duan, Y., Dwivedi, R., Edwards, J., Eirug, A., Galanos, V., Ilavarasan, P. V., Janssen, M., Jones, P., Kar, A. K., Kizgin, H., Kronemann, B., Lal, B., Lucini, B., & Williams, M. D. (2021, April 1). Artificial Intelligence (AI): Multidisciplinary perspectives on emerging challenges, opportunities, and agenda for research, practice and policy. *International Journal of Information Management, 57*, 101994. doi:10.1016/j.ijinfomgt.2019.08.002

Emily, M. (2020). Climbing towards NLU: On Meaning, Form, and Understanding in the Age of Data. In *Proceedings of the 58th Annual Meeting of the Association for Computational Linguistics. Association for Computational Linguistics*. ACL. 10.18653/v1/2020.acl-main.463

FiratM. (2023). How Chat GPT Can Transform Autodidactic Experiences and Open Education? doi:10.31219/osf.io/9ge8m

Fullan, M., Azorín, C., Harris, A., & Jones, M. (2023). Artificial intelligence and school leadership: Challenges, opportunities and implications. *School Leadership & Management*, 1–8. doi:10.1080/136 32434.2023.2246856

George, A. S., & George, A. H. (2023). A review of ChatGPT AI's impact on several business sectors. *Partners Universal International Innovation Journal*, *1*(1), 9–23.

Gozalo-Brizuela, R., & Garrido-Merchan, E. C. (2023). *ChatGPT is not all you need. A State of the Art Review of large Generative AI models*. arXiv preprint arXiv:2301.04655.

Grant, N., & Metz, C. (2022). A new chat bot is a 'code red' for Google's search business. *New York Times*.

Guzman, A. L., & Lewis, S. C. (2020). Artificial intelligence and communication: A Human–Machine Communication research agenda. *New Media & Society*, *22*(1), 70–86. doi:10.1177/1461444819858691

Henderson, P., Hashimoto, T., & Lemley, M. (2023). Where's the Liability in harmful AI Speech? *J. Free Speech L.*, *3*, 589.

Hohenstein, J., Kizilcec, R., Difranzo, D., Aghajari, Z., Mieczkowski, H., Levy, K., Naaman, M., Hancock, J., & Jung, M. (2023). Artificial intelligence in communication impacts language and social relationships. *Scientific Reports*, *13*(1), 5487. doi:10.1038/s41598-023-30938-9 PMID:37015964

Howard, J., & Ruder, S. (2018). *Universal language model fine-tuning for text classification*. arXiv preprint arXiv:1801.06146. doi:10.18653/v1/P18-1031

Huang, W., Hew, K. F., & Fryer, L. K. (2022). Chatbots for language learning—Are they really useful? A systematic review of chatbot-supported language learning. *Journal of Computer Assisted Learning*, *38*(1), 237–257. doi:10.1111/jcal.12610

ICML. (n.d.). *Clarification on Large Language Model Policy LLM*. ICML. https://icml.cc/Conferences/2023/llm-policy

Intelligence, N. M. (2023). *The AI writing on the wall*. Editorial.

Javaid, M., Haleem, A., & Singh, R. P. (2023). ChatGPT for healthcare services: An emerging stage for an innovative perspective. BenchCouncil Transactions on Benchmarks. *Standards and Evaluations*, *3*(1), 100105.

Javaid, M., Haleem, A., Singh, R. P., & Suman, R. (2021). Substantial capabilities of robotics in enhancing industry 4.0 implementation. *Cognitive Robotics*, *1*, 58–75. doi:10.1016/j.cogr.2021.06.001

Jeon, J., Lee, S., & Choe, H. (2023). Beyond ChatGPT: A conceptual framework and systematic review of speech-recognition chatbots for language learning. *Computers & Education*, *206*, 104898. doi:10.1016/j.compedu.2023.104898

Kayande, U., De Bruyn, A., Lilien, G. L., Rangaswamy, A., & Van Bruggen, G. H. (2009). How incorporating feedback mechanisms in a DSS affects DSS evaluations. *Information Systems Research*, *20*(4), 527–546. doi:10.1287/isre.1080.0198

Khurana, D., Koli, A., Khatter, K., & Singh, S. (2023). Natural language processing: State of the art, current trends and challenges. *Multimedia Tools and Applications*, *82*(3), 3713–3744. doi:10.1007/s11042-022-13428-4 PMID:35855771

Kietzmann, J., Paschen, J., & Treen, E. R. (2018). Artificial Intelligence in Advertising: How Marketers Can Leverage Artificial Intelligence Along the Consumer Journey. *Journal of Advertising Research*, *58*(3), 263–267. doi:10.2501/JAR-2018-035

Kim, S. W., & Lee, Y. (2023). Investigation into the Influence of Socio-Cultural Factors on Attitudes toward Artificial Intelligence. *Education and Information Technologies*. doi:10.1007/s10639-023-12172-y

Kingma, D. P., & Ba, J. (2014). *Adam: A method for stochastic optimization*. arXiv preprint arXiv:1412.6980.

Krugman, P. (2022). Does ChatGPT mean robots are coming for the skilled jobs. *The New York Times*. http://bit. ly/3HdnAp2

Lee, S. B. (2020). Chatbots and communication: The growing role of artificial intelligence in addressing and shaping customer needs. *Business Communication Research and Practice*, *3*(2), 103–111. doi:10.22682/bcrp.2020.3.2.103

Lock, S. (2022). What is AI chatbot phenomenon ChatGPT and could it replace humans. *The Guardian, 5*.

Ma, L., & Sun, B. (2020). Machine learning and AI in marketing–Connecting computing power to human insights. *International Journal of Research in Marketing*, *37*(3), 481–504. doi:10.1016/j.ijresmar.2020.04.005

Manning, C. D., Surdeanu, M., Bauer, J., Finkel, J. R., Bethard, S., & McClosky, D. (2014, June). The Stanford CoreNLP natural language processing toolkit. In *Proceedings of 52nd annual meeting of the association for computational linguistics: system demonstrations* (pp. 55-60). ACL. 10.3115/v1/P14-5010

Medhat, W., Hassan, A., & Korashy, H. (2014). Sentiment analysis algorithms and applications: A survey. *Ain Shams Engineering Journal*, *5*(4), 1093–1113. doi:10.1016/j.asej.2014.04.011

Mekni, M. (2021). An artificial intelligence based virtual assistant using conversational agents. *Journal of Software Engineering and Applications*, *14*(9), 455–473. doi:10.4236/jsea.2021.149027

Michael, J., & Hughes, T. (2021). *Tech-Powered Sales: Achieve Superhuman Sales Skills*. HarperCollins Leadership.

Miller, A. (2019). The intrinsically linked future for human and Artificial Intelligence interaction. *Journal of Big Data*, *6*(1), 38. doi:10.1186/s40537-019-0202-7

Murtarelli, G., Gregory, A., & Romenti, S. (2021). A conversation-based perspective for shaping ethical human–machine interactions: The particular challenge of chatbots. *Journal of Business Research*, *129*, 927–935. doi:10.1016/j.jbusres.2020.09.018

Nair, M. M., Tyagi, A. K., & Sreenath, N. (2021, January). The future with industry 4.0 at the core of society 5.0: Open issues, future opportunities and challenges. In *2021 international conference on computer communication and informatics (ICCCI)* (pp. 1-7). IEEE.

Nazir, A., & Wang, Z. (2023). A Comprehensive Survey of ChatGPT: Advancements, Applications, Prospects, and Challenges. *Meta-Radiology*, *1*(2), 100022. doi:10.1016/j.metrad.2023.100022 PMID:37901715

Open A. I. (n.d.). *OpenAI Blog*. OpenAI. https://openai.com/blog/.

Pham, S. T., & Sampson, P. M. (2022). The development of artificial intelligence in education: A review in context. *Journal of Computer Assisted Learning*, *38*(5), 1408–1421. doi:10.1111/jcal.12687

Phul, H., & Mangi, A. (2023). *Service Marketing Acts As Sales Booster: Exploring The Impact On Cosmetic Business*. Research Gate.

Radford, A., Wu, J., Child, R., Luan, D., Amodei, D., & Sutskever, I. (2019). *Language Models Are Unsupervised Multitask Learners*. OpenAI Blog. https://life-extension.github.io/2020/05/27/GPT

Reverberi, C., Rigon, T., Solari, A., Hassan, C., Cherubini, P., Antonelli, G., Awadie, H., Bernhofer, S., Carballal, S., Dinis-Ribeiro, M., Fernández-Clotett, A., Esparrach, G. F., Gralnek, I., Higasa, Y., Hirabayashi, T., Hirai, T., Iwatate, M., Kawano, M., Mader, M., & Cherubini, A. (2022). Experimental evidence of effective human–AI collaboration in medical decision-making. *Scientific Reports*, *12*(1), 14952. doi:10.1038/s41598-022-18751-2 PMID:36056152

Ribas, J. (2023). *Building the New Bing*. LinkedIn. https://www.linkedin.com/pulse/building-new-bing-jordi-ribas

Roco, M. C., & Bainbridge, W. S. (2002). Converging technologies for improving human performance: Integrating from the nanoscale. *Journal of Nanoparticle Research*, *4*(4), 281–295. doi:10.1023/A:1021152023349

Roose, K. (2022). The brilliance and weirdness of ChatGPT. *The New York Times*.

Rudolph, J., Tan, S., & Tan, S. (2023). ChatGPT: Bullshit spewer or the end of traditional assessments in higher education? *Journal of Applied Learning and Teaching*, *6*(1).

Schwartz, R., Dodge, J., Smith, N. A., & Etzioni, O. (2020, November). Green AI. *Communications of the ACM*, *63*(12), 54–63. doi:10.1145/3381831

Sheehan, B., Jin, H. S., & Gottlieb, U. (2020). Customer service chatbots: Anthropomorphism and adoption. *Journal of Business Research*, *115*, 14–24. doi:10.1016/j.jbusres.2020.04.030

Skjuve, M., Følstad, A., & Brandtzaeg, P. B. (2023). The user experience of ChatGPT: findings from a questionnaire study of early users. *Proceedings of the 5th International Conference on Conversational User Interfaces*. ACM. 10.1145/3571884.3597144

Strubell, E., Ganesh, A., & McCallum, A. (2019). Energy and Policy Considerations for Deep Learning in NLP. In *Proceedings of the 57th Annual Meeting of the Association for Computational Linguistics*. ACM. 10.18653/v1/P19-1355

Tai, M. C. (2020, August 14). The impact of artificial intelligence on human society and bioethics. *Tzu-Chi Medical Journal*, *32*(4), 339–343. doi:10.4103/tcmj.tcmj_71_20 PMID:33163378

Torfi, A., Shirvani, R. A., Keneshloo, Y., Tavaf, N., & Fox, E. A. (2020). *Natural language processing advancements by deep learning: A survey*. arXiv preprint arXiv:2003.01200.

Twyman, M. (2017). Black Lives Matter in Wikipedia: Collective memory and collaboration around online social movements. In *Proceedings of the 2017 ACM Conference on Computer Supported Cooperative Work and Social Computing*. ACM.

Vaswani, A., Shazeer, N., Parmar, N., Uszkoreit, J., Jones, L., Gomez, A. N., & Polosukhin, I. (2017). Attention is all you need. *Advances in Neural Information Processing Systems*, 30.

White House. (n.d.). *Blueprint for An AI Bill of Rights*. The White House. https://www.whitehouse.gov/ostp/ai-bill-of-rights/

Wu, T., He, S., Liu, J., Sun, S., Liu, K., Han, Q. L., & Tang, Y. (2023). A brief overview of ChatGPT: The history, status quo and potential future development. *IEEE/CAA Journal of Automatica Sinica, 10*(5), 1122-1136.

Wu, Y., Schuster, M., Chen, Z., Le, Q. V., Norouzi, M., Macherey, W., Krikun, M., Cao, Y., Gao, Q., Macherey, K., & Klingner, J. (2016). *Google's neural machine translation system: Bridging the gap between human and machine translation.* arXiv preprint arXiv:1609.08144.

Yogesh, K. (2023). "So what if ChatGPT wrote it?" Multidisciplinary perspectives on opportunities, challenges and implications of generative conversational AI for research, practice and policy. *International Journal of Information Management, 71*. doi:10.1016/j.ijinfomgt.2023.102642

Yue, B., & Li, H. (2023). The impact of human-AI collaboration types on consumer evaluation and usage intention: A perspective of responsibility attribution. *Frontiers in Psychology, 14*, 1277861. doi:10.3389/fpsyg.2023.1277861 PMID:38022995

Zaimah, N. R., Hartanto, E. B., & Zahro, F. (2024). Acceptability and Effectiveness Analysis of Large Language Model-Based Artificial Intelligence Chatbot Among Arabic Learners. *Mantiqu Tayr: Journal of Arabic Language, 4*(1), 1–20.

Chapter 3
Algorithmic Issues, Challenges, and Theoretical Concerns of ChatGPT

Pradnya Patil
ⓘ https://orcid.org/0000-0001-8313-8635
K.J. Somaiya Institute of Technology, Mumbai, India

Kaustubh Kulkarni
ⓘ https://orcid.org/0000-0002-1270-0878
K.J. Somaiya College of Engineering, Somaiya University, Mumbai, India

Priyanka Sharma
ⓘ https://orcid.org/0000-0002-9503-1170
Swami Keshvanand Institute of Technology, Management, and Gramothan, India

ABSTRACT

Large language model (LLM) ChatGPT has made tremendous progress in natural language processing (NLP), especially in human-quality text production, multilingual translation, and content creation. However, because of its extensive use, algorithmic issues, challenges, and theoretical queries come up. Fairness, bias, explainability, generalization, originality, inventiveness, and safety are the main topics of this study's examination of ChatGPT's intricate theoretical and algorithmic components. It looks into the possibility of explainability, transferability, generalization, bias in the data, and the model's capacity to provide original and imaginative content. It also covers possible issues including harmful use, disseminating incorrect information, and offensive or misleading content. These limitations can be addressed so that ChatGPT can be improved to provide LLMs that are more dependable, accountable, and long-lasting while posing no needless risks.

DOI: 10.4018/979-8-3693-6824-4.ch003

INTRODUCTION

Recent years have witnessed a notable improvement in the field of Natural Language Processing (NLP), with ChatGPT pushing the frontiers of conversational AI. However, alongside these advancements come algorithmic issues, challenges, and theoretical concerns that demand careful consideration and investigation. This chapter delves into the critical aspects surrounding ChatGPT, exploring the motivations behind addressing these issues, outlining proposed solutions, and providing an overview of the chapter's contents.

ChatGPT embodies a significant milestone in the development of conversational AI, leveraging large-scale transformer architectures to generate human-like responses across various domains and topics. As these models become more pervasive in applications such as customer service, education, and entertainment, it becomes imperative to examine the algorithmic intricacies that underpin their functionality.

The motivation behind studying algorithmic issues, challenges, and theoretical concerns in ChatGPT stems from the dual objectives of advancing the capabilities of conversational AI while ensuring ethical and responsible deployment. Biases, fairness, interpretability, and performance optimization are among the key motivations driving this exploration, aiming to enhance the robustness, inclusivity, and reliability of AI-generated conversations.

The proposed work in this chapter encompasses a comprehensive analysis of algorithmic issues such as bias amplification, stereotypical responses, lack of diversity, contextual bias, data source bias, fairness, and equity within ChatGPT. Additionally, solutions and mitigation strategies, including bias detection techniques, fairness-aware training algorithms, data augmentation approaches, and contextual calibration methods, will be discussed and evaluated.

The chapter begins by contextualizing the significance of algorithmic issues and theoretical concerns in the context of ChatGPT's development and deployment. It then delves into a detailed examination of each identified challenge, providing insights into their underlying causes and potential impact on conversational AI systems. Following this, proposed solutions and mitigation strategies will be presented, drawing from both existing research and innovative approaches tailored to ChatGPT's architecture and capabilities. Finally, an overarching overview will synthesize the key findings, implications, and future directions in addressing algorithmic issues and theoretical concerns to foster the responsible and effective use of ChatGPT and similar conversational AI models.

LITERATURE REVIEW

Brief Overview of ChatGPT

A complex neural network architecture, trained on a sizable corpus of online text data, is at the core of ChatGPT. One of the pioneering works that laid the foundation for ChatGPT's architecture is the seminal paper (Brown et al., 2020), wherein the authors introduced the concept of large-scale language models as few-shot learners. This breakthrough highlighted the remarkable ability of models like ChatGPT to generalize across diverse language tasks with minimal task-specific training data. Furthermore, Radford et al.(Wu & Lode, 2020) elucidated the unsupervised multitask learning capabilities inherent in language models, providing insights into the underlying mechanisms driving ChatGPT's remarkable versatility.

Significance of Understanding Algorithmic Issues and Theoretical Concerns

As ChatGPT and similar language models continue to permeate various facets of society, understanding the algorithmic issues and theoretical concerns associated with these systems becomes paramount. Mittelstadt et al. (Mittelstadt et al., 2016) pioneered the discourse on the ethics of algorithms, emphasizing the need to scrutinize the societal implications of algorithmic decision-making processes. Additionally, Barocas, Hardt, and Narayanan (Solon Barocas, Moritz Hardt, 2020) shed light on the challenges surrounding fairness in machine learning, highlighting the potential for algorithmic biases to perpetuate societal inequities. These seminal works underscore the critical importance of questioning the ramifications of deploying AI systems similar to ChatGPT in real-world contexts on ethical and societal aspects.

Purpose of the Chapter in the Context of Real-Time Data Decisions With AI

In light of the rapid proliferation of AI technologies, the need to address real-time data decisions with AI becomes increasingly pressing. Zou et al. (Zou & Schiebinger, 2018) shed light on the pervasive issue of algorithmic bias, highlighting instances where AI systems exhibit discriminatory behaviors along gender and racial lines. Furthermore, Mitchell et al.(Mitchell et al., 2019) advocate for improved transparency and responsibility in AI model reporting, emphasizing the importance of model cards as a means to document and communicate the performance characteristics of AI systems. Against this backdrop, this chapter seeks to elucidate the intricate interplay between algorithmic decision-making and real-time data processing, with a specific focus on the theoretical underpinnings and ethical considerations surrounding ChatGPT.

Algorithmic Overview of ChatGPT

Description of the Underlying Transformer Architecture

The transformer architecture was created by Vaswani et al. (2017) in their seminal work "Attention is All You Need," which represents a radical paradigm shift in the field of natural language processing. Conventional sequence-to-sequence models, such Convolutional Neural Networks (CNNs) and Recurrent Neural Networks (RNNs), frequently have trouble preserving contextual information between sequences and capturing dependencies on previous inputs. On the other hand, the transformer design makes use of attention processes to analyze input sequences in parallel, which makes learning complicated language patterns more effective and efficient.

The transformer design is based on the self-attention mechanism, which allows the model to analyze individual words by calculating their relative importance. The attention mechanism aids in improving the model's ability to grasp long-range relationships by narrowing in on relevant portions of the input sequence and removing irrelevant information. Transformers are consequently well-suited for a range of NLP applications as they excel at tasks requiring the understanding of word connections and context.

One key innovation introduced by (Vaswani et al., 2017) is the idea of "multi-head attention," which applies the self-attention process repeatedly in tandem, each with its own set of learnable parameters. Multi-head attention helps the model catch a wider range of linguistic patterns and relationships by enabling it to attend to distinct segments of the input sequence concurrently. This parallel processing capability not only improves the model's performance but also enables efficient training on large-scale datasets.

Another notable aspect of the transformer architecture is its use of position-wise feedforward networks, which apply separate linear transformations to every position in the sequence of inputs. This design lets the model capture position-specific information and learn complex nonlinear associations between words within the sequence. Position-wise feedforward networks help the transformer describe extended dependencies and encode rich contextual details in the input representation when combined with the self-attention mechanism.

The transformer architecture has emerged as a key concept in NLP, offering unparalleled capabilities in modeling sequential data with complex dependencies. The paper by (Devlin et al., 2019) introduced a groundbreaking extension to the transformer architecture with their paper "BERT: Pre-training of Deep Bidirectional Transformers for Language Understanding." An important development in natural language processing (NLP) is Bidirectional Encoder Representations from Transformers (BERT), particularly for language comprehension problems.

The transformer architecture is the primary component of BERT, which leverages attention mechanisms to capture contextual information and dependencies across input sequences. Unlike traditional unidirectional models, BERT adopts a bidirectional approach, allowing the model to consider both left and right context when encoding every word in the input sequence. This bidirectional encoding scheme enables BERT to capture richer semantic representations and better understand the nuances of natural language.

One of the important innovations introduced by BERT is the concept of masked language modeling, where the model's job is to predict the masked tokens based on the surrounding context after a subset of the input sequence's tokens are masked during pre-training. This technique encourages the model to learn bidirectional representations by considering both the left and right context of every token, thereby improving its ability to capture contextual information and perform language understanding tasks.

Additionally, BERT incorporates the concept of next sentence prediction, where pairs of sentences are provided as input during pre-training, and the model is trained to determine if the second sentence comes after the first. This objective encourages the model to learn association between sentences and understand the flow of discourse within a given context.

The pre-training methodology proposed by (Devlin et al., 2019) enables BERT to learn general-purpose language representations from huge amounts of unlabeled text data, paving the way for fine-tuning on downstream NLP tasks with limited labeled data. By pre-training on varied linguistic contexts and domains, BERT learns rich and contextualized representations of words and sentences, helping it to achieve cutting-edge performance across a wide range of NLP benchmarks.

Like GPT, there are many other architectures like BERT, Transformer, T5, ViT, DETR, Transformer XL, and BERT variants. This comparison is shown in the Table 1.

Training Methodology and Data Used

In their pioneering work, (Radford et al., 2018) present an approach to enhancing language understanding through generative pre-training. This work signifies a significant milestone in NLP, offering insights into the training methodology and data utilized to pre-train large-scale language models.

Radford et al. propose a training methodology consisting of two steps; unsupervised pre-training followed by supervised fine-tuning. During the pre-training phase, the model is fed vast amounts of unlabeled text data, allowing it to learn rich and contextually relevant representations of language. The authors leverage a generative approach to pre-training, wherein the model is trained to predict the next

Table 1. Comparison of various transformer architectures

Architecture	Key Components	Main Innovations	Applications
Transformer (Vaswani et al., 2017)	Encoder-decoder, multi-head self-attention	Original transformer model	Machine translation
BERT (Kowsher et al., 2022)	Bidirectional, MLM pre-training, NSP task	Bidirectional pre-training	NLP tasks (e.g., sentiment analysis)
GPT (Radford et al., 2018)	Unidirectional, autoregressive training	Language model for text generation	Text generation
BERT Variants (Yan et al., 2022)	Various improvements on BERT architecture	Parameter efficiency, compressed architectures	Named Entity Recognition
Transformer-XL(Elnaggar et al., 2022)	Segment-level recurrence, longer context modeling	Address fixed-length context limitation	Long-range dependency tasks
T5(Raffel et al., 2020)	Unified text-to-text framework	Text-to-text format for all tasks	Multitask learning
ViT(Dosovitskiy et al., 2021)	Self-attention for image processing	Applied transformers to computer vision	Classify Images
DETR(Carion et al., 2020)	Transformers for Detecting the objects	Replaced CNN-based detectors	Object detection

word in a sequence given its context. In order to achieve this goal, the model is encouraged to recognize both sequential and hierarchical connections in the input data. enabling it to acquire a deeper understanding of linguistic structures.

One of the key innovations introduced by (Radford et al., 2018) is the use of a transformer-based architecture for language modeling. Transformers leverage attention mechanisms to capture contextual information and dependencies across input sequences, enabling more efficient and effective learning of language patterns. By leveraging transformers for generative pre-training, Radford et al. demonstrate significant improvements in language understanding tasks, surpassing previous benchmarks in various NLP benchmarks.

Radford et al. (Radford et al., 2018) discussed the training approach in addition to the significance of data selection and preparation in the pre-training phase. To guarantee the trained model's robustness and generalizability, the authors stress the importance of having a variety of representative datasets. They pre-train their language model using a variety of proprietary and publicly accessible text corpora, covering a broad spectrum of linguistic contexts and domains.

The pre-training process outlined by Radford et al. (Radford et al., 2018) culminates in fine-tuning on downstream NLP tasks, where the pre-trained model is adapted to specific tasks with labeled data. Fine-tuning enables the model to leverage its learned representations for tasks such as sentiment analysis, text classification, and named entity recognition, among others.

In the pursuit of training large-scale language models, Shoeybi et al.(M. Shoeybi, 2020) introduced a groundbreaking approach with their paper titled "Megatron-LM: Training Multi-Billion Parameter Language Models Using Model Parallelism." This work represents a significant advancement in the field of NLP, offering insights into the training methodology and data utilized to train massive language models capable of capturing rich linguistic patterns.

The central innovation proposed by Shoeybi et al. (M. Shoeybi, 2020) revolves around the use of model parallelism to scale up training to unprecedented levels. Traditional approaches to training Large Language Models (LLM) often face scalability challenges due to memory constraints and computational overhead. Megatron-LM addresses these challenges by distributing the model across multiple accelerators and leveraging model parallelism to enable efficient training of multi-billion parameter language models.

At the heart of Megatron-LM lies the concept of data parallelism combined with model parallelism. Data parallelism involves distributing batches of training data across multiple devices and synchronizing model updates to ensure consistency across parallel computations. Model parallelism, on the other hand, involves partitioning the model parameters across multiple devices and orchestrating communication between devices to compute gradients and update model parameters effectively.

Shoeybi et al.(M. Shoeybi, 2020) present a novel approach to implementing model parallelism in the context of training large language models. By partitioning the model parameters and computation graph across multiple accelerators, Megatron-LM enables efficient utilization of computational resources and scales training to unprecedented levels. This approach not only accelerates training but also enables the exploration of larger model architectures and datasets, leading to improvements in model performance and generalization.

In addition to the training methodology, Shoeybi et al. (M. Shoeybi, 2020)discuss the importance of data selection and preprocessing in training LLMs. The authors leverage a diverse range of text corpora, including publicly available datasets and proprietary sources, to pre-train Megatron-LM on a wide variety of linguistic contexts and domains. This diverse training data ensures that the model learns robust and generalizable representations of language, enabling it to perform effectively across different NLP tasks and domains.

The training process outlined by Shoeybi et al (M. Shoeybi, 2020)culminates in fine-tuning on downstream NLP tasks, where the pre-trained Megatron-LM model is adapted to specific tasks with labeled data. Fine-tuning enables the model to leverage its learned representations for tasks such as text classification, language generation, and sentiment analysis, among others.

Transfer Learning and Fine-Tuning Process

In their paper "Exploring the Limits of Transfer Learning with a Unified Text-to-Text Transformer," Raffel et al. (Raffel et al., 2020)present a comprehensive investigation into the efficacy and limitations of transfer learning in the context of text understanding tasks. This work sheds light on the transfer learning and fine-tuning process, offering insights into the strategies employed to adapt pre-trained language models to specific downstream tasks.

A popular machine learning technique called "transfer learning" uses information from one job to enhance performance on another. Transfer learning has shown to be very useful in the field of NLP, allowing researchers to fine-tune massive language models on downstream tasks with sparse labelled data after pre-training them on enormous volumes of unlabeled text data.

The work by (Raffel et al., 2020) propose an integrated text-to-text transformer architecture for transfer learning that transforms all natural language processing jobs into text-to-text issues. This formulation allows for a consistent and generalizable approach to transfer learning, wherein both pre-training and fine-tuning involve mapping input text to output text. By unifying the representation of tasks as text transformations, Raffel et al. (Raffel et al., 2020)demonstrate improvements in the transfer learning performance on a variety of NLP tasks, such as language production, question answering, and text classification.

The fine-tuning process outlined by Raffel et al. (Raffel et al., 2020) involves adapting a pre-trained language model to a specific downstream task by fine-tuning its parameters on task-specific data.

Fine-tuning typically involves updating the parameters of the pre-trained model using gradient-based optimization methods to minimize a task-specific loss function, such as Adam optimization or stochastic gradient descent (SGD).

One key insight provided by Raffel et al. (Raffel et al., 2020) is the importance of task-specific pre-processing and tokenization strategies during fine-tuning. Different downstream tasks may require different pre-processing and tokenization techniques to represent input data effectively for the pre-trained language model. By carefully designing task-specific pre-processing pipelines, researchers can maximize the compatibility between the pre-trained model and the downstream task, thereby improving fine-tuning performance.

Additionally, Raffel et al. (Raffel et al., 2020) highlight the potential benefits of multi-task learning during fine-tuning, wherein the pre-trained language model is simultaneously fine-tuned on multiple related tasks. Multi-task learning allows the model to leverage shared representations across tasks, enabling more efficient transfer of knowledge and improved generalization performance.

Wolf et al. present a comprehensive overview of the transformers library, in their paper (Wolf et al., 2020) which has become a cornerstone in NLP research and applications. This work sheds light on the transfer learning and fine-tuning process, offering insights into the strategies employed to adapt pre-trained language models to specific downstream tasks.

By allowing researchers to use pre-trained language models to obtain state-of-the-art performance on a variety of tasks, transfer learning has completely changed the area of NLP. Hugging Face's transformers library offers a consistent framework for using transformer-based models that have already been trained, making it easier to transfer learning and fine-tune across a variety of NLP applications.

One of the key contributions of the transformer library is its support for a diverse range of pre-trained transformer models, including BERT, GPT, RoBERTa, and DistilBERT, among others. These pre-trained models serve as powerful starting points for transfer learning, capturing rich linguistic patterns and semantic representations from huge amounts of unlabeled text data.

The transformers library helps with the fine-tuning process, which is adjusting the parameters of a pre-trained language model based on task-specific input to tailor it to a particular downstream job. To minimize a task-specific loss function, fine-tuning usually entails changing the parameters of the pre-trained model using gradient-based optimization techniques, such as Adam optimization or stochastic gradient descent (SGD).

One notable feature of the transformer's library is its support for task-specific model architectures and configurations, enabling researchers to fine-tune pre-trained models for a diverse array of NLP tasks, comprising question answering, text classification, language generation, and named entity recognition. By providing a flexible and extensible framework for fine-tuning pre-trained models, the transformers library has made cutting-edge NLP more accessible to everybody and has accelerated progress in the field.

Moreover, the transformers library provides a rich set of tools and utilities for data preprocessing, model evaluation, and inference, streamlining the fine-tuning process and enabling researchers to focus on developing task-specific solutions. This ecosystem of tools and resources has fostered a vibrant community of NLP practitioners and researchers, driving innovation and collaboration in the field.

KEY ALGORITHMIC ISSUES

Bias and Fairness

Discussion on Biases in Training Data

Work by (Bolukbasi et al., 2016) delve into the pervasive issue of biases present in word embeddings, a central component of many NLP systems, including language models like ChatGPT.

Word embeddings are vector representations of words in a continuous dense vector space. They have become a cornerstone in NLP research, enabling algorithms to capture semantic relationships and contextual information between words. However, work by (Bolukbasi et al., 2016)highlight a critical limitation of word embeddings: their susceptibility to encoding and perpetuating societal biases present in the training data.

The study by Bolukbasi et al. (Bolukbasi et al., 2016) underscores the insidious nature of biases embedded in word embeddings, as exemplified by the association between gender-neutral professions and gender-specific terms. Through careful analysis, the authors reveal troubling patterns in word embeddings, such as the tendency to associate female gender pronouns with domestic roles and male gender pronouns with technical or professional occupations. This gender bias reflects and reinforces societal stereotypes and inequalities, posing significant ethical and societal concerns for NLP systems.

Furthermore, Bolukbasi et al. (Bolukbasi et al., 2016)demonstrate the downstream impact of biased word embeddings on NLP applications, including search engines, sentiment analysis, and machine translation. Biases present in word embeddings can propagate and amplify throughout the entire system, leading to biased outcomes and discriminatory behaviors in AI-driven decision-making processes.

To address the pervasive issue of biases in word embeddings, Bolukbasi et al. (Bolukbasi et al., 2016) propose a novel debiasing technique aimed at neutralizing gender-specific associations present in the embedding space. By orthogonalizing word embeddings along gender dimensions, the authors aim to mitigate gender bias while preserving semantic relationships between words. This debiasing approach represents a crucial step towards developing fairer and more equitable NLP systems that uphold principles of diversity, equity, and inclusion.

The study by Bolukbasi et al. (Bolukbasi et al., 2016)underscores the importance of critically examining and addressing biases in training data, particularly in the context of language models like ChatGPT. Biases present in word embeddings can have far-reaching implications, shaping the behavior and decision-making processes of AI systems and perpetuating societal inequalities.

The authors (Dixon et al., 2018)in their paper "Measuring and Mitigating Unintended Bias in Text Classification" shed light on the pervasive issue of biases inherent in training data, particularly in the context of text classification tasks. Published in the arXiv preprint, the study addresses the critical need to measure and mitigate unintended biases that can distort the outcomes of text classification algorithms, including those used in NLP systems like ChatGPT.

The authors recognize that training data, often collected from real-world sources, may inadvertently reflect and perpetuate societal biases and stereotypes. These biases can manifest in various forms, including gender, race, ethnicity, religion, and socio-economic status, among others. Left unaddressed, biased training data can lead to discriminatory outcomes and reinforce existing inequalities in NLP systems and other AI-driven applications.

Authors (Dixon et al., 2018)employ a systematic approach to identify and quantify unintended biases present in training data for text classification tasks. By analyzing large-scale datasets spanning diverse domains and topics, the authors identify patterns of bias that may influence the performance of text classification algorithms. These biases can manifest in the form of skewed distributions, underrepresentation of certain demographic groups, or language that perpetuates stereotypes and prejudices.

· To mitigate unintended biases in text classification, Dixon et al. (Dixon et al., 2018)propose a series of mitigation strategies aimed at promoting fairness, transparency, and accountability in AI systems. One such strategy involves augmenting training data with diverse examples representing underrepresented groups and perspectives. By enriching the training data with a more balanced representation of diverse voices, algorithms can learn to make more informed and equitable decisions across different demographic groups.

Furthermore, the authors advocate for the use of fairness-aware learning algorithms that explicitly optimize for fairness objectives alongside traditional performance metrics. Fairness-aware algorithms can mitigate biases by penalizing discriminatory behaviors and promoting equitable outcomes across different demographic groups. By integrating fairness considerations into the learning process, algorithms can strive to uphold principles of fairness and non-discrimination in their decision-making processes.

The study by(Dixon et al., 2018) emphasizes how crucial it is to measure and reduce unintentional biases in training data for tasks involving text categorization. By proactively addressing biases at the data level and algorithmic level, researchers and practitioners can help build more inclusive and equitable AI systems that serve diverse communities and uphold principles of fairness and social justice.

Challenges in Addressing Bias in Responses

Work by (Bender et al., 2021) delve into the challenges surrounding bias in responses generated by LLMs in their paper. The study sheds light on the complex interplay between model size, training data, and the perpetuation of biases in language generation tasks, raising critical questions about the ethical implications of deploying LLMs like ChatGPT.

LLMs have shown themselves to be quite adept at producing text that is human-like for a variety of applications, including conversation production and text completion. However, Bender et al. (Bender et al., 2021)caution against the uncritical deployment of such models, highlighting the risks associated with biases inherent in the training data and the potential for LLMs to amplify and perpetuate these biases in their generated responses.

One of the key challenges identified by (Bender et al., 2021) is the phenomenon of "stochastic parroting," wherein LLMs mimic and reproduce biases present in the training data, often without discernment or critical evaluation. This blind reproduction of biases can lead to harmful and discriminatory outcomes, reinforcing stereotypes, prejudices, and inequalities in the text generated by these models.

Moreover, Bender et al. (Bender et al., 2021) argue that the sheer scale and complexity of LLMs exacerbate the challenges of addressing bias in responses. Traditional mitigation strategies, such as debiasing techniques and fairness-aware training algorithms, may be insufficient to fully address the nuanced and context-dependent nature of biases in language generation tasks. As a result, biases in responses generated by LLMs can persist despite efforts to mitigate them, posing significant ethical and societal risks.

The work by (Bender et al., 2021) underscores the need for improved accountability and transparency and avoiding omissions of the information in the development and deployment of LLMs. While these models offer unprecedented capabilities in natural language understanding and generation, their potential for harm cannot be overlooked. Bender et al. (Bender et al., 2021) advocate for critical examination and evaluation of LLMs, including assessments of their impact on fairness, diversity, and inclusion in language generation tasks.

Furthermore, Bender et al. (Bender et al., 2021) call for interdisciplinary collaboration and engagement across diverse stakeholders, including researchers, policymakers, industry practitioners, and civil society organizations, to address the complex challenges surrounding bias in responses generated by LLMs. By fostering dialogue and collaboration, stakeholders can work together to develop ethical guidelines, best practices, and regulatory frameworks to promote fairness, accountability, and transparency in the deployment of AI-driven systems.

Ian Tenney et. al. (Tenney et al., 2019) examine the intricate relationship between contextualized word representations and biases in language generation tasks in their study. The study sheds light on the challenges associated with addressing biases in responses generated by language models like ChatGPT.

Transformer-based language models have made contextualized word representations popular, which are able to capture the relationships and contextual information between words in a phrase. These representations make it possible to generate language that is more contextually relevant and sophisticated, but they also make it more difficult to detect and reduce biases in the training set.

One of the key challenges identified by Tenney et. al. (Tenney et al., 2019) is the opacity of contextualized word representations, which makes it difficult to interpret and understand the underlying factors contributing to biases in language generation tasks. Unlike traditional word embeddings, which represent words as fixed vectors independent of context, contextualized word representations encode dynamic and context-dependent information, making it challenging to isolate and analyze biases at the word level.

To address the challenge of interpreting biases in contextualized word representations, Tenney et. al. (Tenney et al., 2019) propose a probing approach aimed at uncovering the underlying sentence structure and syntactic information encoded in the representations. By designing probing tasks that target specific linguistic phenomena, such as subject-verb agreement or syntactic dependency parsing, researchers can gain insights into the information captured by contextualized word representations and identify potential sources of biases.

The study by Tenney et. al. (Tenney et al., 2019) underscores the importance of understanding the role of context in shaping biases in language generation tasks. Language models' word selection and generation can be impacted by small biases found in the training data, which can appear inside a phrase. By probing contextualized word representations, researchers can elucidate the mechanisms underlying biases and develop targeted strategies for mitigating them.

Furthermore, Tenney et. al. (Tenney et al., 2019) advocate for interdisciplinary collaboration and methodological diversity in the study of biases in language generation tasks. Addressing biases in responses requires a multifaceted approach that integrates insights from computational linguistics, cognitive science, and social sciences. By drawing on diverse perspectives and methodologies, researchers can develop a more holistic and nuanced understanding of biases in language generation tasks and devise effective strategies for mitigating them.

Strategies for Mitigating Bias

Xie et al. (Xie et al., 2020) present a novel approach to mitigating bias in machine learning models through self-training with a noisy student in their paper. Their study offers insights into effective strategies for mitigating bias and improving the fairness of machine learning models, including those used in NLP systems like ChatGPT.

Bias in machine learning models, including language models like ChatGPT, can arise from various sources, including skewed training data, inherent biases in the learning algorithm, and feedback loops that perpetuate and amplify existing biases. Left unaddressed, these biases can lead to unfair and discriminatory outcomes, reinforcing societal inequalities and exacerbating disparities in access and opportunity.

To mitigate bias in machine learning models, Xie et al. (Xie et al., 2020)propose a self-training approach that leverages a noisy student model to improve classification performance on ImageNet, a widely used benchmark dataset in computer vision tasks. The noisy student model is trained on noisy, augmented data generated by adding perturbations to the original training data, thereby simulating real-world variations and challenges.

One key insight provided by Xie et al. (Xie et al., 2020) is the importance of incorporating diverse and representative training data to mitigate bias in machine learning models. By augmenting the training data with noise and perturbations, the noisy student model learns to generalize more robustly and adapt to variations in the input space, thereby reducing the risk of overfitting to biased or spurious patterns in the data.

Furthermore, Xie et al. (Xie et al., 2020)emphasize the role of self-training as a form of iterative learning that enables the model to continually refine and improve its performance over time. Through self-training, the noisy student model gradually reduces its reliance on noisy labels and learns to distill more accurate and discriminative representations from the training data, leading to improvements in classification accuracy and generalization performance.

The study by Xie et al. (Xie et al., 2020)underscores the importance of incorporating principled regularization techniques and data augmentation strategies to mitigate bias in machine learning models. By introducing controlled noise and perturbations into the training process, researchers can encourage models to learn more robust and generalizable representations of the underlying data distribution, thereby reducing the risk of bias and improving fairness in model predictions.

In their paper, Roselli et. al. (Roselli et al., 2019)emphasizes that while AI holds immense potential to revolutionize various industries, the presence of bias can lead to unfair outcomes and perpetuate existing societal inequalities.

The authors (Roselli et al., 2019) begin by highlighting the significance of bias in AI, explaining how biases present in training data, algorithms, and decision-making processes can result in discriminatory practices. They stress that bias in AI systems often reflects societal biases encoded in the data used for training, posing challenges for fairness and equity.

One key aspect discussed in the paper (Roselli et al., 2019) is the role of data preprocessing in mitigating bias. The authors advocate for careful examination of training data to identify and address biases at the source. They suggest techniques such as data augmentation, sampling strategies, and feature engineering to reduce bias and improve the representativeness of datasets used for training AI models.

Furthermore, the paper (Roselli et al., 2019) explores the importance of algorithmic transparency and interpretability in understanding and addressing bias in AI systems. The authors argue that transparent algorithms enable stakeholders to scrutinize model behavior, identify bias patterns, and intervene when necessary. They advocate for the development of explainable AI techniques that provide insights into the decision-making process of AI models.

Another crucial aspect discussed in the paper (Roselli et al., 2019)is the necessity of inclusion and diversity in teams developing AI. The authors stress that diverse teams may successfully detect and

Table 2. Types of bias and their potential solutions

Challenge	Potential Solution
Training Data Bias	- Curating training data to be more balanced and representative. - Techniques like data augmentation to create more inclusive datasets.
Model Architecture Bias	- Designing model architectures that are less susceptible to amplifying biases in the data. - Research on bias detection and mitigation methods within the model itself.
Evaluation and Monitoring	- Developing robust benchmarks to identify and measure bias in LLM outputs. - Continuously monitoring LLM outputs for signs of bias and taking corrective actions.
Transparency and Explainability	- Making the training data and model inner workings more transparent to identify potential biases. - Developing methods to explain how LLMs arrive at their outputs, allowing for bias detection and mitigation.
User Education and Awareness	- Educating users about the potential for bias in LLM outputs and how to interpret them critically. - Providing tools and techniques for users to identify and mitigate bias in LLM outputs.

lessen prejudices since they bring a range of viewpoints and experiences to the table. They demand that women, minorities, and other marginalized groups be represented more in AI research and development.

Additionally, the paper(Roselli et al., 2019) investigates the moral ramifications of bias in AI and advocates for the creation of moral standards and legal frameworks to control the creation and application of AI systems. The authors emphasize the significance of ethical factors, such as responsibility, transparency, justice, and privacy, in AI design.

Table 2 summarizes the discussion in previous sections for various challenges and potential solutions.

Explainability and Interpretability

Addressing the Black-Box Nature of Deep Learning Models

ChatGPT, the impressive language model by OpenAI, has won over people all over the world with its capacity to produce prose of human caliber, translate across languages, and even compose other forms of creative material. But behind the surface, there's a basic problem: deep learning models are black boxes. As Yoshua Bengio argues in his paper "On the Black Box Problem of AI and a Possible Solution" (2018), the complex internal workings of these models often remain opaque, hindering our understanding of how they arrive at their outputs. This opacity, known as the "black-box problem", poses significant hurdles for the trustworthiness and reliability of ChatGPT and other AI systems.

The black-box problem primarily stems from the intricate web of interconnected neurons within deep learning models. Each neuron performs a simple calculation on its inputs, but the sheer number of neurons and their interconnections create a dizzying tapestry of computations, ultimately masking the reasoning behind the final output. This lack of transparency becomes especially concerning when ChatGPT makes seemingly nonsensical or even harmful outputs. Without insights into its decision-making process, it's difficult to pinpoint errors, mitigate bias, or even debug unintended consequences.

The implications of this opacity extend beyond technical complexities. In applications where AI interacts directly with humans, such as healthcare or autonomous driving, explainability becomes crucial for building trust and accountability. Imagine a medical diagnosis delivered by a black-box AI with no explanation for its reasoning. The patient remains in the dark, unable to assess the validity of the diagnosis or challenge potential biases embedded within the model. Similarly, an autonomous vehicle making potentially life-altering decisions on the road demands transparency to ensure responsible development and public trust.

Fortunately, researchers are actively addressing the black-box problem and exploring various avenues for enhancing explainability and interpretability in deep learning models. One promising approach involves dissecting the internal representations learned by the model. By visualizing these representations and their evolution during the computation process, one can gain insights into the features and concepts the model relies on to generate its outputs. Techniques like attention mechanisms and gradient-based visualization offer valuable glimpses into the model's "thought process."

Another approach delves into counterfactual reasoning, asking "what if?" questions to understand how the model's output changes when specific input features are modified. This allows the researchers to pinpoint the factors influencing the model's decisions and identify potential biases that might be driving undesirable outcomes. For instance, by testing how ChatGPT's responses change with variations in gender-related keywords, one can identify and address potential gender biases within the model.

The quest for explainability and interpretability in deep learning models like ChatGPT is an ongoing journey. While significant challenges remain, the growing arsenal of techniques and the unwavering dedication of researchers offer promising avenues for demystifying the black box and paving the way for more trustworthy and reliable AI systems. By studying the inner workings of these powerful models one can truly foster trust, mitigate bias, and unlock the full potential of AI for the benefit of humanity.

The black-box nature of deep learning models has long been a topic of concern and investigation within the machine learning community. In their comprehensive primer, Bau et al. (2020) delve into the intricacies of neural network interpretability, shedding light on the challenges posed by the opacity of deep learning models and the importance of understanding their decision-making processes.

Deep learning models, particularly neural networks, have demonstrated remarkable capabilities across various domains, including image recognition, natural language processing, and autonomous driving. However, the internal workings of these models often remain elusive, with complex interactions between layers of neurons and learned representations contributing to their black-box nature.

Bau et al. (2020) highlight the inherent trade-offs associated with the complexity of deep learning models. While deep neural networks excel at capturing intricate patterns and features in high-dimensional data, their opacity poses challenges for understanding how decisions are made and interpreting model predictions. This lack of transparency can hinder trust, accountability, and adoption of deep learning systems in critical domains.

One key insight provided by Bau et al. is the distinction between global and local interpretability in neural networks. The capacity to comprehend a model's general behavior and functioning across a variety of inputs and circumstances is known as global interpretability. Local interpretability, on the other hand, focuses on explaining individual predictions and understanding the factors that influence specific model outputs.

It takes a multidisciplinary approach that includes model design, training tactics, and post-hoc interpretability techniques to address the black-box aspect of deep learning models. Bau et al. discuss a variety of methods for enhancing interpretability, including visualization techniques, saliency maps, and attention mechanisms, which provide insights into the inner workings of neural networks and help elucidate the factors driving model predictions.

Furthermore, Bau et al. emphasize the importance of integrating interpretability into the entire machine learning pipeline, from model development to deployment and evaluation. By incorporating interpretability as a core design principle, researchers and practitioners can foster transparency, accountability, and trust in deep learning systems, thereby enabling more responsible and ethical AI-driven decision-making processes.

The primer by Bau et al. serves as a comprehensive guide for navigating the complex landscape of neural network interpretability. By demystifying the black-box nature of deep learning models and providing practical insights into interpretability techniques, the primer empowers researchers, practitioners, and stakeholders to critically evaluate and understand the decisions made by neural networks.

The black-box nature of deep learning models presents significant challenges in understanding and interpreting their decision-making processes. In their seminal paper, Ribeiro et al. (2016) provide a unified view of machine learning interpretability, shedding light on the complexities of deep learning models and the implications for transparency and accountability in AI systems.

Deep learning models, particularly neural networks, have achieved remarkable success in various domains, including computer vision, natural language processing, and healthcare. However, the internal mechanisms governing these models often remain opaque, with complex interactions between layers of neurons and learned representations contributing to their black-box nature.

Ribeiro et al. (2016) highlight the critical importance of interpretability in understanding the behavior and functionality of machine learning models, especially in high-stakes applications where decisions have significant real-world consequences. The lack of transparency in deep learning models can hinder trust, accountability, and adoption in domains such as healthcare, finance, and criminal justice.

One key insight provided by Ribeiro et al. is the distinction between global and local interpretability in machine learning models. Global interpretability refers to the ability to understand the overall behavior and functionality of a model across different inputs and contexts. Local interpretability, on the other hand, focuses on explaining individual predictions and understanding the factors that influence specific model outputs.

It takes a multifaceted strategy that includes model design, training tactics, and post-hoc interpretability techniques to address the black-box aspect of deep learning models. Ribeiro et al. discuss a variety of methods for enhancing interpretability, including feature importance analysis, model-agnostic techniques, and post-hoc explanation methods, which provide insights into the decision-making processes of complex machine learning models.

Furthermore, Ribeiro et al. emphasize the importance of transparency and accountability in the development and deployment of machine learning systems. By integrating interpretability as a core design principle, researchers and practitioners can foster trust and confidence in AI-driven systems, enabling more informed decision-making and oversight.

The unified view presented by Ribeiro et al. serves as a roadmap for navigating the challenges of machine learning interpretability. By providing a comprehensive framework for understanding and evaluating interpretability techniques, the paper empowers researchers, practitioners, and stakeholders to critically assess the reliability and robustness of machine learning models.

Table 3 shows the challenges and potential solutions for explainable AI.

CONCLUSION

This chapter delves into the intricate algorithmic issues, challenges, and theoretical concerns surrounding ChatGPT and similar AI models. Through an exhaustive examination, it becomes evident that the landscape of AI-driven conversations is fraught with complexities and implications that necessitate

Table 3. Challenges and potential solutions for explainable AI

Challenge	Potential Solution
Lack of Interpretability: Difficulty understanding how models arrive at their predictions.	**Explainable AI (XAI) Techniques** (Machlev et al., 2022): Feature attribution methods to understand which features contribute most to a prediction. - Counterfactual explanations to show how changing an input would affect the output.**Visualizations**: Creating visualizations of the model's internal workings to aid understanding.
Limited Debugging Capabilities: Difficulty diagnosing errors or unexpected model behaviour.	**Input Perturbation Analysis:** Observing how small changes to the input affect the output to identify potential issues.**Gradient-based debugging:** Analysing the gradients of the loss function to understand how changes in the input affect the model's predictions.
Difficulties in Trust and Reliability: Difficulties in trusting models for critical decision-making due to lack of transparency.	**Uncertainty Quantification**: Estimating the uncertainty associated with model predictions to provide users with a sense of confidence.**Guardrails and Human Oversight:** Implementing safety measures and human oversight to ensure responsible use of models.
Potential for Bias: Black-box models can amplify biases present in the training data.	**Fairness-aware training and evaluation techniques:** Ensuring training data is balanced and representative and developing metrics to detect and mitigate bias in model outputs.Explainability techniques can help identify how biases might be influencing model behaviour.

careful consideration. The algorithmic overview provided insights into the foundational components of ChatGPT, elucidating its transformer architecture, training methodologies, and transfer learning techniques. Understanding these aspects is crucial for comprehending the model's capabilities and limitations, thereby informing decisions regarding its deployment and usage.

The chapter delved into the limitations of transfer learning, highlighting how pre-trained models like ChatGPT may struggle to adapt effectively to new domains, potentially leading to inaccurate outputs. To mitigate this, careful domain-specific fine-tuning and continuous monitoring are necessary to ensure the model's performance aligns with intended purposes. Furthermore, the exploration of algorithmic issues such as biases and fairness underscored the challenges in ensuring equitable and inclusive AI interactions. Proactive measures and continuous refinement are needed to address biases within training data and responses, promoting ethical standards and diversity in conversational outcomes. The opaque theoretical underpinnings of LLMs like ChatGPT raise concerns about interpretability, accountability, and the potential for manipulation. Therefore, further research into explainable AI techniques is crucial to bridge this gap and enhance transparency. In conclusion, navigating the algorithmic landscape of ChatGPT requires a cautious and nuanced approach, with a focus on recognizing and addressing these challenges for responsible use in real-time data decisions. By fostering transparency, mitigating bias, and refining our understanding of complex algorithms, we can unlock AI's true potential for societal benefit.

The future scope of research on algorithmic issues, challenges, and theoretical concerns surrounding ChatGPT and similar AI models is vast and promising. Key areas for exploration include advancing explainable AI techniques tailored for LLMs, developing robust methods for bias mitigation and fairness, deepening understanding of ethical considerations and governance frameworks, enhancing domain adaptation and transfer learning capabilities, fostering interdisciplinary collaboration, implementing continuous monitoring and evaluation mechanisms, and prioritizing user-centric design for AI-driven conversational systems. By focusing on these areas, researchers can contribute to the responsible deployment and ethical use of AI while unlocking its full potential for societal benefit.

REFERENCES

Bender, E. M., Gebru, T., McMillan-Major, A., & Shmitchell, S. (2021). On the dangers of stochastic parrots: Can language models be too big? *FAccT 2021 - Proceedings of the 2021 ACM Conference on Fairness, Accountability, and Transparency*. ACM. 10.1145/3442188.3445922

Bolukbasi, T., Chang, K. W., Zou, J., Saligrama, V., & Kalai, A. (2016). Man is to computer programmer as woman is to homemaker. Debiasing word embeddings. *Advances in Neural Information Processing Systems*.

Brown, T. B., Mann, B., Ryder, N., Subbiah, M., Kaplan, J., Dhariwal, P., Neelakantan, A., Shyam, P., Sastry, G., Askell, A., Agarwal, S., Herbert-Voss, A., Krueger, G., Henighan, T., Child, R., Ramesh, A., Ziegler, D. M., Wu, J., Winter, C., & Amodei, D. (2020). Language models are few-shot learners. *Advances in Neural Information Processing Systems*.

Carion, N., Massa, F., Synnaeve, G., Usunier, N., Kirillov, A., & Zagoruyko, S. (2020). End-to-End Object Detection with Transformers. Lecture Notes in Computer Science (Including Subseries Lecture Notes in Artificial Intelligence and Lecture Notes in Bioinformatics). Springer. doi:10.1007/978-3-030-58452-8_13

Devlin, J., Chang, M. W., Lee, K., & Toutanova, K. (2019). BERT: Pre-training of deep bidirectional transformers for language understanding. *NAACL HLT 2019 - 2019 Conference of the North American Chapter of the Association for Computational Linguistics: Human Language Technologies - Proceedings of the Conference*. ACL.

Dixon, L., Li, J., Sorensen, J., Thain, N., & Vasserman, L. (2018). Measuring and Mitigating Unintended Bias in Text Classification. *AIES 2018 - Proceedings of the 2018 AAAI/ACM Conference on AI, Ethics, and Society*. ACM. 10.1145/3278721.3278729

Dosovitskiy, A., Beyer, L., Kolesnikov, A., Weissenborn, D., Zhai, X., Unterthiner, T., Dehghani, M., Minderer, M., Heigold, G., Gelly, S., Uszkoreit, J., & Houlsby, N. (2021). AN IMAGE IS WORTH 16X16 WORDS: TRANSFORMERS FOR IMAGE RECOGNITION AT SCALE. *ICLR 2021 - 9th International Conference on Learning Representations*.

Elnaggar, A., Heinzinger, M., Dallago, C., Rehawi, G., Wang, Y., Jones, L., Gibbs, T., Feher, T., Angerer, C., Steinegger, M., Bhowmik, D., & Rost, B. (2022). ProtTrans: Toward Understanding the Language of Life Through Self-Supervised Learning. *IEEE Transactions on Pattern Analysis and Machine Intelligence*, *44*(10), 7112–7127. doi:10.1109/TPAMI.2021.3095381 PMID:34232869

Kapadiya, D., Shekhawat, C., & Sharma, P. (2023). A Study on Large Scale Applications of Big Data in Modern Era. In *International Conference on Information Management & Machine Intelligence (ICIMMI2023)*. ACM. https://doi.org/10.1145/3647444.364788

Kowsher, M., Sami, A. A., Prottasha, N. J., Arefin, M. S., Dhar, P. K., & Koshiba, T. (2022). *Bangla-BERT: Transformer-based Efficient Model for Transfer Learning and Language Understanding*. IEEE. doi:10.1109/ACCESS.2022.3197662

Machlev, R., Heistrene, L., Perl, M., Levy, K. Y., Belikov, J., Mannor, S., & Levron, Y. (2022). Explainable Artificial Intelligence (XAI) techniques for energy and power systems: Review, challenges and opportunities. In Energy and AI, 9. doi:10.1016/j.egyai.2022.100169

Maharajan, K., Kumar, A. V., El Emary, I. M., Sharma, P., Latip, R., Mishra, N., Dutta, A., Manjunatha Rao, L., & Sharma, M. (2023). Blockchain Methods and Data-Driven Decision Making With Autonomous Transportation. In R. Kumar, A. Abdul Hamid, & N. Binti Ya'akub (Eds.), *Effective AI, Blockchain, and E-Governance Applications for Knowledge Discovery and Management* (pp. 176–194). IGI Global. doi:10.4018/978-1-6684-9151-5.ch012

Merlin Mancy, A., Kumar, A. V., Latip, R., Jagadamba, G., Chakrabarti, P., Sharma, P., Musirin, I. B., Sharma, M., & Kanchan, B. G. (2024). Smart Healthcare System, Digital Health and Telemedicine, Management and Emergencies: Patient Emergency Application (PES) E-Governance Applications. In R. Kumar, A. Abdul Hamid, N. Binti Ya'akub, H. Sharan, & S. Kumar (Eds.), *Sustainable Development in AI, Blockchain, and E-Governance Applications* (pp. 124–151). IGI Global. doi:10.4018/979-8-3693-1722-8.ch008

Mitchell, M., Wu, S., Zaldivar, A., Barnes, P., Vasserman, L., Hutchinson, B., Spitzer, E., Raji, I. D., & Gebru, T. (2019). Model cards for model reporting. *FAT* 2019 - Proceedings of the 2019 Conference on Fairness, Accountability, and Transparency*. ACM. 10.1145/3287560.3287596

Mittelstadt, B. D., Allo, P., Taddeo, M., Wachter, S., & Floridi, L. (2016). The ethics of algorithms: Mapping the debate. *Big Data & Society*, 3(2). doi:10.1177/2053951716679679

Prasad, G. A., Kumar, A. V., Sharma, P., Irawati, I. D., D. V., C., Musirin, I. B., Abdullah, H. M., & Rao L, M. (2023). Artificial Intelligence in Computer Science: An Overview of Current Trends and Future Directions. In S. Rajest, B. Singh, A. Obaid, R. Regin, & K. Chinnusamy (Eds.), Advances in Artificial and Human Intelligence in the Modern Era (pp. 43-60). IGI Global. doi:10.4018/979-8-3693-1301-5.ch002

Radford, A., Narasimhan, K., Salimans, T., & Sutskever, I. (2018). *Improving Language Understanding by Generative Pre-Training*. OpenAI.Com.

Raffel, C., Shazeer, N., Roberts, A., Lee, K., Narang, S., Matena, M., Zhou, Y., Li, W., & Liu, P. J. (2020). Exploring the limits of transfer learning with a unified text-to-text transformer. *Journal of Machine Learning Research*, 21.

Rawat, P., Bhardwaj, A., Lamba, N., Sharma, P., Kumawat, P., & Sharma, P. (2023). Arduino Based IoT Mini Weather Station. *SKIT Research Journal*, 13(2), 34–41. doi:10.47904/IJSKIT.13.2.2023.34-41

Roselli, D., Matthews, J., & Talagala, N. (2019). Managing bias in AI. *The Web Conference 2019 - Companion of the World Wide Web Conference*. ACM. 10.1145/3308560.3317590

Sethi, S. S., & Sharma, P. (2023). New Developments in the Implementation of IoT in Agriculture. *SN Computer Science*, 4(5), 503. doi:10.1007/s42979-023-01896-w

Sharma, P. (2023). *Utilizing Explainable Artificial Intelligence to Address Deep Learning in Biomedical Domain, Medical Data Analysis and Processing using Explainable Artificial Intelligence*. Taylor & Francis. doi:10.1201/9781003257721-2

Sharma, P., & Bhatnagar, N. (2023). Passenger Authentication and Ticket Verification at Airport Using QR Code Scanner. *SKIT Research Journal, 13*(2), 10–13. doi:10.47904/IJSKIT.13.1.2023.10-12

Sharma, P., & Dadheech, P. (2023). Modern-age Agriculture with Artificial Intelligence: A review emphasizing Crop Yield Prediction. *EVERGREEN Joint Journal of Novel Carbon Resource Sciences & Green Asia Strategy, 10*(4), 2570–2582. doi:10.5109/7160906

Sharma, P., Dadheech, P., Aneja, N., & Aneja, S. (2023). Predicting Agriculture Yields Based on Machine Learning Using Regression and Deep Learning. *IEEE Access : Practical Innovations, Open Solutions, 11*, 111255–111264. doi:10.1109/ACCESS.2023.3321861

Sharma, P., Dadheech, P., & Senthil Kumar Senthil, A. V. (2023). AI-Enabled Crop Recommendation System Based on Soil and Weather Patterns. In R. Gupta, A. Jain, J. Wang, S. Bharti, & S. Patel (Eds.), *Artificial Intelligence Tools and Technologies for Smart Farming and Agriculture Practices* (pp. 184–199). IGI Global. doi:10.4018/978-1-6684-8516-3.ch010

Sharma, P., & Jain, M. K. (2023). Stock Market Trends Analysis using Extreme Gradient Boosting (XGBoost*). International Conference on Computing, Communication, and Intelligent Systems (ICCCIS)*, Greater Noida, India. 10.1109/ICCCIS60361.2023.10425722

Sharma, P., Kapadiya, D., & Bhardwaj, A. (2023). Efficient Note Sharing Model for Collaborative Learning. *SKIT Research Journal, 13*(2), 42–46. doi:10.47904/IJSKIT.13.2.2023.42-46

Sharma, P., & Rathi, Y. (2016, June 5). Efficient Density-Based Clustering Using Automatic Parameter Detection. *Efficient Density-Based Clustering Using Automatic Parameter Detection*. Springer. . doi:10.1007/978-981-10-0767-5_46

Sharma, P., Sharma, C., & Mathur, P. (2023). *Machine Learning-based Stock Market Forecasting using Recurrent Neural Network*. 2023 9th International Conference on Smart Computing and Communications (ICSCC), Kochi, Kerala. 10.1109/ICSCC59169.2023.10335083

Shoeybi, M. (2020). Megatron-LM: Training Multi-Billion Parameter Language Models Using Model Parallelism. *ArXiv:1909.08053 [Cs]*.

Tanwar, A., Sharma, P., Pandey, A., & Kumar, S. (2023). Intrusion Detection System Based Ameliorated Technique of Pattern Matching. In *Proceedings of the 4th International Conference on Information Management & Machine Intelligence (ICIMMI '22)*. Association for Computing Machinery, New York, NY, USA. 10.1145/3590837.3590947

Tenney, I., Xia, P., Chen, B., Wang, A., Poliak, A., Thomas McCoy, R., Kim, N., Van Durme, B., Bowman, S. R., Das, D., & Pavlick, E. (2019). What do you learn from context? Probing for sentence structure in contextualized word representations. *7th International Conference on Learning Representations, ICLR 2019*.

V., M. V., Kumar, A. S., Sharma, P., Kaur, S., Saleh, O. S., Chennamma, H., & Chaturvedi, A. (2023). AI-Equipped IoT Applications in High-Tech Agriculture Using Machine Learning. In A. Khang (Ed.), *Handbook of Research on AI-Equipped IoT Applications in High-Tech Agriculture* (pp. 38-64). IGI Global. . doi:10.4018/978-1-6684-9231-4.ch003

Vaswani, A., Shazeer, N., Parmar, N., Uszkoreit, J., Jones, L., Gomez, A. N., Kaiser, Ł., & Polosukhin, I. (2017). Attention is all you need. *Advances in Neural Information Processing Systems, 2017-December*.

Wolf, T., Debut, L., Sanh, V., Chaumond, J., Delangue, C., Moi, A., Cistac, P., Rault, T., Louf, R., Funtowicz, M., Davison, J., Shleifer, S., Von Platen, P., Ma, C., Jernite, Y., Plu, J., Xu, C., Le Scao, T., Gugger, S., & Rush, A. M. (2020). Transformers: State-of-the-Art Natural Language Processing. *EMNLP 2020 - Conference on Empirical Methods in Natural Language Processing, Proceedings of Systems Demonstrations*. ACL. 10.18653/v1/2020.emnlp-demos.6

Wu, X., & Lode, M. (2020). Language Models are Unsupervised Multitask Learners (Summarization). *OpenAI Blog*. OpenAI.

Xie, Q., Luong, M. T., Hovy, E., & Le, Q. V. (2020). Self-training with noisy students improves imagenet classification. *Proceedings of the IEEE Computer Society Conference on Computer Vision and Pattern Recognition*. IEEE. 10.1109/CVPR42600.2020.01070

Yan, A., McAuley, J., Lu, X., Du, J., Chang, E. Y., Gentili, A., & Hsu, C. N. (2022). RadBERT: Adapting Transformer-based Language Models to Radiology. *Radiology. Artificial Intelligence*, 4(4), e210258. doi:10.1148/ryai.210258 PMID:35923376

Zou, J., & Schiebinger, L. (2018). AI can be sexist and racist — It's time to make it fair. *Nature*, 559(7714), 324–326. doi:10.1038/d41586-018-05707-8 PMID:30018439

Chapter 4
Applications Areas, Possibilities, and Limitations of ChatGPT

Roheen Qamar

 https://orcid.org/0000-0003-4169-9455

Quaid-e-Awam University of Engineering, Sciences, and Technology, Pakistan

Baqar Ali Zardari

Quaid-e-Awam University of Engineering, Sciences, and Technology, Pakistan

ABSTRACT

AI developments have led to the creation of complex language models like ChatGPT, which can produce text that appears human. Although ChatGPT has limitations, it can be helpful in elucidating concepts and offering basic guidance. It cannot access original medical databases or offer the most recent scientific knowledge. Public opinion in a number of areas, including healthcare, education, manufacturing, artificial intelligence (AI), machine revolution, science, industry, and cyber security, has been scrutinizing ChatGPT. However, there hasn't been as much research done on the analysis of ChatGPT studies in these settings. The present chapter looks at the various potential applications, difficulties, and upcoming projects for ChatGPT. A synopsis of studies on ChatGPT in the literature on applications is given by this review. The authors also offer a thorough and original assessment of ChatGPT's future concerns in Diff applications, including their promise and limitations.

INTRODUCTION

ChatGPT, launched by OpenAI on November 30, 2022, is a chatbot that allows users to adjust conversation length, structure, style, information level, and language using a large-scale language model. It uses large data and an efficient architecture to analyze user requests and respond in natural language, a significant advancement in artificial intelligence and natural language processing. This chapter provides a quick overview of ChatGPT and its potential influence on many businesses.

ChatGPT offers many services for education, healthcare practitioners, and patients. For students, it may provide assistance and coaching by answering questions and sketching details to clarify hard con-

DOI: 10.4018/979-8-3693-6824-4.ch004

Figure 1. ChatGPT

cepts. As a teaching tool, the statement has the potential to transform .biomedical science education. ChatGPT in dentistry and healthcare can improve diagnosis, support decision-making, record digital data, analyze images, prevent diseases, reduce treatment errors, and facilitate research.

ChatGPT, the fastest-growing consumer software program in history, gained over 100 million users by January 2023, raising OpenAI's worth to $29 billion. Rival programs like Bard, Ernie Bot, LLaMA, Claude, and Grok emerged, while Microsoft introduced Bing Chat using OpenAI's GPT-4. Concerns were raised about ChatGPT's potential to undermine human intelligence, facilitate plagiarism, or spread false information. It can produce human-like writing and perform tasks like text completion and translation.

. This analysis examines the history, uses, main obstacles, and potential future developments of ChatGPT, a prominent artificial intelligence language model developed by Open AI. ChatGPT is a conversational Chabot that uses neural network architecture to process and comprehend natural language, making it applicable in various fields such as customer service, healthcare, and education. It marks a new era in AI's widespread use and application. (Kocoń, J. et al, 2023, pp. 101861)

ChatGPT, an advanced language model from the OpenAI family, uses deep learning techniques to generate interactive, instantaneous responses based on a large dataset of billions of words, resulting in responses similar to human inputs, making it one of the largest available to the public.

ChatGPT, an AI technology, can generate contextually relevant responses to various inputs, offering potential applications in the medical field. It can assist professionals with clinical and laboratory diagnoses, propose study participants, and inform medical personnel about updates. It can also develop virtual assistants to support patients in managing their health. However, ethical and legal concerns arise, such as intellectual property infringements, complicated legal issues, and the need for transparency in AI data. (Mokmin et al, 2021, pp. 6033-6049).

ChatGPT is a deep learning language model that mimics human speech using deep learning techniques. It is part of the OpenAI generative pre-training transformer model family and is one of the largest available. It can provide contextually relevant responses for various inquiries using a large corpus of text data. AI's usage in healthcare and medical research has been limited, but its potential in data management and customer support is crucial.

ChatGPT is a deep learning language model that mimics human responses to natural language inputs. It is part of the Open AI generative pre-training transformer model family and uses a large corpus of text data to provide contextually relevant responses. Although AI is used in other fields like data management and customer service, its use in healthcare and medical research is relatively new, making it crucial for healthcare systems. (Liebrenz et al, 2023, pp. 105-106).

There are many useful applications available on ChatGPT. The usage of ChatGPT for creating scientific publications has been covered in a number of studies; one study even shows that ChatGPT can generate formal research articles. The writers discovered that the language reads well, seems to have a classic tone, and is well-chosen. It could be feasible to utilize ChatGPT as a search engine that answers questions immediately, saving users from having to visit websites to obtain the answers. This would reduce the time writers need to spend looking for articles and using different selection criteria to find the ones that best match their study, making it easier for them to create research papers. Additionally, it might serve as a mediator during an ideation session, assisting in the selection of a topic and initiating a research project. (Issom, D. Z et al, 2021, pp. 600333)

A study involving ChatGPT and traditional plagiarism detection methods found that ChatGPT-generated articles can bypass traditional methods. The chatbot produced 50 medical research abstracts from prestigious journals, which were then subjected to an AI output detector and plagiarism detection technologies. Despite the AI-output checker detecting plagiarism in 66% of the generated abstracts, none were found, indicating that ChatGPT-generated articles can be more effective in detecting plagiarism.

ChatGPT is being used to create virtual assistants to assist patients in managing their health, making medical records easier for doctors and nurses. These assistants can automatically summarize patient encounters and medical histories, extract relevant information from patient data, and aid in clinical trial recruitment. ChatGPT can also be used for evaluating clinical skills, providing updates and advancements in medical fields, and increasing health literacy among students and young people. It can also be used for clinical decision assistance and patient monitoring, advising seeking medical advice when necessary. This technology has the potential to revolutionize healthcare and improve patient care. (Casas, J., et al, 2020, pp. 280-286).

ChatGPT'S PROS AND CONS

ChatGPT is a crucial tool for various applications, offering flexibility, natural language understanding, and context retention. However, it also has its pros and cons. Its potential for conversational AI is significantly enhanced by its flexibility. To fully understand how ChatGPT is shaping artificial intelligence, further study and improvements are needed. The moral implications of ChatGPT's use are also discussed. (Han, J. et al, 2022, pp. 830).

Pros of Chat Bot	Cons of Chat Bot
1. Natural language understanding	1. limited context learning
2. Accessibility	2. biased output
3. Versatility	3. Misi information propagation
4. Time saving	4. privicy risk
5. Continuous learning	5. dependency of risk data
6. Language translation	6. limited contextual understanding
7. Innovation catalyst	7. over reliance on training data
8. Enhance learning experience	8. generating misinformation
9. Creative collaboration	9. dependency on prompt phrasing
10. Mental health support	10. lack of real understanding
11. Context Retention	
12. Transfer learning and fine tuning	
13. Massive scale data processing	
14. Adaptability to domain	
15. Zero shot and few shot learning	

ChatGPT'S CHALLENGES

While ChatGPT can assist you with many procedures, some AI ethical problems may impact its application. Here are some issues that might develop while using ChatGPT or other generative AI technologies.

- **Potential for bias.**

   ChatGPT can produce biased and unjust results based on its training data.

- **Risk of Misuse**

   ChatGPT might be used to spread disinformation, such as creating fake news or engaging in destructive talks. ChatGPT's code creation capabilities enable it to build malware that constitutes a cyber-security hazard.

- **Data Privacy**

   ChatGPT can save and utilize certain personal information for training reasons. This implies that if proper safeguards are not taken, sensitive or confidential data may be compromised.

- **Plagiarism**

   ChatGPT's training is based on publicly available data, including publications and journals. As a result, it can exploit these works to create answers without crediting the creators.

- **Subject to Errors**

   ChatGPT may not always operate as expected. Some of its replies can be erroneous and misleading, particularly if the publicly available data it uses is wrong.

- **Complex Reasoning**

   ChatGPT can do a variety of functions, but it cannot reason like humans, restricting its skills to specialized jobs (Hargreaves et al, 2023, pp. *33*, 69)

APPLICATION AREAS IN ChatGPT

1. ***ChatGPT in Education*** There is a lot of interest in using ChatGPT in education because of its potential to improve students' learning experiences. This method might provide students quick feedback, customize solutions to meet their needs, and make complex concepts easier for them to understand by providing brief, individualized answers. This makes it a potentially helpful tool that supports students' cognitive growth and engagement by tailoring to their preferred learning style and offering continuous support for their process of information acquisition .(P. Sharma et al, 2023,

pp. 317-322). OpenAI's ChatGPT, a conversational chatbot, uses natural language processing to provide human-like responses to user input. Despite its widespread use, it poses new challenges and risks to the educational sector. Its ability to provide accurate answers may lead to AI-assisted cheating, as it can be used to complete written assignments and tests on students' behalf. (Lo, C. K et al, 2023, pp. 410). As a result, ChatGPT use on campus is prohibited at several educational institutions. Mhlanga has examined ChatGPT's effects on the field of education. He found that teachers had concerns about using ChatGPT in the classroom after looking through eight ChatGPT publications. They expressed worry that students might outsource their work to ChatGPT because of its speed in producing relevant texts. emphasized how important it is to use ChatGPT responsibly and ethically as a result (Dharmi Kapadiya et al, 2023, pp.6).

2. ***ChatGPT in Industry*** ChatGPT may be utilized in the industrial sector to create quality control plans, estimate maintenance needs, lower risks, improve communications, and optimize processes3. Within the oil and gas sector, ChatGPT may be utilized to educate both new and existing staff members on all industry-related subjects, respond to technical inquiries, onboard new hires, offer training simulations, and disseminate information throughout the organization4.Additionally, ChatGPT may perform tasks that have historically been performed by people, such copywriting, resolving customer care issues, producing news articles, and drafting legal documents (Vaishya, R., et al, 2023, pp. 102744).

3. ***CHATGPT in Manufacturing*** There are several intricate jobs in the manufacturing sector that need for a high level of expertise to do. The swift advancement of artificial intelligence, especially the creation of potent big language models like ChatGPT, has created new avenues for information sharing through dialogue. With its encyclopedic knowledge base and well-structured response approach, ChatGPT is poised to transform the whole industry. It's still unknown, though, how far ChatGPT can take its skills and how they can fit into the industry's next revolution (Rane, N. et al, 2023, pp. 4). The industrial sector may see several changes as a result of ChatGPT, which may be used to create optimization plans, predictive maintenance schedules, mitigate risks, improve communications (making them quicker and more effective), and offer quality control by identifying abnormalities in the information that is now accessible. By adopting this technology, manufacturers would be able to enhance quality, save costs, make better decisions, and ultimately increase customer happiness. In addition to enabling quicker diagnosis and offering tailored advice, the chatbot can respond quickly to frequently asked questions from clients. As a result, it may maximize reaction times while providing the user with helpful information that enables manufacturers to improve customer connections through more responsiveness, customization, and better service. Although ChatGPT and other AI technologies have a lot to offer the industrial sector, there are also a lot of worries and difficulties with them. Sensitive data may be compromised by hacks targeting AI systems. It is the duty of manufacturers to guarantee AI system security (Fui-Hoon et al, 2023, pp. 277-304). Furthermore, there is a tendency for AI to replace automated work more and more, raising ethical questions about choices made with these technologies in the absence of a person. Thus, in order to deliver a secure service, manufacturers have to think about adding people to check and rectify AI findings (Ren, R et al, 2023, pp. 12430-12464) .

4. ***CHATGPT Generative AI*** Any form of artificial intelligence (AI) that may be used to produce fresh, unique information using patterns and examples it has learnt is known as generative AI. Text, pictures, videos, code, and artificial data can all be included in this material. DALL-E, Midjourney, and ChatGPT are a few examples. AI trained on trees can generate images based on

real-world patterns, often converting human-written cues into output. Generative AI models, such as ChatGPT, can create new content like audio, code, images, text, simulations, and videos. Recent breakthroughs in this field have the potential to significantly change the way we approach content creation. (Mancy et al, 2024, pp. 124-151).

5.   **CHATGPT in Machine Revolution** *OpenAI developed ChatGPT, a advanced natural language processing tool using Deep Learning and Machine Learning algorithms.it has completely changed how people interact with computers. When users input, ChatGPT creates remarkably human-like discussions. Thus, ChatGPT's effectiveness is on its capacity to recognize textual patterns, evaluate contextual information, and generate replies that resemble real-world dialogue. Its ability to grasp syntactic and semantic components via the application of deep learning algorithms yields output that sounds natural. Furthermore, by being exposed to a large volume of user interactions, its adaptive learning capabilities enables it to continually update and enhance its comprehension of language. To keep up with the revolution of Artificial Intelligence (AI) influence on life areas, including economic, financial, military, and cyber security, this study offers a historical overview of ChatGPT. In the end, an analysis is conducted to compare ChatGPT versions with alternative AI platforms, highlighting their respective strengths, weaknesses, and efficacy (Leaver. et al, 2023, pp. 26)*

Figure 2. ChatGPT in machine revolution

Figure 3. ChatGPT in science

6.   CHATGPT in Science

A large language model (LLM) that has gained attention in the scientific community is called ChatGPT. This algorithm of Artificial intelligence (AI) has the potential toproduce content that is similar to that of a person, whether it prose, poetry, computer code, or even editing research papers 1. The most recent developments in generative AI have researchers thrilled, but they are also concerned about how they could affect science 1.

Computational biologists Casey Greene and Milton Pividori carried out an experiment in which they requested assistance from ChatGPT to enhance three of their scientific publications in December 2023. Even in one biology publication, their assistant found an error in an equation reference. Less than US$0.50 was charged for each document, and the finished documents were simpler to read (Zhai, et al, 2023, pp. 42-46)

In addition to editing publications, scientists may develop or review code and generate ideas via ChatGPT. Many scholars even utilize it as a virtual assistant or secretary.

Large language models, or LLMs, are what are often referred to as ChatGPT, a GPT-3 version that became well-known after it was released under license in November 2020. Other generative AIs are capable of creating sounds or pictures. One of the highly anticipated generative AI chatbot-style technologies, ChatGPT, can generate believable, fluid prose. (Alıcı et al, 2023, pp. *4412215*).

7.   CHATGPT in Cyber Security

Cyber security professionals are fascinated with using various technologies to carry out their responsibilities in the security field. However, the quick development of ChatGPT raised a lot of questions regarding potential hackers using this technology for their own gain. Nevertheless, several cyber security concepts— such include creating malware that may be fraudulently exploited, social engineering, im-

Figure 4. ChatGPT in A.I.

personation, and creating a list of the most popular passwords for 2023—are now simpler to understand thanks to this improvement. Furthermore, according to the cyber security hub society, hackers have used ChatGPT to create malware scripts and phishing emails (Fitria, T et al, 2023, pp. 44-58).

8.   CHATGPT in Artificial intelligence

ChatGPT is an AI system developed by OpenAI that uses deep learning algorithms to create natural language conversations resembling human ones. It is part of the generative pre-trained transformer (GPT) family and is commonly used in conversational AI applications for composing tales, summarizing lengthy texts, and answering queries. (Cao et al, 2023, pp. 177-191).

LITERATURE REVIEW

(Cao et al, 2023, pp. 177-191) Numerous studies have been conducted to demonstrate ChatGPT's benefits and effects on human life, particularly in the areas of AI, finance, the military, education, and cyber security. ChatGPT has the potential to have a big influence on global financial matters. Large volumes of financial data may be analyzed using it, and it can help with algorithmic trading, fraud detection, and risk evaluation. Additionally, GPT could support automated content production and chat bots to enhance customer care and comply with regulations. But for responsible deployment, ethical issues and problems with algorithmic bias and data privacy must be properly addressed.

(Priyanka et al, 2023, pp. 10-13) the most recent advancement in artificial intelligence (AI) technology is ChatGPT, a widely used big language model inside the open AI firm. Even while ChatGPT satisfies academic and professional requirements, it is open to all users without charge. With plans to reach 100 million users, it has completely transformed the information technology industry and now has 57 million active monthly users. This enables it to correctly read user input and produce the suitable answer instantly. This platform has been deemed the most popular application by users, indicating remarkable success. The Internet's fastest-growing customer base will gain knowledge about ChatGPT's features, operation, and essential words throughout the summary.

(Li, J et al, 2023, pp. 108013) A research comparing ChatGPT's performance to the USMLE was carried out by Open-ended questions created by the writers were transformed into multiple-choice, single-answer questions. According to the study, ChatGPT can answer more than 60% of questions correctly without the need for direct assistance from human trainers. Confidence in ChatGPT's dependability and comprehensibility grew as a result of its clear rationale and pertinent clinical findings. The authors suggested integrating ChatGPT into clinical decision-making procedures and utilizing it to support human learners in medical education. The study's overall findings demonstrate ChatGPT's potential as a tool to advance clinical decision-making and medical education.

(Aydın et al, 2023, pp. 22) Authors utilized ChatGPT to rewrite abstracts from Google Scholar's most referenced publications on the topic of "Digital Twin in Healthcare," as part of a literature analysis. In order to evaluate ChatGPT's understanding of the subject, relevant subjects were asked of it. The authors manually checked the ChatGPT-generated articles' plagiarism rates with those of pertinent texts that were available online and in academic libraries, using an authenticated plagiarism tool. While ChatGPT's paraphrases revealed high rates of plagiarism, its replies to discussion-relevant questions revealed low rates. The writers came to the conclusion that ChatGPT's paraphrasing did not result in original articles and proposed that future academic publishing techniques should need less human labor so that academics may concentrate on their work.

(Rane, N et al, 2023, pp. 16) The article discusses the use of computational systems biology in stem cell research, emphasizing its role in understanding biological mechanisms. It emphasizes the need for multidisciplinary interactions between computational and experimental biologists. Deep learning and machine learning approaches are also discussed. The article also discusses the potential of AI-powered chatbots like ChatGPT to improve patient outcomes by encouraging contact between patients and doctors.

(Cao, et al, 2023, pp. 1287) the primary barrier to using AI for mental risk assessment, according to the scientists, is ethical concerns. The need of adhering to the biomedical ethical principles of beneficence, impartiality, non-maleficence, and respect for autonomy is emphasized. A second research on the moral authority of ChatGPT highlights its inconsistency and capacity to contaminate judgment while also demonstrating that it has the potential to improve users' moral judgment. Users misjudge its influence, therefore in order to fully comprehend its advice, appropriate use and digital literacy training are required.

(Fitria, et al, 2023, pp. 44-58) A review of the major literature on AI-assisted psychosis risk screening in teens highlights two different approaches: analysis of large-scale social media data and chat bot-based screening. The scientists claim that ethical issues are the primary barrier to applying AI for mental risk assessment. It is stressed how crucial it is to uphold the beneficence, impartiality, non-maleficence, and respect for autonomy biomedical ethical standards.

FEATURES OF CHATBOT

ChatGPT, a chatbot, is versatile and can simulate human conversationalists, create and debug programs, write poetry, compose music, and answer test questions. It can also translate and summarize text, play games like chat rooms, tic tac toe, ATM simulations, and Linux system imitations.(Aljanabi et al, 2023, pp. 62-64).

ChatGPT, unlike Instruct GPT, aims to minimize deceptive responses. It frames answers as hypothetical scenarios, using information about Columbus' voyages and modern world facts, including opinions about his actions. Instruct GPT acknowledges the premise's veracity, while ChatGPT frames it as counterfactual.. (Raval, et al, 2020, pp. 2).

LIMITATIONS OF CHATBOT

About ChatGPT, OpenAI states that it "sometimes writes plausible-sounding but incorrect or nonsensical answers". This is known as "hallucination" and is a common occurrence with large language models. (Lecler et al, 2023, pp. 269-274)

ChatGPT's incentive model is vulnerable to over-optimization, a condition linked to optimization known as Goodhart's law, as it depends on human monitoring. By 2023, events will be known to Chat-GPT-3.5 (free) through January 2022 and ChatGPT-4 (premium) through April 2023 (Parikshit et al, 2023, pp. 34-41)

Like other technologies, ChatGPT is not without its limits. Even though it can produce well-reasoned and contextually relevant answers, it occasionally produces incorrect or unsuitable ones, particularly when provided with insufficient or unclear information. Furthermore, ChatGPT may have trouble comprehending sarcasm, colloquial language, and other nonliteral terms that people employ in daily discussion. Lastly, ChatGPT occasionally produces repeated or unrelated replies, especially when it comes across a subject on which it has not been taught (Priyanka et al, 2023, pp. 42-46).

ChatGPT'S OPEN POSSIBILITIES

OpenAI's ChatGPT-3 language model has the potential to revolutionize human-technology communication by accurately reading and producing language similar to a person's. Its ability to improve natural language processing and understanding is exciting, making it useful for chatbots, virtual assistants, and other conversational interfaces. As more people interact with technology through text and speech, ChatGPT-3's significance is highlighted in various categories.(Sharma et al, 2023, pp. 45-55).

1. **Academic Writing** ChatGPT-3 is a valuable tool in academic writing, saving time and effort by generating summaries, extracting key points, and providing citations, but should not replace human intelligence. (P. Mathur et al, 2023, pp. 600-605).
2. **Chat GPT as a Search Engine** ChatGPT-3 is a search engine that understands natural language queries, provides contextually relevant information, and generates new text for content creation. However, its cost and accuracy may be limited, and it is currently only available to select developers and researchers.(Dadheech et al, 2023, pp. 111255-111264)

3. **Coding** ChatGPT-3 is a powerful tool for coding that understands natural language inputs, making the process more intuitive and user-friendly. It provides contextually relevant information, saving developers time and generating new code for large projects. However, it has limitations such as its limited user base, high cost, and inability to fully understand programming languages. Additionally, it is not yet capable of handling certain queries, such as debugging or performance optimization. Despite these limitations, ChatGPT-3 remains a valuable tool for developers and researchers (Sethi, S. et al, 2023, pp. 503) .

4. **Detect Security Vulnerabilities** ChatGPT-3 is a valuable tool for security professionals and researchers, enabling the detection of security vulnerabilities. It understands natural language inputs, making the detection process more intuitive. It provides contextually relevant information, saving time and providing relevant information. ChatGPT-3 generates code snippets for exploit generation, but its cost and accessibility may be prohibitive for small businesses and individuals, and it's not yet fully understanding security vulnerabilities.it cannot handle certain queries like reverse engineering or malware analysis (Tanwar. et al, 2022, pp. 1-4).

5. **Social** ChatGPT-3 is a valuable tool for marketers, businesses, and individuals, assisting with social media tasks. It understands natural language inputs, making content creation more intuitive. It provides contextually relevant information, saving time and providing relevant content. ChatGPT-3 can generate new text for engaging posts, making it useful for businesses and organizations. However, its cost and accessibility limit its potential user base, as it is only available to a select group of developers and researchers (Rathi,. et al, 2022, pp. 1-4).

ChatGPT'S FUTURE

AI is expected to significantly impact several medical and dentistry sectors in the future years. It might be difficult to grasp the full extent of these impacts. AI is still in its early stages, therefore more study is needed to properly appreciate its potential advantages.

ChatGPT can process information quickly and provide evidence-based decision-making, reducing human error. It can also aid in disease diagnosis, prognosis, and personalized treatment plans.

ChatGPT has a bright future ahead of it in terms of creating even more advanced language models since it has so much opportunity for development. We may expect ChatGPT to become more sophisticated and potent as technology advances. (Sharma, P.. et al, 2023, pp. 19-38).

Context awareness is one of the main areas where ChatGPT is still under development. Though it is unable to completely comprehend the context in which those words and phrases are being used, ChatGPT can now produce answers based on the words and phrases that it receives. We can anticipate ChatGPT being considerably better at recognizing context as technology advances, which will result in more precise and pertinent replies (Prasad, A. et al, 2023, pp. 43-60).

ChatGPT demands great accuracy to prevent mistakes that might jeopardize patient safety. While ChatGPT contains a large quantity of material, students with limited backgrounds may struggle to identify inaccurate information. Clear rules and verification methods must be established and properly tested by relevant staff (Maharajan, et al,2023, pp. 176-194)

Multi-modal learning is an area where ChatGPT is still being developed. This speaks to the capacity to integrate many forms of input into the learning process, such pictures and movies. By doing this,

ChatGPT will be able to produce replies that are more complex and nuanced and take into consideration a wider variety of data (Kumar, et al,2023, pp. 38-64).

Beyond these fields of study and development, further specialized language models tailored to certain industries or use cases may be created. For example, a language model designed specifically for legal or medical terminology could be significantly more precise and efficient than a general-purpose model such as ChatGPT (Sharma, et al,2023, pp. 184-199).

All things considered, ChatGPT has a very bright future ahead of it. There is a great deal of opportunity for developing ever more complex and powerful language models. We may anticipate ChatGPT becoming even more practical and commonplace as the technology develops further, with applications in a variety of sectors and use cases (Rathore, et al,2023, pp. 63-68).

The emergence of powerful conversational AI systems such as ChatGPT demonstrates the fast growth of technology and its capacity to change the way we operate. While it is true that such technology may eliminate certain employment, it has the ability to generate new possibilities and increase efficiency in a variety of industries. However, it is crucial to acknowledge the necessity for effective implementation and regulation to guarantee that these technologies are utilized ethically and responsibly (Rasul,, et al,2023, pp.1-6).

OpenAI is constantly refining Chat GPT. Their aim involves making it more context-aware, which will further boost its responsiveness and accuracy in real-time communication, reflecting future advancements in artificial intelligence (Aydin, et al,2023, pp. 118-134).

Chat GPT is more than simply a technology fad; it exemplifies human creativity and our relentless drive of development. It has the potential to change many aspects of society, from how we communicate to how we do business. However, as we enter this new era, it is critical that we proceed with prudence, ensuring that we use AI for the advancement of mankind while remaining true to our basic beliefs. The future looms, and with Chat GPT, it appears brighter than ever (Forman, N.,, et al,2023, pp.1-7).

CONCLUSION

The development of ChatGPT and related models has revolutionized human-computer interactions as Conversational AI is expanding rapidly, with ChatGPT making significant contributions to scientific research and paving the way for future technological advancements.

We have examined the history, uses, benefits, drawbacks, moral dilemmas, and potential future developments of ChatGPT in this survey. However, there hasn't been as much focus on the analysis of ChatGPT research conducted in these settings. This chapter looks at ChatGPT's many potential applications, difficulties, and upcoming projects. An overview of ChatGPT works in the application literature is given by our study.

REFERENCES

AlıcıU. I.OksuztepeA.KilinccekerO.KaraarslanE. (2023). OpenAI ChatGPT for Smart Contract Security Testing: Discussion and Future Directions. *Available at* SSRN 4412215.

Aljanabi, M., Ghazi, M., Ali, A. H., & Abed, S. A. (2023). ChatGpt: Open possibilities. *Iraqi Journal For Computer Science and Mathematics*, *4*(1), 62–64.

Aydin, Ö., & Karaarslan, E. (2023). Is ChatGPT leading generative AI? What is beyond expectations? *Academic Platform Journal of Engineering and Smart Systems*, *11*(3), 118–134. doi:10.21541/apjess.1293702

Cao, X. J., & Liu, X. Q. (2022). Artificial intelligence-assisted psychosis risk screening in adolescents: Practices and challenges. *World Journal of Psychiatry*, *12*(10), 1287–1297. doi:10.5498/wjp.v12.i10.1287 PMID:36389087

Cao, Y., Li, S., Liu, Y., Yan, Z., Dai, Y., Yu, P. S., & Sun, L. (2023). A comprehensive survey of ai-generated content (aigc): A history of generative ai from gan to chatgpt. *arXiv preprint arXiv:2303.04226*.

Cao, Y., & Zhai, J. (2023). Bridging the gap–the impact of ChatGPT on financial research. *Journal of Chinese Economic and Business Studies*, *21*(2), 177–191. doi:10.1080/14765284.2023.2212434

Casas, J., Tricot, M. O., Abou Khaled, O., Mugellini, E., & Cudré-Mauroux, P. (2020, October). Trends & methods in chatbot evaluation. In *Companion Publication of the 2020 International Conference on Multimodal Interaction* (pp. 280-286). ACM. 10.1145/3395035.3425319

Fitria, T. N. (2023, March). Artificial intelligence (AI) technology in OpenAI ChatGPT application: A review of ChatGPT in writing English essay. In *ELT Forum. Journal of English Language Teaching*, *12*(1), 44–58.

Fitria, T. N. (2023, March). Artificial intelligence (AI) technology in OpenAI ChatGPT application: A review of ChatGPT in writing English essay. In *ELT Forum. Journal of English Language Teaching*, *12*(1), 44–58.

. Forman, N., Udvaros, J., & Avornicului, M. S. (2023). ChatGPT: A new study tool shaping the future for high school students. *Future, 5*(6), 7.

Fui-Hoon Nah, F., Zheng, R., Cai, J., Siau, K., & Chen, L. (2023). Generative AI and ChatGPT: Applications, challenges, and AI-human collaboration. *Journal of Information Technology Case and Application Research*, *25*(3), 277–304. doi:10.1080/15228053.2023.2233814

Han, J. W., Park, J., & Lee, H. (2022). Analysis of the effect of an artificial intelligence chatbot educational program on non-face-to-face classes: A quasi-experimental study. *BMC Medical Education*, *22*(1), 830. doi:10.1186/s12909-022-03898-3 PMID:36457086

Hargreaves, S. (2023). 'Words Are Flowing out Like Endless Rain into a Paper Cup': ChatGPT & Law School Assessments. *Legal Educ. Rev.*, *33*(1), 69. doi:10.53300/001c.83297

Issom, D. Z., Hardy-Dessources, M. D., Romana, M., Hartvigsen, G., & Lovis, C. (2021). Toward a conversational agent to support the self-management of adults and young adults with sickle cell disease: Usability and usefulness study. *Frontiers in Digital Health*, *3*, 600333. doi:10.3389/fdgth.2021.600333 PMID:34713087

Kapadiya, D., Shekhawat, C., & Sharma, P. (2023). A Study on Large Scale Applications of Big Data in Modern Era. In *International Conference on Information Management & Machine Intelligence (ICIMMI2023)*. ACM, New York, NY, USA. https://doi.org/10.1145/3647444.364788

Kocoń, J., Cichecki, I., Kaszyca, O., Kochanek, M., Szydło, D., Baran, J., Bielaniewicz, J., Gruza, M., Janz, A., Kanclerz, K., Kocoń, A., Koptyra, B., Mieleszczenko-Kowszewicz, W., Miłkowski, P., Oleksy, M., Piasecki, M., Radliński, Ł., Wojtasik, K., Woźniak, S., & Kazienko, P. (2023). ChatGPT: Jack of all trades, master of none. *Information Fusion, 99,* 101861. doi:10.1016/j.inffus.2023.101861

Kumar, A. S., Sharma, P., Kaur, S., Saleh, O. S., Chennamma, H. R., & Chaturvedi, A. (2023). AI-Equipped IoT Applications in High-Tech Agriculture Using Machine Learning. In *Handbook of Research on AI-Equipped IoT Applications in High-Tech Agriculture* (pp. 38–64). IGI Global.

Leaver, T., & Srdarov, S. (2023). ChatGPT Isn't Magic: The Hype and Hypocrisy of Generative Artificial Intelligence (AI) Rhetoric. *M/C Journal, 26*(5).

Lecler, A., Duron, L., & Soyer, P. (2023). Revolutionizing radiology with GPT-based models: Current applications, future possibilities and limitations of ChatGPT. *Diagnostic and Interventional Imaging, 104*(6), 269–274. doi:10.1016/j.diii.2023.02.003 PMID:36858933

Li, J., Dada, A., Puladi, B., Kleesiek, J., & Egger, J. (2024). ChatGPT in healthcare: A taxonomy and systematic review. *Computer Methods and Programs in Biomedicine, 245,* 108013. doi:10.1016/j.cmpb.2024.108013 PMID:38262126

Liebrenz, M., Schleifer, R., Buadze, A., Bhugra, D., & Smith, A. (2023). Generating scholarly content with ChatGPT: Ethical challenges for medical publishing. *The Lancet. Digital Health, 5*(3), e105–e106. doi:10.1016/S2589-7500(23)00019-5 PMID:36754725

Lo, C. K. (2023). What is the impact of ChatGPT on education? A rapid review of the literature. *Education Sciences, 13*(4), 410. doi:10.3390/educsci13040410

Maharajan, K., Kumar, A. S., El Emary, I. M., Sharma, P., Latip, R., Mishra, N., & Sharma, M. (2023). Blockchain Methods and Data-Driven Decision Making With Autonomous Transportation. In Effective AI, Blockchain, and E-Governance Applications for Knowledge Discovery and Management (pp. 176-194). IGI Global. doi:10.4018/978-1-6684-9151-5.ch012

Mancy, A. M., Kumar, A. S., Latip, R., Jagadamba, G., Chakrabarti, P., Sharma, P., . . . Kanchan, B. G. (2024). Smart Healthcare System, Digital Health and Telemedicine, Management and Emergencies: Patient Emergency Application (PES) E-Governance Applications. In Sustainable Development in AI, Blockchain, and E-Governance Applications (pp. 124-151). IGI Global.

Mokmin, N. A. M., & Ibrahim, N. A. (2021). The evaluation of chatbot as a tool for health literacy education among undergraduate students. *Education and Information Technologies, 26*(5), 6033–6049. doi:10.1007/s10639-021-10542-y PMID:34054328

. Prasad, A., Kumar, A. S., Sharma, P., Irawati, I. D., Chandrashekar, D. V., Musirin, I. B., & Abdullah, H. M. A. (2023). Artificial Intelligence in Computer Science: An Overview of Current Trends and Future Directions. *Advances in Artificial and Human Intelligence in the Modern Era,* 43-60.

. Rane, N. (2023). ChatGPT and Similar Generative Artificial Intelligence (AI) for Smart Industry: role, challenges and opportunities for industry 4.0, industry 5.0 and society 5.0. *Challenges and Opportunities for Industry, 4.*

Rane, N. (2023, October 16). Contribution and Challenges of ChatGPT and Similar Generative Artificial Intelligence in Biochemistry, Genetics and Molecular Biology. *Genetics and Molecular Biology*.

Rasul, T., Nair, S., Kalendra, D., Robin, M., de Oliveira Santini, F., Ladeira, W. J., & Heathcote, L. (2023). The role of ChatGPT in higher education: Benefits, challenges, and future research directions. *Journal of Applied Learning and Teaching*, *6*(1).

. Rathore, B. (2023). Future of AI & generation alpha: ChatGPT beyond boundaries. *Eduzone: International Peer Reviewed/Refereed Multidisciplinary Journal*, *12*(1), 63-68.

Raval, H. (2020). Limitations of existing chatbot with analytical survey to enhance the functionality using emerging technology. [IJRAR]. *International Journal of Research and Analytical Reviews*, *7*(2).

Rawat, P., Bhardwaj, A., Lamba, N., Sharma, P., Kumawat, P., & Sharma, P. (2023). Arduino Based IoT Mini Weather Station. *SKIT Research Journal*, *13*(2), 34–41. doi:10.47904/IJSKIT.13.2.2023.34-41

Ren, R., Zapata, M., Castro, J. W., Dieste, O., & Acuña, S. T. (2022). Experimentation for chatbot usability evaluation: A secondary study. *IEEE Access : Practical Innovations, Open Solutions*, *10*, 12430–12464. doi:10.1109/ACCESS.2022.3145323

Sethi, S. S., & Sharma, P. (2023). New Developments in the Implementation of IoT in Agriculture. *SN Computer Science*, *4*(5), 503. doi:10.1007/s42979-023-01896-w

Sharma, P. (2023). Utilizing Explainable Artificial Intelligence to Address Deep Learning in Biomedical Domain. In *Medical Data Analysis and Processing using Explainable Artificial Intelligence* (pp. 19–38). CRC Press. doi:10.1201/9781003257721-2

Sharma, P., & Bhatnagar, N. (2023). Passenger Authentication and Ticket Verification at Airport Using QR Code Scanner. *SKIT Research Journal*, *13*(2), 10–13. doi:10.47904/IJSKIT.13.1.2023.10-12

. Sharma, P., & Dadheech, P. (2023). *Modern-age Agriculture with Artificial Intelligence: A review emphasizing Crop Yield Prediction*.

Sharma, P., Dadheech, P., Aneja, N., & Aneja, S. (2023). Predicting Agriculture Yields Based on Machine Learning Using Regression and Deep Learning. *IEEE Access : Practical Innovations, Open Solutions*, *11*, 111255–111264. doi:10.1109/ACCESS.2023.3321861

Sharma, P., Dadheech, P., & Senthil, A. S. K. (2023). AI-Enabled Crop Recommendation System Based on Soil and Weather Patterns. In *Artificial Intelligence Tools and Technologies for Smart Farming and Agriculture Practices* (pp. 184–199). IGI Global. doi:10.4018/978-1-6684-8516-3.ch010

Sharma, P., & Jain, M. K. (2023). Stock Market Trends Analysis using Extreme Gradient Boosting (XGBoost*). International Conference on Computing, Communication, and Intelligent Systems (ICCCIS)*, Greater Noida, India. 10.1109/ICCCIS60361.2023.10425722

Sharma, P., Kapadiya, D., & Bhardwaj, A. (2023). Efficient Note Sharing Model for Collaborative Learning. *SKIT Research Journal*, *13*(2), 42–46. doi:10.47904/IJSKIT.13.2.2023.42-46

Sharma, P., & Rathi, Y. (2016). Efficient density-based clustering using automatic parameter detection. In *Proceedings of the International Congress on Information and Communication Technology: ICICT 2015,* (pp. 433-441). Springer Singapore. 10.1007/978-981-10-0767-5_46

Sharma, P., Sharma, C., & Mathur, P. (2023). *Machine Learning-based Stock Market Forecasting using Recurrent Neural Network.* 2023 9th International Conference on Smart Computing and Communications (ICSCC), Kochi, Kerala, India. 10.1109/ICSCC59169.2023.10335083

Tanwar, A., Sharma, P., Pandey, A., & Kumar, S. (2022, December). Intrusion Detection System Based Ameliorated Technique of Pattern Matching. In *Proceedings of the 4th International Conference on Information Management & Machine Intelligence* (pp. 1-4). ACM. 10.1145/3590837.3590947

Vaishya, R., Misra, A., & Vaish, A. (2023). ChatGPT: Is this version good for healthcare and research? *Diabetes & Metabolic Syndrome, 17*(4), 102744. doi:10.1016/j.dsx.2023.102744 PMID:36989584

Zhai, X. (2023). ChatGPT for next generation science learning. *XRDS: Crossroads. The ACM Magazine for Students, 29*(3), 42–46.

Chapter 5
Insights and Future Prospects for ChatGPT:
A Productive Computational Intelligence Approach on the Administration of Human Resources

Saumendra Das

https://orcid.org/0000-0003-4956-4352

GIET University, India

Udaya Sankar Patro

https://orcid.org/0009-0009-9198-3578

Rayagada Autonomous College, India

Tapaswini Panda

https://orcid.org/0009-0003-8327-9990

Debasis Pani

https://orcid.org/0009-0002-1706-5751

Gandhi Institute of Advanced Computer and Research, India

Hassan Badawy

https://orcid.org/0000-0001-6536-150X

Luxor University, Egypt

ABSTRACT

Using regenerative artificial intelligence (AI) models, ChatGPT and its variations have quickly gained attention in scientific and public debate about the possible advantages and disadvantages they may have in economics, a republic, the community, and the environment. It is unclear if these advancements will create new jobs or eliminate existing ones, or if they redistribute human labour by producing additional knowledge and choices that may be insignificant or functionally unimportant. In light of the swift progress in productive neural networks (AI) as well as their arising consequences for job procedures worldwide and HR management in especially, this HRMJ argument writing generates jointly a variety of opinions concerning how we may improve HRM academic discourse. Giving a synopsis of the most recent advances in the discipline and creating a collection of possibilities for study are the main goals of this approach. By assuming tangible proof, we hope to advance the comprehension of artificial intelligence and push beyond the borders of what is currently known as science.

DOI: 10.4018/979-8-3693-6824-4.ch005

INTRODUCTION

The Emergence of Artificial Intelligence: Exploring the Knows and Hidden

Over the past ten years, artificial intelligence (AI) tools and digital platforms—or at least devices and networks that assert "intelligent status"—have established a necessary component of commercial organizations and civilization. This results from AI algorithms' greater cognitive and mathematical powers compared to humans (von Krogh, Roberson, and Gruber, 2023), their capacity to simplify corporate operations, harvest information from huge data, and to make forecasts and suggestions. It is contradictory due to the fact it generates fresh data as well as judgments that must be taken in areas that may be of tremendous significance or mere insignificance, taking stuff out from people's hands while giving people additional duties to do.

However, like a number of contemporary technical developments, it may be challenging to separate myth form reality, and AI has shown to be more effective in certain domains that some (e.g., producing written material that appears believable on the surface) (e.g., creating robotics with true agility). It is still unclear if artificial intelligence that regenerates devalue or kills, provides employment or generates new ones.

The different kinds of AI, including automated robotic procedures (such as autonomous machines in warehouses), techniques involving computer vision, recognizing words, deep-learning and machine-learning computations, and machine learning, have opened up a wide range possibilities and distinctive advantages for organizations to rethink company operations and procedures, develop ways to operate and customer experiences (like based on information flexible and target choices, handling projects, and other areas), and more (Rawat et al., 2023).

The amount of HRM scholarship on AI has grown over the last five years (Budhwar et al., 2022; Chowdhury et al., 2023; Edwards et al., 2022; Malik, Budhwar, & Kazmi, 2022). The beneficial effects of using artificial intelligence (AI) machine learning techniques for encouraging variation (Daugherty et al., 2018), recruiting fresh hires (Pan et al., 2022), variables influencing HRM managers' use of AI (Suseno et al., 2022), the growing significance of machines to improve staff work environments (Malik, Budhwar, Patel, & Srikanth, 2022), and the implications of Duties and the Law have all been emphasised recently. Recently published studies have examined the possible advantages and disadvantages of artificial intelligence for human resource management and HRM practises and standards (Margherita, 2022; Pereira et al., 2023). Nevertheless, it is also associated with the reducing skills of expert labour (Xue et al., 2022) and may lead to immoral decisions being made by managers.

Nevertheless, as artificial intelligence (AI) algorithms and varieties have quickly developed, they have also presented exciting new possibilities as well as challenges for users in business and academia. This is associated with generating artificial intelligence (AI), that has gained popularity ever since ChatGPT (Generative Pre-trained Transformers), a standard bot, was initially made available for use by the public in the month of November 2022. This was promptly followed by ChatGPT-4, a more advanced version released in the month of March 2023 (OpenAI Blog, 2022; Das & Nayak, 2022). Since its debut, ChatGPT has grown significantly in Favor thanks to its capacity to produce interesting, humanoid responses to practically any query posed.

The ChatGPT-human connection is natural and natural because the bot may respond to additional inquiries, accept responsibility for errors, and reject improper demands. In comparison to traditional AI algorithms built on machine learning that can find similarities in enormous data sets and formulate projections, ChatGPT marks a considerable divergence. This capacity for prediction may be seen in engines for searches like Google in 2010, which provide completion suggestions to improve the Caliber of search outcomes. ChatGPT, nevertheless, goes above simple forecasting. Artificial models for languages are used.

Allowing it to produce completely unique material depending just on the answer prompts given by a user (Sethi & Sharma, 2023). This writing There are many different types of content, including reports, writing, screenplays, business concepts, programming codes, and studies. Advertising efforts and texts. The calibre of its intake determines the Caliber of its product, assuming either the instructional data that it has seen and the user-provided cues of tasks that has to be accomplished (Sharma, Dharmi & Ajay, 2023).

The "mind" of the ChatGPT, the computer's programming model, uses artificial intelligence for development (Sharma & Rathi, 2016). The phrase "generative intelligence" refers to the use of ML models to produce new content, such as writing, music, video, photographs, software programmes, and studies, which makes use of enormous learning information collections (Kapadiya et al, 2023). But the Caliber, rapidity, and applicability of the initial database will determine how contextually relevant new information produced is (Boston Management Centre The term generative AI, 2023; McKinsey & Prominent Research, 2023). As an illustration, the GPT4 model underwent training utilizing just 45 gigabytes of info that had been collected from the internet as a whole up to 2021 (Open AI GPT 4 Technology Conclusion, 2023). As a result, it is doubtful that the replies will offer accurate and current data.

To better understand ChatGPT's progress, let's look at its past (Figure 1). In order to predict the next word in a string of letters that makes up a phrase, massive linguistic networks (LLMs) are constructed utilising massive volumes of textual data. LLMs do this by determining relationships between concepts throughout the characters itself. Nevertheless, the historical context, significance, as well as effectiveness of the results were constrained by the original LLMs' sequential and independent processing of every sentence in a block of text. As a result, converters were created in 2018 and have the ability to concurrently process every word within an information set while assigning varied values to various textual components to increase the results' accuracy and value (Uszkoreit, 2017). This characteristic made it possible to effectively handle very huge datasets, which encouraged the creation of GPT frameworks.

GPT-1, GPT-2, GPT-3, Instruct-GPT, and ChatGPT were all released by Open Artificial Intelligence in 2018; they followed in 2019, 2020, 2022, then February 2023, correspondingly. because their debut, GPT platforms have been trained using enormous datasets (the GPT-3 training data set is approximately 575 GB in size) and a significant number of variables (the GPT-3 learning database has 175 million variables) in order to enable these individuals to reply to questions that are asked. Nevertheless, since there were no safety controls, GPT-3 would provide inaccurate outputs with incorrect data (known as illusions), that could contain hazardous and offensive messages and generate unnecessary findings.

The following contributed the integration of supervision and reinforced machine learning (ML) approaches to include input from humans in the development manage, producing results suited to users' purpose and the meaning provided by the prompting (Ouyang et al., 2023; Prasad et al., 2023; Maharajan et al., 2023).

As a result, the GPT-3 model was improved by engaging actual contracts to offer a labelled development information set, whereby the employees will supply the algorithm with a suitable answer for every argument (gathered from previous GPT-2 user prompts). Of obviously, this cannot rule out the prospect of prejudices or poor decisions on the part of the aforementioned subcontractors. This model evolved into GPT3.5. Utilizing the method of reinforcement learning incorporating feedback from humans (RLHF) approach, it was improved to more effectively handle a variety of stimuli (Ouyang et al., 2023). In order

Figure 1. Evolution of ChatGPT
(Rehana, H., Çam, N. B., Basmaci, M., Zheng, J., Jemiyo, C., He, Y., ... & Hur, J., 2023)

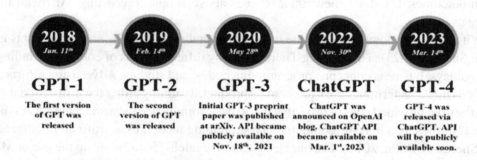

Evolution of GPT Models. GPT: generative pre-trained transformer. API: application programming interface.

for the artificial intelligence (AI) to determine which response was the most pertinent, subcontractors graded several model-generated comments for a particular question in the form of an incentive mechanism built with contrast information (Schulman et al., 2017). In simple terms, this made it possible for people (or, more specifically, a small number of people) to direct the system's development procedure and enhance its capacity to provide excellent replies (Tanwar et al., 2022; Das et al., 2022; Kumar et al., 2023).

Machine learning is a very dynamic field of AI study that has seen significant expansion in the past few years (Sharma, Sharma & Mathur, 2023). Deep learning has become a significant advancement in the field of machine learning, which is characterized by the use of artificially generated neural networks to acquire knowledge from data. Deep learning is currently used. In order to get cutting-edge efficiency across multiple areas, such as photo and audio honor, processing of natural languages, and video game play, extensive efforts are required. Contextual learning is an artificial learning approach that emphasizes

Figure 2. ChatGPT development
(https://www.officetimeline.com/blog/artificial-intelligence-
ai-and-chatgpt-history-and-timelines)

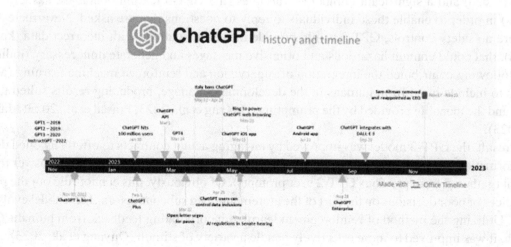

learning via iterative experimentation. The use of reinforced learning is being seen in several domains, including but not limited to video games, machine learning, as well as control algorithms (Prasad, et al., 2023).

In order to improve the connection of the results of the algorithm and user intents, the GPT-4 paradigm was developed. This entails improving the algorithm's output's correctness and lowering the likelihood of offensive words, although this hasn't really addressed AI's very boring literary approach. GPT-4 has outperformed the prior version GPT-3.5 in both historical precision and mistake rates, yet this doesn't negate the ability for it to produce inaccuracies on command. Additionally, it offers more steering flexibility, enabling customers to customize the car's colour and appearance to their tastes. Furthermore, GPT-4 purportedly has improved barriers for avoiding incorrect answers, exhibiting a stronger dedication to moral dilemmas.

Those safeguards, nevertheless, are constrained to the guidelines and public standards established by the creators. You can use a variety of techniques for jailbreaking GPT4, which serves as a means to utilize certain queries to get around restrictions and unlocked capabilities that might allow GPT4 to distribute false facts and display immoral behaviour (Lloyds, 2023). GPT-4 can handle both written content and visual content, contrast the previous versions, whose only handle text. This enables GPT-4 to evaluate a photograph's subject matter and relate it to a textual query, offering a more thorough grasp of the environment. It must be emphasized, though, that GPT-4 is intended solely for picture analysis, not creating pictures nevertheless, is generally accepted that AI is capable of producing research papers in addition to pastiches of other artistic genres (Das et al., 2022).

As the aforementioned techniques are transparent is regard to the fact of where they are unable to clarify why the replies originated as the location of their training data is likewise unclear, the veracity of answers produced by creative AI systems like GPT4 is constrained. Additionally, there are severe social and image hazards for businesses wishing to employ the results of artificial intelligence because to the systems' capacity to create erroneous information (often jokingly referred to as "hallucinations"). For instance, during a demonstration in February 2023, the market value of Google dropped $100 billion as a result of Bard, a Google artificial intelligence (AI) chatbot, responding incorrectly on Twitter (Thorbecke, 2023; Sharma, 2023; Sharma et al., 2023).

The ability to deceive and provide erroneous data may be a feature of various of the more well-known artificially intelligent systems, or it may be a decision made autonomously and consciously by the current; either scenario would bring up major moral issues.

The linguistic instruction site Duolingo uses the GPT-4 framework within its setting of commercial projects, and adaptive equipment company Be Mine uses it to develop a remedy for people with blindness to help them become cognizant of the world around them (Derico & Kleinman, 2023). GPT-4 is being used by Stripe, the payments device, to protect message boards of spammers and deception in 2023, and Bing, a subsidiary of Microsoft, is adopting it to enhance the search engine functionality (Stripe Newsroom, 2023).

GPT-4 is being used by Morgan Stanley to streamline employee support procedures (Davenport, 2023), and IBM has adopted it to offer tailored suggestions to users for the purpose to assist them in addressing their problems (Yakar, 2023).

This is significant that the government of Denmark worked with Open Artificial Intelligence to use GPT-4 to safeguard the written language of Icelandic. GPT-4 is now part of Microsoft Office 365, enabling users to swiftly summarise lengthy paragraphs in Microsoft or create a complete presentation using PowerPoint with only one text prompt (Microsoft Blog, 2023). Although generative AI's early commercial applications show off its potential, the tool's eventual acceptability and uptake will be contingent on how well-founded ethical and security issues can be addressed (Mancy et al., 2024).

The widespread use of ChatGPT increased interest along with competition in marketplaces for chatbots that use artificial intelligence. The declaration by Microsoft that it will invest $10 billion in Open Artificial Intelligence has considerably heightened this trend and encouraged other tech firms to enter the race. Alphabet recently unveiled "Project Magi" and the experimental service "Bard" (Data Scientist, 2023), while Meta recently released LLAMA, an artificial intelligence algorithm that includes 65 billion characteristics, both of which aim to revolutionise the web search experience. Google has also entered the race with its ChatGPT-like products known as "Ernie Bot" in English or "Wenxin Yiyan" in Chinese.

Additionally, the chatbot that uses artificial intelligence Character. ai has the ability to mimic notable persons or fictitious creatures. A South Korean internet search engine company called Naver has declared that "Search GPT" will debut in the primary half of 2023. A Russian tech firm named Yandex has stated intentions to make "YaLM 2.0" available in Russian by the end of 2023. We thus predict that as additional competitors continuing to make inroads into the artificial intelligence industry, the methodology may grow stronger and complex, expanding its commercial uses and possible economic dangers (Das et al., 2023).

However, as everyone that's had the misfortune of interacting with an automated online communication consumer reaction chat framework is going to be understanding, these platforms are becoming increasingly better at producing merely reliable plaid and pancake and hitting out undesirable inquiries than actually helping individuals resolve challenges (Das et al., 2021).

Despite to the hoopla surrounding generating artificial intelligence systems like GPT-4, organizations entail a significant challenge in operationalizing and training these technologies inside their current company procedures, that will result in a number of ramifications for human resources management. In order to put into perspective, the outcomes and fit them with the specific requirements of the companies, the instruction procedure is labour-intensive (Sharma and Dadheech, 2023).

It also presents questions about the sort of education; there's a gap among technical competence with a system that uses AI and practical expertise in the managerial or operational domains it is intended to support (Das, 2022). Furthermore, Dr. Geoffrey Hinton, known as the "Godfather of AI," that recently left Google, for example, has voiced his concerns regarding the dangers of artificial intelligence (AI), like the dissemination of deceptive data, manipulation of social buildings, disruption of the employment market, risks associated with cyberspace, and misuse by criminals in unanticipated ways that may cause geo-political conflicts as well as cause great damage to people (Guardian New).

For example, the original versions, that was released in November 2022, raises questions concerning prejudice, actual damage, the training of creative artificial intelligence models, or the behaviour of ChatGPT (Bidle, 2022). Control and understanding of the new dangers and opportunities offered by smart technology are still considerably in their development. In one example, a US senators group requested the creation of a brand-new oversight organization to oversee the artificial intelligence (AI) sector in response to the chief executive officer of OpenAI's statements. Nevertheless, given the speed at which technology is developing, legislators gazed how well such a body could keep up with the changes (Clayton, 2023).

While AI may speed up the investigation manage, it also introduces serious hazards because its propensity to fabricate data if provided the opportunity or when instructed to perform so. Additionally, it creates space for computerized study review (Gendron et al., 2022). In order to avoid occurrences of outsourced to machine learning, this automatic review can be helpful in checking the portrayal of numerous real perspectives in interviews, assuring the validity of data shown in rows, and even establishing the authorship of a publication (Sharma et al., 2023). The likelihood of humans exercising judgment cantered around implicit and subjective understanding may be reduced as a result, and enabling computers to choose whether research is suitable exposes both academics and practise to completely novel dangers (Sharma & Bhatnagar, 2023).

Customs of intellectual food may be dropped in these advances if guiding surrounding a variety of educational talents becomes unnecessary (Gendron et al., 2022); the former could be difficult to reestablish if the effects of a still mainly untested technological advances demonstrate detrimental or potentially harmful.

The current developments and debates around artificial intelligence (AI) that generates show that it has the potential to change HRM positions, procedures, and behaviours. Understanding how businesses might use this potential to add value is essential. We think that crucial analysis and comprehension of the consequences of the latest wave of artificial intelligence (AI) models may be greatly aided by human resources management studies. Through doing this, HRM may act as a catalyst for the prudent and intentional use of artificial intelligence (AI), that will provide beneficial HR results.

Corporate Benefits of Artificial Intelligence Generation and HRM Results

What valuable lessons can we draw from commercial past concerning technological innovation and its consequences for company? (Savvas Papagiannidis and Stephanie Decker)

Jaap Paauwe and Paul Boselie's article, "Take Resource-based Perspective: ChatGPT and Strategies to Implement it in HRM,"

- The consequences of AI for generation for HRM-Related Outcomes: Academic Benefits of Analyse

   (Vijay Pereira and David Guest)

Artificial Intelligence for Generation: Skill, Efficiency, and Staff Administration

- Staff Wellness and Participation, Workplace Relationships (Andrew J. Knoblich and Steven Rogelberg)
- Which of the following are the consequences and difficulties for labour relations of ChatGPT and other creative based on artificial intelligence instruments?

(Ashish Malik and Greg J. Bamber)

- ChatGPT Evaluation Advice and Recruitment. (Angelo DeNisi and Arup Varma)

   On Possibilities & Hazards of Creative Writing AI: An Internationally Human Resources Administration Research Program (Rosalie L. Tung): Generative AI - International Human Resources Management (EDI, and Long-Term HRM)

- Fang Lee Cooke and Charmi Patel's paper, "ChatGPT, EDI, and Implications for HRM,"

- Sustainable administration of human resources with AI that generates (Shuang Ren and Prasanta Kumar Dey)

  Academia Study Methods and Artificial Intelligence for Generation

- Using Artificial Intelligence (AI) as a Methodological Assistant: confidence, and Confirm (Herman Anguini's and Jose R. Beltran)
- Observations and Suggestions from a Study Procedures' Discussion employing ChatGPT

COMMERCIAL RESPONSES OF GENERATIVE AI WITH HRM

Since Chat-GPT's debut, users have reacted in a number of ways to the topic of generating Intelligence. LLMs, which were hitherto the purview of specialists, are becoming the subject of more widespread discussion about the prospects of employment & the significance of labour in general. Stresses surrounding cutting-edge technology are nothing novel; for example, when locomotives first became a mode of public transportation, worries were voiced that the fast pace may drive customers insane (Milne-Smith, 2016).

Comparable health issues were raised by smartphones due to possible undetectable irradiation (FDA, 2022) or, more seriously, the risk for malformed fingertips following excessive usage of smartphones, or the "smartphone Pinky" (Taylor, 2020). However, excessively gushing assessments of new technology can prove that they were similarly exaggerated.

For instance, although being developed more than 40 years ago, the method of 3D printing is just now beginning to gain widespread business acceptance (PWC., 2016), and referred to as MOOCs did not substantially change or disrupt the way schooling is provided in the world (Borden, 2014). A rebuttal of hyperbole with little later impact may be found for every historical instance of a disruptive innovation. It is evident that technological advancement is not disrupting society as a whole on its own; rather, it merely does so over time in tandem with increased productivity, the adoption of new requirements, and the development of new types of businesses. And as the dot-com bubble and crash have demonstrated, it might be more challenging to comprehend ways to economically utilize an innovation then knowing it (Decker).

We are unsure of how prevalent as well as economically feasible autonomous machines is going to get whilst the argument over its place in our competent, instructive, and private life continues on. Could it turn into a semi-public commodity where the majority of users may get AI technologies for free or at a reasonable cost via SaaS (software-as-a-service)? bundles, or would the most effective artificial intelligence (AI) models be so expensive that they stay the exclusive domain following their first release?

of substantial, funded adequately businesses that use it covertly or without oversight? Right now, it appears like AI might been widely used.

For example, Copilot, an AI employee, is going to be made instantaneously accessible to a billion of people globally when Ms introduces it as part of their Office Suite (Spataro, 2023). The inclusion of artificial intelligence (AI) that generates in commonly used office packages will work as a catalyst for achieving the two essential goals.

The perception of utility alongside perceived usability are key determinants of technological acceptability (Davis, 1989). Therefore, this may normalize its application and shape public opinions of the upcoming regulations for dynamic artificial intelligence.

A more basic concern is if AI can mostly support human judgment in the face with data stress, or if it will eventually replace the work of humans and choices. In the most recent financial institution analysis (Hatzis et al., 2023) it was expected that the two alternatives would result in major financial benefits. Over the next ten years, artificial intelligence with generative capabilities may increase US employment efficiency by slightly about 112 percentage points a lot of assimilation. These standards rely on how challenging tasks AI will eventually be able to accomplish the number of occupations that finally get computerized, indicating: the greatest positive among these possibilities assumes that Many of the occupations presently done by individuals will become outdated (Das et al., 2023).

Since the dawn of industrialization, significant improvements in efficiency have been experienced driven by automation and cooperation in machines. At the end of the 20th century, Charlie Chaplin's film Modern Times film comically depicted humanity's dependence on machinery. James Cameron's Cyborg trilogy in the early 21st century brought this fear of being subjugated by computers to its natural conclusion. Historical economists have emphasized that substantial rises in productivity via innovation rely on a variety of reasons (Crafts, 2010), and that historically, industry has benefited most from considerable efficiency advances (Panda et al., 2024). Despite smaller increases frequently being seen in the hospitality sector (Bosworth & Collins, 2008), AI technologies could offer a significant improvement in this area, since the possibility exists for big computational languages to quickly replace people in the operations industries.

Additionally, given that the hospitality economy dominates most modern industrialized nations, the effect on volunteering in addition to working in an administrative capacity.

Even in situations when occupations are not eliminated, they could possibly be downgraded. AI may improve output, nevertheless it can also (what is frequently poor) in our capacity for thinking objectively. Comparing directly between AI and humans may give the false sense of security that humanity is "greater" than them. For example, we are concerned because AI may deliver inaccurate responses to inquiries, as if people could just offer accurate responses. Similar to how we worry about prejudice in human beings, we worry about bias in AI. LLMs have received training in interpersonal interaction and online writing, and they take in the prejudices that we as humans have. Civilizations had previously developed electronic reproduction.

This also become easier given the severe disparities in the world finances, African nations' AI employees provide the majority among the cheap labour needed for training the LLMs. 2023 (Perrigo). It can reinforce our preconceptions instead of making us work to overcome them. Positively, it could serve as a way to show us what we are capable of. However, doing so requires a rigorous examination of the manner in which artificial intelligence algorithms operate.

Calls for "explainable AI" might understate the level of intricacy required for effective models of artificial intelligence. Future dependence on artificial intelligence (AI) might affect our capacity for autonomous and analytical thinking. We aren't going to be equipped to critically evaluate AI-based conclusions absent the proper education, training, and expertise, so we could just comply to cover up our inexperience. The result might be a cycle of feedback. The potential for confronting AI will decrease as more people trust it. Such a difficulty will have an impact on everybody in the organization, not only those who participate in routine, minimal duties.

Depending on AI can provide homogeneous labour outcomes that won't be anticipated to lose value as time passes, presuming that AI is widely used so that organizations are able to stay viable. On the one together, value decreases when a product is made simpler to create, particularly when people aren't as important to the process as they once were.

On the other hand, whatever is the comparative benefit if decreasing the obstacles to producing results in everybody producing comparable or even identical results? This is especially problematic if there's a lack of diversity in the development and management of artificial intelligence (AI) platforms since there exist just a few artificial intelligence vendors and technologies made accessible for end customers. In an ironic twist, this may lead to a rise in what people think of human generated outputs.

With the expansion of craft businesses and goods, including the pervasive emergence of small-scale brewing that mix "old" craft know-how with affordable cutting-edge brewing appliances (and tax incentives in many nations), we can already see it. On the opposite hand, people will never be able to match the speed of technology. despite the fact that the product is of a high Caliber, the pace that it is produced is unlikely to be comparable. Both human responses and computer productions cannot match each other's speed of production. Due to this, task-level employee contributions are going to be undervalued through their supervisors, which will have a cascade impact.

The following is going to have an impact on how activities are completed as well as on leadership and oversight. Histories is unsuited themselves to making predictions for the future since there are numerous, complex, and contentious different paths for each technological advancement (Pomeranz, 2009). Our economy, our workplaces, and even our private lives are now set to be significantly impacted by AI. The environmental consequences of AI, which are now being operated in enormous data centres and use a substantial amount of energy, have seldom been mentioned in our present-day debates of the technology (Bender et al., 2021).

Although industrialization has possibly previously resulted in enormous advances in income and social security, however there's little question about how it has additionally caused the rise in consumption of resources that's generating the present environmental catastrophe.

McKenna, 2011. From an ecological standpoint, AI keeps us on our current journey of rapidly increasing pollution that results from every day per-person consumption of energy.

The Results of Generative Artificial Intelligence in HRM: Academic Implications of Analysis

The most recent advancement in artificial intelligence, known as "generative AI," is currently characterized as representing an evolution in thinking and a new phase of industrial growth defined as "Industry 4.0." It stands out because it transfers information management between individuals to robots, possibly changing where it comes from. Additionally, there are requests to halt growth until these ramifications are given more careful consideration because of the repercussions of this for leadership, staff, and the community as general (Shet & Pereira, 2021). This implies that generating AI's potential effects and results, both at work and elsewhere, remain unpredictable. As a result, it presents HRM experts with an extensive new study topic since it has the ability to have an impact on a variety of aspects of the operations, written material, and results.

The ability to hold an infinite amount of data and convey it in a cohesive, usable manner is the key characteristic of computational AI, which is represented, for instance, in ChatGPT and Troubadour. It can carry out a variety of tasks that used to necessitate human intervention. As a result, it makes a compelling case to business by offering to make excellence, well researched data available in large quantities more far quicker that people can.

We provide two analytical structures for human resources management scholars interested in the results of generating AI. The initial strategy is the stakeholder approach put forth by Beer et al. in 1984, which contends that human resources should prioritize a variety of customers, including board members, staff members, the judiciary, neighbours, and labour organizations, while pursuing the core objectives of company efficiency, satisfaction with work, and a healthy society. This is due, in part, to the belief that, so far, AI has mostly served to advance effectiveness and adaptability in the benefit of investors while harming the needs of additional stakeholders by promoting their best interests. The probable influence of artificial intelligence (AI) generative goes far outside the realm of work.

The promotion of Industry 5.0 is where an additional and supplementary analytical paradigm may be discovered. A resetting is necessary to guarantee that Technology 4.0, which includes artificial intelligence (AI) that is generative, serves harmony with the needs of all parties at job and in the world, as illustrated by results consistent with expanding the standard of employment and an excellence of life for citizens as a whole. This is recognized between schoolwork, authorities such as those in Japan and the European Commission, and even in the scientific community. To guarantee that advancements are adequately human-centric, suggestions have been made for the revitalization of a technological-societal viewpoint (Bednar & Welch, 2020).

The socio-technical method has the ability to meet the major goals of the many stakeholders because it recognizes institutional flexibility for the creation of employment (Trist et al., 1963).

The key objectives defined by Beer et al. in 1984—organizational performance, satisfaction with work, and society well-being—may offer an outline for studies regarding artificial intelligence with generative capabilities when those analytical concerns are kept in view. We can then select particular results who can serve as this focus. By doing so, we will take into account both possible advantages and disadvantages, keep mindful of the particular HR function's accountability for overseeing personnel administration, and deal with the characteristics of Industrial 5.0.

In times past, businesses have tried to adopt new technologies to obtain an edge over their competitors. There is no reason to think that AI, and particularly generative artificial intelligence, will make a difference. When viewed via the conceptual framework of the Understanding Based View (KBV), a particular aspect of the resource-centred perspective of the firm, we predominantly view that businesses have distinctive collections of particular understanding skills and assets (knowledge related to generative AI), which need to be properly handled so that they maximize appreciate through its optimum installation, while recognizing and building their expertise capability and collection of assets for the foreseeable future (Grant, 2017).

Thus, by using artificial intelligence to analyse and arrive at decisions more effectively in a variety of HR activities, the department of human resources may enhance its own procedures and outcomes while contributing overall company performance. Possible examples of this are the prompt delivery of semi-standard data from areas like job postings, resumes, recruitment shapes, and processes. Bots, which stand for "interactive robots," have a lot of promise for education and advancement since they can handle tasks like answering queries from workers typically handled by HR contact centres. Evidence-driven HRM have been promoted for a while.

The accessibility of data backed by evidence that can be used to base human resources choices and enhance the results of HR is a possible benefit of generating AI. This could put into use internally generated HR analytical data to give insight into employee turnover and absenteeism, and much information about human resources, as well as outside proof by relying upon careful evaluations of the effects of legislation and additional initiatives to enhance personnel administration. Lowering the amount of time required to gather HR data might free up time for essential HR tasks such as assisting supervisors, handling employee issues, and adding to planning for the types of results to prioritize for personnel managing.

Such represents a potential; reality could prove harder given worries regarding the reliability of the information created by AI, staff satisfaction with chatbots, and asymmetry in the socio-technical ecosystem.

ChatGPT's Public Asset Oriented Perspective and HRM

Given the correct conditions, people (human resources) may be an asset of sustainable competitive edge, according to the theory of human capital and resource-based perspective (RBV) theories, which are the foundations of modern strategic human resources management, or SHRM (Boon et al., 2018). Digital technology and technical advancements like ChatGPT have the potential to be disrupting and potentially result in a Schumpeter jolt similar to the advent of electronic photographs in the 1990s as opposed to widely used picture film rolls. In Barney's (1991) famous RBV paper, destabilizing technical advancements and Schumpeter surprises are characterized as occurrences that undermine businesses' long-standing advantages over rivals. How competitive is ChatGPT as a technology? What effect does ChatGPT have on HRM specialists and SHRM (strategic human resources management) experts?

Creating policy statements on extended absences owing to sickness, hiring and choosing employees, training procedures, evaluating job candidates and resumes, and creating job postings are a few examples of how ChatGPT is used in the Strategic Human Resources Management sector.

Renkema and colleagues, 2023; Renkema, 2022. Renkema (2023) brings up a number of intriguing points, including the following:

Susskind & Susskind's (2022) question is: If there are no human resources management specialists, how is new HRM information created? Being no longer required and being taken over by technology? A shortage, mimicry, worth, substitutes and displacement in HRM economy render us immediately consider the Strategic Human Resources Management as well as the centred around resources viewpoint.

According to Chaudhary (2023), ChatGPT can boost HR procedures in a number of domains, such less expensive remedies, simpler human resources administration and statistical analysis, superior worker satisfaction thanks to feedback from surveys, and simpler hiring & induction.

In this analysis, we concentrate on the potential implications of ChatGPT employing the conventional RBV (Paauwe & Boselie, 2003) A distinct philosophical framework we refer to as the "Open resource-focused approach to SHRM 1". The main objective is to present an investigation proposal for investigating the distinctiveness of the Strategic Human Resources Management and the human resources department organizational ramifications.

RESOURCE-BASED VIEW

The strategy based on resources is one professional the oldest and most prevalent ideas in SHRM, according to a review of the previous 30 years of study (Paauwe, 2004). Gazing at the effects of ChatGPT becoming extensively used shortly, we predict an enormous decrease of the opportunities to use the Strategic Human Resources Management to maintain an edge over others. In light of the four circumstances, As stated by Barney (1991), they are going to become obsolete:

- Worth: Because ChatGPT is openly accessible to every individual, there is little to no chance of creating and collecting royalties considering that there aren't any intellectual rights. For everyone who understands how to use and use the program, there are additionally rentals and advantages available.

- A shortage no longer exists. The same is becoming true for all of the open-source programs, not only ChatGPT.
- Imitation: Historically, the hypothesis of RBV was based on this concept, particularly with regard to gaining a "marketing edge." 'Causal confusion', 'path dependence', and 'social intricacy' are circumstances that help to clarify how things happen via people' (Pfeffer, 1994). This type of safe-guarding for an edge in competition won't be valid anymore. Accessible is ChatGPT for all people.
- Replacement: Once more, this circumstance is no longer relevant. ChatGPT offers a variety of chances for modifying or substituting procedures for human resources management and skilled HRM actions.

Negatively, ChatGPT may mark the conclusion to Human resources management (HR serving as an option in whole or in part to maintain an edge over others. However, advances in technology have repeatedly shown to contributing to fresh accomplishments, which is what we as a species also want to emphasize ChatGPT's prospective advantages advancements from a different perspective.

Open Resource-Based Viewpoint: The Constructive Viewpoint

In execution, we are moving toward greater accessibility to programs, which will benefit all businesses and reduce costs for employees who have access, such as in the fields of independent contractors and (Through online channels) the gig sector. Worker competencies are overdue and will expand Via a variety of not competing and confidentiality agreements, the company serves as a business to safeguard its employees.

Let's start by listing some benefits from the standpoint of the HR department. ChatGPT can be highly beneficial for enhancing HR's affordability. Consider tasks like creating descriptions for jobs and reviewing applicants. creating educational courses, creating somewhat structured job interviews depending on employment needs and -materials like course descriptions and more boarding instructions.

Additionally, ChatGPT may be used to "outsource" the development of policies papers, like issues pertaining to tardiness, flexible scheduling, and boosting staff loyalty, without accruing extra expenditures and preserving a significant number of personnel sessions or costly consulting fees companies. This change might give the initially migrating businesses a temporary edge over others and people in general. Hazards associated regarding the 'outsourcing' of human resources management processes and responsibilities include in respect to:

- Erroneous or deceptive material: Using ChatGPT may result in insufficient, out-of-date, or incorrect data, and therefore human judgment cannot be overlooked.
- Context and ChatGPT: Ignoring or ignoring the circumstances might result in the absence of situational knowledge of the particular firm, with a variety of detrimental effects on wise decisions and accurate replies.
- Outdated data: ChatGPT was created and calibrated with data that was already available. This suggests that current and forthcoming improvements are not taken into account. Uncertainty surrounds the scope to which ChatGPT and machine learning in general independently produce new understandings and knowledge.

- Prejudice and inequality: Examples from big companies that impact how they approach artificial intelligence recruiting Racial discrimination and a propensity to favour male applicants are red flags, according to cognitive ability or ChatGPT.
- The right to privacy, Information Safety and Security, and Regulation 2: Sharing Data through a Chatbot May Introduce It the Illegal Parties Information theft or breach of privacy may come from abuse by strangers or other individuals.
- Regulatory and moral problems: Whatever are the potential ramifications of employing avatars with machine learning from a legal as well as ethical standpoint?

Whose IP does created material have? Would here be national legislation or industry-specific rules that restrict or prevent using ChatGPT?

A different resource-centred method to analysing the effects of ChatGPT on the Strategic Human Resources Management may be seen of as having the "essential circumstances" outlined in the overview aforementioned possible concerns. Multidisciplinary development will be made possible and intensified by capabilities that are becoming accessible at all stages of life. businesses, as well as society overall, to provide rent that is accessible to everyone. This is how we are moving in the right path. The strategy of human resources management's ability to provide satisfaction with work, managerial efficiency, and social health in line beyond the corporation's permanent or ultimately financial objectives The Harvard model's repercussions.

- Given ChatGPT's capacity to take over all manner of HRM procedures and operations of employees in HRM and staff members, organizational success may be realized through increased focus on HRM supply and productivity enhancements.
- Improved access to data and personal expertise exchange are two approaches to improve satisfaction with work. and immediate employee participation via ChatGPT's conversational interaction.
- Open and widespread knowledge exchange via ChatGPT contributes to the health of society.

HRM collaboration and expertise transmission amongst businesses and between people, especially HRM experts, can benefit from an open resource-based view utilizing ChatGPT. A alternate strategy for attaining advantages in competition might be to encourage collaboration, sharing of information, and expertise exchange across various firms.

A multiple levels and multi-sector view on the benefit to the organisations concerned. Open assets may be included in Development that is produced through teamwork, including competing together (cooperation in a setting where there is competition). and at a period where distinct companies are frequently not effective at sharing understanding, addressing and resolving significant corporate & social problems.

The "traditional" dependent on resources perspective is heavily concentrated on the long-term advantageous position of a single business. Our common based on resources solution to the Strategic Human Resources Management focuses on the long-term gains for businesses, people (workers and citizens), and community. Aside from that Applying an analytical strategy that utilizes open resources continues to assist a company maintain its competitiveness. opportunity resulting from distinctiveness and intentional focusing of the human resources department on important issues for the corporation, taking the environment into consideration.

Strategic Planning management and professionals in human resources management can concentrate on human resources management concepts that are important and require particular focus, which might include developing and changing company culture, fostering a sense of mental security, enhancing the standard of cooperation both internally and externally with organizations, freelancers, customers, and vendors, and constructively influencing the performance of these groups. impacting how agile you are. Regardless of the various routine duties associated with HRM (such as candidate screening and manuals) By using ChatGPT on a variety of Human resources management (HR concerns, such as creating guides, flexibility is created to strategically concentrate on more effective and difficult tasks for organizations.

The ability of human resources management professionals to concentrate on the issues that are important but also hard to solve via ChatGPT makes them distinctive. The simple fact that HR professionals are aware about a company's both inside and outside circumstances will allow them to Participants can modify and personalize the conversation with GPT-generated findings and guidelines to fit their own circumstances. the company. This suggests that while having access to free assets, hiring managers may still deliver the enterprise having distinctive information that is hence organizational-specific.

OBJECTIVES OF THE STUDY

The Harvard Business School's three long-lasting effects of business performance, staff happiness, and society happiness are used to further explore the collaborative, dependent upon resources vision of the company. To achieve this, we must first make clear the conceptual foundations. fundamental preconditions, and premises of this new conceptual paradigm. enhancing longevity balance implications pertaining to this research topic is on our minds:

- Using a numerous a case study analysis approach, the influence of collaborative creativity using ChatGPT on the efficiency of organizations in a particular industry or demographic.
- The integration of ChatGPT to the human resources management department will revolutionize it in terms of procedures for managing HR positions, and the limited room for individuality, resulting in a continuous advantage in competitiveness via SHRM.
- The extent in which readily accessible programs, like ChatGPT, benefits everyone—not those with special privileges (the core staff or "happy few"—but also disadvantaged workforce categories, people of ethnic minorities, and technological novices.
- The dehumanizing and digitization of companies and work as a result of the ChatGPT human interface's effects on the well-being of workers.
- Relevance and Originality: Using freely accessible applications, such as ChatGPT, while attaining originality by incorporating ambient information and observations that are organization- and sector-specific.

The Results of Generation AI in Human Resources Management

Academic Significance of the Investigation

The most recent advancement in artificial intelligence, referred to as "generative AI," has been characterized as representing an evolution in thinking and a new phase of industrial growth described as "Industry 4.0." It stands out because it transfers expertise control between human beings to robots, possibly changing where it came from. There were requests to halt expansion until these ramifications are given more careful consideration because of the consequences of this for leadership, staff, as well as society as general (Shet & Pereira, 2021). This implies that dynamic AI's potential effects and results, both at place of employment and elsewhere, remain unpredictable.

As a result, it presents HRM academics with a rich new study topic since it has the potential to have an impact on a variety of aspects including the content, procedures, and results of HRM activities. Although these HRM components are interconnected, in this article we will concentrate on taking possible repercussions into account.

The ability to hold an infinite amount of information and to present it in a cohesive, usable manner is the key characteristic of generative artificial intelligence, which is represented, for instance, in ChatGPT and Bard. It can carry out a variety of tasks that used to necessitate human involvement. As a result, it makes a compelling case to business by offering to make effectiveness, well analyzed data available in large quantities and much faster than people can.

We provide two analytical structures for human resources management investigators interested in the results of creative AI. The first is the stakeholder strategy put forth by Beer et al. in 1984, which contends that human resource management should prioritize a variety of participants, including board members, staff members, the governing body, community members, and labor organizations, while pursuing the primary goals of company efficiency, satisfaction with work, and a healthy society. This is due, in part, to the belief that, so far, AI has mostly served to advance effectiveness and adaptability in the benefit of investors at the expense of other stakeholders by promoting their highest goals. The boundless influence of artificial intelligence (AI) generative goes far outside the walls of work.

The promotion of Industry 5.0 is where an additional and supplementary analytic paradigm may be discovered. A resetting is necessary to guarantee that Industry 4.0, which includes Artificial Intelligence (serves the best interests of all parties at employment and to the community, as demonstrated by effects consistent with expanding the standard of job life and the power source quality of existence for citizens across all sectors. This is recognized among schoolwork, leaders such as those in Japan and the European Commission, and many others in the scientific community. To guarantee that advancements are adequately human-centric, suggestions have been made for the revitalization of a technological-society viewpoint (Bednar & Welch, 2020).

The key objectives defined by Beer et al. in 1984—organizational performance, staff happiness, and society well-being—may offer a focus to studies on generative artificial intelligence when these analytical concerns are kept in view. We can then select particular results that can serve as this focus. To do that was the case we will take into account both possible advantages and disadvantages, keep in mind this particular HR function's accountability for overseeing personnel operations, and tackle the characteristics of Sector 5.0.

In past decades, businesses have tried to adopt new technologies to obtain an edge over their competitors. There is no reason to think that AI, and particularly artificial intelligence (AI) that generates data, will make a difference.

We mainly perceive that businesses have distinctive collections in peculiar information capacities and assets (information regarding creative AI), which need to be accomplished in order to optimize worth through the best use, while determining and building the necessary the capacity along with wealth of resources for the future (Grant, 1996). This is according to the philosophical prism of the Understanding Based View (KBV), an instance of the resource-centred perspective of the firm. Thus, by using artificial intelligence (AI) to analyse and make decisions more effectively in a variety of HR activities, the HR function may enhance its own processes and results while also contributing to the success of the company. Possible examples of this include the prompt delivery of semi-standard knowledge in areas like resumes, salaries, recruitment forms, and processes.

Bots, which stand for "interactive robots," have a lot of promise for education and growth since they can handle tasks like answering employee questions typically handled by HR contact centre's. Evidence-driven human resources management have been promoted for a while. The accessibility of based on research data on whom to base HR choices and enhance human resources results could be beneficial as a result of generating AI. This can take into use inner HR analytical data to give insights into labour turnover, absenteeism, and many data related to human resources, as well as outside proof by relying on methodical evaluations of the effect of regulations and additional initiatives aimed at improving people administration.

Getting human resources data together more quickly might free up valuable time for essential HR tasks like helping line managers, handling worker problems, and adding to planning for the kinds of achievements to prioritize for employee's administration. This represents the commitment, but the truth can be trickier and raise doubts about its veracity reliance on AI-generated information, staff satisfaction with robots, and a disparity in the socio-technical structure.

EMPLOYEE RELATIONS, WELL-BEING, TALENT, AND PERFORMANCE MANAGEMENT WITH GENERATIVE AI

Impact of ChatGPT on staff involvement, happiness, and workplace relations

Introduction

Conversational representatives and chatbot with AI capabilities, like ChatGPT, are being adopted by businesses more often to improve across various sectors, stakeholder relationships, participation, and happiness (McKinsey Global Institute, 2017). ChatGPT will have various effects depending on the environment, but it has the potential to significantly change how HRM is done. a majority of business contexts (Edlich et al., 2018; OpenAI, 2023) employ technology and processes. Currently, ChatGPT may be used as a part of a customized network of apps, incorporated into workplaces. Depending on its use case, ChatGPT can offer individualized help on request, creative answers to challenging questions, and advice on a wide range of subjects (Hatzius et al., 2023).

ChatGPT Employment Relations Consequences

In the context of HRM, ChatGPT offers the ability to automate a number of routine procedures. For instance, Edlich (2018) showed the use of intelligent models and chatbot in HR customer service centre's that answered-to-answered questions from employees, handled benefits management, and administered record-keeping. Using the current context, use eyes can profit by having utilization of assets, data, and amenities upon request. The outcomes of the analytics can also assist leaders make more informed choices and produce better HRM support, which will affect employment relations. Using ChatGPT-enabled interfaces, one essential factor that is likely to influence workplace interactions is trust.

Workplace interactions are expected to be regulated with the usage of ChatGPT interface inasmuch as personnel regard technological innovation as a suitably leveraged, capable, and trusted resource (Yadav

Figure 3. ChatGPT's response on "can I trust you"?
(Authors' own contributions)

Figure 3. ChatGPT's response on "can I trust you"?
(Authors' own contributions)

et al., 2022), since trust is a key component in the connection between workers and their employers. Figure 3 displays some of its restrictions for exploration.

The reply from ChatGPT to the question, "Can I trust you?" The model then lists a number of its flaws in reply.

Worker Wellbeing

Woebot, a publicly traded approachable robot that employs a form of cognitive behavioural therapy to give emotional wellness assistance for its users (Fitzpatrick et al., 2017), is another noteworthy instance of a powered by artificial intelligence chatbots. throughout Respondents in a randomised controlled experiment where Woebot was employed as a therapy strategy for 2 weeks), depression symptoms were significantly reduced (Fitzpatrick et al., 2017). Woebot is not, however Its role as a ChatGPT-enabled software serves as an example of the possible effects that ChatGPT may have on employees. in terms of mental health, wellness. The reply of ChatGPT to the query "I'm feeling depressed" is shown in Figure 3. The model starts off by showing compassion. It then identifies its limits before making broad suggestions. On the other hand, implementing ChatGPT at work might have a detrimental effect on staff morale. For employees who are concerned about job instability, the incorporation of ChatGPT can make them more anxious (OpenAI, 2023). I'm concerned about how the integration will go, as seen in Figure 4 of ChatGPT's answer to the user query of ChatGPT will result in my employment termination. Once more, the representation shows compassion prior to offering recommendations.

Employee Participation

Staff participation may be affected in either direction by ChatGPT, similar to how well employees are doing.

The job of humans may be improved by AI & predictive algorithms like ChatGPT in a variety of ways, including from giving writing assistance to call centre improving to delivering services on demand. The benefits of an AI enhancement for employees might include possibilities. For fulfilment, better productivity, creative discovery, and independence. These results, in turn, might increase happiness at

Figure 4. ChatGPT response on "I am feeling depressed"
(Authors' own contributions)

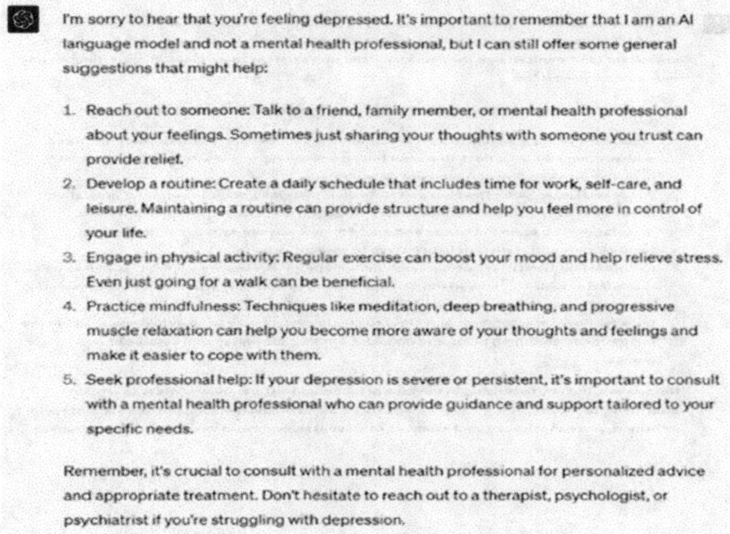

I'm sorry to hear that you're feeling depressed. It's important to remember that I am an AI language model and not a mental health professional, but I can still offer some general suggestions that might help:

1. Reach out to someone: Talk to a friend, family member, or mental health professional about your feelings. Sometimes just sharing your thoughts with someone you trust can provide relief.
2. Develop a routine: Create a daily schedule that includes time for work, self-care, and leisure. Maintaining a routine can provide structure and help you feel more in control of your life.
3. Engage in physical activity: Regular exercise can boost your mood and help relieve stress. Even just going for a walk can be beneficial.
4. Practice mindfulness: Techniques like meditation, deep breathing, and progressive muscle relaxation can help you become more aware of your thoughts and feelings and make it easier to cope with them.
5. Seek professional help: If your depression is severe or persistent, it's important to consult with a mental health professional who can provide guidance and support tailored to your specific needs.

Remember, it's crucial to consult with a mental health professional for personalized advice and appropriate treatment. Don't hesitate to reach out to a therapist, psychologist, or psychiatrist if you're struggling with depression.

work and productivity in general. Psychologists have determined that contentment with life is connected to participation (Cheng et al., 2022). In this manner, ChatGPT usage might potentially improve staff involvement.

OpenAI (2023) has drawn focus on the potential for greater inequity and uneven effects that might arise from the deployment of ChatGPT, nevertheless. Personnel may be affected differently by the potential for job loss or role redefining. Workers may have a hard time adjusting to new procedures. These difficulties might affect workers' squandered time, anger, and mistrust. In this sense, ChatGPT use is likely to have a detrimental impact the level of employee involvement.

OBJECTIVE FOR INVESTIGATION

A thorough investigation is necessary since the implementation of ChatGPT in businesses is expected to change human resources management procedures and processes, with both beneficial and detrimental effects on relationships with employers, employee welfare, and participation on the topic at hand, required. The study program that is presented below is expected to reveal ChatGPT's hidden expertise.

Studying Stakeholders Expectations & ChatGPT Adoption Due to numerous failures in chatbot performance, Cheng et al (2022) observed a low degree of customer willingness to accept and utilize chatbots. Chatbot interacts with people. The notion of "products" received various degrees of acceptance in a 2022 IPSOS survey. and AI-based services offered more advantages than disadvantages. Flstad and Brandtzaeg (2017) investigated in more detail the many purposes for employing chatbots. Therefore, we provide with the following research inquiries:

Figure 5. ChatGPT response on a human being questioning about loss of job
(Authors' own contributions)

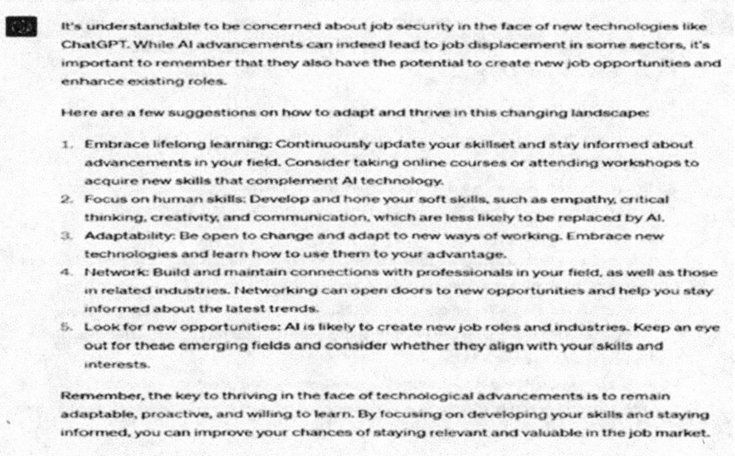

It's understandable to be concerned about job security in the face of new technologies like ChatGPT. While AI advancements can indeed lead to job displacement in some sectors, it's important to remember that they also have the potential to create new job opportunities and enhance existing roles.

Here are a few suggestions on how to adapt and thrive in this changing landscape:

1. Embrace lifelong learning: Continuously update your skillset and stay informed about advancements in your field. Consider taking online courses or attending workshops to acquire new skills that complement AI technology.
2. Focus on human skills: Develop and hone your soft skills, such as empathy, critical thinking, creativity, and communication, which are less likely to be replaced by AI.
3. Adaptability: Be open to change and adapt to new ways of working. Embrace new technologies and learn how to use them to your advantage.
4. Network: Build and maintain connections with professionals in your field, as well as those in related industries. Networking can open doors to new opportunities and help you stay informed about the latest trends.
5. Look for new opportunities: AI is likely to create new job roles and industries. Keep an eye out for these emerging fields and consider whether they align with your skills and interests.

Remember, the key to thriving in the face of technological advancements is to remain adaptable, proactive, and willing to learn. By focusing on developing your skills and staying informed, you can improve your chances of staying relevant and valuable in the job market.

- What variables influence the successful implementation of ChatGPT in work environments, and how can businesses get over possible roadblocks?
- How effectively does ChatGPT work at enhancing employee welfare, interaction, and participation sectors and environments?
- Which traits and abilities continue to be distinctive and necessary among human staff members?

The list of investigation issues in the aforementioned plan is not all-inclusive. These inquiries, nevertheless may shed light on the most beneficial procedures, advantages, hazards, and results connected with human resources management and the influence on labour relations given the current and imminent rapid use of this sort of gadgetry in work environments wellness and commitment of employees.

A number of problems with ChatGPT OpenAI's most current model, GPT-4, were brought to light by research on the Safety, Ethicality, and Equity Considerations of ChatGPT OpenAI (2023). Notably, GPT-4 created biased and untrustworthy content, was able to encourage initiatives, and could offer details on how to sell illegal goods and services (OpenAI, 2023) to organize violent assaults. Even with the potential for a wide range of advantages, it is crucial that academics and professionals thoroughly and critically analyse the effects of integrating this technology. As

As a result, we suggest the following research inquiries:

- What possible difficulties with privacy and security are connected to adopting ChatGPT at work, and how can businesses reduce these risks?
- How can businesses use ChatGPT in their work environments ethically, and what are the ethical issues involved make certain that ChatGPT usage complies with moral principles and rules?
- To what extent can ChatGPT usage affect company culture, as well as how can businesses ensure that ChatGPT is used effectively corresponds with their customs and principles?
- How can businesses quantify and monitor the long-term impacts of adopting ChatGPT in the workplace determine what is happening?

Which are the consequences and difficulties for staff relations of ChatGPT along with other creative AI-driven tools?

Numerous scholars utilize a single frame to guide them while conducting their study on HRM. In contrast, the majority of labour contracts (ER) academics use radical or inclusive frame for reference while conducting research. Understanding various types of dispute resolution frameworks for HRM and ER. The ER sector takes into account a variety of features of individuals at work, including as conversations, job oversight, negotiations, and opposing interests. conflicts of interests and authority involving bosses and staff members, as well as their agents (lawyers, executives, organizations and employers' organizations. The responsibilities of "third parties" like arbitrators, decision-makers, other stakeholders and governmental organization.

Equal treatment, reliability, confidence and openness are crucial components of emergency response. What is the repercussions and applications of ChatGPT alongside additional creative powered by AI ER tools within this setting? Developments similar to ChatGPT use artificial intelligence, LLM, and machine learning (ML) techniques to simulate human-looking chat interaction. The consequences for administrators and managers attempting to symbolize, inform, and train employees have sparked a great deal of debate and growing research topics. These outages have generated curiosity in how such technologies powered by AI may affect places of employment, ER those who matter, and HRM as well as other stakeholders. We mention some of the early repercussions associated with AI-driven tools for ER because innovations in this field are progressing quickly. Stakeholders may make use of innovations:

- develop potential scenarios and tailored, individualized training programs for staff to fill skill shortages already present and anticipated as a result of artificial intelligence (AI) applications
- generate stories that might improve staff knowledge and skills.
- automates some language-processing-intensive processes, such as evaluating contractual agreements and other paperwork.
- develop guidelines for safety procedures and relationships at work.
- examine and disseminate data from HR analytics.
- synthesize recommendations, comments, criticism, and observations from the workforce.
- raise the public's consciousness of the problems associated with disparities, openness, and legal systems.
- open up new career options in logical, ethical, data analysis, and ethical AI fields.

Others who participate in union negotiations might utilize these developments to help in their studies and claim building and more planning. Negotiating parties may, for instance, employ ChatGPT-like technologies to support their study. cases faster and more broadly than they might if not for example, to gather examples, produce arguments and address drafts. Additionally, union officials and leaders may use these technologies to support the interactions between members, as well as member acquisition and retention. Despite the rhetoric used by huge technology organizations may assert that the inventions like ChatGPT encourage independence and other benefits, yet there may also negative consequences (Sharma & Jain, 2023).

Such innovations are not a cure-all; they are not without drawbacks, potential negative aspects, and difficulties (van Dis et al., 2023). This is particularly true since staff may be subject to obligations under the law and moral as well as duties on the part of bosses, who ought to speak with them prior to implementing significant changes to working circumstances.

Depending on the national and local circumstances (for more information on the Australian setting, see. Utilizing these advancements improperly, for instance, may:

- prompt higher levels of work instability and precariousness, which frequently manifest as hidden or overt issues in ER conflicts.

Why exacerbate inequality in work environments, particularly given that consumers of these advances might not be aware of their restrictions.

- create negative, false, or incorrect results that may undermine public confidence in management, labour organizations, and businesses credibility.

may result in legal issues when utilized to make ER choices where there is a chance of erroneous input or output.

- bring up legal and moral issues of responsibility, covert monitoring, confidentiality, and creativity personal information about workers.

For a lack of openness, for example, complicated permission difficulties may arise if partners weren't informed. Afterwards for using a staff member's information for purposes not initially disclosed in the permission, particularly if data is input

- provide false narratives by sometimes not being fully in touch to the surroundings, intent, subtlety, or style of the person using it or the job; and generate unsuitable or irrelevant replies.
- develop new employment, many of which aren't currently available, that may need for high-tech expertise or be part of the "gig economy" Unions provide coverage.
- increase emotional distress in workers and reduce their feeling of happiness.

Since there may be benefits and drawbacks for various consumers, customers, and circumstances, it is important to employ these technologies carefully and ethically. Developments like ChatGPT that use techniques like autonomous information filtering and validation need have human control and involvement.

This is required to guarantee excellence, accuracy, and adherence with the legislation, treaties and workplace agreements, and moral conduct. Employees are inclined to get resentful if they believe These technologies or algorithms are controlling or representing them. We believe that the majority of employees rather than impersonal organizations, individuals prefer to be controlled and governed by people with whom they can communicate techniques or technology.

We urge ER players to make it possible for staff to have a say in how technology is utilized, given that numerous breakthroughs similar to ChatGPT will continue being created and impact ER in many ways. whichever the situation, management ought to speak with labour unions or additional staff organizations. Generally, innovations If the innovations integrate open co-design and sustainable development, they will be executed more successfully, fairly, and ecologically. cooperation that includes stakeholders like workers and their elected representatives. To combat, this should be promoted.

It's tempting for executives, technocrats, specialists, and executives across major tech businesses to use these creative openly and covertly using based on artificial intelligence techniques inside a single frame of view.

From the aforementioned, we deduce various future study goals. First, researchers in HRM and Em ought to select a useful frame for comparison and cautiously evaluate how to overcome concerns about privacy and fair reuse. The manner in which might ownership of information, monetization, and selection be (co-)regulated, for instance? Second, who needs to participate in evaluating and confirming what was generated material and answers? Third, assuming they concur that negotiation-related factors or are there additional ER-related topics that are "off-limits" or off-limits to ChatGPT-like innovations? What is "decent work"? mean in this situation, as well as can it grow and endure? Fifth, who must be held responsible for subpar or incorrect information choices?"

Sixth, how will these advances affect the nature of labour in the future? The seventh, who is hurt, Who gains from inventions like ChatGPT, and who determines how the pain and gains are distributed? Last, Companies may utilize these advances to replace positions such as company, information scientists, and computer engineers. In summary, individuals who utilize ChatGPT and related developments should bear in mind that, while they are evolving and having the potential to be very beneficial, they are also becoming more complicated. On the contrary side, entrepreneurs should pay attention to the adage "garbage in, garbage out" (GIGO) from computers science and practice prompt design including ask the proper questions. If not, illogical (junk) input information and searches could result in illogical output!

TALENT MANAGEMENT USING CHATGPT

The growth of artificially intelligent (AI) and Watson-enabled products like ChatGPT is a positive development, but if allowed unchecked, it might pose a threat to our way of life. In this regard, a Swiss Bank investigation had found that ChatGPT was the app with the fastest overall growth rate (see Ortiz, 2023). Researchers like Prikshat et al. (2022) have stated that "AI-augmented HRM can improve workflow and productivity, decrease costs, and improve reliability in Hr functions," which is not surprising. In fact, given how quickly artificial intelligence-powered technologies like ChatGPT are developing, these programs may benefit enterprises and society in a variety of ways. Organizations that chose to disregard ChatGPT, in our opinion, do so at their own volition.

The crucial field of staff planning is one wherein AI might make significant progress given the depth, length, and ongoing growth of the function (see, for instance, DeNisi. Since the task of management role calls for raters to establish their decisions on a wealth of both quantitative and qualitative information ChatGPT may be quite helpful in facilitating the analysis of complicated data for numerical information. But here is the part where the There is risk. Companies must be vigilant since ChatGPT and other solutions that use AI are dependent on what data they have access to. extremely cautious & precise about what data the bot has access to.

A few recent instances aid in demonstrating the necessity for prudence. A powered by AI bot named Sydney once attempted to persuade a New York Times writer to divorce his wife. A similarly absurd result included Chrome's competitor to ChatGPT, Bard, who advocated for the authorities to intervene and split up YouTube as a result of its perceived monopolistic status (see Prakash, 2023). The idea is that businesses and employees must pick up the ante or track and control either official datum as well as informal talk inside their enterprises when it involves adopting ChatGPT for evaluations. If human resources directors are prepared to accept the ChatGPT dispute, they may benefit from ChatGPT in a number of ways, including performance oversight.

In fact, we want to make it easier for HR professionals to take the initiative and find areas of performance oversight whereby the bot may assist management (who are often the ones conducting the ratings) in performing their jobs more effectively. In recent years, provide a business, explored with adopting ChatGPT in their performance administration procedure, particularly for assessments of performance (see Parisi, 2022). Their initial results look good; the software was very effective at creating performance assessments by grilling the ratee's coworkers with pertinent questions. However, as CEO emphasized, ChatGPT has yet to get ready to provide comments to specific workers.

The difficulty of organizational performance both in academia and practice to create a clear relationship between personal achievement and organization-level results is another issue that academics studying perform monitoring frequently raise (DeNisi & Murphy, 2017). ChatGPT may be capable to help businesses correlate individual level performance with organisational results by analysing achievement-related data and looking at how the many elements related to personal successes tie in with company achievements.

Of naturally, as we all understand, at the moment this connection is at best shaky, with the intermediary stage more akin to a black hole become which knowledge comes from and the decisions are made, even if it is unclear how the facts are translated into specific decisions. We think this offers academics studying the following fields:

In fact, there are additionally a number of additional aspects of performance administration because ChatGPT is still in its early stages. that demand intellectual research. First, the amount in which the bot can help businesses may depend on the rater's acquaintance with computers and readiness to integrate ChatGPT into the procedure for rating. Next, Performance oversight is considered to be an incubator for prejudice, and tools like these bots may make this situation worse. difficulty. In fact, studies demonstrate that utilizing chatbots alongside other technologies powered by AI enhances the human beings' propensity for immoral behaviour (see, for instance, Kim et al., 2022). The moral implications of Investigations of the employment of the bot are warranted.

In addition, it is well acknowledged that supervisor-subordinate interactions are important in determining sub evaluations and consequences associated with them (see Varma, Jaiswal, et al., 2022). Researchers would be doing also to look around at the circulation, reports, and volume of failure to deliver and data concerning performance in order to determine if ChatGPT is able to distinguish between pertinent and unimportant data and the extent to where it bases its recommendations on outcomes pertinent data. This is because the majority, if not all, personal assistant systems do not particular apply this component in the psychological procedure. Lastly, it's critical to look at how various eras of staff members inside firms perceive and respond to ChatGPT differently.

CONCLUSION

As alongside any novel invention, HRM and its investigation of it, as well as the economic and social landscape as a whole, may be affected indefinitely by AI. Despite it clearly has an opportunity to be advantageous, its full effects are not yet recognized. In fact, it's debatable if there is any real AI at this point; yet, even complex systems comprising data collection and addressing issues systems may bring significant prospects and dangers. The various topical speeches within the HRMJ points of view revision serve as an initial stop on this road trip of discovering as opposed to offering just one collection of conclusive ideas or judgments. At HRMJ, we aim to encourage a deeper comprehension and disagreement approximately AI along with its impacts on the research and application of human resource management.

To sum up, we think that ChatGPT have the capacity to make life simpler for assessors, though the bot has to be continuously controlled and users require instruction on how to properly utilize the software.

To assess creative artificial intelligence's efficacy as a methodological helper carefully, we performed a case investigation. ChatGPT includes some helpful features, including the ability to develop ideas, propose hypotheses, choose study designs, metrics, and data-analytic techniques, as well as offer basic assistance on how to carry out ethical investigations and present findings.

However, ChatGPT also has constraints associated with restricted data for training, leading to the generation of excessive, inadequate, or too ambiguous suggestions, such as reiterating mistakes in methodology from previous studies and providing suggestions in ethical standards for research that tend to be too broad despite not being adequately enforceable or particulars. Therefore, we draw the conclusion that artificial intelligence (AI) that generates information may be employed in addition to researcher judgment, but not as a substitute for it.

REFERENCES

Agrawal, A., Gans, J., & Goldfarb, A. (2022). ChatGPT and how AI disrupts industries. *Harvard Business Review*. https://hbr.org/2022/12/chatgpt-and-how-ai-disrupts-industries

Aguinis, H., Banks, G. C., Rogelberg, S. G., & Cascio, W. F. (2020). Actionable recommendations for narrowing the science-practice gap in open science. *Organizational Behavior and Human Decision Processes*, *158*, 27–35. doi:10.1016/j.obhdp.2020.02.007

Aguinis, H., Ramani, R. S., & Alabduljader, N. (2018). What you see is what you get? Enhancing methodological transparencyin management research. Academy of management annals. *The Academy of Management Annals*, *12*(1), 83–110. doi:10.5465/annals.2016.0011

Aguinis, H., & Solarino, A. M. (2019). Transparency and replicability in qualitative research: The case of interviews with eliteinformants. *Strategic Management Journal*, *40*(8), 1291–1315. doi:10.1002/smj.3015

AI Research Assistant Elicit. (2023). *Elicit uses language models to help you automate research workflows, like parts of literature review*. Elicit. https://elicit.org/.

Appel, G., Neelbauer, J., & Schweidel, D. A. (2023). Generative AI has an intellectual property problem. *Harvard Business Review*. https://hbr.org/2023/04/generative-ai-has-an-intellectual-property-problem

Aust, I., Matthews, B., & Muller-Camen, M. (2020). Common good HRM: A paradigm shift in sustainable HRM? *Human Resource Management Review*, *30*(3), 100705. doi:10.1016/j.hrmr.2019.100705

Bamber, G. J., Cooke, F. L., Doellgast, V., & Wright, C. F. (2021). *International and comparative employment relations: Globalcrises and institutional responses* (7th ed.). SAGE.

Bandura, A. (1999). Moral disengagement in the perpetration of inhumanities. Personality and social psychology review. *Personality and Social Psychology Review*, *3*(3), 193–209. doi:10.1207/s15327957pspr0303_3 PMID:15661671

Barney, J. (1991). Firm resources and sustained competitive advantage. *Journal of Management, 17*(1), 99–120. doi:10.1177/014920639101700108

Bednar, P. M., & Welch, C. (2020). Socio-technical perspectives on smart working: Creating meaningful and sustainable systems. *Information Systems Frontiers, 22*(2), 281–298. doi:10.1007/s10796-019-09921-1

Beer, M., Spector, B. A., Lawrence, P. R., Mills, D. Q., & Walton, R. E. (1984). *Managing human assets: The groundbreaking harvard business school program.* Free Press.

Bell, E., Dacin, M. T., & Toraldo, M. L. (2021). Craft imaginaries–past, present and future. Organization theory, 2(1), Bell, E., Mangia, G., Taylor, S., & Toraldo, M. L. (Eds.). (2018). The organization of craft work: Identities, meanings, and materiality Routledge.

Bender, E. M., Gebru, T., McMillan-Major, A., & Shmitchell, S. 2021. On the dangers of stochastic parrots: Can language models be too big? *FAccT 2021-proceedings of the 2021 ACM conference on fairness, accountability, and transparency* (pp. 610–623). ACM. doi:10.1145/3442188.3445922

Bidle, S. (2022). The internet's new favourite AI proposes torturing Iranians and surveilling mosques. *The Intercept Voices.* https://theintercept.com/2022/12/08/openai-chatgpt-ai-bias-ethics/.

Bing, M. (2023). Introducing the new bing. *Your AI-powered copilot for the web.* https://tinyurl.com/4vzmnrx7

Blau, F. D., & Kahn, L. M. (2007). The gender pay gap: Have women gone as far as they can? Academy of management perspectives. *The Academy of Management Perspectives, 21*(1), 7–23. doi:10.5465/amp.2007.24286161

Bolina, J. (2023). How to defend against the rise of ChatGPT? Think like a poet. *Washington Post.* https://www.washingtonpost.com/opinions/2023/04/20/chatgpt-poetry-ai-language/

Boon, C., Eckardt, R., Lepak, D. P., & Boselie, P. (2018). Integrating strategic human capital and strategic human resource management. *International Journal of Human Resource Management, 29*(1), 34–67. doi:10.1080/09585192.2017.1380063

Borden, J. (2014). MOOCs are dead - long live the MOOc. *WIRED magazine, 2014.* https://www.wired.com/insights/2014/08/moocs-are-dead-long-live-the-mooc/

Bosworth, B., & Collins, S. M. (2008). Accounting for growth: Comparing China and India. *The Journal of Economic Perspectives, 22*(1), 45–66. doi:10.1257/jep.22.1.45

Brandtzaeg, P. B., & Følstad, A. (2017). Why people use chatbots. In *Internet science: 4th international conference, INSCI 2017* (pp. 377–392). Springer International Publishing. 10.1007/978-3-319-70284-1_30

Breque, M., De Nul, L., & Petridis, A. (2021). *Industry 5.0. Towards sustainable human-centric resilient European industry.* European Director-General for Research and Innovation. https://tinyurl.com/4psv72b2

Broussard, M. (2018). *Artificial unintelligence: How computers misunderstand the world.* MIT Press. doi:10.7551/mitpress/11022.001.0001

Brynjolfsson, E. (1993). The productivity paradox of information technology. *Communications of the ACM, 36*(12), 66–77. doi:10.1145/163298.163309

Brynjolfsson, E., Rock, D., & Syverson, C. (2020). *The productivity J-curve: How intangible complement general purpose technologies.*National Bureau of Economic Research. https://www.nber.org/papers/w25148.

Bubeck, S., Chandrasekaran, V., Eldan, R., Gehrke, J., Horvitz, E., Kamar, E., Lee, P., Lee, Y. T., Li, Y., Lundberg, S., & Nori, H. (2023). *Sparks of artificial general intelligence: Early experiments with gpt-4.* arXiv preprint arXiv:2303.12712. https://doi.org//arXiv.2303.12712 doi:10.48550

Budd, J. W., Pohler, D., & Huang, W. (2022). Making sense of (mis) matched frames of reference: A dynamic cognitive theory of (in) stability in HR practices. *Industrial Relations*, *61*(3), 268–289. doi:10.1111/irel.12275

Budhwar, P., Malik, A., De Silva, M. T., & Thevisuthan, P. (2022). Artificial intelligence–challenges and opportunities for international HRM: A review and research agenda. *International Journal of Human Resource Management*, *33*(6), 1065–1097. doi:10.1080/09585192.2022.2035161

Burger, B., Kanbach, D. K., Kraus, S., Breier, M., & Corvello, V. (2023). On the use of AI-based tools like ChatGPT to support management research. *European Journal of Innovation Management*, *26*(7), 233–241. doi:10.1108/EJIM-02-2023-0156

ChatGPT. (2023). *Interview Participants' ChatGPT Mar. 2023 version*. OpenAI. https://chat.openai.com/.

Chaudhary, M. (2023). *How ChatGPT can Be a game changer in human resource management*. Spiceworks. https://tinyurl.com/mwf63772.

Cheng, X., Zhang, X., Cohen, J., & Mou, J. (2022). Human vs. AI: Understanding the impact of anthropomorphism on consumer response to chatbots from the perspective of trust and relationship norms. *Information Processing & Management*, *59*(3), 102940. doi:10.1016/j.ipm.2022.102940

Chowdhury, S., Dey, P., Joel-Edgar, S., Bhattacharya, S., Rodriguez-Espindola, O., Abadie, A., & Truong, L. (2023). Unlocking the value of artificial intelligence in human resource management through AI capability framework. *Human Resource Management Review*, *33*(1), 100899. doi:10.1016/j.hrmr.2022.100899

Chowdhury, S., Joel-Edgar, S., Dey, P. K., Bhattacharya, S., & Kharlamov, A. (2022). Embedding transparency in artificial intelligence machine learning models: Managerial implications on predicting and explaining employee turnover. *International Journal of Human Resource Management*, 1–32. doi:10.1080/09585192.2022.2066981

Clayton, J. (2023). *Sam altman: CEO of OpenAI calls for US to regulate artificial intelligence*. BBC news. https://www.bbc.com/news/world-us-canada-65616866.

Clayton, U. T. Z. (2023). *Generative AI miniseries - opportunities and risks for Australian organisations, in Ep2: The workplace and employment implications of generative AI – Risky business?*

Cortada, J. W. (2006). The digital hand: How information technology changed the way industries worked in the United States. *Business History Review*, *80*(4), 755–766. doi:10.2307/25097268

Cortada, J. W. (2013). How new technologies spread: Lessons from computing technologies. *Technology and Culture*, *54*(2), 229–261. https://www.jstor.org/stable/24468014. doi:10.1353/tech.2013.0081

Cox, J. (2023). AI anxiety: The workers who fear losing their jobs to artificial intelligence. *BBC Worklife.* https://tinyurl.com/k6j4swez.

Crafts, N. (2010). The contribution of new technology to economic growth: Lessons from economic history. *Revista de Historia Económica, 28*(3), 409–440. doi:10.1017/S0212610910000157

D. (2023). "So what if ChatGPT wrote it?" Multidisciplinary perspectives on opportunities, challenges and implications of generative conversational AI for research, practice and policy. *International Journal of Information Management, 71,* 102642. doi:10.1016/j.ijinfomgt.2023.102642

Das, S. (2022). *Crypto Currency and Its Assemblage during the Period of Covid-19: A State of the Art Review.*

Das, S., & Nayak, J. (2022). Customer segmentation via data mining techniques: State-of-the-art review. Computational Intelligence in Data Mining. *Proceedings of ICCIDM, 2021,* 489–507. doi:10.1007/978-981-16-9447-9_38

Das, S., Nayak, J., Mishra, M., & Naik, B. (2021). Solar photo voltaic renewal energy: analyzing the effectiveness of marketing mix strategies. In *Innovation in Electrical Power Engineering, Communication, and Computing Technology: Proceedings of Second IEPCCT 2021* (pp. 527-540). Singapore: Springer Singapore. 10.1007/978-981-16-7076-3_45

Das, S., Nayak, J., & Naik, B. (2023). An impact study on Covid-19 and tourism sustainability: Intelligent solutions, issues and future challenges. *World Review of Science, Technology and Sustainable Development, 19*(1-2), 92–119. doi:10.1504/WRSTSD.2023.127268

Das, S., Nayak, J., Nayak, S., & Dey, S. (2022). Prediction of life insurance premium during pre-and post-COVID-19: A higher-order neural network approach. *Journal of The Institution of Engineers (India): Series B, 103*(5), 1747-1773. doi:10.1007/s40031-022-00771-1

Das, S., Saibabu, N., & Pranaya, D. (2023). Blockchain and Intelligent Computing Framework for Sustainable Agriculture: Theory, Methods, and Practice. In Intelligent Engineering Applications and Applied Sciences for Sustainability (pp. 208-228). IGI Global.

Das, S., Swapnarekha, H., & Vimal, S. (2022, April). Integration of Blockchain Technology with Renewable Energy for Sustainable Development: Issues. *Challenges and Future Direction. In International Conference on Computational Intelligence in Pattern Recognition* (pp. 595-607). Singapore: Springer Nature Singapore.

Dasborough, M. T. (2023). Awe-inspiring advancements in AI: The impact of ChatGPT on the field of organizational behavior. *Journal of Organizational Behavior, 44*(2), 177–179. doi:10.1002/job.2695

Data Scientist. (2023). *Internet searches will change forever with Google's "Magi".* Data Scientist. https://tinyurl.com/3dj94ryf.

Daugherty, P. R., Wilson, H. J., & Chowdhury, R. (2018). Using artificial intelligence to promote diversity. *MIT Sloan Management Review.* Magazine Winter 2019 Issue/Frontiers/Research Highlight. https://sloanreview.mit.edu/article/using-artificial-intelligence-to-promote-diversity/

Daugherty, P. R., Wilson, H. J., & Michelman, P. (2019). Revisiting the jobs artificial intelligence will create. *MIT Sloan Management Review*. https://mitsmr.com/2QZT4mE

Davenport. (2023). How Morgan Stanley is training GPT to help financial advisors. *Forbes*. https://tinyurl.com/32zsapxz.

Davis, F. D. (1989). Perceived usefulness, perceived ease of use, and user acceptance of information technology. *Management Information Systems Quarterly*, *13*(3), 319–339. doi:10.2307/249008

De Vos, A., Van der Heijden, B. I., & Akkermans, J. (2020). Sustainable careers: Towards a conceptual model. *Journal of Vocational Behavior*, *117*, 103196. doi:10.1016/j.jvb.2018.06.011

Decker, S., Nix, A., Kirsch, D., & Venkata, S. K. (2022). The dotcom archive: Contextualizing email archives. https://dotcomarchive.bristol.ac.uk/.

Deloitte. (2017). *The 2017 Deloitte state of cognitive survey*. Deloitte. https://tinyurl.com/4kn2c35s. Accessed on 08 May 2023.

DeNisi, A., Murphy, K., Varma, A., & Budhwar, P. (2021). Performance management systems and multinational enterprises: Where we are and where we should go. *Human Resource Management*, *60*(5), 707–713. doi:10.1002/hrm.22080

DeNisi, A., Varma, A., & Budhwar, P. S. (2023). Performance management around the globe: Where are we now? In A. Varma, P. Budhwar, & A. DeNisi (Eds.), *Performance management systems: A global perspective* (2nd ed.). Routledge. doi:10.4324/9781003306849-17

DeNisi, A. S., & Murphy, K. R. (2017). Performance appraisal and performance management: 100 years of progress? *The Journal of Applied Psychology*, *102*(3), 421–433. doi:10.1037/apl0000085 PMID:28125265

Derico, B., & Kleinman, Z. (2023). *OpenAI announces ChatGPT successor GPT-4*. BBC News Online. https://www.bbc.com/news/technology-64959346.

Dey, P. K., Chowdhury, S., Abadie, A., Vann Yaroson, E., & Sarkar, S. (2023). Artificial intelligence-driven supply chain resilience in Vietnamese manufacturing small-and medium-sized enterprises. *International Journal of Production Research*, 1–40. doi:10.1080/00207543.2023.2179859

Dey, P. K., Malesios, C., Chowdhury, S., Saha, K., Budhwar, P., & De, D. (2022). Adoption of circular economy practices in small and medium-sized enterprises: Evidence from Europe. *International Journal of Production Economics*, *248*, 108496. doi:10.1016/j.ijpe.2022.108496

Dilmegani, C. (2023). *Generative AI ethics: Top 6 concerns*. Research AIMultiple. https://research.aimultiple.com/generative-ai-ethics/

Dwivedi, Y. K., Kshetri, N., Hughes, L., Slade, E. L., Jeyaraj, A., Kar, A. K., Wright, R., Koohang, A., Raghavan, V., Ahuja, M., Albanna, H., Albashrawi, M. A., Al-Busaidi, A. S., Balakrishnan, J., Barlette, Y., Basu, S., Bose, I., Brooks, L., & Buhalis, Eddleston, K., Hughes, M., & Deeds, D. (2023). *Family business.org's editorial guidelines for the use of generative AI tools*. Family Business.org. https://tinyurl.com/45e3f95y

Edlich, A., Ip, F., & Whiteman, R. (2018). *How bots, algorithms, and artificial intelligence are reshaping the future of corporate.*

Edwards, M. R., Charlwood, A., Guenole, N., & Marler, J. (2022). HR analytics: An emerging field finding its place in the world alongside simmering ethical challenges. *Human Resource Management Journal.* doi:10.1111/1748-8583.12435

Eisenhardt, K. M. (1989). Building theories from case study research. *Academy of Management Review*, *14*(4), 532–550. doi:10.2307/258557

Elsevier. (2023). *The use of AI and AI-assisted technologies in scientific writing.* Elsevier. https://tinyurl.com/5dwsyntf.Accessed on May-12.

Farndale, E., Bonache, J., McDonnell, A., & Kwon, B. (2023). Positioning context front and center in international human resource management research. *Human Resource Management Journal*, *33*(1), 1–16. doi:10.1111/1748-8583.12483

FDA. (2022). *Do cell phones pose a health hazard? US food and drug administration website.* FDA. https://tinyurl.com/ycxyax5p.

Fitzpatrick, K. K., Darcy, A., & Vierhile, M. (2017). Delivering cognitive behavior therapy to young adults with symptoms of depression and anxiety using a fully automated conversational agent (Woebot): A randomized controlled trial. *JMIR Mental Health*, *4*(2), e7785. doi:10.2196/mental.7785 PMID:28588005

Forscey, D., Bateman, J., Beecroft, N., & Woods, B. (2022). *Systemic cyber risk: A primer.* Carnegie Endowment for InternationalPeace.

Francis, J. J., Johnston, M., Robertson, C., Glidewell, L., Entwistle, V., Eccles, M. P., & Grimshaw, J. M. (2010). What is an adequate sample size? Operationalising data saturation for theory-based interview studies. *Psychology & Health*, *25*(10), 1229–1245. https://tinyurl.com/yckywptz. doi:10.1080/08870440903194015 PMID:20204937

Gendron, Y., Andrew, J., & Cooper, C. (2022). The perils of artificial intelligence in academic publishing. *Critical Perspectives on Accounting*, *87*, 102411. doi:10.1016/j.cpa.2021.102411

Gilpin, L. H., Bau, D., Yuan, B. Z., Bajwa, A., Specter, M., & Kagal, L. (2018). October. Explaining explanations: An overview of interpretability of machine learning. In *2018 IEEE 5th International Conference on data science and advanced analytics(DSAA)* (pp. 80–89). IEEE. 10.1109/DSAA.2018.00018

Glaser, B. G., & Strauss, A. L. (1967). *The discovery of grounded theory.*

Goldfarb, B., & Kirsch, D. A. (2019). *Bubbles and crashes: The boom and bust of technological innovation.* Stanford UniversityPress. gpt-4-salesforce-potential-features/.

Graeber, D. (2018). *Bullshit jobs: A theory.* Simon and schuster.

Grant, R. M. (1996). Toward a knowledge-based theory of the firm. *Strategic Management Journal*, *17*(S2), 109–122. doi:10.1002/smj.4250171110

Griffi, A. (2023). *ChatGPT creators try to use artificial intelligence to explain itself – And come across major problems.* Independent. https://tinyurl.com/bdfzbvux.

Guardian News. (2023). Godfather of AI' Geoffrey Hinton quits Google and warns over dangers of misinformation. *Guardian News.* https://tinyurl.com/3se42t5e.

Guest, D., Knox, A., & Warhurst, C. (2022). Humanizing work in the digital age: Lessons from socio-technical systems and quality of working life initiatives. *Human Relations*, *75*(8), 1461–1482. doi:10.1177/00187267221092674

Guest, G., Bunce, A., & Johnson, L. (2006). How many interviews are enough? An experiment with data saturation and variability. *Field Methods*, *18*(1), 59–82. https://journals.sagepub.com/doi/10.1177/1525822X05279903. doi:10.1177/1525822X05279903

Habermas, J. (1984). The theory of communicative action. In *Reason and rationalization of society* (Vol. 1). Heinemann.

Habermas, J. (1992). *Moral consciousness and communicative action.* Polity Press.

Hennink, M. M., Kaiser, B. N., & Marconi, V. C. (2017). Code saturation versus meaning saturation: How many interviews are enough? *Qualitative Health Research*, *27*(4), 591–608. doi:10.1177/1049732316665344 PMID:27670770

Howlett, E. (2023). Third of HR professionals want to use ChatGPT at work, exclusive data reveals. *People Management.* https://tinyurl.com/yu6j8fkf doi:10.1177/014920639101700108

Hyman, L. (2023). *It's not the end of work. It's the end of boring work.* https://tinyurl.com/3tbap77h.

Ioakimidis, V., & Maglajlic, R. A. (2023). Neither 'neo-luddism' nor 'neo-positivism'; rethinking social work's positioning in the context of rapid technological change. *British Journal of Social Work*, *53*(2), 693–697. doi:10.1093/bjsw/bcad081

Kapadiya, D., Shekhawat, C., & Sharma, P. (2023). A Study on Large Scale Applications of Big Data in Modern Era. In *International Conference on Information Management & Machine Intelligence (ICIMMI2023).* ACM, New York, NY, USA. https://doi.org/10.1145/3647444.364788

Keegan, A., & Den Hartog, D. (2019). Doing it for themselves? Performance appraisal in project-based organisations, the role of employees, and challenges to theory. *Human Resource Management Journal*, *29*(2), 217–237. doi:10.1111/1748-8583.12216

Kumar, A. S., Sharma, P., Kaur, S., Saleh, O. S., Chennamma, H. R., & Chaturvedi, A. (2023). AI-Equipped IoT Applications in High-Tech Agriculture Using Machine Learning. In Handbook of Research on AI-Equipped IoT Applications in High-Tech Agriculture (pp. 38-64). IGI Global.

Maharajan, K., Kumar, A. V., El Emary, I. M., Sharma, P., Latip, R., Mishra, N., Dutta, A., Manjunatha Rao, L., & Sharma, M. (2023). Blockchain Methods and Data-Driven Decision Making With Autonomous Transportation. In R. Kumar, A. Abdul Hamid, & N. Binti Ya'akub (Eds.), *Effective AI, Blockchain, and E-Governance Applications for Knowledge Discovery and Management* (pp. 176–194). IGI Global., doi:10.4018/978-1-6684-9151-5.ch012

Mancy, A. M., Kumar, A. S., Latip, R., Jagadamba, G., Chakrabarti, P., Sharma, P., & Kanchan, B. G. (2024). Smart Healthcare System, Digital Health and Telemedicine, Management and Emergencies: Patient Emergency Application (PES) E-Governance Applications. In Sustainable Development in AI, Blockchain, and E-Governance Applications (pp. 124-151). IGI Global. on 12 May 2023. doi:10.4018/979-8-3693-1722-8.ch008

Panda, T., Patro, U. S., Das, S., Venugopal, K., & Saibabu, N. (2024). Blockchain in Human Resource Management: A Bibliographic Investigation and Thorough Evaluation. In Harnessing Blockchain-Digital Twin Fusion for Sustainable Investments (pp. 86-119). IGI Global. doi:10.4018/979-8-3693-1878-2.ch005

Prasad, G. A., Kumar, A. V., Sharma, P., Irawati, I. D., D. V., C., Musirin, I. B., Abdullah, H. M., & Rao L, M. (2023). Artificial Intelligence in Computer Science: An Overview of Current Trends and Future Directions. In S. Rajest, B. Singh, A. Obaid, R. Regin, & K. Chinnusamy (Eds.), Advances in Artificial and Human Intelligence in the Modern Era (pp. 43-60). IGI Global. doi:10.4018/979-8-3693-1301-5.ch002

Prasad, G. A., Kumar, A. V., Sharma, P., Irawati, I. D., D. V., C., Musirin, I. B., Abdullah, H. M., & Rao L, M. (2023). Artificial Intelligence in Computer Science: An Overview of Current Trends and Future Directions. In S. Rajest, B. Singh, A. Obaid, R. Regin, & K. Chinnusamy (Eds.), Advances in Artificial and Human Intelligence in the Modern Era (pp. 43-60). IGI Global. . preprints202302.0069.v doi:10.4018/979-8-3693-1301-5.ch002

Rawat, P., Bhardwaj, A., L. Nitya., Sharma, P., & Sharma., P. K. P. (2023). Arduino Based IoT Mini Weather Station. SKIT Research Journal, Vol. 13, Issue 2, pp. 34-41, https://doi.org/ S0212610910000157 doi:10.47904/IJSKIT.13.2.2023.34-41

Rehana, H., Çam, N. B., Basmaci, M., Zheng, J., Jemiyo, C., He, Y., & Hur, J. (2023). Evaluation of GPT and BERT-based models on identifying protein-protein interactions in biomedical text. arXiv preprint arXiv:2303.17728

Rehana, H., Çam, N. B., Basmaci, M., Zheng, J., Jemiyo, C., He, Y., & Hur, J. (2023). Evaluation of GPT and BERT-based models on identifying protein-protein interactions in biomedical text. arXiv preprint arXiv:2303.17728

Saul, J., & Bass, D. (2023). *Artificial intelligence is booming—So is its carbon footprint.* Bloomberg News. https://tinyurl.com/eruhxdhv.

Saunders, M. N., & Townsend, K. (2016). Reporting and justifying the number of interview participants in organization and workplace research. *British Journal of Management, 27*(4), 836–852. doi:10.1111/1467-8551.12182

Schrage, M., Kiron, D., Candelon, F., Khodabandeh, S., & Chu, M. (2023). AI is helping companies redefine, noy just improve performance. *MIT Sloan Management Review*. https://sloanreview.mit.edu/article/ai-is-helping-companies-redefine-not-just-improve-performance/.

SchulmanJ.WolskiF.DhariwalP.RadfordA.KlimovO. 2017. Proximal policy optimization algorithms. arXiv preprintarXiv:1707.06347.

Schwartz, R., Vassilev, A., Greene, K., Perine, L., & Burt, A. (2022). *Towards a standard for identifying bias in Artificial Intelligence*. Department of Commerce's National Institute of Standards and Technology. doi:10.6028/NIST.SP.1270

Schweizer, K. (2022). Artificial unintelligence: How computers misunderstand the world. *The European Legacy, 27*(7–8), 7–8. science-practice gap in open science. https://doi.org/ doi:10.1080/10848770.2022.2110366

Sethi, S. S., & Sharma, P. (2023). New Developments in the Implementation of IoT in Agriculture. *SN Computer Science, 4*(5), 503. doi:10.1007/s42979-023-01896-w

Sharma, P. (2023). *Utilizing Explainable Artificial Intelligence to Address Deep Learning in Biomedical Domain, Medical Data Analysis and Processing using Explainable Artificial Intelligence*. Taylor & Francis., doi:10.1201/9781003257721-2

Sharma, P., & Bhatnagar, N. (2023). Passenger Authentication and Ticket Verification at Airport Using QR Code Scanner. *SKIT Research Journal, 13*(2), 10–13. doi:10.47904/IJSKIT.13.1.2023.10-12

Sharma, P., & Dadheech, P. (2023). Modern-age Agriculture with Artificial Intelligence: A review emphasizing Crop Yield Prediction. *EVERGREEN Joint Journal of Novel Carbon Resource Sciences & Green Asia Strategy, 10*(4), 2570–2582. doi:10.5109/7160906

Sharma, P., Dadheech, P., Aneja, N., & Aneja, S. (2023). Predicting Agriculture Yields Based on Machine Learning Using Regression and Deep Learning. *IEEE Access : Practical Innovations, Open Solutions, 11*, 111255–111264. doi:10.1109/ACCESS.2023.3321861

Sharma, P., Dadheech, P., & Senthil Kumar Senthil, A. V. (2023). AI-Enabled Crop Recommendation System Based on Soil and Weather Patterns. In R. Gupta, A. Jain, J. Wang, S. Bharti, & S. Patel (Eds.), *Artificial Intelligence Tools and Technologies for Smart Farming and Agriculture Practices* (pp. 184–199). IGI Global. doi:10.4018/978-1-6684-8516-3.ch010

Sharma, P., Dharmi, K., & Ajay, B. (2023). Efficient Note Sharing Model for Collaborative Learning. *SKIT Research Journal., 13*(2), 42–46. doi:10.47904/IJSKIT.13.2.2023.42-46

Sharma, P., & Jain, M. K. (2023, November). Stock Market Trends Analysis using Extreme Gradient Boosting (XGBoost). In *2023 International Conference on Computing, Communication, and Intelligent Systems (ICCCIS)* (pp. 317-322). IEEE. 10.1109/ICCCIS60361.2023.10425722

Sharma, P., & Rathi, Y. (2016, June 5). Efficient Density-Based Clustering Using Automatic Parameter Detection. Efficient Density-Based Clustering Using Automatic Parameter Detection | SpringerLink. doi:10.1007/978-981-10-0767-5_46

Sharma, P., Sharma, C., & Mathur, P. (2023). Machine Learning-based Stock Market Forecasting using Recurrent Neural Network. *9th International Conference on Smart Computing and Communications (ICSCC)*, Kochi, Kerala, India. 10.1109/ICSCC59169.2023.10335083

Shet, S. V., & Pereira, V. (2021). Proposed managerial competencies for Industry 4.0–Implications for social sustainability. *Technological Forecasting and Social Change, 173*, 121080. doi:10.1016/j.techfore.2021.121080

Stahl, G. K., Brewster, C. J., Collings, D. G., & Hajro, A. (2020). Enhancing the role of human resource management in corporate sustainability and social responsibility: A multi-stakeholder, multidimensional approach to HRM. *Human Resource Management Review, 30*(3), 100708. doi:10.1016/j.hrmr.2019.100708

Suddaby, R., Ganzin, M., & Minkus, A. (2017). Craft, magic and the Re-enchantment of the world. *European Management Journal, 35*(3), 285–296. doi:10.1016/j.emj.2017.03.009

Suseno, Y., Chang, C., Hudik, M., & Fang, E. S. (2022). Beliefs, anxiety and change readiness for artificial intelligence adoption among human resource managers: The moderating role of high-performance work systems. *International Journal of Human Resource Management, 33*(6), 1209–1236. doi:10.1080/09585192.2021.1931408

Susskind, R. E., & Susskind, D. (2022). *The future of the professions: How technology will transform the work of human experts, updated edition*. Oxford University Press.

Tanwar, A., Sharma, P., Pandey, A., & Kumar, S. (2022, December). Intrusion Detection System Based Ameliorated Technique of Pattern Matching. In *Proceedings of the 4th International Conference on Information Management & Machine Intelligence* (pp. 1-4). ACM. 10.1145/3590837.3590947

Taylor, A. (2020). Smartphone pinky' and other injuries caused by excessive phone use. *The conversation, 2020*. https://tinyurl.com/6keemvsk.

Tcharnetsky, M., & Vogt, F. (2023). *The OSQE model: The ai cycle against the shortage of skilled professionals: A holistic solution approach based on artificial intelligence in times of demographic change*. https://doi.org// doi:10.20944

Teicher, J., Van Gramberg, B., & Bamber, G. J. (2023). Understanding workplace conflict and its management in the context of COVID-19. In A. Avgar, D. Hann, R. Lamare, & D. NashLERA Research Volume Series (Eds.), The evolution of workplace dispute resolution: International perspectives. Labor and Employment Relations Association.

The Economist. (2020). Businesses are finding AI hard to adopt. *The Economist*. https://tinyurl.com/2p8ne738.vAccessed on 12 May 2023.

The Royal Society. (2019). *Explainable AI: The basics - POLICY BRIEFING*. The Royal Society. https://tinyurl.com/wkkevmu9.

Thompson, E. P. (1966). *The making of the English working class*. Victor Gollancz Ltd.

Thorbecke, C. (2023). *Google shares lose $100 billion after company's AI chatbot makes an error during demo*. CNN Business. https://edition.cnn.com/2023/02/08/tech/google-ai-bard-demo-error/index.html.

Trist, E., Higgin, G., Murray, H., & Pollock, A. (1963). *Organizational choice*. Tavistock Publications.

Uszkoreit, J. (2017). *Transformer: A novel neural network architecture for language understanding*. Google Research Blog. https://ai.googleblog.com/2017/08/transformer-novel-neural-network.html.

Vallance, C. (2023). AI could replace equivalent of 300 million jobs – report. *BBC News Technology, 28*. https://www.bbc.com/news/technology-65102150.

van Dis, E. A. M., Bollen, J., Zuidema, W., van Rooij, R., & Bockting, C. (2023). ChatGPT: Five priorities for research. *Nature*, *614*(7947), 224–226. doi:10.1038/d41586-023-00288-7 PMID:36737653

Varma, A., Dawkins, C., & Chaudhuri, K. (2022). Artificial intelligence and people management: A critical assessment throughthe ethical lens. *Human Resource Management Review*, *33*(1), 100923. doi:10.1016/j.hrmr.2022.100923

Varma, A., Jaiswal, A., Pereira, V., & Kumar, Y. L. N. (2022). Leader-member exchange in the age of remote work. *Human Resource Development International*, *25*(2), 219–230. doi:10.1080/13678868.2022.2047873

Venkata, S. K., Decker, S., Kirsch, D. A., & Nix, A. (2021). EMCODIST: A context-based search tool for email archives. In 2021 IEEE international conference on big data (big data). IEEE. 10.1109.

Vincent, J. (2023). Meta open-sources multisensory AI model that combines six types of data. *Verge*. https://tinyurl.com/2s3jucwd

von Krogh, G., Roberson, Q., & Gruber, M. (2023). Recognizing and utilizing novel research opportunities with artificial intelligence. *Academy of Management Journal*, *66*(2), 367–373. doi:10.5465/amj.2023.4002

Wang, Z., Cai, S. A., Ren, S., & Singh, S. K. (2023). Green operational performance in a high-tech industry: Role of green HRM and green knowledge. *Journal of Business Research*, *160*, 113761. doi:10.1016/j.jbusres.2023.113761

Westerman, J. W., Rao, M. B., Vanka, S., & Gupta, M. (2020). Sustainable human resource management and the triple bottom line: Multi-stakeholder strategies, concepts, and engagement. *Human Resource Management Review*, *30*(3), 100742. doi:10.1016/j.hrmr.2020.100742

Willig, C., & Rogers, W. S. (2017). *The SAGE handbook of qualitative research in Psychology* (2nd ed.). Sage. doi:10.4135/9781526405555

Wilson, H. J., Daugherty, P., & Bianzino, N. (2017). The jobs that artificial intelligence will create. *MIT Sloan Management Review*, *58*(4), 14. http://mitsmr.com/2odREFJ

Wolf, Z. B. (2023). AI can be racist, sexist and creepy. What should we do about it? CNN what matters. https://tinyurl.com/yc4u46d3

Xue, M., Cao, X., Feng, X., Gu, B., & Zhang, Y. (2022). Is college education less necessary with AI? Evidence from firm-level labor structure changes. *Journal of Management Information Systems*, *39*(3), 865–905. doi:10.1080/07421222.2022.2096542

Yadav, R., Chaudhary, N. S., Kumar, D. & Saini, D. (2022). Mediating and moderating variables of employee relations and sustainable organizations: A systematic literature review and future research agenda. *International journal of organizational analysis*. doi:10.1108/IJOA-12-2021-3091

Yakar, T. (2023). *GPT-4 and Salesforce potential features*. ApexHours website. https://www.apexhours.com/

Zu, D. (2023). *Collective action and AI: The next stage in accelerating digital transformation*. University of Bremen.

Chapter 6
Bibliographical Survey of Extensive Uses of AI-Based Tools in Real-Time Intelligent Bidding in Electricity Markets

Ajay Bhardwaj

Swami Keshvanand Institute of Technology, Management, and Gramothan, Jaipur, India

Sarfaraz Nawaz

Swami Keshvanand Institute of Technology, Management, and Gramothan, Jaipur, India

ABSTRACT

The successful implementation of the electricity market model has challenged the conventional way of operating the power system. In the electricity market model, power system is restructured to promote private companies to participate in a market structure where companies can sign a binding contract with large customers or can participate into pool market structure. Generation companies (GENCOs) and customers submit their bids in blocks in a pool market structure. GENCOs can achieve profit through strategic bidding due to the competitive nature of market structure. For this objective to realize, historical data of bidding of other participants should be modeled. This chapter addresses the application of dynamic programming, game theory and various AI based tools to form strategic bidding in the real time electricity market. To extend the analysis, a comparison of methods of designing bidding strategies has been presented. Based on this comparison, a critical review has been carried out to investigate the leading methods of strategic bidding.

INTRODUCTION

Conventional power systems, consisting of vertical integrated utility suffer from rigidity, organizational complexity, management difficulties and risk of failure. The regulations which were followed earlier in these systems are not much relevant at the present time. Advanced technologies, research, integration

DOI: 10.4018/979-8-3693-6824-4.ch006

Figure 1. Evolution of deregulated power system

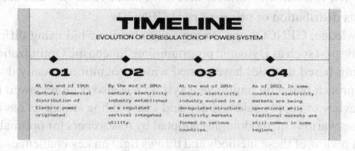

of renewable sources and enhancement in security of power system and revenues demanded deregulation of power system. Deregulation or restructuring of power system required leniency in government policies and encouragement of private firms to participate in the operation of power system (David & Wen, 2000). This led to inception of market structure where public and/or private firms participate to sell produced power in blocks. These evolutionary changes are depicted in the timeline diagram in Fig. 1. Customer participation is of great significance here to improve energy efficiency and reliability. Large customers can play a vital role in the market structure as they can bid to purchase electricity. In a pool market structure, the market operator records the bid submitted by market participants and determines Market Clearing Price (MCP) (David, 1993). MCP is an equilibrium price determined from the supply and demand curve and it is the maximum price at which energy can be sold or purchased. Prices remain close or moving towards MCP in a competitive market structure. But due to the oligopolistic nature of electricity markets, large companies can exercise market power and influence MCP.

GENCOs can also enter into long-term bilateral transactions with large customers. There are many benefits yet there are many challenges in horizontal structure also such as electricity markets are not perfectly competitive. Only a few power generation companies can participate, which indicates the oligopolistic nature of market structure. In this oligopolistic pool market structure, GENCOs submit their bid to Market Operator who dispatches the feasible trading solution (Ansari & Rahimi-Kian, 2015)

GENCOs can increase their profits by predicting rival GENCO's behavior. Historical data is needed to model this complex problem. The profit, which is to be maximized, can be calculated by:

$$\varphi_j = \sum_{i=1}^{n} C_{ji} P_{ji} - GC_j \tag{1}$$

The price and quantity offered are denoted by C_{ji} and P_{ji} respectively where i is bid in blocks for j^{th} generator. Product of these two is noted as revenue. φj denotes profit and generator cost is given by GCj.

To gain profit, GENCOs have to be aware of their rival's behavior which can be predicted using normal Probability Density Function. The distribution of prices of bids can be modeled as:

$$PDF\left(\widetilde{C}_i^n\right) = \frac{1}{2\pi\sigma_i^n} \exp\left(-\frac{(\widetilde{C}_i^n - \mu_i^n)}{2(\sigma_i^n)^2}\right) \tag{2}$$

$\widetilde{C}_i^n$ is the price which is a random variable here with mean value μ_i^n and standard deviation σ_i^n. The function represents distribution of prices of rival GENCOs.

Based on this knowledge, GENCOs can strategically plan their bid using different approaches addressed by authors in the past such as Dynamic programming, Stochastic Optimization and Game Theory approach. Deep learning-based methods have gained wide recognition recently due to their robust and reliable nature. An approach based on multi agent system has also been reviewed to show the efficacy of these methods. A review of supply side and demand side bidding strategies has also been presented.

This article addresses various methodologies adopted by researchers for optimal bidding of power. It also represents critical review of these methods and throws light on key challenges and research gaps on the same. This paper is organized in five sections. Section I presents introduction of the subject matter. Section II represents various methodologies proposed by researchers for strategic bidding. Section III and IV represent critical review and comparison among these methods, respectively. Section V presents concluding remarks on the topic.

BIDDING STRATEGIES

Dynamic Programming Based Approach

Dynamic programming (DP) is a mathematical optimization approach proposed by Richard Bellman in 1950s. This approach breaks a complex problem into sub problems and solves it by simplifying the problem in recursive manner.

Dynamic programming approach has been utilized to plan strategic bidding in electricity markets. (David, 1993 ; Ansari & Rahimi-Kian, 2015).

In power markets of the England-Wales type, a DP-based solution to the strategic bidding problem was presented (David, 1993). For a thorough grasp of these considerations, the study presented in the paper examined a variety of issues regarding electricity markets. In their research, a bidding mechanism for this market that encourages each supplier to submit a set price bid for each block of generation capacity was suggested.

An example of a risk-constrained bidding model for GENCOs participating in an energy market with pools is given in (Ansari & Rahimi-Kian, 2015). The strategic bidding problem was formulated using the DP algorithm. The uncertainty in the system demand is considered by the bidding model. The bidding methodology incorporates risk management as well.

Stochastic Optimization Approach

Stochastic optimization methods have a random probability distribution or pattern, and they use lots of historic data to illustrate the likelihood of occurrence of an event. These methods gained wide attention due to their accuracy being close enough to the exact solution.

In the unfavorable setting of oligopolistic electricity markets, A stochastic optimization approach addressing bidding problem was developed by Wen and David (2001). Analysis of potential market power suggests that if suppliers bid strategically, the market clearing price (MCP) could be higher than levels that are competitive.

E. S. Huge et al. (1999) suggested a heuristic-based method to solve the optimal bidding strategy. The technique was applied for market clearing and bidding. The approach was also applied to a normal unit commitment problem while taking into consideration several limitations, including minimum start-up and shut-down periods, start-up costs, and spinning reserve requirements.

MC approach has been proposed in the work of Li Ma et al. (2002) to solve optimal bidding problem. Based on the provincial power market in Zhejiang, the authors created a model of bidding strategy. The Genetic Algorithm (GA) was used to identify the problem's global optimal solution. Power system network restrictions and intertemporal operational constraints for starting and stopping generators were not considered.

The spot market's multistage probabilistic bidding decision problem was handled in the work of H. Song et al. (2000). The Markov decision process, a discrete stochastic optimization technique, was used to formulate the decision-making issue. Operating restrictions on the power system were disregarded in their work, and the decision-action makers were viewed as risk-neutral.

In a day-ahead energy market, the difficulty of creating a bidding strategy was addressed by Wen and David (2001). The spinning reserve market's bidding strategy was proposed in the work of Wen and David (2002). Their work did not consider inter-temporal operational limitations, and the market model did not accurately reflect the actual market dynamics.

Genetic programming (GP) with finite state automata was used by C.W. Richter et al. (1999) to propose bidding strategies. They did not include in predicted prices or information on unit commitment programs in their work.

Fuzzy Adaptive Particle Swarm Optimization (FAPSO), which P. Bajpai et al. (2007) suggested, can be used to create bidding strategies in spot markets with uniform prices.

R. Herranz et al. (2012) found a solution to the issue of strategic bidding in an unpredictable short-term power market. The parameters determining the optimum purchase strategy were optimized using GA.

A mathematical model was put forth by S. J. Kazempour et al. (2015) for large consumers to modify pool prices in order to improve the benefits of determining bidding tactics. They did not model risk management in their work.

To increase GENCOs' profits, the biogeography-based optimization (BBO) method was utilized in the work of P. Jain et al. (2012). The suggested technique created bid prices for the GENCO whose profit was to be maximized before stochastically predicting bid prices of rivals.

An approach based on the hunting behavior of grey wolves was proposed in the work of A. Bhardwaj et al. (2017) to design an optimal bidding strategy to maximize the revenue of generating companies. The technique was based on the social hierarchy of grey wolves which was illustrated by S. Mirjalili (2014) and C. Muro et al. (2011). Authors ignored the inter-temporal operating constraints.

Game Theory Based Approach

Development of game theory to solve optimization problems began with two-person zero sum games proposed by John Von Neumann. Game theory is an approach which describes interaction between market players. Players may form their own strategy to gain individual maximum profit, or they can interact to form a tactical strategy which enhances profit of everyone. The game theory approach has been extensively used in social science, economics and computer science. Researchers working in the field of economics of restructured power systems have applied this technique to form bidding strategy in electricity markets.

A game theory-based approach was proposed by R. W. Ferrero et al. (1997) to simulate bidding price in a restructured competitive market environment. The power pool was completely expected to be unregulated, with perfect circumstances adjusted. By coordinating bid methods and sharing benefits, participants boosted their benefits while the network imposed further limits on bids.

R.W. Ferrero et al. (1998) presented a game theory method to describe pool market participants' bidding tactics. Deregulated power markets are modeled using this method. Participants competed against one another in a non-cooperative game with incomplete knowledge of rivals' actions. The strategic bidding problem with incomplete information was solved by Nash Equilibrium (NE) and tested on two participants in pool market.

C. A. Berry et al. (1999) proposed an approach to examine non-cooperative behavior among participants and calculated NE under different market structures. The findings demonstrated that higher consumer prices at the second node were a direct outcome of increased competition at the first node, which also led to a general decline in consumer surplus.

F. S. Wen et al. (2001) introduced a strategy for predicting the best energy output to increase the profit of power producers in an oligopoly electricity market with imperfect information environment. The optimal supply quantity of each power provider was determined by the authors using the Cournot non-cooperative game theory approach. It was demonstrated that in an oligopolistic setting of power markets, the estimations of production cost functions of competitors play a significant effect.

A game theory application was put up by J. B. Park et al. (2001) to examine power transactions in a deregulated electricity market. The author modelled the electrical market as a non-cooperative game with comprehensive information, with NE providing the basis for the solution.

In a bilateral market where power producers made their bids known to loads, H. Song et al. (2002) investigated bidding tactics. For the generators in their paper, NE bid prices were calculated using network optimization techniques.

Simulations of a pool-based electricity market and identification of equilibrium patterns can be found in the work of S. de la Torre et al. (2003). The piecewise constant price-demand curves were used to represent the load elasticity.

It is cumbersome to characterize real market behavior for bidders and network operators to analyze market power and bidding strategies. S. de la Torre et al. (2004) presented a three-step methodology to find the equilibria of pool-based electricity market.

Electricity markets are not fully competitive due to transmission constraints and market concentration. Because of this, producing companies can use their market dominance to charge more than their actual marginal cost of electricity. To examine these markets, B. F. Hobbs et al. (2000) proposed a strategy-gaming model in which a single firm model was represented as a computer program with equilibrium constraints.

P. F. Correia et al. (2001) proposed a solution to strategic bidding problem by NE. Authors addressed the problem of finding NE in centralized electricity market.

An algorithm to determine a market participant's individual wellbeing was put forth by J. D. Weber et al. (2002). NE discovered market equilibrium points in their research. The author's approach calculated the best adjustment in each bidder's offer by using the price and dispatch sensitivities provided by the hessian matrix and gradient of the optimal power flow (OPF).

Due to the challenging problem's exponential order of numerous equilibria in controlled power markets, P. F. Correia et al. (2003) addressed it in their work. They used an example to show the issue and the continuation approach to resolve it.

A. Haurie et al. (1992) proposed an approach in which participants can interact before the game starts. This co-operative approach was applied to the case of New England power system in their work.

The cost of transmission network facility is of much concern while deciding bidding strategy. The work of Tsukamoto and Iyoda (1996) considered the transmission losses while maximizing profits for power producers. Tsukamoto and Iyoda (1996) allocated the transmission cost to wheeling transactions and proposed MW-Mile method. They incorporated a nucleolus scheme in the co-operative game theory to deal with conflicting matters while selecting bid. To increase profitability in the power system, X. Bai et al. (1997) introduced an open access transmission approach. The suggested approach was based on a Nash bargaining game for power flow analysis, where the best price and resource allocation for each transaction were chosen to optimize the interests of parties. X. Guan et al. (2001) presented an explicit examination of gaming and price increases in the power market.

L. A. Barroso et al. (2006) addressed the issue of finding NE in short-term electricity markets. The NE problem was converted into a mixed integer linear problem by the authors using a binary expansion approach. The 95 GW Brazilian system was used to test the strategy.

Multi Agent System Based Approaches

Machine learning and deep learning concepts derived from core area of artificial intelligence have been drawing attention these days due to their accuracy in prediction of a future event (Prasad et al., 2023). These concepts find their application in various areas such as agriculture (Sharma et al., 2023; Vinshon et al., 2023; Sharma et al., 2023) density-based clustering (Sharma et al., 2023), Pattern Matching (Tanwar et al., 2023) and biomedical domain (Sharma et al., 2023).

Multi Agent System (MAS) evolved from machine and deep learning concepts are computerized systems based on interactions among multiple intelligent agents having the ability to acquire knowledge and sharing this knowledge with other agents to find an effective solution of a problem. This technique produces promising results and finds its application in online trading, disaster response, target surveillance and social structure modeling.

An agent-based simulation model was suggested by Danial Esmaeili Aliabadi et al. (2017) to achieve learning dynamics of competing GENCOs in the recurrent market. Although the results of the simulation indicated that the market had reached Nash equilibrium, capacity withholding is not considered in this study.

In order to analyze the bidding behaviors of all the participants in the power markets, Jidong Wang et al. (2019) found the gaps in the models of a single electrical firm. In order for agents to learn about, inform, and adapt to their surroundings through interaction, authors employed the reinforcement learning algorithm. Due to consideration of fewer factors in the analysis of hybrid model, actual situation of electricity markets has not been grasped in this work.

Kiran Purushothaman et al. (2020) proposed agent-based modeling of restructured power system with learning capabilities of generator. Authors used stochastic reinforcement learning algorithm to train the strategic bidding of generators. They maintained that an agent-based model would enable the generators to outbid their competitors and wield greater market control.

Kiran P. et al. (2020) emphasized the need to use reinforcement learning approach to solve bidding problem in restructured power system. In this approach, GENCOs are modeled as agents and GENCO learns the market environment as an agent and obtains profits by learning the behavior of other agents. Authors used their technique for GENCOs to attain high profits even with micro grid integration. The approach is applicable to small and medium scale systems only. The effect of distributed energy resources are not taken into account in this study.

Peer to peer bilateral transactions do not incur broker fees, but they present difficulties in striking a balance between cooperative and competitive negotiating tactics (Imran et al., 2020). Authors solved these challenges by developing utility based and adaptive agent tracking strategies for bilateral transactions. The strategy developed in this work can be used to evaluate the performance of small-scale systems only. More generators and loads should be included to test the market performance.

Electricity markets are the present need to realize carbon neutrality. Optimal bidding strategies play a significant role here to stabilize the complex structure of power system. Jiahui Wu et al. (2022) proposed Multi-Agent Reinforcement Learning (MARL) to simulate the optimal bidding framework.

In a competitive market environment, each generating unit aims to maximize the revenue by bidding effectively, but preventive maintenance scheduling is a critical aspect here due to imposed safety and reliability constraints. It is uncertain to fulfill these constraints while being unaware of the rival behavior. A multi-agent based deep learning approach was proposed to tackle these issues in the work of P. Rokhforoz et al. (2023). Contingency of the network and integration of renewable sources were ignored in the authors' work.

S. Li et al. (2022) reinforced the fact that Virtual Power Plant (VPP) is critical for stabilizing the power grids, but adequate energy dispatch is a huge challenge. Authors provided solutions to these problems by proposing a multi-agent system based optimal bidding strategy to model the bidding process in the VPPs. The technique incorporates Self-Adaptive Global Optimal Harmony Search Algorithm to effectively handle the problem of multi-operator participation in scheduling VPPs. The profit gained is distributed to the operators which optimize the Distributed Energy Resources (DERs). The scheduling problem of DERs after bidding was considered a major concern by the authors which was not addressed in their research.

Jidong Wang et al. (2023) proposed multi-agent simulation (MAS) based method to simulate competitive bidding problem of the electricity market. Authors prepared a MAS model and applied an Improved Experience Weighted Attraction (IEWA) algorithm to solve strategic bidding problem. Authors also compared this technique with other reinforcement learning algorithms to check accuracy and rationality of the proposed method.

Bidding Strategy Based on Area of Application

Researchers developed bidding strategies depending upon the area of application such as supply side and demand side. In this article, the supply side has been subdivided into pool market, bilateral market, and ancillary services market.

M. Shahidehpour, M. Alomoush (2001) and M. Shahidehpour et al. (2002) discussed that Power suppliers and major consumers submit bids and offers in sealed envelopes for pool trading, after which the pool operator implements the economic dispatch and establishes the price for electricity. Encouragement of customers in the bidding process is quite significant to reap the true benefits of a market environment.

Demand side bidding defines active participation of customers in the bidding process, and it prevents abuse of market power which is a major concern for market operators.

Supply Side Bidding Strategies

Pool Market

The pool market is the place where energy suppliers submit their bid to market operator. The market operator performs simulations on the data received in the form of bids and dispatches market clearing prices (MCP).

In a competitive electricity market, Vasileios P. Gountis et al. (2004) suggested a framework for developing bidding strategies for GENCOs. The predicted profit was computed using MC simulation, and the best bidding strategy was determined using GA. For more accurate individual decision-making models, risk aversion was taken into consideration.

A method was put forth by Claudia P. Rodriguez et al. (2004) to discover a bidding strategy made up of curves with the best offer blocks where just data on anticipated demand and market clearing prices were needed.

Karl Seeley et al. (2000) examined the impact of energy market regulations on strategic behavior. Through gaming in a non-congested system, their research demonstrated the potential for mid-price suppliers to cause congestion issues. In this paper, a constant marginal cost was assumed.

To maximize the profits of the suppliers, S. Hao et al. (2000) proposed an ideal bidding strategy which consists of the solution of differential equations. In their work, ramping restrictions were disregarded.

Karush-Kuhn-Tucker conditions are used to solve non-linear constrained algebraic equations. Wang Xian et al. (2004) integrated these conditions to present solution to the problem of strategic bidding. The results of this study showed that producing companies may employ overproduction in crowded locations to assert their market dominance.

Sinan Yörükoğlu et al. (2018) proposed a mathematical model for the exact solution of clearing day ahead markets. They introduced the concept of paradoxically accepted/rejected orders placed by the market participants. This mathematical model is defined in two different forms, each of which supports a different kind of paradoxical processing. Authors overlooked the alternative objectives in their work such as minimization of Market Clearing Price (MCP) or maximization of equilibrium quantities.

F. Lisi et al. (2015) emphasized the need to assess the appropriate approach to model system components of electricity market time series in day ahead markets. They compared the deterministic and the stochastic approach for prediction of loads and prices. They concluded that both approaches have their strengths and weaknesses and hence advised to use both approaches and pick the one that suits the particular model.

Mostafa Kazemi et al. (2015) simulated the bidding curve of a supplier participating in a day-ahead electricity market. The information gap choice theory was used to model the market uncertainty related to power.

Bilateral Market

Bilateral transactions are also made between two parties in bilateral markets. The regulations of this contract are formed and defined in the presence of both parties, and they should abide by them. Bilateral contracts are generally long-term contracts.

The cost at which transmission services are accessed and whether generators sell through bilateral agreements, or a central auction constitute the challenges surrounding restructuring (B. E. Hobbs, 2001). Bilateral trade is thought to be a good option from the perspective of a dynamic incentive to competition and short- and long-term stability in the supply (M. Marmiroli et al., 2002). These problems affect the type and outcome of competition among GENCOs.

The binary expansion (BE) method is described in the work of M. V. Pereira et al. (2005) as a solution to the optimal bidding problem. The nonlinear bidding problem's variable products were transformed by the authors using the BE method into a mixed integer linear programming (MILP) problem that can be addressed by computer systems. On case studies using configurations taken from an 80 GW Brazilian system, the technique was used.

Ancillary Service Market

Ancillary services, such as reactive power support, spinning reserves, load frequency management, etc., can be bought through auction-based competitive marketplaces, just like energy. Certain auxiliary services are necessary to maintain the security and dependability of the system.

A unique solution to model bidding pattern of spinning reserve market was proposed in the work of F. A. Campos et al. (2016). The day-ahead market opportunity cost was considered when constructing the reserve cost curve.

Reactive power ancillary services were designed for a competitive energy market in the work of K. Bhattacharya and J. Zhong (2001). A bidding framework was then built after using generator reactive power capability parameters to analyze the reactive power prices. Through MC simulations, uncertainty in reactive demand and in reactive bids from involved parties was integrated, and the anticipated reactive power purchase strategy was established.

J. Zhong and K. Bhattacharya (2002) settled the reactive power market using the same framework and a compromise programming strategy based on a modified OPF model. The Cournot model of an oligopolistic electrical market was proposed in the work of D. Chattopadhyay (2004) to address the co-optimization of several commodities, particularly energy and frequency control ancillary services.

Demand Side Bidding Strategies

Since transmission is still a monopoly and the generation side of the energy market is primarily competitive, the power suppliers are primarily the focus of the electricity market, notwithstanding the importance of demand side bidding in preventing abuse of market power. Because consumers lack the financial incentives and the technical knowledge necessary to contribute effectively to such a difficult and time-consuming undertaking, they have little control over how energy markets are designed. Electricity markets would become more effective and competitive with active demand side participation.

Demand side bidding would additionally support efficient resource allocation (D. S. Kirschen, 2003). Electricity demand has very little price elasticity, which leads to significant price jumps and GENCOs' exploitation of market dominance. Demand side bidding is an option for large consumers in some electricity markets, including those in California, New Zealand, and Spain, to respond to electricity pricing. The maximizing of social welfare is used in this instance to clear bids. The minimum price technique should be used if demand side bidding is not allowed since in this situation, the purchasers are passive, and the government should defend their interests (G. Strbac and D. Kirschen, 1999).

On the demand side, there has not been a lot of research on strategic bidding. Using linear bidding functions, David et al. (2001) explored the best simultaneous bidding techniques for generators and large clients.

Conejo et al (2018) 's discussion of the difficulties in constructing electricity markets because of changes in system design, including the increasing penetration of weather-dependent renewable energy sources and the unpredictability of load demand, highlighted some of these issues. By introducing load aggregators or utilities that manage the flexibility of one or more forms of load, they placed a major emphasis on the integration of the demand side in the market model.

Manisha et al. (2023) presented a two-level optimization method to address strategic bidding of generation companies and large customers. Authors focused on maximizing social welfare and calculated MCP and profits by applying four different evolutionary algorithms. Comparison of results showed Non-Dominated Sorting genetic Algorithm (NSGA-III) to be most superior.

CRITICAL REVIEW

The primary causes of the oligopolistic nature of the electricity markets include the high cost of energy, a lack of suppliers, an imbalance between supply and demand, as well as the political and economic problems specific to certain regions. In these marketplaces, GENCO's bid is intended to maximize profit. Market settlement between supplier and client bids establishes the market clearing price (MCP).

The best pay-as-MCP (PAMCP) bidding technique for a GENCO depends on accurate MCP prediction, which in an oligopolistic market and cannot be regarded as deterministic. The bidding practices of other rivals constitute a significant source of uncertainty for a strategically bidding GENCO since it is influenced by suppliers' bidding activity.

The most common energy producers in the world are thermal generating units, which are divided into groups based on their capacity and fuel type having different production costs, operating limitations, and operating cost components. A unit's manufacturing cost, which varies with fuel cost and efficiency, accounts for most of its marginal cost.

Thus, the price being paid for a unit's fuel storage determines its best bidding approach. Additionally, operating restrictions and operating cost elements have an impact on a unit's bid strategy when it is built over a period. There is a wealth of literature on the best bid strategy for a GENCO in an oligopolistic market, but there is a dearth of analysis for realistic, diverse fuel generating units with realistic fuel pricing.

Numerous studies on the creation of the best bidding strategy for GENCO have identified three general solution methods. The first set includes traditional optimization methods like Lagrange relaxation and dynamic programming, among others. If used, these strategies require nonlinear simplification because they cannot solve real-world problems with many constraints and non-differentiable goals.

Another strategy is grounded in game theory and presupposes that rival GENCO's cost functions and full bid details are available to the public. Practically, this is untrue. Additionally, there are numerous Nash equilibriums for vast numbers of players. Heuristic algorithms based on Artificial Intelligence

Table 1. Critical review of the methods adopted by researchers for strategic bidding

S. No.	Name of Method	Critical Review
1.	Dynamic Programming	• Dynamic programming uses recursion which requires a large memory. • Notable risk of error in run-time while optimizing realistic non-differentiable, multi-constraint and multi-objective problems. • Execution speed is very low. • Allocates memory to store the solution of each sub-problem. There is uncertainty about the utilization of these stored values later in execution.
2.	Stochastic Optimization Approach	• Reasonable accuracy is achieved while handing multi-objective problems. • Allows less optimal local decision to be made hence probability of converging to a global optimum solution is remarkably high. • Convergence is slow in multi-stage convex problems. • Reliable Solution Tools • Higher computational cost which increases with sample size.
3.	Game Theory Approach	• Game theory is unable to incorporate the situations of falling into Nash Equilibrium. • Unrealistic assumptions are made in Game theory such as players are opaque to one another which translates into error in result. • Additional complexity increases as the number of rivals increases in the actual business. • Cumbersome to achieve winning strategy as realistic conditions are compromised. • Electricity markets are oligopolistic hence incorporating high level of uncertainty is not easy considering limitations of methods based on Game theory.
4.	Multi Agent System (MAS)	• Agents typically have imprecise local information and visibility. • There is no need for centralized planning or control, even when random components are frequently present in the system or among variable agents. • It is more adaptable, reliable, and straightforward to use than the other approaches mentioned here. • Additional information about the effectiveness of suppliers, load serving entities, market operators, and market regulations is provided by MAS. • The MAS algorithm can help with important decisions including capacity growth, scheduling maintenance, and creating bidding tactics.

(AI) can tackle such difficult issues in their original forms, producing correct solutions, as the third set of approaches.

These techniques explore a large search space and frequently produce a quick and extremely close to the ideal result. The use of methods like GA, EP, PSO, and their variations, among others, is documented in the literature. These imply that these can be considered as trustworthy solution tools as the complexity and limitations of EMs increase.

The performance of suppliers, load serving organizations, market operators, and market regulations is further revealed through multi agent systems. An algorithm created for MAS can help with crucial decisions including capacity growth, scheduling maintenance, and devising intelligent strategy.

COMPARATIVE ANALYSIS

Customer satisfaction is the basic need which must be catered to while designing a power system. The need for restructuring was vital to fulfill this important aspect of a modern power system as it gives rise to competition between power producers. Power producers frame bidding strategies to gain maximum profit in such a competitive environment. The incomplete information about rival bids is a biggest catch in this process. This paper has addressed the issue of strategic bidding in a lucid manner.

Figure 2. Number of research articles reviewed for different methods adopted by researchers

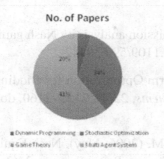

Figure 3. Number of research articles reviewed for different application sides

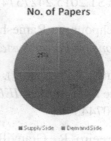

The literature review is carried out for different methods applied for strategic bidding, and different application side for carrying out the strategy i.e. (demand side, supply side). Figures show the no. of papers reviewed per parameter.

CONCLUSION

The purpose of this review paper was to review the trends in formulation of bidding strategies adopted by different generating companies at different sides of the market. From the review, it has been observed that the strategic bidding problem is a potential research area. Stochastic optimization based approaches are based on Monte Carlo simulations and application of meta-heuristic optimization approaches. The cost models of rivals are modelled through normal distribution of the bids. On the other hand, Game theory-based approaches provide logic but not winning strategies. Application of dynamic programming methods are limited to differentiable and continuous functions. Bidding strategies are different for supply side and demand side, a comparison between the both has been presented. Bidding strategies for Ancillary market has also been discussed. Multi Agent Systems gives further insights into electricity markets. Algorithms developed for MAS can support critical decision making such as capacity expansion, maintenance scheduling and designing of bidding strategies.

ACKNOWLEDGMENT

We would like to thank Swami Keshvanand Institute of Technology, Management & Gramothan and Rajasthan Technical University, Kota for the infrastructure provided to complete this review article.

REFERENCES

Aliabadi, D. E., Kaya, M., & Şahin, G. (2017, January). An agent-based simulation of power generation company behavior in electricity markets under different market-clearing mechanisms. *Energy Policy*, *100*, 191–205. doi:10.1016/j.enpol.2016.09.063

Ansari, B., & Rahimi-Kian, A. (2015). A Dynamic Risk-Constrained Bidding Strategy for Generation Companies Based on Linear Supply Function Model. *IEEE Systems Journal*, 9(4), 1463–1474. doi:10.1109/JSYST.2015.2427374

Bai, X., Shahidehpour, S., Ramesh, V., & Yu, E. (1997). Transmission analysis by Nash game method. *IEEE Transactions on Power Systems*, 12(3), 1046–1052. doi:10.1109/59.630442

Bajpai, P., & Singh, S. N. (2007). Fuzzy Adaptive Particle Swarm Optimization for Bidding Strategy in Uniform Price Spot Market. *IEEE Transactions on Power Systems*, 22(4), 2152–2160. doi:10.1109/TPWRS.2007.907445

Barroso, L., Carneiro, R., Granville, S., Pereira, M., & Fampa, M. (2006, May). Nash Equilibrium in Strategic Bidding: A Binary Expansion Approach. *IEEE Transactions on Power Systems*, 21(2), 629–638. doi:10.1109/TPWRS.2006.873127

Berry, C. A., Hobbs, B. F., Meroney, W. A., O'Neill, R. P., & Stewart, W. R. Jr. (1999, September). Understanding how market power can arise in network competition: A game theoretic approach. *Utilities Policy*, 8(3), 139–158. doi:10.1016/S0957-1787(99)00016-8

Bhardwaj, A., Saxena, A., & Manglani, T. (2017). Optimal Bidding Strategy for Profit Maximization of Generation Companies under Step-Wise Bidding Protocol. *Int. J. Eng. Technology*, 9(2), 797–805. doi:10.21817/ijet/2017/v9i2/170902060

Bhattacharya, K., & Zhong, J. (2001, May). Reactive power as an ancillary service. *IEEE Transactions on Power Systems*, 16(2), 294–300. doi:10.1109/59.918301

Campos, F. A., Munoz San Roque, A., Sanchez-Ubeda, E. F., & Portela Gonzalez, J. (2016, July). Strategic Bidding in Secondary Reserve Markets. *IEEE Transactions on Power Systems*, 31(4), 2847–2856. doi:10.1109/TPWRS.2015.2453477

Chattopadhyay, D. (2004, February). Multicommodity Spatial Cournot Model for Generator Bidding Analysis. *IEEE Transactions on Power Systems*, 19(1), 267–275. doi:10.1109/TPWRS.2003.821436

Conejo, A. J., & Sioshansi, R. (2018, June). Rethinking restructured electricity market design: Lessons learned and future needs. *International Journal of Electrical Power & Energy Systems*, 98, 520–530. doi:10.1016/j.ijepes.2017.12.014

Correia, P., Overbye, T., & Hiskens, I. (2003, November). Searching for noncooperative equilibria in centralized electricity markets. *IEEE Transactions on Power Systems*, 18(4), 1417–1424. doi:10.1109/TPWRS.2003.818692

Correia, P., Weber, J., Overbye, T., & Hiskens, I. (n.d.). Strategic equilibria in centralized electricity markets. 2001 IEEE Porto Power Tech Proceedings (Cat. No.01EX502).

David, A. K. (1993). Competitive bidding in electricity supply. *IEEE Proceedings C - Generation, Transmission and Distribution, 140* (5), pp. 421-426. 10.1049/ip-c.1993.0061

David, A. K., & Wen. (2000). *Strategic bidding in competitive electricity markets: a literature survey. 2000 Power Engineering Society Summer Meeting*, Seattle, WA. 10.1109/PESS.2000.866982 de la Torre, S., Conejo, A., & Contreras, J. (2003, November). Simulating oligopolistic pool-based electricity markets: A multiperiod approach. *IEEE Transactions on Power Systems*, *18*(4), 1547–1555. doi:10.1109/TPWRS.2003.818746

de la Torre, S., Contreras, J., & Conejo, A. (2004, February). Finding Multiperiod Nash Equilibria in Pool-Based Electricity Markets. *IEEE Transactions on Power Systems*, *19*(1), 643–651. doi:10.1109/TPWRS.2003.820703

Ferrero, R., Rivera, J., & Shahidehpour, S. (1998). Application of games with incomplete information for pricing electricity in deregulated power pools. *IEEE Transactions on Power Systems*, *13*(1), 184–189. doi:10.1109/59.651634

Ferrero, R., Shahidehpour, S., & Ramesh, V. (1997). Transaction analysis in deregulated power systems using game theory. *IEEE Transactions on Power Systems*, *12*(3), 1340–1347. doi:10.1109/59.630479

Gountis, V. P., & Bakirtzis, A. G. (2004). Bidding strategies for electricity producers in a competitive electricity marketplace. *IEEE Transactions on Power Systems*, *19*(1), 356–365. doi:10.1109/TPWRS.2003.821474

Guan, X., Yu-Chi, Ho., & Pepyne, D. (n.d.). Gaming and price spikes in electric power markets. Pica 2001. Innovative Computing for Power - Electric Energy Meets the Market. *22nd IEEE Power Engineering Society. International Conference on Power Industry Computer Applications* (Cat. No.01CH37195). 10.1109/MPER.2001.4311547

Hao, S. (2000). A study of basic bidding strategy in clearing pricing auctions. *IEEE Transactions on Power Systems*, *15*(3), 975–980. doi:10.1109/59.871721

Haurie, A., Loulou, R., & Savard, G. (1992). A two-player game model of power cogeneration in New England. *IEEE Transactions on Automatic Control*, *37*(9), 1451–1456. doi:10.1109/9.159591

Herranz, R., Munoz San Roque, A., Villar, J., & Campos, F. A. (2012, August). Optimal Demand-Side Bidding Strategies in Electricity Spot Markets. *IEEE Transactions on Power Systems*, *27*(3), 1204–1213. doi:10.1109/TPWRS.2012.2185960

Hobbs, B. (2001, May). Linear complementarity models of Nash-Cournot competition in bilateral and POOLCO power markets. *IEEE Transactions on Power Systems*, *16*(2), 194–202. doi:10.1109/59.918286

Hobbs, B., Metzler, C., & Pang, J. S. (2000, May). Strategic gaming analysis for electric power systems: An MPEC approach. *IEEE Transactions on Power Systems*, *15*(2), 638–645. doi:10.1109/59.867153

Huse, E. S., Wangensteen, I., & Faanes, H. (1999). Thermal power generation scheduling by simulated competition. *IEEE Transactions on Power Systems*, *14*(2), 472–477. doi:10.1109/59.761868

Jain, P., Agarwal, A., Gupta, N., Sharma, R., Paliwal, U., & Bhakar, R. (2012, July). Profit maximization of a generation company based on Biogeography based Optimization. *2012 IEEE Power and Energy Society General Meeting*. IEEE. 10.1109/PESGM.2012.6345445

Jong-Bae Park, Kim, B. H., Jin-Ho Kim, Man-Ho Jung, & Jong-Keun ParkJong-Bae Park. (2001). A continuous strategy game for power transactions analysis in competitive electricity markets. *IEEE Transactions on Power Systems*, *16*(4), 847–855. doi:10.1109/59.962436

Kazemi, M., Mohammadi-Ivatloo, B., & Ehsan, M. (2015, January). Risk-Constrained Strategic Bidding of GenCos Considering Demand Response. *IEEE Transactions on Power Systems*, 30(1), 376–384. doi:10.1109/TPWRS.2014.2328953

Kazempour, S. J., Conejo, A. J., & Ruiz, C. (2015, March). Strategic Bidding for a Large Consumer. *IEEE Transactions on Power Systems*, 30(2), 848–856. doi:10.1109/TPWRS.2014.2332540

Kirschen, D. (2003, May). Demand-side view of electricity markets. *IEEE Transactions on Power Systems*, 18(2), 520–527. doi:10.1109/TPWRS.2003.810692

Li, S., Huo, X., Zhang, X., Li, G., Kong, X., & Zhang, S. (2022, October 20). A Multi-Agent Optimal Bidding Strategy in Multi-Operator VPPs Based on SGHSA. *International Transactions on Electrical Energy Systems*, 2022, 1–13. doi:10.1155/2022/7584424

Lisi, F., & Pelagatti, M. M. (2018, August). Component estimation for electricity market data: Deterministic or stochastic? *Energy Economics*, 74, 13–37. doi:10.1016/j.eneco.2018.05.027

Ma, Li, Fushuan, Wen & David, A. K. (2002). A preliminary study on strategic bidding in electricity markets with step-wise bidding protocol. IEEE/PES Transmission and Distribution Conference and Exhibition, 3, pp. 1960-1965.

Marmiroli, M., Tsukamoto, Y., & Yokoyama, R. (2002). Innovative generation scheduling algorithm for multi bilateral electricity market. *Proceedings. International Conference on Power System Technology*, (pp. 1383-1386). IEEE. 10.1109/ICPST.2002.1067756

Mirjalili, S., Mirjalili, S. M., & Lewis, A. (2014, March). Grey Wolf Optimizer. *Advances in Engineering Software*, 69, 46–61. doi:10.1016/j.advengsoft.2013.12.007

Muro, C., Escobedo, R., Spector, L., & Coppinger, R. (2011, November). Wolf-pack (Canis lupus) hunting strategies emerge from simple rules in computational simulations. *Behavioural Processes*, 88(3), 192–197. doi:10.1016/j.beproc.2011.09.006 PMID:21963347

P., K., & Vijaya Chandrakala, K. (2020, December). New interactive agent based reinforcement learning approach towards smart generator bidding in electricity market with micro grid integration. *Applied Soft Computing, 97*, 106762.

Pereira, M., Granville, S., Fampa, M., Dix, R., & Barroso, L. (2005, February). Strategic Bidding Under Uncertainty: A Binary Expansion Approach. *IEEE Transactions on Power Systems*, 20(1), 180–188. doi:10.1109/TPWRS.2004.840397

Prasad, G. A., Kumar, A. V., Sharma, P., Irawati, I. D., D. V., C., Musirin, I. B., Abdullah, H. M., & Rao L, M. (2023). Artificial Intelligence in Computer Science: An Overview of Current Trends and Future Directions. In S. Rajest, B. Singh, A. Obaid, R. Regin, & K. Chinnusamy (Eds.), Advances in Artificial and Human Intelligence in the Modern Era (pp. 43-60). IGI Global.

Purushothaman, K., & Chandrakala, V. (2020). Roth-Erev Reinforcement Learning Approach for Smart Generator Bidding towards Long Term Electricity Market Operation Using Agent Based Dynamic Modeling. *Electric Power Components and Systems*, 48(3), 256–267. doi:10.1080/15325008.2020.1758840

Richter, C. W., Sheble, G. B., & Ashlock, D. (1999). Comprehensive bidding strategies with genetic programming/finite state automata. *IEEE Transactions on Power Systems*, *14*(4), 1207–1212. doi:10.1109/59.801874

Rodriguez, C., & Anders, G. (2004, May). Bidding Strategy Design for Different Types of Electric Power Market Participants. *IEEE Transactions on Power Systems*, *19*(2), 964–971. doi:10.1109/TP-WRS.2004.826763

Rokhforoz, P., Montazeri, M., & Fink, O. (2023, April). Safe multi-agent deep reinforcement learning for joint bidding and maintenance scheduling of generation units. *Reliability Engineering & System Safety*, *232*, 109081. doi:10.1016/j.ress.2022.109081

Saini, M., Bhardwaj, A., & Nawaz, S. (2023, April 7). Multi-Objective Optimal Bidding Approach for both Small & Large Customers in Competitive power Market. *2023 IEEE 8th International Conference for Convergence in Technology (I2CT)*. IEEE.

Seeley, K., Lawarree, J., & Liu, C. C. (2000). Analysis of electricity market rules and their effects on strategic behavior in a noncongestive grid. *IEEE Transactions on Power Systems*, *15*(1), 157–162. doi:10.1109/59.852115

Shahidehpour, M., & Alomoush, M. (2001). *Restructured electric power systems: Operation, trading and volatility*. Marcel Dekker, Inc.

Shahidehpour, M., Yamin, H., & Li, Z. (2002). *Market operations in electric power systems: Forecasting, scheduling and risk management*. John Wiley. doi:10.1002/047122412X

Sharma, P. (2023). *Utilizing Explainable Artificial Intelligence to Address Deep Learning in Biomedical Domain, Medical Data Analysis and Processing using Explainable Artificial Intelligence*. Taylor & Francis.

Sharma, P., Dadheech, P., Aneja, N., & Aneja, S. (2023). Predicting Agriculture Yields Based on Machine Learning Using Regression and Deep Learning. *IEEE Access : Practical Innovations, Open Solutions*, *11*, 111255–111264. doi:10.1109/ACCESS.2023.3321861

Sharma, P., Dadheech, P., & Senthil Kumar Senthil, A. V. (2023). AI-Enabled Crop Recommendation System Based on Soil and Weather Patterns. In R. Gupta, A. Jain, J. Wang, S. Bharti, & S. Patel (Eds.), *Artificial Intelligence Tools and Technologies for Smart Farming and Agriculture Practices* (pp. 184-199). IGI Global. 10.4018/978-1-6684-8516-3.ch010

Song, H., Liu, C.-C., & Lawarree, J. (2002). Nash equilibrium bidding strategies in a bilateral electricity market. *IEEE Transactions on Power Systems*, *17*(1), 73–79. doi:10.1109/59.982195

Song, H., Liu, C. C., Lawarree, J., & Dahlgren, R. W. (2000). Optimal electricity supply bidding by Markov decision process. *IEEE Transactions on Power Systems*, *15*(2), 618–624. doi:10.1109/59.867150

Strbac, G., & Kirschen, D. (1999). Assessing the competitiveness of demand-side bidding. *IEEE Transactions on Power Systems*, *14*(1), 120–125. doi:10.1109/59.744498

Tanwar, A., Sharma, P., Pandey, A., & Kumar, S. (2022, December 23). Intrusion Detection System Based Ameliorated Technique of Pattern Matching. *Proceedings of the 4th International Conference on Information Management & Machine Intelligence*. ACM. 10.1145/3590837.3590947

Tsukamoto, Y., & Iyoda, I. (1996, May). Allocation of fixed transmission cost to wheeling transactions by cooperative game theory. *IEEE Transactions on Power Systems*, *11*(2), 620–629. doi:10.1109/59.496131

V., M. V., Kumar, A. S., Sharma, P., Kaur, S., Saleh, O. S., Chennamma, H., & Chaturvedi, A. (2023). AI-Equipped IoT Applications in High-Tech Agriculture Using Machine Learning. In A. Khang (Ed.), *Handbook of Research on AI-Equipped IoT Applications in High-Tech Agriculture* (pp. 38-64). IGI Global.

Wang, J., Wu, J., & Che, Y. (2019, August). Agent and system dynamics-based hybrid modeling and simulation for multilateral bidding in electricity market. *Energy*, *180*, 444–456. doi:10.1016/j.energy.2019.04.180

Wang, J., Wu, J., & Kong, X. (2023). Multi-agent simulation for strategic bidding in electricity markets using reinforcement learning. *CSEE Journal of Power and Energy Systems*, *9*(3), 1051–1065.

Weber, J., & Overbye, T. (2002, August). An individual welfare maximization algorithm for electricity markets. *IEEE Transactions on Power Systems*, *17*(3), 590–596. doi:10.1109/TPWRS.2002.800899

Wen, F. (2001). Optimal bidding strategies and modeling of imperfect information among competitive generators. *IEEE Transactions on Power Systems*, *16*(1), 15–21. doi:10.1109/59.910776

Wen, F., & David, A. (2001). Oligopoly Electricity Market Production under Incomplete Information. *IEEE Power Engineering Review*, *21*(4), 58–61. doi:10.1109/39.916353

Wen, F., & David, A. (2001, January). Optimal bidding strategies for competitive generators and large consumers. *International Journal of Electrical Power & Energy Systems*, *23*(1), 37–43. doi:10.1016/S0142-0615(00)00032-6

Wen, F. S., & David, A. K. (2001). Strategic bidding for electricity supply in a day-ahead energy market. *Electric Power Systems Research*, *59*(3), 197–206. doi:10.1016/S0378-7796(01)00154-7

Wen, F. S., & David, A. K. (2002). Optimally co-ordinated bidding strategies in energy and ancillary service markets. *IEE Proceedings. Generation, Transmission and Distribution*, *149*(3), 331–338. doi:10.1049/ip-gtd:20020211

Wu, J., Wang, J., & Kong, X. (2022, October). Strategic bidding in a competitive electricity market: An intelligent method using Multi-Agent Transfer Learning based on reinforcement learning. *Energy*, *256*, 124657. doi:10.1016/j.energy.2022.124657

Xian, W., Yuzeng, L., & Shaohua, Z. (2004, August). Oligopolistic Equilibrium Analysis for Electricity Markets: A Nonlinear Complementarity Approach. *IEEE Transactions on Power Systems*, *19*(3), 1348–1355. doi:10.1109/TPWRS.2004.831237

Yörükoğlu, S., Avşar, Z. M., & Kat, B. (2018, October). An integrated day-ahead market clearing model: Incorporating paradoxically rejected/accepted orders and a case study. *Electric Power Systems Research*, *163*, 513–522. doi:10.1016/j.epsr.2018.07.007

Zhong, J., & Bhattacharya, K. (2002, November). Toward a competitive market for reactive power. *IEEE Transactions on Power Systems*, *17*(4), 1206–1215. doi:10.1109/TPWRS.2002.805025

Chapter 7
The Impact of ChatGPT on the Revolution of Educational Trends

Soumya P. S.
Karpagam Academy of Higher Education, India

S. Mythili
Karpagam Academy of Higher Education, India

ABSTRACT

The way that education is taught has changed dramatically since ChatGPT, a cutting-edge conversational AI model, was integrated into classrooms. This study looks into ChatGPT's wide-ranging implications on teaching strategies and outcomes. ChatGPT is an adaptation of technology that allows both teachers and students to create personalized, in-demand learning experiences. The major portion of technological changes in education are caused by the integration of chat GPT. This chapter analyses how chat GPT is involved in the way of teaching learning process and how it affects the revolution of education.

INTRODUCTION

Modern machine learning model ChatGPT is well known for its ability to comprehend natural language. With incredible fluency and coherence, ChatGPT can comprehend, produce, and react to human language because to its transformer architecture, which it was trained on a massive quantity of text data. It is a flexible tool for a range of applications, including customer service, education, and entertainment, because to its capacity to have conversations, respond to inquiries, and deliver contextually relevant information. More natural interactions between humans and machines are made possible by ChatGPT, a notable development in the field of artificial intelligence because to its versatility and ability to comprehend complex linguistic patterns.

Like ChatGPT, other Machine learning models find wide-ranging applications in several sectors, where their skills are utilized to address particular issues and enhance processes. Machine learning models are

DOI: 10.4018/979-8-3693-6824-4.ch007

used in healthcare to improve patient care and outcomes through the diagnosis of diseases, creation of individualized treatment plans, medication development, and analysis of medical imaging. (Mancy et al., 2023). These models are used in the financial industry to improve efficiency and security through the use of fraud detection, risk assessment, algorithmic trading, and customer relationship management. Stock market forecasters use data from the prior year to estimate future stock values. The different machine learning models make the forecast. (*Stock Market Trends Analysis Using Extreme Gradient Boosting (XGBoost)*, 2023) A range of machine learning, deep learning, and hybrid techniques to accurately predict agricultural yields that will support the country's economic growth. range of hybrid, ML, and DL. Techniques for accurately predicting agricultural yields that will support the country's economic expansion *(Sharma,Dadheech,2023)*

With the ability to provide instructors and students with individualized, easily accessible, anytime assistance with ChatGPT, education is set to enter an exciting period. This AI chatbot improves education in general by providing tailored learning experiences, helping with homework, and providing teachers with data-driven insights. It also helps with the globalization of education, guarantees accessibility for students with disabilities, and makes language learning easier. Chat GPT uses data analysis to assist in the development of more effective teaching strategies and superior instructional materials as we transition to a more data-driven learning environment. As education changes in the digital era, striking a balance between the benefits of AI and the upkeep of interpersonal ties and oversight is crucial. Leading a role in this revolution is Chat GPT, which is changing how we both learn and impart knowledge. To maintain the essential role that human interaction and guidance play in the learning process, a balance between the advantages of AI in education and ethical concerns must be achieved. As such, ChatGPT has a significant influence on education and presents opportunities as well as problems for transforming the way people learn in the future.

LITERATURE REVIEW

The outcomes of some research on the application of ChatGPT in education are explained in detail.

Recently, the examination of a review of the literature revealed both beneficial and detrimental effects of ChatGPT in the classroom. Personalized learning experiences, better teaching methods, and more student engagement are among the benefits. Among the detrimental effects are worries about privacy, Academic honesty and the possibility of prejudice (De Castro, 2023)

Another article "ChatGPT and AI Text Generators: Should Academia Adapt or Resist?" It may be concluded that educators need to think creatively about how to adapt the subjects they teach as well as the skills they want to teach their pupils. AITGs such as ChatGPT can and should be embraced as a partner that expands our understanding and speeds up smarter, more efficient work. (*Harvard Business Publishing Education*, n.d.)

Another study advised that ChatGPT be included into English language courses to encourage students' desire to study independently while yet being supervised by teachers. It is recommended that educators demonstrate to their pupils the advantages of ChatGPT rather than making them dread its drawbacks. The absence of corroborating qualitative data that would have enhanced the study is a problem that needs to be mentioned. (Ali et al., 2023)

Undoubtedly, ChatGPT is frightening the public, but it's also going to help identify those with genuine talent and help express who an individual is at their best because a lot of the answers provided by

ChatGPT will match those of the person using its content. The real portion of the content, which is the key to education, will then highlight the realities in education.*(Dr.C. Karthikeyan,2023)*

EFFECTS OF ChatGPT ON STUDENT LEARNING

Personalized Learning

ChatGPT allows students to have individualized learning experiences by analysing individual student data to determine their needs. It is a useful strategy for promoting the customized learning of students. It does this through several important ways:

- *Personalized Content:* Chat GPT can assess a student's knowledge and preferred learning styles by examining their responses and interactions. Subsequently, it adapts educational resources to suit the distinct requirements of every learner, guaranteeing that the information aligns with the student's cognitive proficiency and rate of learning. When themes are customized, students learn them more effectively.
- *Adaptive Feedback:* Chat GPT provides prompt and adaptive responses. In the event that a student answers a question incorrectly, the AI can offer clarifications, additional examples, or alternative strategies until the learner grasps the material. It tailors its solutions to the specific challenges a learner is facing in order to encourage a deeper understanding of the material.
- *Individualized Practice:* Learners are able to complete tests and practice questions according to their proficiency level. By identifying areas in which a student needs more practice and offering relevant exercises to help their learning, Chat GPT can make the educational process more efficient and engaging.
- *Improvement Monitoring:* Chat GPT can track a student's growth and performance over time. Teachers and students can focus on areas that need improvement and have a better understanding of each other's strengths and limits by using this data to create learning profiles.
- *Targeted Suggestions*: Based on each student's individual learning goals and preferences, Chat GPT might suggest additional materials such as books, videos, or articles. These recommendations could enhance the learning process by providing supplementary resources that are relevant to the demands of the students.
- *Independent Learning*: With Chat GPT, students may study at their own flow, taking as much time as necessary to grasp a concept or covering the material more rapidly. This flexibility provides for various ways of learning and interests

Homework Assistance

It's important to remember that teachers and other educators continue to play a critical role in shaping kids' educational pathways, even though Chat GPT may be a helpful tool for helping students with their assignments. It is necessary in a variety of ways to assist kids with their homework:

- *Rapid Responses*: Chat GPT offers students accurate and prompt responses when they are struggling with a concept or issue on their project. Because of this prompt assistance, students experience less frustration and maintain their enthusiasm in their work.

- *Clarifications and explanations*: Chat GPT can do not just simply provide answers; it can also explain the solutions and the underlying concepts, which will help students comprehend the material. This promotes deeper learning and comprehension.

- *Practice and Examples:* Students can strengthen their comprehension and hone their problem-solving abilities by using Chat GPT to produce extra practice problems and examples linked to the homework. Mastery requires this further practice.

- *Topic Coverage*: Chat GPT is an adaptable tool that may assist in a range of topics, such as arithmetic, physics, language, and history. For students who require assistance with multiple subjects, it can serve as a one-stop shop. With Chat GPT available to them 24/7, students can provide assistance outside of the designated classroom hours. Because assistance is offered around-the-clock, it can accommodate different study schedules and time zones and is particularly useful when needed.

- *Independence & Self-Reliance:* By utilizing Chat GPT, students can enhance both their degree of independence and problem-solving skills. They learn how to solve problems on their own and get more confidence in their ability to finish assignments.

- *Reduced Stress*: By ensuring that students have the resources they need to do their work successfully, Chat GPT's homework assistance helps reduce the stress that comes with challenging assignments.

- *Consistency:* Chat GPT provides uniform and consistent assistance, ensuring that each student receives the same level of guidance. You can maintain educational equity and ensure that no student is left behind by doing this.

Availability

Chat GPT is essential for increasing student accessibility since it provides a range of customizable tools and functionalities. Through text-to-speech conversion, language support, and reading assistance, it makes instructional content more accessible for students with visual impairments, language barriers, or reading difficulties. By its adaptable features, which ensure a comfortable and friendly experience, students may modify the learning environment to their preferences. Chat GPT ensures that educational resources are accessible to students with impairments and those who prefer various learning modes by creating alternative formats and providing transcripts or subtitles for multimedia content. This encourages diversity, expands equitable access to education, and improves the effectiveness with which all students engage with the course materials.

Language Training

For students attempting to learn a language, ChatGPT is a valuable resource. Above all, it provides a venue for practicing conversations. Through text-based exchanges, students can enhance their language skills in a casual environment by taking part in dialogues and getting responses that mimic real-world conversations. Along with enhancing their speaking and listening abilities, it can boost students' confidence in speaking the language and offer immediate feedback on vocabulary, grammar, and pronunciation, helping them to identify and fix errors—an essential part of language learning.

Chat GPT can assist with grammatical correction. It may identify and highlight vocabulary and grammar errors in students' written responses and provide suggestions and explanations for improvement. Students can ensure that their written communication is more exact and well-organized by using this function to assist them write better. Additionally, it can provide translations and synonyms, enabling students to express themselves more effectively and expand their vocabulary. In essence, Chat GPT aids students in their language learning process by offering helpful resources, encouraging feedback, and opportunities for language practice.

Instant Support

Chat GPT is a vital resource for students seeking immediate assistance, offering direction and responses to their questions at the very moment they require it. The availability of assistance to pupils 24/7 ensures that they can seek it out when it's most convenient for them to study and pose queries. For anyone who needs to rapidly get information or has complex homework questions or inquiries about challenging subjects, Chat GPT is a fast and trustworthy resource. Giving students the flexibility to find solutions and insights in real time enhances their educational experience overall, reduces academic stress and frustration, and encourages independent learning.

Study Materials

Chat GPT is a great place for students to find educational materials. It can recommend works of literature, films, audiobooks, and other instructional materials related to the subjects. By introducing them to a range of additional material, this tool helps students understand a subject better and saves them time when looking for reliable sources. By offering practice tests, flashcards, and study strategies tailored to each student's needs, it can help students make the most of their study time and review efficiently. It also gives students access to a wide range of study resources that will help them achieve academic success and encourage a more thorough and effective approach to studying.

Lifelong Learning

Chat GPT plays a significant role in supporting students' pursuit of lifelong learning in various ways. First and foremost, it is an extensive and user-friendly information source that covers a wide range of topics and questions. Those that are always eager to learn new things will find this to be quite beneficial. For those who are learning a new language, taking up a new hobby, or exploring a completely uncharted territory, Chat GPT can provide explanations and insights.

It can make recommendations for books, online courses, and other educational items, assisting users in finding the most relevant and up-to-date resources for their self-directed learning trips. It can also assist with research by pointing students in the direction of reliable papers, studies, and articles that will strengthen their understanding of a particular topic. Self-paced learning is made possible by Chat GPT, encouraging lifelong learning. Individuals can pursue their interests at their own speed because to its support for a variety of schedules and learning methods. This flexibility may be especially useful for people who lead busy lives, have demanding work, or have obligations to their families. Generally speaking, Chat GPT provides individuals with the means, guidance, and resources need to embark on a lifetime path of personal development. This adds value and fulfilment to learning new things.

Data-Driven Observations: Chat GPT Can Assist Students in Gaining Data-Driven Insights in a Number of Ways

- *Performance tracking*: By compiling and analysing data on interactions, responses, and progress over time, Chat GPT offers a comprehensive view of a student's educational experience.
- *Identifying Negative aspects*: Chat GPT evaluates a student's performance to pinpoint areas in which a student may be struggling or making mistakes a lot. This makes it easier to identify regions that require greater care.
- *Customized Recommendations*: Chat GPT can make use of data-driven insights to provide students recommendations for study materials, practice questions, or other teaching strategies that are appropriate for their particular needs.
- *Performance Evaluation*: Students can set goals and assess their degree of advancement over time by using the data provided by Chat GPT to track their own development.
- *Feedback Analysis*: By using Chat GPT's feedback analysis tool, which offers feedback on the Caliber of work and responses, students can learn how to enhance their learning process and discover their strengths and areas for improvement.
- *Adaptive learning*: Chat GPT can modify the speed and degree of difficulty of the content in response to data, ensuring that students are appropriately challenged and continue to develop a deeper understanding of the subject.

EDUCATIONAL FUNCTIONS OF ChatGPT IN TEACHING

Improvement of Materials

By satisfying a variety of learning demands and expanding the availability of educational resources, Chat GPT works with instructors to provide a more engaging and productive learning environment for their students.

- *Resource Creation*: Lesson plans, assessments, and assignments can all be created by teachers using Chat GPT. This AI tool helps teachers create content efficiently and rapidly, saving them time.
- *Customization of content:* Chat GPT is able to satisfy the individual demands of each learner by tailoring information to fit their own learning style and aptitude.
- *Multilingual Support:* To enable a diverse spectrum of students to access educational content, Chat GPT can assist with resource changes and translations into many languages.
- *Recommendation of Supplementary Materials*: To improve the learning experience and allow teachers access to a greater selection of resources, Chat GPT can make recommendations for additional books, movies, or interactive activities.
- *Accessibility elements*: Chat GPT can incorporate elements such as text-to-speech conversion and topic summaries to ensure that instructional materials are inclusive and appropriate for students with impairments.

- ***The discovery of Resources:*** By using Chat GPT to locate and choose instructional resources from a vast body of knowledge, teachers may keep current on the newest teaching pedagogies and methodologies.

Content Creation

Chat GPT gives teachers an adaptable and effective platform to produce a variety of educational materials, which substantially helps them in content creation. It aids in making sure that lesson plans, homework assignments, and tests are organized properly and meet learning goals. Instructors can utilize Chat GPT to simplify complex concepts into language that students can grasp. By expediting the process of locating and choosing extra materials, this AI technology helps teachers stay up to date with the latest teaching materials. Additionally, it offers bilingual assistance, making it easier to communicate with a varied student group. It might recommend cutting-edge instructional techniques and materials to deliver engaging and effective instruction. Teachers may use more of their time and energy to delivering excellent instruction and improving their students' educational experiences by making use of Chat GPT's capabilities.

Innovative Teaching Methods and Tutoring Support

In many respects, ChatGPT is a helpful tool for innovative teaching techniques and tutoring support. To begin with, students can gain from personalized and adaptable learning opportunities. ChatGPT may assess each student's individual needs through one-on-one conversations, answer questions, and provide answers in a conversational manner. This gives students the freedom to learn at their own pace and in a way that best suits their learning styles. It might give pupils instant feedback, which is important for their growth in identifying and correcting their mistakes.

When classes are not in session, ChatGPT can serve as a constant tutor, providing support and resources. It can help students with their homework, provide more practice problems, and even utilize a range of teaching techniques to make complex concepts easier to understand. With dependable and practical assistance, ChatGPT can close knowledge gaps and help learners understand the subject matter more thoroughly. Additionally, teachers can benefit from technology by having repetitive chores like handling administrative work and grading assignments automated, which frees them up to focus more on teaching and mentoring their students. Thus, ChatGPT advances innovative and successful teaching techniques while offering priceless tutoring support.

Automating Administrative Tasks

ChatGPT can assist teachers free up time to focus on teaching and student engagement rather than managing their workload by automating administrative tasks in the classroom. ChatGPT can be useful in this situation in the following ways:

- ***Feedback and Grading***: ChatGPT can automate the grading of assignments, tests, and quizzes. By putting up exact grading criteria, it may evaluate and provide comments on student work, including essays, short responses, and multiple-choice questions. Teachers gain a lot from this, particularly in large courses where efficiency is crucial.

- *Administration Communication*: ChatGPT can handle routine administration communication tasks, such as informing students of approaching deadlines, announcing announcements in class, and even responding to their frequent administrative questions. It can efficiently manage email correspondence, reducing the related workload.
- *Data management*: ChatGPT can support students with their data management and record-keeping needs. It can help in monitoring student achievement, maintaining and organizing attendance data, and generating dashboards or reports that educators can utilize to monitor their students' development.
- *Scheduling and Calendar Management*: ChatGPT helps teachers keep their calendars organized by helping with meeting, appointment, and class session planning, scheduling, and administration. When unanticipated events conflict with the regular class schedule, it can also assist with rescheduling or make-up class scheduling.
- *Resource Organization*: By using ChatGPT to gather and arrange educational resources, such as links to online articles, videos, or other learning materials, teachers may find it simpler to locate and share pertinent content with their students.

Data Analysis

Instructors can get a lot of help from ChatGPT in deciphering the vast amounts of instructional data they generate. Test results, attendance logs, and student performance statistics can all be processed and understood with its assistance. With ChatGPT's insights and reports, educators may effectively adjust their teaching tactics and interventions. These tools can also be used to identify patterns and identify specific areas where students could be performing below expectations. It can also make recommendations on the resources or instructional strategies that could be most beneficial for a particular set of students' needs. With ChatGPT, teachers can make data-driven decisions and are better equipped to guide and support students as they work toward more challenging learning goals.

Accessibility

ChatGPT can significantly improve the accessibility of instruction by offering inclusive and customized learning help. With choices for text-to-speech and speech-to-text capabilities, it can be a helpful tool for students with disabilities, making instructional information more accessible.

THE PROS AND CONS

There are several advantages of ChatGPT for education. It can help students by providing them with customized, one-on-one support for their questions, clarifications, and even specialized learning resources. This personalized assistance can be highly beneficial, especially in big courses where it might be challenging for teachers to satisfy each student's unique needs. Furthermore, ChatGPT can be an extremely useful tool for self-directed learning, offering students practice questions, explanations, and demonstrations outside of planned class periods. It can also automate administrative tasks like grading and correspondence, giving teachers more time for mentoring and instruction. Additionally, ChatGPT can promote diversity by offering accessibility features that facilitate the accessibility of educational resources for students with disabilities.

There are a few possible drawbacks to take into account. If the remarks made by ChatGPT are not always true or suitable for the situation, students could be misled. It is devoid of the human connection and empathy that come from being a teacher, and strong connections between educators and students require human interaction. Over-reliance on ChatGPT could lead to students losing their capacity for critical thought and problem-solving if they only employ automated solutions for their class requirements. Privacy and data security issues can arise from the possibility that using ChatGPT will need providing personal information to the technology provider. To sum up, even if ChatGPT offers a lot of educational advantages, it is essential to use it as an additional tool in conjunction with human educators.

DISCUSSIONS

There were more benefits than drawbacks to using ChatGPT. The impact of ChatGPT on teaching and learning was well covered above. This paper aims to identify the ways in which ChatGPT has influenced the area of education. A significant effort that can provide important insights into the possible advantages and difficulties of incorporating artificial intelligence technology into educational settings is researching ChatGPT's effects on education.

The strengths of this study are a thorough analysis of ChatGPT's effects on education would highlight a number of important advantages. First off, a thorough approach that included qualitative and quantitative data would offer a sophisticated comprehension of the issue. Confounding variable control and statistical analysis would increase the validity of the study's results. And also it make sure the results are applicable to actual educational contexts and that they are relevant.

ANALYSIS

Numerous advantages and uses for ChatGPT are shown by a survey looking at its usage in educational settings. The survey emphasizes how crucial it is to uphold ethical principles like data protection and making sure ChatGPT enhances human contact in learning environments rather than diminishes it.

The usage of ChatGPT by a thousand students is demonstrated in the following survey.

The survey of students about the use of ChatGPT, is depicted above. Out of 1000 students, 645 students answered Strongly agree for Question 1, which was about personalized learning. 577 were strongly agree for Question 2 which was about providing additional documents. But in the case of fifth and sixth question most of the people disagree, which was about the negative impacts of ChatGPT. By analysing the report, It is clear that students made greater use of ChatGPT's benefits than drawbacks.

The following table shows how one hundred instructors are using ChatGPT.

The survey of teachers about the use of ChatGPT, is shows above. Out of 100 teachers, 67 teachers answered Strongly agree for Question 1, which was about data management and documentation. 52 were strongly agree and 37 for agree for Question 2 which was about additional resources. But in the case of fifth and sixth question most of the people disagree, which was about the negative impacts of ChatGPT. By analysing the report, It is evident that educators utilized ChatGPT's advantages above its disadvantages.

Table 1. Usage of ChatGPT

Sl No	Questions	Strongly Agree	Agree	Disagree	Neutral
1	IS ChatGPT really helped for personalized learning?	645	210	114	31
2	ChatGPT provides additional materials to enhance the learning	577	321	16	86
3	ChatGPT really support for homework assistance	712	168	98	22
4	It is motivating and interesting	430	215	194	161
5	It provides negative impact of education	204	86	451	259
6	Can facilitate malicious use	65	119	519	243

Figure 1. Survey results on students' use of chatGPT

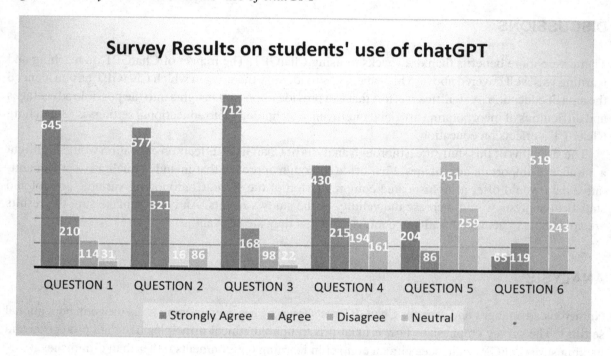

Table 2. Instructors' use of chatGPT

Sl No	Questions	Strongly Agree	Agree	Disagree	Neutral
1	IS ChatGPT helped for data management and documentation?	67	29	1	3
2	ChatGPT provides additional resources to enhance teaching?	52	37	8	3
3	Is ChatGPT really helped for administration communication?	71	22	2	5
5	It provides negative impact of education	20	15	65	0
6	Can facilitate malicious use	12	9	71	8

Figure 2. Survey results on teachers' use of chatGPT

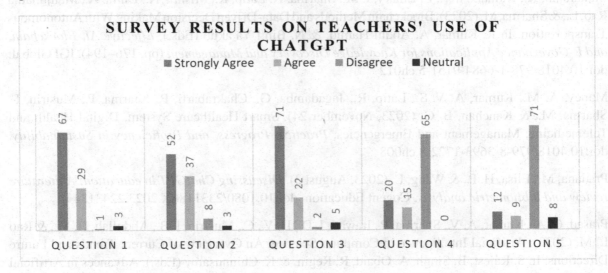

CONCLUSION

It is impossible to dispute ChatGPT's impact on the transformation in educational practices. It has brought in a new era of accessible and personalized learning experiences with resources and support tailored to each student's needs. Technology has not only made instructors' administrative tasks easier, but it has also enhanced their teaching methods and raised student achievement. Even though ChatGPT has made things better, it's important to remember that technology cannot replace real teachers and the close bonds they foster with their students. There is little doubt that ChatGPT will influence education in the future. The key to success is ensuring that students receive a thorough and well-rounded education by judiciously integrating new technology with traditional teaching methods. For educators, organizations, and legislators to properly embrace ChatGPT while upholding the core principles and values of education, they must remain adaptable, inquisitive, and imaginative.

REFERENCES

Ali, J. K. M., Shamsan, M. A. A., Hezam, T. A., & Mohammed, A. A. Q. (2023, March 7). Impact of ChatGPT on Learning Motivation. *Journal of English Studies in Arabia Felix*. doi:10.56540/jesaf.v2i1.51

De Castro, C. A. (2023, May 7). A Discussion about the Impact of ChatGPT in Education: Benefits and Concerns. *Journal of Business Theory and Practice*. https://doi.org/ doi:10.22158/jbtp.v11n2p28

Kaid Mohammed Ali, J. (2022). The Impact of Online Learning amid [Pandemic on Student Intrinsic Motivation and English Language Improvement. Dirasat: Human and Social Sciences.]. *COVID*, 19.

Kapadiya, D., Shekhawat, C., & Sharma, P. 2023. A Study on Large Scale Applications of Big Data in Modern Era. In *International Conference on Information Management & Machine Intelligence (ICIMMI2023)*. ACM. https://doi.org/10.1145/3647444.364788

Maharajan, K., Kumar, A. V., El Emary, I. M., Sharma, P., Latip, R., Mishra, N., Dutta, A., Manjunatha Rao, L., & Sharma, M. (2023). Blockchain Methods and Data-Driven Decision Making With Autonomous Transportation. In R. Kumar, A. Abdul Hamid, & N. Binti Ya'akub (Eds.), *Effective AI, Blockchain, and E-Governance Applications for Knowledge Discovery and Management* (pp. 176–194). IGI Global. doi:10.4018/978-1-6684-9151-5.ch012

Mancy, A. M., Kumar, A. V. S., Latip, R., Jagadamba, G., Chakrabarti, P., Sharma, P., Musirin, I., Sharma, M., & Kanchan, B. G. (2023, November 24). Smart Healthcare System, Digital Health and Telemedicine, Management and Emergencies. *Practice, Progress, and Proficiency in Sustainability*. doi:10.4018/979-8-3693-1722-8.ch008

Pradana, M., Elisa, H. P., & Wang, L. (2023, August 3). *Discussing ChatGPT in education: A literature review and bibliometric analysis.* Cogent Education. doi:10.1080/2331186X.2023.2243134

Prasad, G. A., Kumar, A. V., Sharma, P., Irawati, I. D., D. V., C., Musirin, I. B., Abdullah, H. M., & Rao L, M. (2023). Artificial Intelligence in Computer Science: An Overview of Current Trends and Future Directions. In S. Rajest, B. Singh, A. Obaid, R. Regin, & K. Chinnusamy (Eds.), Advances in Artificial and Human Intelligence in the Modern Era (pp. 43-60). IGI Global. https://doi.org/ doi:10.4018/979-8-3693-1301-5.ch002

Rawat, P., Bhardwaj, A., Lamba, N., & Sharma, P. (2023). Praveen Kumawat, Prateek Sharma, "Arduino Based IoT Mini Weather Station". *SKIT Research Journal*, *13*(2), 34–41. doi:10.47904/IJSKIT.13.2.2023.34-41

Sethi, S. S., & Sharma, P. (2023). New Developments in the Implementation of IoT in Agriculture. *SN Computer Science*, *4*(5), 503. doi:10.1007/s42979-023-01896-w

Sharma, P. (2023). *Utilizing Explainable Artificial Intelligence to Address Deep Learning in Biomedical Domain, Medical Data Analysis and Processing using Explainable Artificial Intelligence.* Taylor & Francis. doi:10.1201/9781003257721-2

Sharma, P., & Bhatnagar, N. (2023). Passenger Authentication and Ticket Verification at Airport Using QR Code Scanner. *SKIT Research Journal*, *13*(2), 10–13. doi:10.47904/IJSKIT.13.1.2023.10-12

Sharma, P., & Dadheech, P. (2023). Modern-age Agriculture with Artificial Intelligence: A review emphasizing Crop Yield Prediction. *EVERGREEN Joint Journal of Novel Carbon Resource Sciences & Green Asia Strategy*, *10*(4), 2570–2582. doi:10.5109/7160906

Sharma, P., Dadheech, P., Aneja, N., & Aneja, S. (2023). Predicting Agriculture Yields Based on Machine Learning Using Regression and Deep Learning. *IEEE Access : Practical Innovations, Open Solutions*, *11*, 111255–111264. doi:10.1109/ACCESS.2023.3321861

Sharma, P., Dadheech, P., & Senthil Kumar Senthil, A. V. (2023). AI-Enabled Crop Recommendation System Based on Soil and Weather Patterns. In R. Gupta, A. Jain, J. Wang, S. Bharti, & S. Patel (Eds.), *Artificial Intelligence Tools and Technologies for Smart Farming and Agriculture Practices* (pp. 184–199). IGI Global. doi:10.4018/978-1-6684-8516-3.ch010

Sharma, P., Kapadiya, D., & Bhardwaj, A. (2023). Efficient Note Sharing Model for Collaborative Learning. *SKIT Research Journal*, *13*(2), 42–46. doi:10.47904/IJSKIT.13.2.2023.42-46

Sharma, P., & Rathi, Y. (2016, June 5). Efficient Density-Based Clustering Using Automatic Parameter Detection. *Efficient Density-Based Clustering Using Automatic Parameter Detection*. SpringerLink. . doi:10.1007/978-981-10-0767-5_46

Tanwar, A., Sharma, P., Pandey, A., & Kumar, S. 2023. Intrusion Detection System Based Ameliorated Technique of Pattern Matching. In *Proceedings of the 4th International Conference on Information Management & Machine Intelligence (ICIMMI '22)*. Association for Computing Machinery, New York, NY, USA. 10.1145/3590837.3590947

V., M. V., Kumar, A. S., Sharma, P., Kaur, S., Saleh, O. S., Chennamma, H., & Chaturvedi, A. (2023). AI-Equipped IoT Applications in High-Tech Agriculture Using Machine Learning. In A. Khang (Ed.), *Handbook of Research on AI-Equipped IoT Applications in High-Tech Agriculture* (pp. 38-64). IGI Global. . doi:10.4018/978-1-6684-9231-4.ch003

Chapter 8
Beyond Boundaries:
Role of Artificial Intelligence and ChatGPT in Transforming Higher Education

Shikha Arora

https://orcid.org/0000-0001-8712-2905

Christ University, India

ABSTRACT

The goal of the proposed chapter is to give readers a thorough understanding of the complex effects of ChatGPT on higher education. It will cover the short- and long-term benefits that ChatGPT offers, as well as limitations that may affect both educators and learners. The chapter will also highlight a wide range of ethical issues and challenges that arise while using ChatGPT. Research in this area is very limited and the literature review reveals that there are benefits as well as limitations of using ChatGPT in the domain of higher education but the fact is that it is going to grow further which makes it an urgent need for the policymakers and stakeholders to explore and understand how ChatGPT should be integrated into higher education to deliver more value to the educators and learners. The proposed chapter will cover the evolution of ChatGPT, its growing popularity and impact, benefits it offers, the associated disadvantages and the road ahead.

INTRODUCTION

Artificial intelligence (AI) is proving to be a disruptive force across several industries, catalyzing innovative breakthroughs that are reshaping the manner that we live and work. One domain where AI's impact is particularly profound is education, an essential component of societal evolution and individual development. The amalgamation of AI tools into educational systems aims to redefine the learning experience for students, the teaching methods for educators, and the overall functioning of institutions. By tailoring learning and development experiences to individual needs, automating administrative tasks, and facilitating instantaneous feedback, AI is dramatically changing the educational landscape, enhancing

DOI: 10.4018/979-8-3693-6824-4.ch008

its inclusivity and effectiveness. However, as AI advances, it has become imperative that we consider its ramifications and adopt safeguards to ensure its responsible use.

One prominent application of AI in the field of education is natural language processing (NLP), exemplified by intelligent chatbots that have transformed customer service across various industries. In education, the application of chatbots is continuously on the rise, with studies revealing their potential to enhance students' learning experiences. In November 2022, the launch of ChatGPT marked a pivotal moment in adopting AI in education. Its exceptional comprehension and responding abilities captured the attention of a diverse audience and sparked debates within the entire educational community including basic level and higher level of education (Holmes et al., 2023). A more conversational and natural method of computer interaction is made possible by the language model known as ChatGPT. The term GPT, "Generative Pre-trained Transformer," refers to a group of natural language models created via open artificial intelligence (AI). Because of its capacity to generate unique outcomes, this is often referred to as generative AI.

Through the application of natural language processing and Internet data, ChatGPT enables users with textual responses based on artificial intelligence in response to prompts or requests.

For these models to produce coherent and convincing human-like output in response to a query or statement, they must first learn to predict the next word in a phrase using vast text datasets. Regarding ChatGPT, the system has been fed 570 GB of data, or 300 billion words, and has about 175 billion parameters.

ChatGPT can be viewed as a "computer robot" with the capability to converse like human beings. Its intuitive UI aids in this. Data, analysis, and even opinions can be requested via ChatGPT. However, because its interpretation is based on the statistical examination of billions of documents on the Internet, the algorithm that powers it does not choose a finite perspective (Oreshin et al., 2020).

Currently, the most recent free version of ChatGPT, GPT-3.5, is the foundation, and it is predicted that the upgraded versions will be more functional, with enhanced writing skills and the ability to analyze various kinds of data.

While educators have shown apprehensions and issues about potential academic dishonesty, several school districts and several institutions have prohibited its use on students' devices and institutional networks. However, it is becoming increasingly clear that incorporating AI tools into the present system of imparting education offers significant benefits, including smart tutoring systems, customized learning, and automated grading.

AI would be a game changer as it holds great potential in transforming education, extending it beyond chatbots, and includes need-based learning, practical and smart tutoring systems, automated assessment, and improved teacher-student collaboration. AI's scalability enables personalized learning, where algorithms adapt the educational process to meet individual students' needs. Intelligent tutoring systems interact with students, providing timely and accurate feedback. Automated grading can relieve instructors of the additional time consuming tasks of grading, permitting them to devote extra time to students, thereby enhancing learning outcomes.

AI's advantages in education are numerous. It enhances learning outcomes, increases cost and time efficiency, extends quality education globally, and offers other significant advantages. Customized learning and intelligent tutoring systems, in particular, help underserved populations access valuable learning opportunities. Automation of grading allows teachers to provide more specific need-based support. However, along with several benefits, specific risks and challenges also emerge(Amirov and Bilalova, 2020; Alasadi et al., 2023).

Figure 1. Comprehensive dimensions of AI
(Regona et al, 2022)

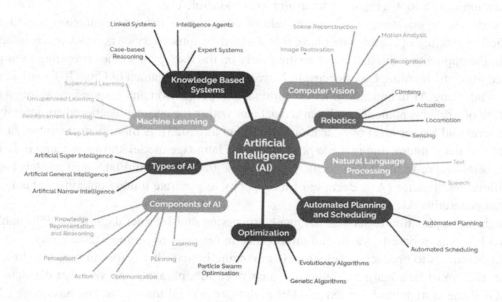

The integration of AI in the education sector necessitates a careful consideration of potential hazards. Young students, more susceptible to misinformation, require a cautious approach to AI implementation. Concerns about security and privacy, discrimination, and the teacher-student relationship are essential issues to address. Protecting students' personal information, minimizing biases in AI algorithms, and establishing comprehensive strategies are essential components of responsible AI utilization in education.

Despite the potential challenges, it has been witnessed that new technologies, when embraced and accompanied by appropriate safeguards, often yield more benefits than harm. The way forward involves not hindering AI's progress in education but rather integrating it with safeguards to harness its full potential. AI can revolutionize higher education, offering solutions to existing problems and making more meaningful and quality education accessible to all (Johnson, 2014; Rasul et al., 2023).

This chapter explores the role of AI in the Education system in the Indian context and the potential benefits it can bring. It highlights the need for AI interventions in various education segments, from personalized learning to teacher support. AI possesses the tremendous ability to address the low availability of quality teachers in India and make education more accessible to students in remote areas. AI in remote proctoring can also simplify the examination process, ensuring fairness and integrity.

The introduction of AI into higher education is completely transforming the ways how teachers and students are trained. This study is a sincere attempt to uncover the various facets of AI and ChatGPT in education, exploring its applications, advantages, and challenges to provide a holistic understanding of AI's role in higher education and its implications for the future.

Literature Review: Artificial Intelligence in Education (AIEd)

The incorporation of AIEd is marked by its potential to emulate human reasoning, decision-making, and problem-solving capabilities. Researchers define AI as a technology-driven system that replicates human-

Figure 2. Research in the domain of AI is expanding at a fast pace

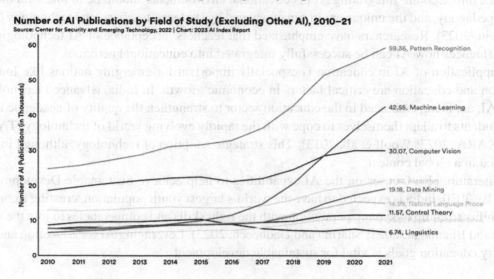

Number of AI Publications by Field of Study (Excluding Other AI), 2010–21
Source: Center for Security and Emerging Technology, 2022 | Chart: 2023 AI Index Report

like cognition and can execute tasks such as learning, reasoning, and self-correction. This integration of AI into education has attracted significant attention in recent years, with AI being synonymous with machine intelligence or computational intelligence (Park et al., 2021; Rakitov, 2018)

AI has been extensively applied to various domains, ranging from chess-playing algorithms and speech recognition systems to even diagnosing medical conditions. AI's ability to emulate human intelligence is a driving force behind its increasing application in the domain of education.

AI in Education (AIEd) represents one of the most promising and novel intersections of AI and educational technology. AIEd aims to mitigate the limitations associated with time and space, offering the benefit of portability. With AI learning systems, learners have the flexibility to access educational materials at their own convenience, engage in practice, and gather information at any time or place. These AI systems not only provide a wealth of learning materials but also offer guidance tailored to individual learners based on their specific environments (Regona et al., 2022; Renz et al, 2020).

A review of AIEd research papers published from 2011 to 2022 identified several key application areas, including profiling and prediction, assessment and evaluation, adaptive systems, personalization, and Intelligent Tutoring Systems (ITSs). ITSs, for instance, assume a significant role in offering personalized learning interfaces and materials by analyzing students' unique learning characteristics and statuses. This facilitates the selection of appropriate teaching learning strategies and approaches customized to individual learners' progress, offering timely guidance and assistance to enhance learning effectiveness (Sijing and Lan, 2018; Tahiru, 2021). Additionally, AI-based educational systems leverage big data analysis to create user learning models, targeting large-scale data sources in learning environments.

AI's Impact on Education and Sustainability Goals

AI technologies in education provide valuable insights into students' learning processes, enabling educators to provide proactive support and guidance when needed. The use of AI technologies can also enhance the quality of education and address sustainability goals. However, several considerations need to be taken into account. Integrating AI in educational environments should be in line with the learning content, pedagogy, and the unique environment shaped by students, teachers, and technology (Adeshola & Adepoju, 2023). Researchers have emphasized that teachers' acceptance of AI technologies significantly influences how AI can be successfully integrated into educational activities.

The application of AI in education is especially important for emerging nations like India, where population and education are critical factors in economic growth. In India, advanced technologies, including AI, are being embraced in the education sector to strengthen the quality of academic inputs and enable students to adapt themselves to cope with the rapidly evolving world of technology (TALAN and KALINKARA, 2023; Woolf et al., 2013). This strategic adoption of technology, although in progress, is essential in a global context.

The literature also focuses on the AI capabilities to help achieve Sustainable Development Goals (SDGs). By 2030, India is expected to have the world's largest youth population, creating a considerable responsibility to equip the young population with the right skills and competencies to join the workforce (Sharma and Bhatnagar, 2023; Sharma and Dadheech, 2023). Leveraging AI for education and addressing quality education goals is vital for sustainable development.

Specific Applications of AI in Education

Artificial intelligence (AI) has many applications in the educational sector, offering innovative ways to deliver the teaching and learning experience.

Real-time Text-to-Speech and Text Translation: AI technology can effectively bridge language gaps by seamlessly translating educational content into various regional languages. It makes learning materials more accessible and ensures that language diversity is accommodated, enabling a more conducive learning environment (Sharma et al., 2023; Tanwar et al., 2023).

Biometric Authentication: AI-driven biometric authentication simplifies administrative tasks like attendance tracking. Additionally, it serves as an essential indicator for monitoring participation rates and maintaining gender balance, contributing to the overall inclusiveness of educational settings.

Chatbots: Integrating chatbots into educational platforms can provide instant responses to student queries. This not only eases the workload of educators but also enhances student engagement and satisfaction by providing timely and personalized support.

Automated Grading and Personalization: AI, mainly through Natural Language Processing (NLP), streamlines the grading process, covering objective and subjective assessments. This not only saves time for educators but also improves the efficiency and accuracy of grading. It can analyze individual student needs and challenges to create personalized learning pathways (Sharma and Rathi, 2016; Sharma, 2023). These pathways offer customized content, feedback, and recommendations, effectively acting as a personalized tutor, thus improving learning outcomes and engagement.

Supervised Classification Models: AI can predict students at risk of dropping out by collecting and analyzing data at various stages of their educational journey. This early intervention can significantly reduce dropout rates and increase higher education enrolment (Prasad et al., 2023; Maharajan et al., 2023). Further, AI can be vital in addressing gender inequalities in education and supporting students with disabilities. For instance, it can assist visually impaired students through speech-to-text systems and identify speech patterns to aid students with conditions like autism.

These AI tools can revolutionize education, improving its efficiency, inclusivity, and accessibility for teachers and students in the long run. By utilizing these technologies, the education industry may adjust and progress to fulfill the varied requirements of students in the contemporary day.

Research Questions

RQ 1: Are AI systems evolving to adapt effectively across a wider spectrum of learning conditions, variables, and individual learning styles, moving beyond the predominant scenarios?

RQ 2: To what degree do AI technologies function as enhancers of human control and judgment in the context of student learning, rather than serving as replacements?

RQ 3: How can users be adequately informed and educated about the legal and ethical ramifications of sharing their data with AI-driven educational technologies, and what strategies can be employed to mitigate potential privacy risks effectively?

RQ 4: To what extent do educational technologies consider and address the intricate social dynamics of collaborative learning and working environments, and are there indications that technology is promoting oversimplification or the narrowing of human interactions in these contexts?

Opportunities and Risks Associated With the Use of ChatGPT

Owing to its ability to generate and analyse huge amount of information at a phenomenal speed, ChatGPT can serve as a game changer for administering various teaching and learning processes. Along with other forms of AI, ChatGPT could enhance the process and experience of learning for students as well as the educators. It can be used as a standalone tool, or it can be integrated into other systems and platforms used by Higher Educational Institutions (Sharma and Jain, 2023; Kapadiya et al., 2023). It can perform multiple tasks ranging from very simple to advanced technical like basic research, calculations, analysis and therefore it can be used to augment teaching and learning.

Along with the multiple opportunities being offered by ChatGPT, there are several associated risks also. The introduction and integration of AI in education requires a careful consideration of potential hazards. Young students and scholars are more vulnerable to misinformation and therefore a cautious approach to AI implementation should be adopted. Privacy and security concerns, bias and discrimination, and the teacher-student relationship are important issues to address (Merlin et al., 2024; Rawat et al., 2023). Protecting students' personal information, minimizing biases in AI algorithms, and establishing comprehensive strategies are essential components of responsible AI integration in education.

Generative AI, employing models such as GPT-3 and BERT, holds the transformative potential to revolutionize education across various applications. These text generation models offer innovative approaches to the teaching and learning processes within higher education.

TEXT GENERATION MODELS

Content Creation

Generative AI involves content generation, a process where artificial intelligence models, such as GPT (Generative Pre-trained Transformer) and similar architectures, generate new, coherent, and contextually relevant content based on the provided input. These models are designed to produce text that resembles human-written content. Content generation in generative AI finds applications in various tasks, including the creation of educational materials like study guides, lesson plans, and articles. This capability enables educators to consistently generate high-quality resources.

Automated Grading

Leveraging artificial intelligence models, often constructed on generative architectures like GPT (Generative Pre-trained Transformer), enables the automated grading of assignments, quizzes, and exams. Here's a detailed breakdown of the automated grading process:

- **Data Collection:** Compile a dataset containing sample graded assignments along with corresponding grading rubrics or correct answers. Train the generative AI model, such as GPT, using this dataset.
- **Model Training:** Select and train a generative AI model suitable for the grading task. Adjust models like GPT to comprehend the relationships between questions, prompts, and accurate answers based on the provided dataset.
- **Specify Grading Standards:** Clearly define the standards, guidelines, and grading criteria the generative AI model should follow when evaluating answers. This step is crucial to ensure that grading aligns with the intended standards.
- **Grading System Integration:** Integrate the trained generative AI model into the platform or grading system used by educational institutions. This may involve creating APIs or integrating the model into an existing Learning Management System (LMS).
- **Student Submission:** Students submit their assignments and tests using the integrated platform. Submissions may include code, text responses, or other relevant materials.
- **Analysis of Responses:** The generative AI model examines each student's response using the predetermined grading criteria. It considers elements like accuracy, applicability, thoroughness, and adherence to rules.
- **Scoring and Feedback Generation**: The model assigns a score to each response and provides students with feedback. Feedback may include explanations for correct answers, identification of mistakes in incorrect answers, and suggestions for improvement.
- **Human Oversight and Validation:** Implement a system of human oversight to verify the grades generated by AI. Human reviewers ensure fairness, check for accuracy, and address any potential biases in the grading process.
- **Security Measures:** Implement security measures to detect and prevent cheating and plagiarism. This may involve using additional algorithms or tools to maintain the integrity of the assessment process.

Question Generation

To promote active learning and assist educators in assessing students' understanding, GPT models can generate practice problems and quiz questions.

Tutoring and Homework Assistance

Utilizing artificial intelligence technologies for tutoring and homework assistance involves providing personalized and interactive support to students. Here are key aspects of this approach:

- **Virtual Tutors:** Develop virtual tutors powered by AI to assist students across various subjects. These online tutors guide students through course materials, explain concepts, and address inquiries.
- **Adaptive Learning:** Implement adaptive learning systems that assess student performance and tailor tutoring sessions based on individual strengths and limitations. AI adjusts the difficulty level of questions and provides focused support.
- **Real-time Feedback:** AI offers immediate feedback on student answers, aiding comprehension of errors and directing them towards correct solutions. This real-time feedback enhances the learning process.
- **Multimodal Learning:** Enhance tutoring sessions with multimedia components such as interactive simulations, videos, and diagrams. AI recommends relevant multimedia resources based on each learner's unique preferences.
- **Determining Learning Styles:** Employ AI algorithms to identify students' learning preferences and styles. Customize tutoring strategies to ensure each student grasps the covered material.
- **Interactive Chatbots:** Introduce interactive chatbots for homework assistance. By interacting with these chatbots, students can get support, extra materials, and detailed instructions on how to solve problems.
- **Language Translation Support:** Utilize AI for language translation, grammar correction, and contextual examples to aid students in understanding and completing language learning assignments.
- **Scaffolded Learning:** AI provides scaffolded learning support, cascading down complicated issues into simple steps that can be managed easily. This approach helps students develop a more comprehensive understanding of the covered concepts.
- **Reinforcement of Concepts:** AI identifies areas where students may struggle and suggests additional readings or activities to reinforce key concepts.
- **Help with Programming:** Leverage models like OpenAI Codex, trained on a vast amount of code from various sources to assist users in coding. Integrate Codex into tools or programming environments for code writing support.

Integration into Existing Systems

Generative AI can significantly enhance diverse facets of teaching and learning within existing educational systems, offering valuable support.

- **Learning Management Systems (LMS):** Integrating generative AI into Learning Management Systems (LMS) platforms holds the potential to enhance support, streamline communication, and introduce interactive elements, creating a more dynamic and engaging learning experience for both educators and learners.

- **Advising and Counselling Services:** Generative AI is crucial in offering academic guidance by assisting students in course planning, primary selection, and career navigation. Leveraging field trends and historical data, the AI delivers personalized recommendations. Additionally, the technology facilitates tailored counseling sessions conducted by virtual counseling assistants driven by generative AI. These sessions address various issues, including career-related anxieties, stress management, and academic challenges. Furthermore, AI-powered chatbots are designed to provide students with empathetic emotional support, engaging in private conversations to allow them to express their thoughts and concerns.

- **Library Resources:** Utilizing a generative AI-powered search assistant elevates the overall search experience, aiding users in discovering pertinent resources within the library catalog by comprehending natural language queries. Implement an AI-driven recommendation system suggesting articles, books, and resources personalized based on user preferences, borrowing history, and current trends. Establish a real-time virtual reference desk using generative AI to assist users with research inquiries, guide them to relevant sections, and furnish information about library services.

- **Administrative Support:** Develop a generative AI-driven system adept at efficiently addressing routine questions from staff, instructors, and students, delivering precise answers to frequently asked queries promptly. Establish a virtual help desk powered by generative AI, providing assistance with various administrative tasks and supplying information on campus resources, financial aid, and enrolment details. Leverage generative AI for the automated completion of forms and documentation, expediting administrative procedures like course registration, financial aid applications, and submission processes. Implement an AI system for scheduling appointments with administrative personnel, optimizing resource allocation for timely support to instructors and students.

Security Issues

The integration of generative AI in education introduces several privacy and security concerns that necessitate careful consideration and management. Key areas of concern include:

- **Data Privacy:** Training generative AI often requires large datasets, raising the need to safeguard sensitive student data. Educational institutions should implement robust data privacy policies to protect student identities and personal information.

- **Student Data Protection:** The processing of extensive student data is inherent in generative AI use in educational settings. Institutions must implement strict safeguards against misuse, breaches, and unauthorized access, ensuring compliance with data protection laws such as FERPA and GDPR.

- **Informed Consent:** Ensuring teachers and students are aware of how generative AI is used and obtaining explicit consent for data usage promotes transparency and empowers individuals to decide whether to participate.

- **Algorithmic Bias and Fairness:** Generative AI models may unintentionally reinforce biases present in training data, affecting various aspects of education. Regular audits and assessments are necessary to identify and rectify algorithmic bias.

- **Security of AI Models:** Securing AI models is crucial to prevent unauthorized access or manipulation. Institutions need safeguards to maintain the confidentiality and integrity of models, especially when they involve sensitive data or proprietary algorithms.

- **Third-Party Services:** Educational institutions often rely on third-party services for generative AI solutions. It's essential to ensure these providers adhere to strict security and privacy guidelines, requiring careful selection and screening of reliable partners.

- **Student Tracking and Profiling:** While generative AI can enhance personalized learning experiences, tracking and profiling students should strike a balance to avoid intrusive surveillance that violates privacy rights.

- **Ethical Use of AI:** Establishing standards for the ethical application of generative AI in the classroom, defining acceptable and unacceptable uses, and aligning AI technologies with moral principles and educational ideals are critical considerations.

- **Secure Communication Channels:** Generative AI systems integrated into learning platforms should utilize secure communication channels. Encrypting data transmission enhances protection against interception, especially when dealing with sensitive information.

- **Conduct Regular Audits and Assessments:** Regular audits and assessments of generative AI systems are essential to identify and address security vulnerabilities, privacy issues, and potential shortcomings, ensuring ongoing compliance with evolving security requirements.

Preparing Students for the Future

Preparing Students for the Future: Generative Artificial Intelligence (AI) in education presents a unique opportunity to equip students for the challenges and opportunities that lie ahead.

- **Promoting Digital Literacy:** Exposure to generative AI technologies enhances students' understanding of technology and familiarity with cutting-edge tools shaping diverse industries. Hands-on experience with these applications deepens their comprehension of AI-driven technologies and their practical applications.

- **Problem-solving and Critical Thinking:** Generative AI fosters critical thinking by requiring students to grasp underlying algorithms and make informed decisions about their applications. Utilizing AI tools to solve complex problems not only enhances problem-solving skills but also nurtures an innovative and adaptable mindset.

- **Tailored Educational Experiences:** Generative AI enables personalized learning experiences tailored to the unique needs and preferences of each student. Emphasizing self-directed learning, students can progress at their own pace, a crucial skill for navigating future educational and professional landscapes.

- **Innovation and Creative Expression:** AI-generated tools unlock creativity, facilitating the generation of novel ideas across various disciplines. Collaborating with AI systems allows students to push the boundaries of conventional creativity, fostering an innovative culture.

- **Analytics and Data Literacy:** Interacting with generative AI involves working with data, contributing to the development of students' data literacy. Exposure to data analytics tools integrated into AI systems hones critical thinking and decision-making abilities essential for future career success.

- **Digital Citizenship and Ethical AI Use**: Introducing generative AI into the classroom provides an opportunity to instil responsible AI application. Teaching digital citizenship principles equips students with ethical and responsible attitudes, preparing them to use technology ethically and responsibly in the future.

Finally, the introduction of generative AI into the classroom stimulates the growth of critical thinking, creativity, data analytics, technology literacy, ethical AI use, and adaptability—all vital life skills. For pupils to successfully navigate the difficulties of the future, these abilities are essential. AI in the classroom improves student performance and equips them for success in a world that is becoming more technologically sophisticated. In conclusion, generative AI's significant influence on education presents innovative chances to improve student learning outcomes and the educational process. As we use AI's benefits, we must strike a careful balance between innovation and protecting the rights and privacy of educators and students. Generic artificial intelligence can play a significant role in influencing the course of education if it is implemented carefully, continuously monitored, and adheres to ethical standards. Prioritizing privacy and security safeguards is essential for educational institutions to fully realize the potential of generative AI while protecting teachers and students. For ethical and successful AI integration in education, a robust framework for privacy and security that is characterized by transparent policies, open communication, and continual assessment must be established.

AI- Challenges and Opportunities

Incorporating AI into education has the potential to address key challenges and create opportunities for more accessible and inclusive learning environments. While challenges and complexities exist, AI's role in education, along with its support for sustainability goals, cannot be overstated. The integration of AI technologies into education systems represents a dynamic and transformative development that holds promise for more equitable and effective learning experiences (Arora et al., 2023).

The Emergence of AI in Indian Education

Artificial Intelligence (AI) has recently begun making inroads into the Indian education sector. However, it has yet to reach a level of disruption and radical change. This shift aligns with the National Education Policy (NEP) 2020, which underscores the pivotal role AI will play in India's education system, from kindergarten to higher education. The potential AI offers in improving the learning experience, governance, teaching, and learning outcomes is substantial. AI has the potential to streamline various aspects of education in India, mainly due to the ongoing massification of higher education (Ryu and Han, 2019; Sharonova and Avdeeva, 2021; Sharma et al., 2023). It can play a significant role in providing feedback and guidance to students, enhancing learning analytics, evaluating curricular materials for quality, and facilitating adaptive learning. This infusion of AI into the education sector holds the promise of creating a unique and personalized learning experience.

Administrative Efficiency and Transparency

Administrative processes within educational institutions face challenges in India, including student loan schemes, curriculum updates, and hierarchical decision-making. AI-driven technological platforms can improve efficiency and transparency. For example, in the case of student loans, AI can evaluate variables related to academic and non-academic performance, making the process more efficient and transparent. AI can also identify outdated curricula and recommend updates, ensuring quality education (Villarreal et al., 2023; Mishra et al., 2023; Sharma et al., 2023). Additionally, AI can simplify administrative procedures and enhance the accountability of teachers, thus benefiting the overall teaching-learning process.

Achieving Coherence and Empowering Educators

The Indian education system suffers from a lack of coherence and coordination among various regulatory bodies, educational institutions, and policy-making bodies. For example, the approval process for new courses is cumbersome, leading to delays and fund diversion. To address these macro-level administrative issues, a coherent system that facilitates coordination among stakeholders is essential. AI can significantly alleviate the non-teaching workload of educators, enabling them to focus more on their core teaching activities. Tasks like evaluation, paperwork, interaction with parents, and procurement of study materials can be streamlined through AI-based systems. These platforms can also provide a first-line interaction with parents and grant teachers access to necessary resources for effective feedback and communication.

Today's college students have a remarkable opportunity to engage in interactive and highly personalized learning experiences, thanks to the integration of AI technology (Dilmurod and Fazliddin, 2021; Etzioni & Etzioni, 2017; Sharma et al., 2023). AI, fuelled by extensive data, can craft individualized educational paths for students. Simultaneously, educators can gain valuable insights into various learning styles, enabling them to tailor their teaching methods accordingly.

CHALLENGES

Threat to Intellectual Integrity

Concerns over the heightened possibility of plagiarism and cheating have been raised by HEIs and educators in relation to students using ChatGPT to study for or produce essays and tests. This might have more profound effects on subjects where information retention or textual inputs are more important—areas where ChatGPT excels.

It's possible that ChatGPT's writing will render the current plagiarism detection systems ineffective. Other programmes that can determine whether AI has been employed in literature have already been developed as a result of this. Meanwhile, a number of HEIs worldwide have prohibited ChatGPT because of worries about academic integrity, and others have updated or modified their evaluation procedures to rely more heavily on in-class or unwritten assignments.

Data Protection Considerations

Due to privacy concerns, ChatGPT was blocked for the first time in Italy in April 2023. The nation's data protection body declared that the gathering and archiving of private information for ChatGPT's training had no legal justification. The incapacity of the tool to ascertain a user's age, which means that minors may be exposed to comments that are unsuitable for their age, has also drawn ethical concerns from the authority. This example draws attention to more general concerns about the kind of data being gathered, who is collecting them, and how AI uses them.

Information Processing Bias

It is crucial to remember that ChatGPT lacks ethical standards and is unable to discriminate between good and wrong, genuine and false. This programme exclusively gathers data from online databases and texts that it analyses, which means that any cognitive bias present in the data is also learned. As a result, it is crucial to evaluate the information it yields critically and contrast it with data from other sources.

Geographic Inclusiveness

Regarding ChatGPT's accessibility, there are two key issues. The first is that the tool is unavailable in some nations because of censorship, government laws, or other online limitations. Regarding the unequal distribution of internet availability, cost, and speed, the second problem is more general in nature and has to do with equity and access.

   Accordingly, there hasn't been a global distribution of AI research and development, with certain areas having a considerably lower likelihood of producing resources or knowledge on the subject.

Risk of Commercial Exploitation

OpenAI, a private firm, developed ChatGPT. Although the company has promised to keep ChatGPT free, it has also introduced a subscription option (currently US$20/month) that provides improved dependability and quicker access to tool updates. Since private organisations have long been involved in higher education, caution and regulation are necessary when choosing AI and other tools that are operated by businesses that rely on profit, may not be open source (and thus more accessible and equitable), and may extract data for profit.

The Perspective of Educators, Policymakers, and Learners

The use of AI in higher education has the potential to completely transform how students learn and how teachers support it. Diverse expert opinions exist about the role of AI technologies, their suitability for higher education, and their effects on student growth, learning, evaluation and assessment, and certification—particularly in the context of an education system that is predominately human-driven. While many educators and practitioners see ChatGPT as an essential tool that may support learning and development in novel ways and have advocated for regulation, others see it as a danger to the fundamental goals of education. ChatGPT has experienced the most customer growth since its launch and now serves over 100 million active users despite the digital divide.

Conclusion and Future Research Directions

Adopting these technologies can give businesses in the EdTech sector and higher education institutions a competitive edge. They can better address the growing need for flexible and individualized education if they are open to trying new things. An attractive path for integrating AI and ML in higher education is to take a data-driven strategy with machine learning at its center.

   Though AI and ML have transformed numerous industries, they haven't had much of an impact on higher education. This ground-breaking study provides insightful information about the application of

AI in higher education, a field facing difficulties made worse by the epidemic, including enrollment and financial concerns. However, in order to survive and improve the educational experience for their students, many institutions of higher learning strive to promote innovation.

Despite being a relatively new and rapidly evolving field, AI has deep roots in established disciplines such as computer science, psychology, language science, philosophy, statistics, mathematics, and electrical engineering. The importance of AI is growing, especially as financial and enrolment pressures mount in higher education. This has led to the development of cost-effective technologies that provide personalized support to students, including chatbots and instant self-service solutions, driving innovation in higher education. Furthermore, the use of cutting-edge AI and ML methodologies accelerates technological advancements, effectively condensing a decade's worth of work into a shorter timeframe. AI plays a pivotal role in delivering a consistent and accessible customer experience, although specific sectors, such as healthcare, grapple with ethical considerations related to preserving individuality and black-box models in AI (Au-Yong-Oliveira et al., 2020; Bilad et al., 2023; Sethi and Sharma, 2023).

Affordable and accessible AI holds significant promise, currently positioned at the "lower" end of the AI spectrum. Nevertheless, when implemented effectively, its impact and depth will expand over time. In the context of middle-income countries, this research study sheds light on the opportunities and challenges of implementing AI and ML in higher education institutions (HEIs) and offers lessons that can be applied in these settings (Lytras, 2023; Malinka et al., 2023; Kumar et al., 2023).

Addressing a research gap identified during the literature review, the primary focus is on overcoming the obstacles associated with AI and ML adoption in HEIs, with a particular emphasis on their relevance to low- and middle-income countries, where the existing literature lacks sufficient recommendations. It's important to acknowledge that, like any research endeavor, this study has limitations, including social desirability, generalizability, imprecise measurement, and unexplored questions. Since this is an original research paper, references to prior work are limited, but it does lay the foundation for future research. Subsequent studies should concentrate on proposing concrete AI and ML platforms and projects for Higher Educational Institutions, particularly in low- and middle-income countries, while promoting best practices to effectively address their challenges.

REFERENCES

Adeshola, I., & Adepoju, A. P. (2023). The opportunities and challenges of ChatGPT in education. *Interactive Learning Environments*, 1–14. doi:10.1080/10494820.2023.2253858

Alasadi, E. A., & Baiz, C. R. (2023). Generative AI in Education and Research: Opportunities, Concerns, and Solutions. *Journal of Chemical Education*, *100*(8), 2965–2971. doi:10.1021/acs.jchemed.3c00323

. Amirov, R. A., & Bilalova, U. M. (2020). Prospects for the introduction of artificial intelligence technologies in higher education. *Administrative consulting*, (3). doi:10.22394/1726-1139-2020-3-80-88

Arora, S., Kr Jha, A., & Upadhyay, S. (2023). *Predicting a Rise in Employee Attrition Rates Through the Utilization of People Analytics*. 2023 12th International Conference on System Modeling & Advancement in Research Trends (SMART), Moradabad, India. 10.1109/SMART59791.2023.10428268

Au-Yong-Oliveira, M., Lopes, C., Soares, F., Pinheiro, G., & Guimarães, P. (2020, June). What can we expect from the future? The impact of artificial intelligence on society. In *2020 15th Iberian Conference on Information Systems and Technologies (CISTI)* (pp. 1-6). IEEE. 10.23919/CISTI49556.2020.9140903

. Bilad, M. R., Yaqin, L. N., & Zubaidah, S. (2023). Recent Progress in the Use of Artificial Intelligence Tools in Education. *Jurnal Penelitian dan Pengkajian Ilmu Pendidikan: e-Saintika, 7*(3), 279-314. doi:10.36312/esaintika.v7i3.1377

. Dilmurod, R., & Fazliddin, A. (2021). Prospects for the introduction of artificial intelligence technologies in higher education. *ACADEMICIA: an international multidisciplinary research journal, 11*(2), 929-934. doi:10.5958/2249-7137.2021.00468.7

Etzioni, A., & Etzioni, O. (2017). Incorporating ethics into artificial intelligence. *The Journal of Ethics, 21*(4), 403–418. doi:10.1007/s10892-017-9252-2

Holmes, W., Bialik, M., & Fadel, C. (2023). *Artificial intelligence in education.* Globethics Publications. doi:10.58863/20.500.12424/4273108

Johnson, J. A. (2014). The ethics of big data in higher education. *International Journal of Information Ethics, 21*, 3–10. doi:10.29173/irie365

Kapadiya, D., Shekhawat, C., & Sharma, P. 2023. A Study on Large Scale Applications of Big Data in Modern Era. *In International Conference on Information Management & Machine Intelligence (ICIMMI2023).* ACM. https://doi.org/10.1145/3647444.364788

Lytras, M. D. (2023). Active and Transformative Learning (ATL) in Higher Education in Times of Artificial Intelligence and ChatGPT: Investigating a New Value-Based Framework. In Active and transformative learning in STEAM disciplines: From curriculum design to social impact (pp. 5-23). Emerald Publishing Limited. doi:10.1108/978-1-83753-618-420231001

Maharajan, K., Kumar, A. V., El Emary, I. M., Sharma, P., Latip, R., Mishra, N., Dutta, A., Manjunatha Rao, L., & Sharma, M. (2023). Blockchain Methods and Data-Driven Decision Making With Autonomous Transportation. In R. Kumar, A. Abdul Hamid, & N. Binti Ya'akub (Eds.), *Effective AI, Blockchain, and E-Governance Applications for Knowledge Discovery and Management* (pp. 176–194). IGI Global. doi:10.4018/978-1-6684-9151-5.ch012

Malinka, K., Peresíni, M., Firc, A., Hujnák, O., & Janus, F. (2023, June). On the educational impact of ChatGPT: Is Artificial Intelligence ready to obtain a university degree? In *Proceedings of the 2023 Conference on Innovation and Technology in Computer Science Education* V. 1 (pp. 47-53). 10.1145/3587102.3588827

Merlin Mancy, A., Kumar, A. V., Latip, R., Jagadamba, G., Chakrabarti, P., Sharma, P., Musirin, I. B., Sharma, M., & Kanchan, B. G. (2024). Smart Healthcare System, Digital Health and Telemedicine, Management and Emergencies: Patient Emergency Application (PES) E-Governance Applications. In R. Kumar, A. Abdul Hamid, N. Binti Ya'akub, H. Sharan, & S. Kumar (Eds.), *Sustainable Development in AI, Blockchain, and E-Governance Applications* (pp. 124–151). IGI Global., doi:10.4018/979-8-3693-1722-8.ch008

Michel-Villarreal, R., Vilalta-Perdomo, E., Salinas-Navarro, D. E., Thierry-Aguilera, R., & Gerardou, F. S. (2023). Challenges and opportunities of generative AI for higher education as explained by ChatGPT. *Education Sciences, 13*(9), 856. doi:10.3390/educsci13090856

Mishra, P., Warr, M., & Islam, R. (2023). TPACK in the age of ChatGPT and Generative AI. *Journal of Digital Learning in Teacher Education, 39*(4), 235–251. doi:10.1080/21532974.2023.2247480

Oreshin, S., Filchenkov, A., Petrusha, P., Krasheninnikov, E., Panfilov, A., Glukhov, I., & Kozlova, D. (2020, October). Implementing a Machine Learning Approach to Predicting Students' Academic Outcomes. In *Proceedings of the 2020 1st International Conference on Control, Robotics and Intelligent System* (pp. 78-83). ACM. 10.1145/3437802.3437816

Park, C. S. Y., Haejoong, K. I. M., & Sangmin, L. E. E. (2021). Do less teaching, do more coaching: Toward critical thinking for ethical applications of artificial intelligence. *Journal of Learning and Teaching in Digital Age*, 6(2), 97–100. doi:10.1145/306363.306372

Prasad, G. A., Kumar, A. V., Sharma, P., Irawati, I. D., D. V., C., Musirin, I. B., Abdullah, H. M., & Rao L, M. (2023). Artificial Intelligence in Computer Science: An Overview of Current Trends and Future Directions. In S. Rajest, B. Singh, A. Obaid, R. Regin, & K. Chinnusamy (Eds.), Advances in Artificial and Human Intelligence in the Modern Era (pp. 43-60). IGI Global. https://doi.org/ doi:10.4018/979-8-3693-1301-5.ch002

. Rakitov, A. I. (2018). Higher education and artificial intelligence: euphoria and alarmism. *Vysshee obrazovanie v Rossii= Higher Education in Russia*, 27(6), 41-49.

Rasul, T., Nair, S., Kalendra, D., Robin, M., de Oliveira Santini, F., Ladeira, W. J., & Heathcote, L. (2023). The role of ChatGPT in higher education: Benefits, challenges, and future research directions. *Journal of Applied Learning and Teaching*, 6(1). doi:10.37074/jalt.2023.6.1.29

Rawat, P., Bhardwaj, A., Lamba, N., & Sharma, P. (2023). Praveen Kumawat, Prateek Sharma, "Arduino Based IoT Mini Weather Station". *SKIT Research Journal*, 13(2), 34–41. doi:10.47904/IJSKIT.13.2.2023.34-41

Regona, M., Yigitcanlar, T., Xia, B., & Li, R. Y. M. (2022). Opportunities and adoption challenges of AI in the construction industry: A PRISMA review. *Journal of Open Innovation*, 8(45), 45. doi:10.3390/joitmc8010045

Renz, A., Krishnaraja, S., & Gronau, E. (2020). Demystification of Artificial Intelligence in Education–How much AI is really in the Educational Technology? [iJAI]. *International Journal of Learning Analytics and Artificial Intelligence for Education*, 2(1), 14. doi:10.3991/ijai.v2i1.12675

Ryu, M., & Han, S. (2019). AI education programs for deep-learning concepts. *Journal of the Korean Association of information. Education*, 23(6), 583–590. doi:10.14352/jkaie.2019.23.6.583

Sethi, S. S., & Sharma, P. (2023). New Developments in the Implementation of IoT in Agriculture. *SN Computer Science*, 4(5), 503. doi:10.1007/s42979-023-01896-w

Sharma, P. (2023). *Utilizing Explainable Artificial Intelligence to Address Deep Learning in Biomedical Domain, Medical Data Analysis and Processing using Explainable Artificial Intelligence*. Taylor & Francis. doi:10.1201/9781003257721-2

Sharma, P., & Bhatnagar, N. (2023). Passenger Authentication and Ticket Verification at Airport Using QR Code Scanner. *SKIT Research Journal*, 13(2), 10–13. doi:10.47904/IJSKIT.13.1.2023.10-12

Sharma, P., & Dadheech, P. (2023). Modern-age Agriculture with Artificial Intelligence: A review emphasizing Crop Yield Prediction. *EVERGREEN Joint Journal of Novel Carbon Resource Sciences & Green Asia Strategy*, 10(4), 2570–2582. doi:10.5109/7160906

Sharma, P., Dadheech, P., Aneja, N., & Aneja, S. (2023). Predicting Agriculture Yields Based on Machine Learning Using Regression and Deep Learning. *IEEE Access : Practical Innovations, Open Solutions*, *11*, 111255–111264. doi:10.1109/ACCESS.2023.3321861

Sharma, P., Dadheech, P., & Senthil Kumar Senthil, A. V. (2023). AI-Enabled Crop Recommendation System Based on Soil and Weather Patterns. In R. Gupta, A. Jain, J. Wang, S. Bharti, & S. Patel (Eds.), *Artificial Intelligence Tools and Technologies for Smart Farming and Agriculture Practices* (pp. 184–199). IGI Global, doi:10.4018/978-1-6684-8516-3.ch010

Sharma, P., & Jain, M. K. (2023). Stock Market Trends Analysis using Extreme Gradient Boosting (XGBoost*). International Conference on Computing, Communication, and Intelligent Systems (ICCCIS)*, Greater Noida, India. 10.1109/ICCCIS60361.2023.10425722

Sharma, P., Kapadiya, D., & Bhardwaj, A. (2023). Efficient Note Sharing Model for Collaborative Learning. *SKIT Research Journal*, *13*(2), 42–46. doi:10.47904/IJSKIT.13.2.2023.42-46

. Sharma, P., & Rathi, Y. (2016, June 5). Efficient Density-Based Clustering Using Automatic Parameter Detection. *Efficient Density-Based Clustering Using Automatic Parameter Detection*. SpringerLink. . doi:10.1007/978-981-10-0767-5_46

Sharma, P., Sharma, C., & Mathur, P. (2023). Machine Learning-based Stock Market Forecasting using Recurrent Neural Network. *2023 9th International Conference on Smart Computing and Communications (ICSCC)*, Kochi, Kerala, India. 10.1109/ICSCC59169.2023.10335083

Sharonova, S., & Avdeeva, E. (2021). Dialogue between smart education and classical education. *Language and Dialogue*, *11*(1), 151–170. doi:10.1075/ld.00088.sha

Sijing, L., & Lan, W. (2018, August). Artificial intelligence education ethical problems and solutions. In *2018 13th International Conference on Computer Science & Education (ICCSE)* (pp. 1-5). IEEE. 10.1109/ICCSE.2018.8468773

Tahiru, F. (2021). AI in education: A systematic literature review. [JCIT]. *Journal of Cases on Information Technology*, *23*(1), 1–20. doi:10.4018/JCIT.2021010101

Talan, T., & Kalinkara, Y.TALAN. (2023). The role of artificial intelligence in higher education: Chat-GPT assessment for anatomy course. *Uluslararası Yönetim Bilişim Sistemleri ve Bilgisayar Bilimleri Dergisi*, *7*(1), 33–40. doi:10.33461/uybisbbd.1244777

Tanwar, A., Sharma, P., Pandey, A., & Kumar, S. 2023. Intrusion Detection System Based Ameliorated Technique of Pattern Matching. In *Proceedings of the 4th International Conference on Information Management & Machine Intelligence (ICIMMI '22)*. Association for Computing Machinery, New York, NY, USA. https://doi.org/10.1145/3590837.3590947

Woolf, B. P., Lane, H. C., Chaudhri, V. K., & Kolodner, J. L. (2013). AI grand challenges for education. *AI Magazine*, *34*(4), 66–84. doi:10.1609/aimag.v34i4.2490

Chapter 9

Examining the Paradigm–Shifting Potential of ChatGPT With AI–Enabled Chatbots in Teaching and Learning:
Shaping University 4.0 System

Princi Gupta
JECRC University, India

ABSTRACT

This research investigates the transformative impact of integrating ChatGPT, an advanced language model, in education. Exploring its natural language processing and chatbot capabilities, the study analyzes its influence on personalized learning, student engagement, instructional support, and administrative efficiency. Through case studies, user feedback, and literature, it unveils ChatGPT's paradigm-shifting potential in shaping the future of education. This contributes valuable insights for educators, administrators, and policymakers navigating the digital era, highlighting AI's role in revolutionizing teaching and learning approaches. In the context of University 4.0, the emergence of ChatGPT sparks interest in its capacity to reshape higher education through AI-enabled chatbots, fostering personalized and interactive learning experiences.

INTRODUCTION

Universities are continually looking for new ideas to enhance the teaching and learning expertise for their students in the ever-changing educational landscape. Artificial intelligence (AI) technology advancements have created new opportunities for modernizing static educational systems into dynamic and individualized learning environments (Chukwuere, 2023). The development of chatbots, intelligent conversational agents that can interact with students in a natural and effective way, is one area where AI has shown enormous potential (Mancy, 2024). With an emphasis on their effects on teaching and learning, this study states to

DOI: 10.4018/979-8-3693-6824-4.ch009

Figure 1. How AI Chatbot's functions
(Author's Compilation)

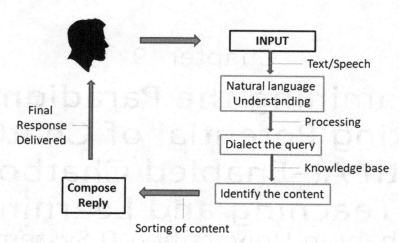

explore the paradigm-shifting capabilities of AI-enabled chatbots in defining the university 4.0 system (Elsen-Rooney, 2023). The term "University 4.0" alludes to the fourth industrial revolution, in which various facets of higher education are automated and digital technologies are integrated (Prasad, 2023). Chatbots powered by AI have the potential to transform the environment of educational sector delivering individualized help, encouraging active interaction, and reducing administrative procedures (Yi, 2020).

Numerous opportunities arise from the incorporation of AI-enabled Chatbots in learning and teaching contexts (Sharma, P., Dadheech, 2023). These Chatbots can serve as online instructors, directing learners along personalized learning pathways, giving immediate feedback, and addressing specific learning needs (Yi, 2020). By using AI algorithms and the processing of natural language abilities, chatbots can adapt to the choices, methods of learning, and pace of students, enhancing the efficacy of the educational process.

Chatbots powered by AI also have the power to promote student involvement and teamwork. Through interactive interactions, chatbots can encourage knowledge exchange, problem-solving, and analytical thinking (Hill-Yardin, 2023). They can act as online discussion partners, igniting the mind's curiosity and encouraging group learning. Additionally, chatbots can offer round-the-clock accessibility, ensuring that students receive ongoing support and direction outside of regular class hours (Yi, 2020).

Figure 1 depicts the functioning of Chatbot. Eliza, the first chatbox designed to play a psychotherapist, was developed in 1966. Smarter chatbots are being developed as a result of technological advancements, like Apple Siri, Smarter Child, IBM Watson, Amazon Alexa, Google Assistant, and Microsoft Cortana. A chatbot typically functions through a combination of several components and technologies. Here is a general overview of how a chatbot functions:

User Input: The user provides textual or spoken commands to the chatbot.

Natural Language Processing (NLP): NLP techniques are employed in processing the user input to understand the context, extract relevant information, and identify the intent behind the user's query or statement.

Intent Recognition: The chatbot determines the user's intent, such as asking a question, seeking information, requesting assistance, or providing feedback.

Information Retrieval: Based on the user's intent, the chatbot retrieves relevant information from its knowledge base or external sources. This can involve searching databases, accessing APIs, or using pre-trained models to gather the required information.

Response Generation: Using the retrieved information, the chatbot generates a response tailored to the user's query or intent. It can employ various techniques, such as natural language generation, template-based responses, or machine learning algorithms to generate a relevant and coherent response.

Output to User: The chatbot delivers the generated response to the user, either as text or speech, to provide assistance, answer questions, or engage in a conversation.

AI-enabled chatbots can simplify administrative procedures in universities in addition to teaching and learning. They can help with activities like course registration, scheduling, and navigating the campus, reducing the workload for administrative employees, and enhancing overall operational effectiveness. Chatbots allow university staff to concentrate on more difficult and valuable work by automating common administrative activities, increasing productivity and resource allocation.

But while AI-enabled chatbots have a lot of potential, integrating them into the university 4.0 system also raises questions about ethics, privacy, and security. This essay will explore these ideas and go through the opportunities and difficulties of implementing AI-enabled chatbots in higher education. In conclusion, this study attempts to investigate how AI-enabled chatbots could reshape the university 4.0 system. These chatbots can revolutionize teaching and learning by leveraging AI, offering individualized guidance, encouraging active interaction, and reducing administrative procedures. The ethical, privacy, and security ramifications of incorporating AI into education must be carefully considered, though. Universities may take advantage of the revolutionary potential of AI-enabled chatbots by solving these issues and building a more efficient and student-centered educational ecosystem.

THEORETICAL FRAMEWORK

AI-Enabled Chatbots: A Review

Particularly, the rapid growth of technologies for deep learning has significantly changed the way we learn and accelerated the advancement of AI. In actuality, artificial intelligence for education (AIEd) has been a unified field of academic research since at least the 1980s.. There are two approaches to AIEd: creating tools for classrooms based on AI and using AI to gather knowledge, evaluate, and improve learning (Biswas, 2023).

The accessibility of artificial intelligence (AI) technology has significantly increased in recent times across many industries, including the field of academics. The use of AI technology appears in a variety of applications, most notably Chatbots, which are computer programs that mimic human speech. Generative Pre-trained Transformer technology is used by ChatGPT, a chatbot that stands out as a particularly advanced and significant intelligent conversational agent. The use of ChatGPT within the setting of tertiary educational institutions is the subject of this manuscript. According to a study by Li, Chen, Yu, Davidson, Hou, Yuan, and Yu (2022), The study's objective was to ascertain whether or not employing chatbots as a teaching tool in language acquisition courses was successful. According to the investigation's findings, using chatbots has significantly increased both student satisfaction and engagement. Chen, Vicki Widarso, and Sutrisno examined the use of chatbots in an online math course and found that it significantly improved student performance and satisfaction (Biswas, 2022). The ChatGPT online platform may offer a chance for higher education institutions to completely rethink their instructional strategy. With its cutting-edge natural language processing capabilities, it is able to actively engage with learners and provide them with personally personalized assistance, guidance, and scholastic support (Surameery, 2023). The ChatGPT platform has the ability to provide helpful answers to student questions, provide constructive criticism of academic work, and advance students' educational achievement. This function is especially useful in situations involving larger classrooms where it is difficult to provide individualized attention (Surameery, 2023).

A new era of innovation and change has been sparked by artificial intelligence (AI), and this includes education. Artificial Intelligence (AI) technologies can completely transform the way that education is now done through the development of new tools and apps (Firat, 2023). AI has several possible applications in higher learning, including raising efficiency and learning outcomes, offering individualized training, giving prompt feedback, and boosting student engagement. AI is already being utilized in education in several applications, such as personalized learning platforms, computerized rating systems, and tutoring systems (Ausa, 2023). These initiatives have a lot of promises to raise student achievement in the classroom and provide teachers with the tools they need to provide more customized training. For example, intelligent tutoring systems can tailor lessons to the needs of individual students by providing them with individualized support and feedback (Ausa, 2023). Customized learning platforms can boost students' motivation and engagement by offering learning opportunities catered to their specific interests and needs. However, despite all of its benefits, implementing artificial intelligence (AI) in academics also presents significant practical and ethical challenges, such as the potential for it to further aggravate the already present disparities in the educational system and the bias-prone nature of AI algorithms. Using automated evaluation resources can help instructors focus on more pressing matters like preparing lessons and assistance for students while simultaneously saving them an enormous amount of time (Firat, 2023). Furthermore, for teachers to effectively incorporate AI into their teaching techniques, they need the right kind of training and assistance (Fuchs, 2023).

The purpose of this paper is to evaluate the literature on artificial intelligence (AI) in education, with a focus on chatbots and ChatGPT—advanced AI systems that can mimic human responses by utilizing natural language models. While there may be benefits to using machine learning in the classroom, there are also considerations that need to be made on the practical and ethical fronts (McGee, 2023). The authors hope to provide useful insights into how intelligence might be successfully incorporated into the classroom for the benefit of both teachers and students by identifying significant study subjects. Furthermore, the authors hope to further the current conversation on the importance of artificial intelligence in education by promoting the moral and responsible use of these technologies to improve teaching and learning processes (Baidoo-Anu, 2023).

INNOVATING EDUCATION: EMPOWERING MINDS WITH CHATGPT

Machine learning can dramatically change how we taught and learn by providing students with individualized learning experiences (Baidoo-Anu, 2023). The phrase "customized learning" describes how educational materials and experiences are produced using technology and tailored to each student's different needs, interests, and skill set. Adaptive learning, personalized recommendations, individualized instruction, and early learning needs assessment are just a few of the ways AI can be utilized for personalized learning (Mijwil, 2023). Overall, by creating experiences that are customized to meet the

Table 1. Key information from each study, focusing on the author, year, main focus, and major findings or contributions

Author	year	Key Focus	Key findings
Biswas	2023	AIEd Overview	Two approaches: AI tools for classrooms and evaluation.
Li et al.	2022	Chatbots in Language	Increased student satisfaction and engagement.
Surameery	2023	ChatGPT in Higher Ed	Actively engages learners, provides personalized assistance.
Firat	2023	AI's Impact on Education	Sparks innovation, applications include tutoring.
McGee	2023	Literature Summary on AI	Focus on chatbots and ChatGPT, emphasizing benefits, ethics.

individual needs of each learner, the use of AI to tailor instruction has the potential to enhance learning outcomes and raise student engagement (McGee, 2023).

In contrast, Generative Pre-trained Transformer (GPT) models leverage a vast amount of publicly accessible digital content data to read and generate text that appears human in several languages (natural language processing; NLP) (Mijwil, 2023). They are talented writers who can effectively (or almost adequately) write a thing as a short paragraph to a four-part research article on almost any subject (V, 2022). These computer models can even engage in human-like dialogue with clients, comparable to chatbots employed in customer support or virtual characters in video games. More recently, a Generative Pre-trained Transformer (GPT)-3 with enhanced capabilities was developed. To achieve task agnosticism and possibly compete with previous state-of-the-art fine-tuning techniques, 175 billion parameters were used to build GPT-3. Ten times as much as any prior non-sparse language model is contained in GPT-3. In the parts that followed, we discussed ChatGPT and how it might improve student learning and instruction. We also discussed the limitations and potential use of ChatGPT by educators to support and improve student learning (Aydın, 2022).

Open AI (San Francisco, CA) released ChatGPT in November 2022. It is a potent machine learning tool that uses the GPT methodology to generate responses to text-based inputs that resemble those of a human. Written discussions, webpages, books, and articles all used as training data for ChatGPT (Lucy, 2021). However, ChatGPT's dialogue optimization technique allows it to respond to commands in a conversational way during fine-tuning (Health, 2023). A class of sophisticated language models known as Generative Pre-trained Transformers (GPTs) uses deep learning to improve the quality of their output. Large datasets are used to train these models. In response to a user's inquiries, GPTs create pertinent phrases and words or make pertinent visuals by spotting patterns and regularities in the data (Lucy, 2021). Communication interpreting, summarizing texts, inquiring about responding to prompts in conversation, writing creatively (poetry or fiction), creating outstanding long- or short-form material (blog posts), explaining complicated topics, ideas, or concepts, repairing mistakes in current code, or creating new code are just a few of the many tasks that ChatGPT can handle (Open AI, 2022). Research demonstrating ChatGPT's ability to pass the Master of Business Administration (MBA) test (Open AI, 2023) and a Law School examination (Open AI, 2022) demonstrate the software's intrinsic talents (O'Connor, 2023).

ChatGPT is a well-liked tool for quickly resolving a variety of problems, from simple to complex themes, due to its capacity to understand natural language queries and produce human-like responses (O'Connor, 2023).For instance, it can succinctly summaries a lengthy scholarly work with just one sentence, words that may even only begin with the letter "q." In addition to identifying the issue, it offers precise answers even while it is programming by self. ChatGPT has rapidly gained popularity as a helpful asset for professionals and students alike (Maharajan, 2023). On March 14, 2023, ChatGPT-4, the most recent version, was published. It is touted to be more potent and capable of carrying out more difficult tasks. Larger and more varied datasets were used to train ChatGPT-4. The model's larger size enables more sophisticated natural language processing capabilities (Cornejo, 2022).It is more versatile and capable of handling difficult jobs thanks to its ability to reason and comprehend prompts across several disciplines. For instance, it provides a detailed description of the image if a user submits an image and wants one. Even handwritten questions are answered and displayed as visuals (Open AI, 2023).

This study's primary focus is ChatGPT, a powerful tool for performing human jobs. I specifically question what kind of education students should receive and what has to be changed to accommodate what they require (Kubo, 2023). According to Stokel-Walker, ChatGPT is a "game changer" with the power to replace several common tasks and test types, such essay writing (Qadir, 2023).The effects could be even greater than anticipated. We must comprehend ChatGPT's potential as well as its limitations in order to determine what skill sets pupils still require in order to flourish in the future. OpenAI developed ChatGPT, a general-purpose conversational chatbot, utilizing the GPT-3 language model. It is designed to generate text that mimics human conversation when responding to a particular dialogue or cue, and it is capable of carrying on conversational, open-ended discussions on a wide range of topics. Unlike the prior linguistic model, ChatGPT was developed in a conversational fashion using learning reinforcement from human feedback (Qadir, 2023). By rating the calibre of the machine responses, humans give feedback (i.e., rewards) and help Proximal Policy Optimization refine the model. Because of the recently introduced technique, ChatGPT may reply to follow-up inquiries, admit errors, disprove erroneous assumptions, and refuse unsuitable requests (Kubo, 2023). Compared with various AI language models, such as Meta has language tool or the RoBERTa model, ChatGPT offers "more creative" responses (Zhai, 2022).

SHAPING EDUCATION 4.0: THE RISE OF EMERGING AI-ENABLED CHATBOTS

The chatbot system is one of the often-used AI tools for assisting with teaching and learning tasks (Tate, 2023). An intelligent agent known as a chatbot is able to connect with a user by responding appropriately to a series of queries. (Tate, 2023). A chatbot, on the other hand, ought to be able to comprehend the subject of the discussion and recognize the emotional and social requirements of others when they arise, just like a dialogue system. It allows users of digital devices to communicate with one another like they were chatting with an actual individual by simulating and interpreting human conversation (Hawley, 2022). Additionally, the size and quality of a chatbot's databases affect its performance, therefore larger databases yield better performance (Ford, 2023). Natural Language Processing (NLP) is used in the development of chatbots. NLP technology enables a machine to comprehend, analyze, and comprehend human natural languages (Ford, 2023).

AI-Enabled Chatbots: Transforming Teaching With Intelligent Assistance

ChatGPT (Open AI's language model) integrated with educational platforms. These systems use AI or chatbot abilities to improve student learning and teaching, automate administrative activities, give students immediate support, and provide individualized help in learning environments (Chukwuere, 2023).

Moodle Chatbot: Moodle is a popular learning management system (LMS) used in educational institutions. The Moodle Chatbot utilizes natural language processing (NLP) and AI to provide personalized assistance, answer queries, deliver course-related information, and facilitate student engagement within the Moodle platform (Chen, 2020).

IBM Watson Assistant for Education: IBM Watson Assistant is an AI-powered chatbot platform that can be customized for educational purposes. It enables educational institutions to build virtual assistants that can provide automated responses to student inquiries, offer support for administrative tasks, deliver personalized learning experiences, and analyze student data for insights (Chen, 2020).

Microsoft Azure Chatbot for Education: Microsoft Azure offers a chatbot framework specifically designed for educational settings. It allows educational institutions to create intelligent virtual assistants that can automate routine tasks, offer personalized support to students, provide information on courses and schedules, and enhance communication between students and faculty (Kim, 2020).

Blackboard Ally's Virtual Assistant: Blackboard Ally is an accessibility-focused platform for educational content. Their Virtual Assistant employs chatbot technology to address accessibility-related queries and provide guidance on creating inclusive digital content. It assists both students and educators in ensuring content accessibility and compliance (Hew, 2023).

AcaBot by Aisera: AcaBot is an AI-powered chatbot developed by Aisera, tailored for educational institutions. It supports various use cases, such as answering repetitively asked queries, assisting with admissions processes, providing course recommendations, and delivering real-time support to students, faculty, and staff (Shidiq, 2023).

Ada Support for Education: Ada Support is an AI chatbot platform that can be applied to educational environments (Shidiq, 2023). It offers automated responses to student inquiries, assists with enrollment processes, provides course information, and supports student engagement. It can also integrate with other educational systems to streamline communication (Hutson, 2022).

Botpress for Educational Institutions: Botpress is an open source chatbot development platform that can be utilized in educational institutions. It allows the creation of custom chatbots that can provide information, answer queries, automate administrative tasks, and facilitate student support, all tailored to the specific needs of the institution (Kom, 2021).

Chabot4Edu by ChabotNL: Chabot4Edu is an AI chatbot designed explicitly for educational institutions. It assists in answering student queries, delivering course-related information, providing study resources, and enhancing communication channels between students, faculty, and staff (Kom, 2021).

Oracle Digital Assistant for Education: Oracle Digital Assistant offers a conversational AI platform that can be employed in the education sector. It enables the development of chatbots that assist with student enrollment, provide course information, support administrative tasks, and offer personalized guidance to students (Lund, 2023).

ChatGPT (OpenAI's Language Model) Integrated With Educational Platforms

ChatGPT, based on Open AI's language model, can be integrated into educational platforms to provide conversational AI capabilities (Tanwar, 2022). It can assist in answering student inquiries, delivering course content, supporting personalized learning experiences, and automating certain administrative tasks. It leverages natural language understanding and generation to create interactive and informative conversations with students (Rudolph, 2023).

These AI tools and chatbots have various functions and implications, including automating administrative tasks, providing personalized support to students, delivering course-related information, enhancing accessibility and inclusivity, improving student engagement, and streamlining communication between stakeholders in educational institutions. They seek to improve student learning and instruction, streamline administrative procedures, and adjust to the changing needs of education in the Web 4.0 era (Lund, 2023).

UNLOCKING NEW FRONTIERS: CHATGPT'S POTENTIAL IN EDUCATION 4.0

Personalized Learning Experience

ChatGPT is a flexible conversational agent because of its capacity to learn from its interactions with humans. ChatGPT can recall and take into account prior discussions when replying. Therefore, over time, it may maintain context while conversing with clients in a more logical and natural way. Because ChatGPT has been trained on a large volume of data, it is able to offer answers that are specific to the situation at hand (McCallum, 2023) Moreover, ChatGPT can react in a variety of tones and patterns according to the user's requirements and preferences. This feature allows users to produce personalized texts in what seems as though there has been or seems like a real conversation with a chatbot that learns from each contact (McCallum, 2023). Students at various skill levels have the option to receive individualized assistance and feedback using ChatGPT (Adamopoulou, 2020) For example, in discussing the significance of debating essay writing for college students, we asked ChatGPT for feedback on an unidentified essay titled "Video Games for Children" in three different contexts, considering the advantageous, beneficial, or and critical aspects of feedback. When given a critical prompt style, ChatGPT produced more critical input; but, when given a complimenting prompt style, it produced more positive and expressive feedback (Kubo, 2023). This means that when giving students personalized feedback, teachers should be very selective about the question prompts they use because, for neurological and emotional reasons, students often do not take feedback seriously when it is merely critical (Khyzhniak, 2021).

Adaptive Real Time Learning

AI can be used to provide students with specialized instruction through techniques like customized planning of lessons or one-on-one coaching (Kumar, 2023). Artificial intelligence (AI) can assist individualized education, a teaching and learning approach that seeks to modify the process of learning to each student's unique needs and abilities. Examples of customized training include self-paced learning, small-group instruction, and one-on-one coaching (Alawi, 2023). When educational software was first created to facilitate self-paced learning in the early days of computer-based education, the history of AI for individualized instruction began (Sharma, 2023). Following that, a wide number of techniques to individualized instruction have been supported by AI, adaptive learning platforms, including intelligent tutoring systems, and customized learning environments (Alawi, 2023). There is some proof that AI can support individualized instruction well. For instance, a review of the literature on AI-based personalized education that was published in the Journal of Educational Computing Research revealed that AI can boost students' performance on a range of metrics, such as test results and course grades. However, the review's authors also stated that additional study is required to completely grasp the capabilities of

AI for individualized instruction and to identify the most effective approaches to use and utilize AI in educational contexts (Aldeman, 2021).

Taking everything into account, artificial intelligence (AI) holds enormous potential for personalized education since it can offer students individualized educational opportunities based on their unique requirements and skills, which may lead to improved learning results. All things considered, AI has a lot of potential for customized instruction since it can give students individualized educational opportunities based on their unique requirements and skills, which could result in better learning outcomes (Aldosari, 2020).

ChatGPT can be used to create adaptive learning systems, which change their teaching strategies based on a student's development and performance (Aleedy, 2022). Based on research conducted by Aleedy, 2022, a dynamic generative model (ChatGPT) based on learning system may be able to assist students' learning coding more efficiently, leading to greater success on programming assessments. The research showed that the algorithm could adjust the degree of complexity of the assignments it generated based on students' past knowledge. It is anticipated that ChatGPT will be an effective tool for improving instruction in general because of its features for interactive learning, adaptive learning, computerized essay assessment, translation of languages, and individualized mentoring (Chen, 2023).

Interactive Process

With ChatGPT, students may create engaging learning experiences by speaking with a virtual tutor (Miao, 2023). In a study by Chen (2023), a conversational agent based on generative algorithms can help learners acquire English as an additional language successfully and boost language competency (Sharma, 2026). The investigation proved the agent's ability to understand students' problems and provide relevant and appropriate responses (Xia, 2022).

Through the utilization of ChatGPT to translate educational resources into many languages, a larger audience can access them (Sethi, 2023). Following a study by Johnson 9 and colleagues, a machine learning algorithm (ChatGPT) developed on a collection of multilingual phrase pairings that was able to translate across languages accurately (Xia, 2022). Furthermore, the model yielded state-of-the-art results on multiple translation benchmarks. The study demonstrated that the algorithm could comprehend text content and translate it between languages with accuracy (Yau, 2023).

Instructional Support

ChatGPT can give teachers and students easy access to information on a range of subjects using a number of platforms (such a website or a mobile app) (Yau. 2023). It is also a more helpful tool than standard search engines because, as opposed to just providing a list of sources, it provides a written response. ChatGPT can locate and condense pertinent material to make it simple for students to obtain in-depth information (Choi et al., 2023). This implies that, from an educational perspective, ChatGPT can free up students' time so they can read and analyze the supplied content more carefully and critically rather than wasting it gathering information. Teachers can identify and develop relevant educational resources with ChatGPT's assistance. It can also assist them in developing lecture plans with constraints and recommendations for instruction (Choi et al., 2023).

Administrative efficiency: Registration and enrollment, student record management, grading and evaluation, and course scheduling. ChatGPT can be used to grade essays, freeing up teachers' time to concentrate on other aspects of teaching (Sharma, 2023). A study found that a machine learning algorithm (ChatGPT) built on a collection of human-graded compositions could correctly assess high school students' essays (Ogawa, 2023), with a 0.86 correlation to ratings from people. The study showed that the model could provide feedback that was similar to that of human graders and could identify important components of well-written essays.

Enhancing student engagement: ChatGPT, which offers personalized feedback, enables the improvement of student engagement, creating a highly interactive and engaging learning environment for students (Ogawa, 2023). The development of the illusion of immediacy is made possible by ChatGPT's real-time reaction, which raises students' motivation levels and encourages their propensity to take part in class more (Arai, 2023).

Improving accessibility: Consider enhancing accessibility by integrating ChatGPT as one potential improvement (Arai, 2023). ChatGPT has the ability to facilitate the involvement of various student populations who encounter linguistic or physical challenges to obtaining course material or participating fully in the learning process by integrating functions like real-time translation and speech recognition. People with disabilities and non-native speakers of the instruction's language are two examples of such groups (Dogan, 2023).

Reducing costs: ChatGPT can save educational institutions a substantial amount of money by assisting with the expenses of grading, giving feedback, and answering frequently asked questions (Sharma, 2023). Nonetheless, there are certain issues with ChatGPT's application in higher education institutions. According to some arguments, the use of ChatGPT, a conversational artificial intelligence system, could lower educational standards if teachers place an undue amount of reliance on the tool (Kanayama, 2023). Because ChatGPT requires commanding access to a wealth of student data in order to work optimally, there may be associated problems with privacy and data protection. Currently, ChatGPT has the potential to significantly disrupt higher education institutions in a number of ways. The benefits of using ChatGPT, including the improvement of student engagement, facilitation of accessibility, reduction of costs, and reformulation of the role of educators, are significant and deserve acknowledgement despite any potential reservations (Popova, 2022). To design and implement relevant policies and guidelines that encourage wise management, institutions must conduct a deliberate assessment of the effects resulting from the use of ChatGPT (Kanayama, 2023).

RESULTS AND DISCUSSION

The impact of integrating ChatGPT into higher education is substantial, reshaping key facets of instructional methodologies and student experiences. The provision of individualized feedback mechanisms emerges as a significant outcome, with ChatGPT's ability to carefully analyze and promptly deliver personalized feedback enhancing learning retention and academic performance. This transformative technology also redefines the instructional obligations of educators, enabling a shift from routine tasks to a focus on more complex aspects of teaching, fostering a deeper engagement with students. Moreover, ChatGPT facilitates improved access to course materials, streamlining the learning process and enhancing overall accessibility for students. The observed increase in student participation, engagement, and satisfaction underscores the potential revolution in the traditional educational approach.

However, these promising outcomes coexist with notable limitations. While ChatGPT excels in providing efficient feedback, it cannot replicate the emotional connection essential for effective teaching.

The lack of human creativity makes it difficult to come up with fresh concepts and cutting-edge methods that are essential for the growth of students. Moreover, the danger of relying too much on ChatGPT is recognized, with possible consequences for deteriorating one's ability to think critically and solve problems. It is critical to acknowledge that, in the setting of independent and self-learning, ChatGPT is an emerging technology, necessitating continued research to fully understand both its strengths and weaknesses. Effectively designing the next phase of higher education will require finding a balance between utilizing ChatGPT's advantages and maintaining the importance of human interaction in the classroom.

CONCLUSION

According to the findings and discussions, ChatGPT can have a good impact on the field of education and learning by offering solutions based on the keywords input by the user. However, it's also important to understand that not all of these resources have a positive effect on helping students develop a variety of learning abilities, including the ability to write. Therefore, it's necessary to come up with a plan for professors to employ techniques other than learning via the Internet, which students could misuse to get work done. One strategy that can be employed while putting together tasks related to creative writing is using paper as a means of communication as a form of process oversight and assessment.

By giving students rapid and tailored feedback, making higher education more accessible, redefining the role of the trainer, and boosting student engagement, ChatGPT technology has the potential to drastically alter higher education institutions. Lessening the burden for academics (educators) and allocating more time for other teaching responsibilities may be possible in order to enhance the standard of education and improve student outcomes. However, there are ethical and privacy concerns with ChatGPT use in higher education that need to be addressed. Before using ChatGPT, institutions need to carefully weigh the possible consequences. They also need to establish the rules and guidelines required to make sure the technology is applied responsibly. Subsequent investigations may concentrate on assessing ChatGPT's efficacy in many educational environments and circumstances, while also considering any plausible ethical and privacy issues. In summary, ChatGPT has the power to wreak havoc and profoundly change the landscape of institutions of higher learning. To maximize benefits and minimize potential drawbacks, its implementation calls for considerable thought and caution.

REFERENCES

Adamopoulou, E., & Moussiades, L. (2020). Chatbots: History, technology, and applications. *Machine Learning with Applications*, 2, 100006. doi:10.1016/j.mlwa.2020.100006

Akinwalere, S. N., & Ivanov, V. (2022). Artificial Intelligence in Higher Education: Challenges and Opportunities. *Border Crossing*, 12(1), 1–15. doi:10.33182/bc.v12i1.2015

Alawi, F. (2023). Artificial intelligence: The future might already be here. *Oral Surgery, Oral Medicine, Oral Pathology and Oral Radiology*, 135(3), 313–315. doi:10.1016/j.oooo.2023.01.002 PMID:36774240

Aldeman, N. L. S., de Sá Urtiga Aita, K. M., Machado, V. P., da Mata Sousa, L. C. D., Coelho, A. G. B., da Silva, A. S., da Silva Mendes, A. P., de Oliveira Neres, F. J., & do Monte, S. J. H. (2021). Smartpathk: A platform for teaching glomerulopathies using machine learning. *BMC Medical Education*, *21*(1), 248. doi:10.1186/s12909-021-02680-1 PMID:33926437

Aldosari, S. A. M. (2020). The future of higher education in the light of artificial intelligence transformations. *International Journal of Higher Education*, *9*(3), 145–151. doi:10.5430/ijhe.v9n3p145

Aleedy, M., Atwell, E., & Meshoul, S. (2022). Using AI Chatbots in Education: Recent Advances Challenges and Use Case. *Artificial Intelligence and Sustainable Computing: Proceedings of ICSISCET 2021*, 661-675.

Arai, H., Akagi, K., Nakagawa, A., Onai, Y., Utsu, Y., Masuda, S., & Aotsuka, N. (2023). Clinical and genetic diagnosis of Cowden syndrome: A case report of a rare PTEN germline variant and diverse clinical presentation. *Medicine*, *102*(1), e32572. doi:10.1097/MD.0000000000032572 PMID:36607858

Ausat, A. M. A., Massang, B., Efendi, M., Nofirman, N., & Riady, Y. (2023). Can chat GPT replace the role of the teacher in the classroom: A fundamental analysis. *Journal of Education*, *5*(4), 16100–16106.

AydınÖ.KaraarslanE. (2022). OpenAI ChatGPT generated literature review: Digital twin in healthcare. *Available at* SSRN 4308687. doi:10.2139/ssrn.4308687

Biswas, S. S. (2023). Role of chat gpt in public health. *Annals of Biomedical Engineering*, *51*(5), 868–869. doi:10.1007/s10439-023-03172-7 PMID:36920578

Chen, H. L., Vicki Widarso, G., & Sutrisno, H. (2020). A chatbot for learning Chinese: Learning achievement and technology acceptance. *Journal of Educational Computing Research*, *58*(6), 1161–1189. doi:10.1177/0735633120929622

Chen, Y., Jensen, S., Albert, L. J., Gupta, S., & Lee, T. (2023). Artificial intelligence (AI) student assistants in the classroom: Designing chatbots to support student success. *Information Systems Frontiers*, *25*(1), 161–182. doi:10.1007/s10796-022-10291-4

ChoiJ. H.HickmanK. E.MonahanA.SchwarczD. (2023).Chatgpt goes to law school. *Available at* SSRN.

Chukwuere, J. E. (2023). ChatGPT: The game changer for higher education institutions. *Jozac Academic Voice*, *3*, 22–27.

Chukwuere, J. E. (2023). ChatGPT: The game changer for higher education institutions. *Jozac Academic Voice*, *3*, 22–27.

Cornejo, C., & Alvarez-Icaza, L. (2022). Passivity based control of under-actuated mechanical systems with nonlinear dynamic friction. *Journal of Vibration and Control*, *18*(7), 1025–1042. doi:10.1177/1077546311408469

Dogan, M. E., Goru Dogan, T., & Bozkurt, A. (2023). The use of artificial intelligence (AI) in online learning and distance education processes: A systematic review of empirical studies. *Applied Sciences (Basel, Switzerland)*, *13*(5), 3056. doi:10.3390/app13053056

Elsen-Rooney, M. (2023). NYC education department blocks ChatGPT on school devices, networks. *Retrieved*, (Jan), 25.

Faiz, A., & Kurniawaty, I. (2023). TantanganPenggunaan ChatGPT dalamPendidikanDitinjaudariSudut Pandang Moral. *Edukatif: JurnalIlmuPendidikan, 5*(1), 456–463.

Ford, E. W. (2023). Artificial Intelligence Answers an Editor's Question. *Journal of Healthcare Management, 68*(1), 1–4. doi:10.1097/JHM-D-22-00252 PMID:36602449

Fuchs, K. (2023, May). Exploring the opportunities and challenges of NLP models in higher education: Is Chat GPT a blessing or a curse?In [].Frontiers.]. *Frontiers in Education, 8*, 1166682. doi:10.3389/feduc.2023.1166682

Hawley, J. (2022). THE ROBOTS ARE COMING: What's Happening in Philosophy (WHiP)-The Philosophers, August 2022.

Hew, K. F., Huang, W., Du, J., & Jia, C. (2023). Using chatbots to support student goal setting and social presence in fully online activities: Learner engagement and perceptions. *Journal of Computing in Higher Education, 35*(1), 40–68. doi:10.1007/s12528-022-09338-x PMID:36101883

Hill-Yardin, E. L., Hutchinson, M. R., Laycock, R., & Spencer, S. J. (2023). A Chat (GPT) about the future of scientific publishing. *Brain, Behavior, and Immunity, 110*, 152–154. doi:10.1016/j.bbi.2023.02.022 PMID:36868432

Hutson, M. (2022). Could AI help you to write your next paper?*Nature, 611*(7934), 192–193. doi:10.1038/d41586-022-03479-w PMID:36316468

Kanayama, M., Izumi, Y., Akiyama, M., Hayashi, T., Atarashi, K., Roers, A., Sato, T., & Ohteki, T. (2023). Myeloid-like B cells boost emergency myelopoiesis through IL-10 production during infection. *The Journal of Experimental Medicine, 220*(4), e20221221. doi:10.1084/jem.20221221 PMID:36719648

Khyzhniak, I., Tsybulko, L., Viktorenko, I., &Mohyliova, N. (2021).Implementing the theory of multiple intelligences into project-based multimedia learning at primary school. *Information technologies and learning tools, 82*(2), 18-31.

Kim, J., Merrill, K., Xu, K., & Sellnow, D. D. (2020). My teacher is a machine: Understanding students' perceptions of AI teaching assistants in online education. *International Journal of Human-Computer Interaction, 36*(20), 1902–1911. doi:10.1080/10447318.2020.1801227

Kom, S. (2021). *Teknologipendidikan di abad digital*. Penerbit Lakeisha.

Kubo, K., Tamura, M., Matsumoto, K., Otsuka, M., & Monzen, H. (2023). Independent monitor unit verification for dynamic flattened beam plans on the Halcyon linac. *Journal of Applied Clinical Medical Physics, 24*(1), e13807. doi:10.1002/acm2.13807 PMID:36265085

Kumar, A. S., Sharma, P., Kaur, S., Saleh, O. S., Chennamma, H. R., & Chaturvedi, A. (2023). AI-Equipped IoT Applications in High-Tech Agriculture Using Machine Learning. In *Handbook of Research on AI-Equipped IoT Applications in High-Tech Agriculture* (pp. 38–64). IGI Global.

Lucy, L., & Bamman, D. (2021, June). Gender and representation bias in GPT-3 generated stories. In *Proceedings of the Third Workshop on Narrative Understanding* (pp. 48-55). 10.18653/v1/2021.nuse-1.5

Lund, B. D., & Wang, T. (2023). Chatting about ChatGPT: How may AI and GPT impact academia and libraries? *Library Hi Tech News*, *40*(3), 26–29. doi:10.1108/LHTN-01-2023-0009

Maharajan, K., Kumar, A. S., El Emary, I. M., Sharma, P., Latip, R., Mishra, N., . . . Sharma, M. (2023). Blockchain Methods and Data-Driven Decision Making With Autonomous Transportation. In Effective AI, Blockchain, and E-Governance Applications for Knowledge Discovery and Management (pp. 176-194). IGI Global. doi:10.4018/978-1-6684-9151-5.ch012

Mancy, A. M., Kumar, A. S., Latip, R., Jagadamba, G., Chakrabarti, P., Sharma, P., & Kanchan, B. G. (2024). Smart Healthcare System, Digital Health and Telemedicine, Management and Emergencies: Patient Emergency Application (PES) E-Governance Applications. In Sustainable Development in AI, Blockchain, and E-Governance Applications (pp. 124-151). IGI Global.

McCallum, S. (2023). *ChatGPT banned in Italy over privacy concerns*. BBC News.

McGeeR. W. (2023). Capitalism, Socialism and ChatGPT. *Available at* SSRN 4369953.

Miao, X., Zhao, D., Lin, B., Jiang, H., & Chen, J. (2023). A Differential Protection Scheme Based on Improved DTW Algorithm for Distribution Networks with Highly-Penetrated Distributed Generation. *IEEE Access : Practical Innovations, Open Solutions*, *11*, 40399–40411. doi:10.1109/ACCESS.2023.3269298

Mijwil, M. M., Hiran, K. K., Doshi, R., & Unogwu, O. J. (2023). Advancing Construction with IoT and RFID Technology in Civil Engineering: A Technology Review. *Al-Salam Journal for Engineering and Technology*, *2*(2), 54–62. doi:10.55145/ajest.2023.02.02.007

O'Connor, S., & Chat, G. P. T. (2023). Editorial: Open artificial intelligence platforms in nursing education: Tools for academic progress or abuse. *Nurse Education in Practice*, 66.

Ogawa, H., Konishi, T., Najima, Y., Kito, S., Hashimoto, S., Kato, C., Sakai, S., Kanbara, Y., Atsuta, Y., Konuma, R., Wada, A., Murakami, D., Nakasima, S., Uchibori, Y., Onai, D., Hamamura, A., Nishijima, A., Shingai, N., Toya, T., & Murofushi, K. N. (2023). Phase I trial of myeloablative conditioning with 3-day total marrow and lymphoid irradiation for leukemia. *Cancer Science*, *114*(2), 596–605. doi:10.1111/cas.15611 PMID:36221800

OpenAI. (2022). Chatgpt: Optimizing language models for dialogue. *OpenAI*.

Popova, S., & Izonin, I. (2022). Application of the Smart House System for Reconstruction of Residential Buildings from an Obsolete Housing Stock. *Smart Cities*, *6*(1), 57–71. doi:10.3390/smartcities6010004

Prasad, A., Kumar, A. S., Sharma, P., Irawati, I. D., Chandrashekar, D. V., Musirin, I. B., & Abdullah, H. M. A. (2023). Artificial Intelligence in Computer Science: An Overview of Current Trends and Future Directions. *Advances in Artificial and Human Intelligence in the Modern Era*, 43-60.

Qadir, J. (2023, May). Engineering education in the era of ChatGPT: Promise and pitfalls of generative AI for education. In *2023 IEEE Global Engineering Education Conference (EDUCON)* (pp. 1-9).IEEE. 10.1109/EDUCON54358.2023.10125121

Rudolph, J., Tan, S., & Tan, S. (2023). ChatGPT: Bullshit spewer or the end of traditional assessments in higher education? *Journal of Applied Learning and Teaching*, *6*(1).

Sethi, S. S., & Sharma, P. (2023). New Developments in the Implementation of IoT in Agriculture. *SN Computer Science*, *4*(5), 503. doi:10.1007/s42979-023-01896-w

Sharma, P. (2023). Utilizing Explainable Artificial Intelligence to Address Deep Learning in Biomedical Domain. In *Medical Data Analysis and Processing using Explainable Artificial Intelligence* (pp. 19–38). CRC Press. doi:10.1201/9781003257721-2

Sharma, P., & Dadheech, P. (2023). *Modern-age Agriculture with Artificial Intelligence: A review emphasizing Crop Yield Prediction.*

Sharma, P., Dadheech, P., Aneja, N., & Aneja, S. (2023). Predicting Agriculture Yields Based on Machine Learning Using Regression and Deep Learning. *IEEE Access : Practical Innovations, Open Solutions*, *11*, 111255–111264. doi:10.1109/ACCESS.2023.3321861

Sharma, P., Dadheech, P., & Senthil, A. S. K. (2023). AI-Enabled Crop Recommendation System Based on Soil and Weather Patterns. In *Artificial Intelligence Tools and Technologies for Smart Farming and Agriculture Practices* (pp. 184–199). IGI Global. doi:10.4018/978-1-6684-8516-3.ch010

Sharma, P., & Jain, M. K. (2023, November). Stock Market Trends Analysis using Extreme Gradient Boosting (XGBoost). In *2023 International Conference on Computing, Communication, and Intelligent Systems (ICCCIS)* (pp. 317-322). IEEE. 10.1109/ICCCIS60361.2023.10425722

Sharma, P., & Rathi, Y. (2016). Efficient density-based clustering using automatic parameter detection. In *Proceedings of the International Congress on Information and Communication Technology: ICICT 2015,* Volume 1 (pp. 433-441). Springer Singapore. 10.1007/978-981-10-0767-5_46

Sharma, P., Sharma, C., & Mathur, P. (2023, August). Machine Learning-based Stock Market Forecasting using Recurrent Neural Network. In *2023 9th International Conference on Smart Computing and Communications (ICSCC)* (pp. 600-605). IEEE. 10.1109/ICSCC59169.2023.10335083

Shidiq, M. (2023, May).The use of artificial intelligence-based chat-gpt and its challenges for the world of education; from the viewpoint of the development of creative writing skills. In *Proceeding of International Conference on Education, Society and Humanity* (Vol. 1, No. 1, pp. 353-357). IEEE.

Surameery, N. M. S., & Shakor, M. Y. (2023). Use chat gpt to solve programming bugs. *International Journal of Information Technology & Computer Engineering (IJITC) ISSN: 2455-5290*, *3*(01), 17-22.

Tanwar, A., Sharma, P., Pandey, A., & Kumar, S. (2022, December). Intrusion Detection System Based Ameliorated Technique of Pattern Matching. In *Proceedings of the 4th International Conference on Information Management & Machine Intelligence* (pp. 1-4). ACM. 10.1145/3590837.3590947

Tate, T., Doroudi, S., Ritchie, D., & Xu, Y. (2023). *Educational Research and AI-Generated Writing: Confronting the Coming Tsunami.*

Xia, Q., Chiu, T. K., Lee, M., Sanusi, I. T., Dai, Y., & Chai, C. S. (2022). A self-determination theory (SDT) design approach for inclusive and diverse artificial intelligence (AI) education. *Computers & Education*, *189*, 104582. doi:10.1016/j.compedu.2022.104582

Yau, K. W., Chai, C. S., Chiu, T. K., Meng, H., King, I., & Yam, Y. (2023). A phenomenographic approach on teacher conceptions of teaching artificial intelligence (AI) in K-12 schools. *Education and Information Technologies*, 28(1), 1041–1064. doi:10.1007/s10639-022-11161-x

Yi, C., Wang, J., Cheng, N., Zhou, S., & Xu, B. (2020).Applying wav2vec2.0 to speech recognition in various low-resource languages. *arXiv preprint arXiv:2012.12121*.

Yui, S., Wakita, S., Nagata, Y., Kuribayashi, Y., Asayama, T., Fujiwara, Y., Sakaguchi, M., Yamanaka, S., Marumo, A., Omori, I., Kinoshita, R., Onai, D., Sunakawa, M., Kaito, Y., Inai, K., Tokura, T., Takeyoshi, A., Yasuda, S., Honma, S., & Yamaguchi, H. (2023). Safety and efficacy of high-dose cytarabine MEAM therapy and other treatments for auto-peripheral blood stem cell transplantation: A retrospective comparative study. *Asia Pacific Journal of Clinical Oncology*, 19(1), 136–148. doi:10.1111/ajco.13780 PMID:35599446

ZhaiX. (2022). ChatGPT user experience: Implications for education. *Available at* SSRN 4312418.

ZhaiX. (2022). ChatGPT user experience: Implications for education. *Available at* SSRN 4312418.

Chapter 10
Role of ChatGPT in Smart Cities

Adline R. Freeda
 https://orcid.org/0009-0002-3335-0907
KCG College of Technology, India

Anju A.
KCG College of Technology, India

Krithikaa Venket
 https://orcid.org/0009-0003-8445-4332
KCG College of Technology, India

Dhaya R.
 https://orcid.org/0000-0002-3599-7272
KCG College of Technology, India

R. Kanthavel
PNG University of Technology, Papua New Guinea

ABSTRACT

In smart cities, generative artificial intelligence (AI) models such as ChatGPT have become revolutionary tools in many respects, chiefly due to their ability to process and communicate natural language. These artificial intelligence (AI) systems have greatly enhanced communication and problem-solving skills, leading to increased productivity and efficiency in a variety of fields, including healthcare, education, environmental monitoring, public health, smart grid management, traffic management, citizen engagement, environmental monitoring, and environmental monitoring. This study looks at ChatGPT's and similar Generative AI's changing role in smartcity contexts. It highlights the need for ethical frameworks and regulatory rules by examining the difficulties in putting them into practice. Concurrently, it highlights the enormous potential these technologies provide, from promoting inclusivity to igniting innovation, forming a future in which artificial intelligence augments human capabilities and fosters peaceful co-existence between sentient machines and people.

DOI: 10.4018/979-8-3693-6824-4.ch010

Copyright © 2024, IGI Global. Copying or distributing in print or electronic forms without written permission of IGI Global is prohibited.

INTRODUCTION

A smart city, at its foundation, is an urban area that uses the Internet of Things (IoT) and data-driven technology to enhance many facets of city life. These communities hope to give their residents a smooth and sustainable living environment by incorporating state-of-the-art technology into their infrastructure.

Natural language inquiries can be understood and answered using ChatGPT, an artificial intelligence program that is language-based. It has the ability to comprehend intricate instructions and queries and to respond with precision and speed. Because it helps cities to manage their operations more effectively and respond to citizen requests promptly, it is a crucial tool for smart city initiatives.

Renewable energies and sustainable development are becoming more and more important in smart city and urban development. In order to achieve this, artificial intelligence (AI) applications are becoming more popular. The use of natural language processing (NLP) in smart cities and sustainable urban development is being completely transformed by OpenAI's ChatGPT tool. The creation of more sustainable and effective cities is made possible by the usage of this technology. Urban planners may create conversational interfaces that help people understand the requirements of their communities—both present and future—by utilizing ChatGPT. ChatGPT is transforming the planning and administration of cities. Cities may use this technology to improve the quality of life for its residents while simultaneously becoming more sustainable and efficient. ChatGPT is certain to play a significant role in urban planning and development as long as cities embrace sustainable development and green activities.

ChatGPT's ability to deliver rapid access to coherent information makes it an excellent tool for public sector offices in urban areas, where wait times for information sharing and delivery to residents can be greatly decreased. Generative AI, such as ChatGPT, has the potential to be used in the city's healthcare industry by answering clinical-related questions. This can be a very useful tool when it comes to research-based inquiries. 1

Generative AI may also be subject to a high degree of error or false information, depending on the kind of data it is trained on.

Large Language Models (LLMs) had a major breakthrough with the release of the new GPT model. We integrated the model with Bing's back-end capabilities after seeing the possibility of improving user experience, relevance, and accuracy. Prometheus, an inventive AI model, was developed as a result of this integration. It combines the sophisticated GPT models from OpenAI with the exhaustive Bing index, rating, and answer outcomes in a novel way (Roose, K., 2022).

Growth of ChatGPT

Customers' opinions of ChatGPT were not quite unanimous over the first six weeks of the experiment. According to Roose, these are some of the best publicly accessible computational intelligence tools((Roose, K., 2022). There are many who contend that ChatGPT's capacity to impact decision-making arises from users' capacity to provide automated reactions via the app (Nazir A. et al,2023).On the other hand, according to (Krugman, P., 2022), ChatGPT may have an impact on the requirement for intellectual labor. (Lock, S., 2022). concurs with this viewpoint as well, given that ChatGPT may produce literature that seems to have been created by humans.

Figure 1. Smart city domains

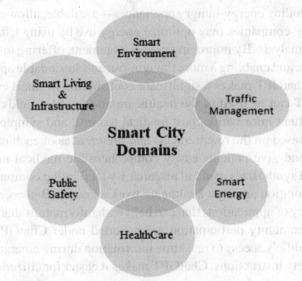

ChatGPT in Smart City Domains

ChatGPT can be quite useful in smart cities. As a sophisticated and interactive communication interface for a range of services and applications, some of the domains that are commonly used to categorize smart city components and application sectors, and they help to illustrate the broad landscape that emerged when analyzing the role of chatGPT in smartcities.

Smart Environment

A network of interconnected items that can coordinate, offer services, and manage complex data is referred to as a smart environment (Mijwil M., et al., 2023) Its goal is to make cities more environmentally friendly and energy efficient. By incorporating ChatGPT into smart environments, user-computer interaction can become more fluid, efficient, and natural, which will improve the general usability and functionality of smart systems.

Traffic Management Users can access real-time traffic updates and information through ChatGPT. This contains information about construction, accidents, alternate routes, and road conditions. By interacting with the system, users can get customized recommendations according to their preferences and location. ChatGPT can provide dynamic and context-aware route recommendations when integrated with navigation systems. Users can get information on public transportation timetables, delays, and route planning from ChatGPT. It is capable of data analysis and adjustment suggestion for better overall traffic management and congestion reduction. ChatGPT is capable of analysing past traffic data and assisting with traffic pattern prediction modelling(Haleem,Abid.,et al,2022).Traffic management systems can take proactive steps to manage traffic by using this information.

Smart Energy: Energy efficiency, sustainability, and management are just a few of the areas in which ChatGPT's involvement in smart energy is diverse. It helps customers gain insight into their usage patterns and make recommendations for optimizing energy use. It also makes voice-activated controls for smart home devices—including energy-hungry appliances—available, allowing for efficient and hands-free administration. Utility companies may optimize energy use by using ChatGPT to help with smart grid data monitoring and analysis. By improving user engagement, offering insightful data, encouraging energy-efficient behaviors, and enabling a more thought-out and sustainable approach to energy management and consumption, ChatGPT makes a significant contribution to smart energy.

HealthCare: ChatGPT can be used in the healthcare and medical fields to help doctors diagnose ailments by looking at patient information, past medical records, and symptoms. It creates individualized treatment programs based on the requirements and preferences of each patient. In order to support evidence-based practice and give patients easily comprehensible medical information and guidance, ChatGPT summarizes and synthesizes medical research.By facilitating communication and information exchange, it makes collaboration amongst healthcare workers easier(Biswas,et al.,2023)..

Public Safety: A variety of applications that can help with information sharing, emergency response, crime prevention, and community participation are included under ChatGPT's role in public safety. ChatGPT facilitates the public's access to real-time information during emergencies, including updates, evacuation routes, and safety instructions. ChatGPT makes it easier for citizens to report occurrences by gathering data that can be sent to the appropriate authorities for a timely reaction (Filali Y., et al,2023; Rane, Nitin., 2023)

Smart Living and Infrastructure: "Smart living" refers to the entire field of administering and improving public services (tourism, culture, education, etc.) that serve to improve the general quality of life of inhabitants, as well as the development of smarter city infrastructures (smart homes, smart buildings, etc.).(P. Sharma, et al,2023) A plethora of facilities for smart buildings are being implemented at a rapid pace thanks to the Internet of Things (IoT). These include air conditioning management, rainwater drainage, security systems for managing authenticated access to buildings, video surveillance and human activity monitoring, alerts for events like fires and gas leaks, and tools for monitoring the structural integrity of buildings (Ketu, Shwet, et al,2022; Mathew, Alex.,2023)

Role of ChatGPT in Predictive Maintenance

Predictive maintenance, or PdM, is a preventative care approach that employs data-driven methods to forecast equipment failure dates so that repairs can be made promptly to avert the malfunction (Dharmi Kapadiya, et al,2023). With the application of technologies, models for predictive maintenance that can foresee possible issues with technology before they arise can be created. To anticipate when a piece of equipment is likely to break, for instance, a model educated on sensor data might help maintenance teams plan ahead for repairs. One technique for employing data analysis to predict and stop equipment problems is called predictive maintenance (Sallam, Malik.,2023). ChatGPT is a machine learning and natural language processing technology that can be trained with past information on equipment failures to offer forecasts and insights in real time. As a natural language recognition model, ChatGPT can be used for predictive maintenance in a number of ways.

By using data analysis tools and methodologies, predictive maintenance is a proactive method that finds anomalies and foresees equipment breakdowns before they happen (Merlin Mancy, A.et al.,2023). Predictive maintenance makes recommendations about when work on maintenance should be done based on real-time data, as opposed to preventative maintenance, which adheres to a predetermined schedule

(Priyanka Sharma, et al,2023a). By averting catastrophic failures and needless maintenance tasks, this technique can drastically lower maintenance expenses and downtime.

Data Evaluation and Processing: ChatGPT can help with the analysis and interpretation of sensor data, maintenance records, and other types of information pertaining to equipment (Parikshit Rawat., et al,2023) The model can offer insights on possible failure sites or abnormalities that might suggest a need for service by analysing the patterns in the data.

Predictive Analytics: ChatGPT can help anticipate failures of equipment or performance degradation by utilizing machine learning algorithms and previous data (Priyanka Sharma, et al,2023b). The model is able to predict when an equipment component is likely to break or need maintenance by looking for developments and patterns in the data.

Decision Support: ChatGPT is a useful tool for engineers and maintenance professionals to make decisions. The model can assist in resource allocation, downtime reduction, and maintenance work prioritization by offering recommendations based on data analysis and predictive models (Priyanka Sharma, et al,2023c).

Notifications and Alerts: ChatGPT can be coupled with monitoring systems to deliver notifications and alerts in real time upon the discovery of abnormalities or possible malfunctions. With this proactive strategy, maintenance personnel may move quickly to resolve minor issues before they become larger ones.

Information Base: ChatGPT can be used as a repository for best practices, maintenance protocols, equipment specs, and troubleshooting manuals. The model has the potential to enhance decision-making and task efficiency for maintenance personnel by giving them immediate access to pertinent information.

Training and Education: Maintenance staff can be trained on equipment-specific procedures, data analysis tools, and predictive maintenance techniques using ChatGPT. The model can assist in enhancing the abilities and expertise of maintenance teams by offering interactive training modules and mimicking real-world events.

Customer Support: ChatGPT can offer customer support by responding to questions on maintenance plans, device status, and troubleshooting techniques in sectors where device uptime is crucial. Customer satisfaction and loyalty can be improved by the model by providing timely and accurate information.

Unlike reactive or preventative maintenance, predictive maintenance aims to find possible problems with technology before they become expensive breakdowns (Priyanka Sharma, et al,2023d). By taking a proactive stance, companies may plan maintenance tasks based on information-driven recommendations, as opposed to depending on time frames or awaiting equipment to malfunction (P. Sharma et al,2023e) Predictive maintenance has many advantages, such as longer equipment life, lower maintenance costs, and less downtime.

The fourth version of OpenAI's Creative Writing Pre-trained Transformer (GPT) models, which are intended to comprehend and produce writing that resembles that of a person, is called ChatGPT-4(Sethi, S.S.,et al 2023) GPT models are renowned for their capacity for deep learning. By providing improved context comprehension, more precise processing of information, and more expressive and subtle language production, ChatGPT-4 outperforms its predecessors (Akshat Tanwar., et al,2023). ChatGPT may be a great tool for predictive maintenance since it can analyse data, forecast equipment failures, help with decision-making, create warnings, act as a knowledge source, assist with training, and provide customer assistance(Sharma, P., & Rathi., 2023) Organizations can increase operational efficiency, lower maintenance costs, and enhance equipment reliability by utilizing conversational AI.

Figure 2. Predictive maintenance

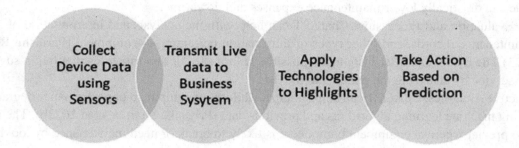

Review of Impact of ChatGPT Adoption in Smart Cities

An overview of ChatGPT adoption's possible effects in smart cities may be found here. Enhanced Public Participation: ChatGPT can act as a digital assistant for residents, giving them details on public transportation, local services, events, and more (Sharma, P., 2023e). The concept has the potential to improve citizen happiness and involvement by providing prompt and customized answers to questions. Effective Service Delivery: ChatGPT has the ability to automate regular questions and duties for city services, including parking, garbage disposal, utility billing, and permits. The system can free up personnel to work on more difficult and value-added tasks by managing these jobs efficiently.

Improved Accessible: ChatGPT can be included into a number of technological platforms and interfaces, such as websites, mobile apps, and kiosks, to offer accessible services and information to people with impairments. All inhabitants' quality of life can be enhanced by the approach by guaranteeing inclusion.

ChatGPT is able to evaluate enormous volumes of information gathered from camera footage, sensors, and other Internet of things devices placed all around the city(Sharma, P., 2023f). The model can assist city officials in making well-informed decisions about public safety, traffic management, infrastructure development, and environmental sustainability by producing conclusions and proposals based on this data.

Safety for the public and emergency response: In times of crisis, such as emergencies, catastrophes, or security situations, ChatGPT can help emergency services by giving them access to real-time information and direction. Through arranging for resources and corresponding with people, the system identifies the risk and predict solutions.

Simplified Governance: ChatGPT may streamline workflows and administrative activities in city departments, including budget planning, human resources, and procurement(Sharma, P., 2023g). The concept can improve accountability and governance through increasing efficiency and transparency.

Environmental Sustainability: ChatGPT can assist with sustainability programs by tracking pollution levels, evaluating environmental data, and encouraging environmentally conscious behavior in the community (Prasad G, A.,2023) The concept has the potential to create an environmentally friendly and more habitable city through increasing awareness and promoting sustainable habits(Maharajan, K., et al,2023).

Promotion of Culture and Tourism: ChatGPT can give visitors and locals information on historical landmarks, local eateries, and cultural events. Through bolstering the city's tourism sector and cultural legacy, the concept can boost economic development and improve the experience for visitors.

Cost Savings: ChatGPT can assist with cost savings by automating repetitive operations and optimizing resource allocation. Cities can increase budget efficiency and save operating expenses by utilizing

Figure 3. Impact of ChatGPT adoption

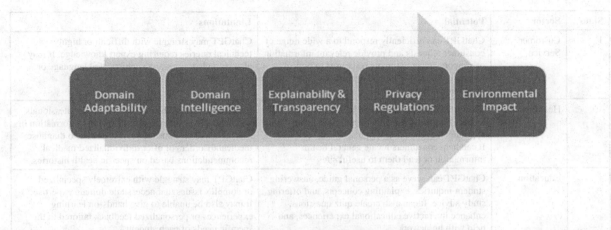

ChatGPT. The concept has the potential to promote long-term sustainability and growth by reallocating savings to prioritized areas including public facilities, social services, and infrastructure development.

Smart city implementations of ChatGPT along with additional conversational AI models have the potential to completely transform urban life and governance through increased citizen involvement, better service delivery, data-driven decision-making, public safety, sustainability, economic growth, and resource allocation optimization. To fully reap the rewards of AI adoption in smart cities, it is imperative to address possible issues with security, confidentiality, bias, and ethical considerations.

ChatGPT's Potential and Limitations Across Multiple Sectors

ChatGPT, like any other AI model, has both benefits and weaknesses in diverse industries. Here's an analysis of its skills and weaknesses in numerous fields (Haleem,Abid.,et al,2022)..

Overall, while ChatGPT excels at answering generic inquiries and giving basic assistance in a variety of industries, its efficacy is limited by a lack of domain-specific knowledge and the inability to do activities requiring real-time data access or specialized expertise. As AI technology advances, overcoming these restrictions will be critical to improving ChatGPT's applicability in a variety of applications.

Challenges of Implementing ChatGPT in Smart Cities

The main challenges of implementing ChatGPT in smart cities are (Tayan, Omar, et al.,2023)

In addition to this there are some more challenges addressed below,

- **Integration with Infrastructure**: Integrating ChatGPT effectively within the existing infrastructure of a smart city, such as mobile apps, websites, or public service interfaces, requires seamless compatibility. Ensuring interoperability and smooth operation can be complex.
- **Continuous Improvement**: Keeping the model updated and relevant to the dynamic needs of a city's residents requires constant monitoring, training, and refinement. Ensuring that ChatGPT stays current and adapts to changing circumstances is an ongoing challenge.
- **Digital Divide and Accessibility**: While AI can enhance citizen services, ensuring equitable access for all residents regardless of their digital literacy, language proficiency, or access to tech-

Table 1. ChatGPT's potential and limitations across multiple sectors

Sl.no	Sector	Potential	Limitations
1	Customer Service	ChatGPT can efficiently respond to a wide range of consumer requests and provide relevant information or support. It can automate responses to typical requests, decreasing human agents' workload and improving response times.	ChatGPT may struggle with difficult or highly technical queries requiring expert knowledge. It may also struggle to interpret sophisticated language or contextual inquiry.
	Healthcare	ChatGPT can provide general health information, answer frequently asked questions, and assist with appointment scheduling or prescription reminders. It can help consumers locate general health information or lead them to useful sites.	ChatGPT is not a substitute for medical professionals and may deliver incorrect or misleading information in crucial health circumstances. It is unable to diagnose medical disorders or offer individualized medical recommendations based on specific health histories.
	Education	ChatGPT can serve as a personal guide, answering student inquiries, explaining concepts, and offering study advice. It can also create quiz questions, enhance interactive educational experiences, and help with homework.	ChatGPT may struggle with extremely specialized or complex issues that necessitate domain expertise. It may also be unable to give hands-on learning experiences or personalized feedback tailored to the specific needs of each student.
	Finance	ChatGPT can provide basic financial advice, such as account balances and transaction history, as well as information on banking goods and services. It can also help with budgeting, cost tracking, and financial guidance.	ChatGPT may not contain real-time financial data or sensitive personal information, which limits its capacity to provide full financial planning and investment advice. It may also lack the regulatory understanding needed to answer legal and compliance-related questions.
	E-commerce	ChatGPT can function as an automated marketing aid, assisting customers in finding products, answering queries about product characteristics or availability, and providing suggestions based on user preferences. It can also help with order management, returns, and refunds.	ChatGPT may struggle with complex product inquiries or comprehensive technical details. It may also be unable to handle transactional operations such as payment processing or inventory management.

nology is crucial. Some segments of the population might struggle to interact effectively with AI-driven systems.

Figure 4. Challenges of implementing ChatGPT in smart cities

Data Privacy and Security
- Smart cities gather vast amounts of data. Maintaining the privacy and security of this data, especially when using AI like ChatGPT, is critical. Ensuring that personal information remains confidential and protected from potential breaches or misuse is a significant challenge.

Accuracy and Reliability
- ChatGPT's responses are based on the data it's trained on. Ensuring accurate and reliable information becomes a challenge if the model encounters queries or scenarios it hasn't been adequately trained for. This can lead to misinformation or incomplete responses.

Contextual Understanding
- While ChatGPT is proficient in understanding language, it might struggle with grasping the specific context of a smart city's environment. Understanding local nuances, regional dialects, or slang can pose challenges in delivering accurate responses.

- **Ethical and Bias Considerations**: AI models can inherit biases from the data they are trained on. Ensuring that ChatGPT's responses are fair, unbiased, and ethical across diverse demographics is essential for its successful implementation in a smart city.

Certainly! Implementing ChatGPT in smart cities can benefit from additional features that enhance its utility and effectiveness:

- **Multilingual Support**: Smart cities often have diverse populations speaking various languages. Adding multilingual support to ChatGPT enables it to cater to a broader range of citizens, breaking language barriers and fostering inclusivity.
- **Real-time Data Integration**: Incorporating real-time data feeds from various city sensors, traffic cameras, weather updates, and public transport schedules can enable ChatGPT to provide up-to-date information, such as traffic updates, weather advisories, or public transportation status.
- **Interactive Mapping and Navigation**: Integrating mapping and navigation capabilities allows ChatGPT to help users find specific locations, plan routes, suggest transportation options, and offer real-time navigation guidance within the city (Dash.,et al,,2022).
- **Service Integration**: Connecting ChatGPT with various city services like utility bill payments, scheduling appointments with government offices, reporting issues (like potholes or malfunctioning streetlights), and accessing emergency services can make it a central hub for citizen interaction.
- **Personalization and User Profiles**: Allowing users to create profiles or accounts within the ChatGPT interface can enable personalized assistance and faster access to frequently used services or information.
- **Voice Recognition and Assistance**: Integrating voice-based interactions with ChatGPT can improve accessibility, allowing citizens to engage hands-free, especially in situations like driving or for those with disabilities.
- **Predictive Analysis for City Planning**: Leveraging ChatGPT's capabilities for analysing historical data and citizen queries can aid in predictive analytics for city planning, helping authorities make informed decisions about future infrastructure and services(Du, Haiping, et al.,2023)
- **Community Engagement and Feedback**: Creating features that facilitate community discussions, gather feedback, and engage citizens in decision-making processes can foster a sense of belonging and involvement within the city's development.
- **Energy and Resource Management Assistance**: Providing tips, suggestions, and information on energy conservation, waste management, and resource optimization can contribute to the city's sustainability goals.

FUTURE OF SMART CITIES WITH CHATGPT

The future of smart cities with ChatGPT looks promising, offering several advancements and transformations (Ketu, Shwet, et al,2022).

- **Enhanced Citizen Engagement**: ChatGPT can serve as a personalized, 24/7 interface for citizens, offering immediate and accurate information on various city services, events, and resources.

Figure 5. Transformation of smart cities with ChatGPT

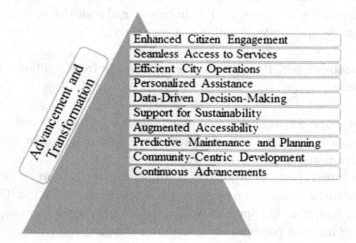

This fosters better engagement between residents and the city administration (Alahi, Md Eshrat E., et al.,2023).

- **Seamless Access to Services**: Citizens can access and interact with city services, pay bills, report issues, and receive real-time updates through a single conversational interface, making city services more accessible and user-friendly (Alahi, Md Eshrat E., et al.,2023).

- **Efficient City Operations**: Integrating ChatGPT with various city systems, such as traffic management, emergency services, waste management, and energy distribution, can optimize operations and response times based on real-time data and citizen queries(Alahi, Md Eshrat E., et al.,2023).

- **Personalized Assistance**: Through machine learning and user profiling, ChatGPT can provide personalized recommendations, services, and information tailored to individual preferences and past interactions, enhancing user experience(Alahi, Md Eshrat E., et al.,2023; Syed, Abbas Shah, et al.,2021)

- **Data-Driven Decision-Making**: ChatGPT can aid city planners and administrators by analyzing citizen queries and data trends, providing valuable insights for informed decision-making regarding infrastructure, services, and resource allocation.

- **Support for Sustainability**: ChatGPT can promote sustainable practices by providing guidance on eco-friendly living, efficient transportation options, waste reduction, and supporting initiatives aligned with the city's environmental goals.

- **Augmented Accessibility**: With voice recognition and multilingual support, ChatGPT can cater to a wider audience, including those with disabilities or language barriers, ensuring equitable access to city services and information.

- **Predictive Maintenance and Planning**: By analyzing ongoing citizen queries and data trends, ChatGPT can anticipate potential issues and aid in proactive maintenance of city infrastructure, reducing downtimes and improving overall efficiency.

- **Community-Centric Development**: ChatGPT can facilitate community discussions, gather feedback, and involve citizens in decision-making processes, fostering a sense of ownership and collaboration in shaping the city's future.
- **Continuous Advancements**: As AI technology evolves, ChatGPT in smart cities will likely see continuous improvements in natural language understanding, context awareness, and adaptability, providing more sophisticated and human-like interactions.

CONCLUSION

By facilitating the development of more effective and sustainable urban environments, generative AI holds the potential to completely transform the future of smart cities. Conversational agents and digital assistants Chatbots and virtual assistants, efficient municipal operations, and citizen-focused services that are tailored to their needs, and are just a few more advantages that generative AI may bring to smart cities. AI's adoption into numerous industries is unavoidable, necessitating a proactive approach to educating individuals about the changing nature of work and collaboration. This technology can be used by smart cities to improve services and better serve their local communities. We can negotiate the developing landscape with resilience and responsibility if we embrace ethical practices, promote openness, and prioritize user education. Smart cities can carefully innovate by utilizing AI to greatly benefit their populations by developing governance systems and being aware of potential threats.

As AI evolves, a commitment to responsible creation, ethical application, and continued study will be critical in realizing its full potential for societal benefit. Finally, the voyage through AI communication reveals a complicated tapestry of possibilities and obstacles. The future of AI communication is dependent not only on technology breakthroughs, but also on a shared commitment to creating an AI environment that is compatible with human values, diversity, and ethical issues.

REFERENCES

Biswas, S. S. (2023). Role of chat gpt in public health. *Annals of Biomedical Engineering*, *51*(5), 868–869. doi:10.1007/s10439-023-03172-7 PMID:36920578

Cowen, T. (2022). *ChatGPT Could Make Democracy Even More Messy*. Bloomberg.

Dash, B., & Sharma, P. (2022). Role of Artificial Intelligence in Smart Cities for Information Gathering and Dissemination - A Review. *Academic Journal of Research and Scientific Publishing.*, *4*(39), 58–75. doi:10.52132/Ajrsp.e.2022.39.4

Du, H., Teng, S., Chen, H., Ma, J., Wang, X., Gou, C., Li, B., Ma, S., Miao, Q., Na, X., Ye, P., Zhang, H., Luo, G., & Wang, F.-Y. (2023). Chat with chatgpt on intelligent vehicles: An ieee tiv perspective. *IEEE Transactions on Intelligent Vehicles*, *8*(3), 2020–2026. doi:10.1109/TIV.2023.3253281

Haleem, A. (2022). An era of ChatGPT as a significant futuristic support tool: A study on features, abilities, and challenges. *BenchCouncil transactions on benchmarks, standards and evaluations*, *2*(4), 100089.

Kapadiya, D., Shekhawat, C., & Sharma, P. (2023). A Study on Large Scale Applications of Big Data in Modern Era. *In International Conference on Information Management & Machine Intelligence (ICIMMI2023)*. ACM. https://doi.org/10.1145/3647444.364788

Ketu, S., & Mishra, P. K. (2022). A contemporary survey on IoT based smart cities: Architecture, applications, and open issues. *Wireless Personal Communications*, *125*(3), 2319–2367. doi:10.1007/s11277-022-09658-2

Krugman, P. (2022). Does ChatGPT mean robots are coming for the skilled jobs. *The New York Times*. http://bit. ly/3HdnAp2

Maharajan, K., Kumar, A. V., El Emary, I. M., Sharma, P., Latip, R., Mishra, N., Dutta, A., Manjunatha Rao, L., & Sharma, M. (2023). Blockchain Methods and Data-Driven Decision Making With Autonomous Transportation. In R. Kumar, A. Abdul Hamid, & N. Binti Ya'akub (Eds.), *Effective AI, Blockchain, and E-Governance Applications for Knowledge Discovery and Management* (pp. 176–194). IGI Global. doi:10.4018/978-1-6684-9151-5.ch012

Mathew, A. (2023). Is Artificial Intelligence a World Changer? A Case Study of OpenAI's Chat GPT. *Recent Progress in Science and Technology*, *5*, 35–42. doi:10.9734/bpi/rpst/v5/18240D

Merlin Mancy, A., Kumar, A. V., Latip, R., Jagadamba, G., Chakrabarti, P., Sharma, P., Musirin, I. B., Sharma, M., & Kanchan, B. G. (2024). *Smart Healthcare System, Digital Health and Telemedicine, Management and Emergencies: Patient Emergency Application (PES)*. E-Governance Applications. doi:10.4018/979-8-3693-1722-8.ch008

Mijwil, M. M., Aljanabi, M., & Chat, G. P. T. (2023, January). Towards Artificial Intelligence-Based Cybersecurity: The Practices and ChatGPT Generated Ways to Combat Cybercrime. *Iraqi Journal For Computer Science and Mathematics*, *4*(1), 65–70. doi:10.52866/ijcsm.2023.01.01.0019

Nazir, A., & Wang, Z. (2023). A Comprehensive Survey of ChatGPT: Advancements, Applications, Prospects, and Challenges. *Meta-Radiology*, *1*(2), 100022. doi:10.1016/j.metrad.2023.100022 PMID:37901715

Prasad, G. A., Kumar, A. V., Sharma, P., Irawati, I. D., D. V., C., Musirin, I. B., Abdullah, H. M., & Rao L, M. (2023). Artificial Intelligence in Computer Science: An Overview of Current Trends and Future Directions. In S. Rajest, B. Singh, A. Obaid, R. Regin, & K. Chinnusamy (Eds.), Advances in Artificial and Human Intelligence in the Modern Era (pp. 43-60). IGI Global. doi:10.4018/979-8-3693-1301-5.ch002

Rawat, P., Bhardwaj, A., Lamba, N., Sharma, P., Kumawat, P., & Sharma, P. (2023). Arduino Based IoT Mini Weather Station. *SKIT Research Journal*, *13*(2), 34–41. doi:10.47904/IJSKIT.13.2.2023.34-41

Sallam, M. (2023). ChatGPT utility in healthcare education, research, and practice: systematic review on the promising perspectives and valid concerns. Healthcare, 11(6).

Sethi, S. S., & Sharma, P. (2023). New Developments in the Implementation of IoT in Agriculture. *SN Computer Science*, *4*(5), 503. doi:10.1007/s42979-023-01896-w

Sharma, P. (2023). *Utilizing Explainable Artificial Intelligence to Address Deep Learning in Biomedical Domain, Medical Data Analysis and Processing using Explainable Artificial Intelligence*. Taylor & Francis., doi:10.1201/9781003257721-2

Sharma, P., & Bhatnagar, N. (2023). Passenger Authentication and Ticket Verification at Airport Using QR Code Scanner. *SKIT Research Journal, 13*(2), 10–13. doi:10.47904/IJSKIT.13.1.2023.10-12

Sharma, P., & Dadheech, P. (2023). Modern-age Agriculture with Artificial Intelligence: A review emphasizing Crop Yield Prediction. *EVERGREEN Joint Journal of Novel Carbon Resource Sciences & Green Asia Strategy, 10*(4), 2570–2582. doi:10.5109/7160906

Sharma, P., Dadheech, P., Aneja, N., & Aneja, S. (2023). Predicting Agriculture Yields Based on Machine Learning Using Regression and Deep Learning. *IEEE Access : Practical Innovations, Open Solutions, 11*, 111255–111264. doi:10.1109/ACCESS.2023.3321861

Sharma, P., Dadheech, P., & Senthil Kumar Senthil, A. V. (2023). AI-Enabled Crop Recommendation System Based on Soil and Weather Patterns. In R. Gupta, A. Jain, J. Wang, S. Bharti, & S. Patel (Eds.), *Artificial Intelligence Tools and Technologies for Smart Farming and Agriculture Practices* (pp. 184–199). IGI Global. doi:10.4018/978-1-6684-8516-3.ch010

Sharma, P., & Jain, M. K. (2023). Stock Market Trends Analysis using Extreme Gradient Boosting (XGBoost*). International Conference on Computing, Communication, and Intelligent Systems (ICCCIS),* Greater Noida, India. 10.1109/ICCCIS60361.2023.10425722

Sharma, P., Kapadiya, D., & Bhardwaj, A. (2023). Efficient Note Sharing Model for Collaborative Learning. *SKIT Research Journal, 13*(2), 42–46. doi:10.47904/IJSKIT.13.2.2023.42-46

Sharma, P., & Rathi, Y. (2016, June 5). *Efficient Density-Based Clustering Using Automatic Parameter Detection. Efficient Density-Based Clustering Using Automatic Parameter Detection.* SpringerLink. . doi:10.1007/978-981-10-0767-5_46

Sharma, P., Sharma, C., & Mathur, P. (2023). *Machine Learning-based Stock Market Forecasting using Recurrent Neural Network.* 2023 9th International Conference on Smart Computing and Communications (ICSCC), Kochi, Kerala, India. 10.1109/ICSCC59169.2023.10335083

Syed, A. S., Sierra-Sosa, D., Kumar, A., & Elmaghraby, A. (2021). IoT in smart cities: A survey of technologies, practices and challenges. *Smart Cities, 4*(2), 429–475. doi:10.3390/smartcities4020024

Tanwar, A., Sharma, P., Pandey, A., & Kumar, S. 2023. Intrusion Detection System Based Ameliorated Technique of Pattern Matching. In *Proceedings of the 4th International Conference on Information Management & Machine Intelligence (ICIMMI '22).* Association for Computing Machinery, New York, NY, USA. https://doi.org/10.1145/3590837.3590947

Lock, S. (2022). What is AI chatbot phenomenon ChatGPT and could it replace humans. *The Guardian, 5.*

V., M. V., Kumar, A. S., Sharma, P., Kaur, S., Saleh, O. S., Chennamma, H., & Chaturvedi, A. (2023). AI-Equipped IoT Applications in High-Tech Agriculture Using Machine Learning. In A. Khang (Ed.), *Handbook of Research on AI-Equipped IoT Applications in High-Tech Agriculture* (pp. 38-64). IGI Global. . doi:10.4018/978-1-6684-9231-4.ch003

Chapter 11
Unveiling Privacy, Security, and Ethical Concerns of ChatGPT

Sachin Lalar
Kurukshetra University, India

Tajinder Kumar
(iD) https://orcid.org/0000-0002-7079-7065
Jai Parkash Mukand lal Innovative Engineering and Technology Institute, India

Rajinder Kumar
Punjab University, India

Shubham Kumar
(iD) https://orcid.org/0000-0001-6095-0815
IIMT University, India

ABSTRACT

The increasing popularity of large-scale language models, such as ChatGPT, has led to growing worries about their safety, potential security threats, and ethical implications. This chapter thoroughly examines ChatGPT, an AI-powered chatbot that utilizes topic modeling and reinforcement learning to generate natural and coherent answers. Even though ChatGPT has enormous promise in a variety of fields, it is crucial to critically assess its security, privacy, and ethical implications. By analyzing possible security flaws in ChatGPT deployment across several scenarios, the chapter begins a thorough investigation. The authors thoroughly examine the security concerns that come with the extensive use of this powerful language model, including exploiting its flaws via adversarial attacks and the unexpected ramifications in real-world applications. Finally, the authors examine the unresolved issues in these domains, encouraging collaborative endeavors to guarantee the advancement of safe and ethically extensive language models.

DOI: 10.4018/979-8-3693-6824-4.ch011

INTRODUCTION

Large language Models (LLMs) demonstrate notable performance improvements compared to smaller models when their parameters reach a certain scale. They excel in producing language outputs that are more accurate and cohesive. LLMs demonstrate superior proficiency in language comprehension and creating activities. They are adept at handling complicated linguistic situations because they have the ability to decipher subtle human language as described by grammatical rules. They have advanced language comprehension and generation skills, which enable them to perceive complex human emotions and adhere to grammatical intricacies with remarkable grace (Jangra et al., 2023). The ability of models such as ChatGPT to engage in coherent and engaging conversations has garnered attention, representing a significant advancement in the field of dialogue systems driven by artificial intelligence (AI). In addition to being highly beautiful, these models are capable of comprehensive representation of the complexity of human language because to their ability to recognize patterns and subtleties seen in large-scale corpora. This learning potential pushes the boundaries of what is possible in the field of natural language generation and interpretation, positioning wide language models as essential tools for language modelling and analysis tasks (Bahdanau et al., 2014). (Alec, et al., 2019).

As their capabilities continue to increase, Expansive Language Models (ELMs) have the potential to become revolutionary tools that will change the face of human-computer communication. LLMs have the capacity to effectively address a wide range of Natural Language Processing (NLP) problems. They can be customized for specific uses such as sentiment analysis, machine translation, and text classification, demonstrating their adaptability and versatility. LLMs, like ChatGPT, are unique in the world of conversational AI applications since they produce replies that mimic those of a person (Sharma & Sharma, 2022). As a large language model, ChatGPT has garnered attention globally for its remarkable capacity to participate in conversations that are both understandable and interesting. One major advantage of LLMs is their capacity to learn from vast corpora. As a result, they are able to document and comprehend a wide range of linguistic nuances and patterns, proving their value as essential instruments for language modelling and analytical tasks (Liu & Lapata, 2019; Radford et al., 2018; Cayir & Navruz, 2021; Lu et al., 2023). Large language models (LLMs) have improved linguistic capacities, as demonstrated by the following examples:

1. **Improved Output Accuracy:**
   ◦ By providing more accurate and coherent language outputs, LLMs outperform smaller models in terms of performance.
2. **Advanced Language Understanding:**
   ◦ LLMs are capable of understanding complex human sentences with the use of grammatical rules because they have enhanced language comprehension and creating abilities.
3. **Versatile Natural Language Processing (NLP):**
   ◦ LLMs exhibit their flexibility and adaptability by effectively handling a wide range of NLP tasks, such as text categorization, sentiment analysis, and machine translation.
4. **Conversational AI Excellence:**
   ◦ Notably, models such as ChatGPT are noticed for their ability to participate in well-structured and lively conversations, demonstrating their potential in conversational AI applications.

5.   Learning from Large-Scale Corpora:

○   LLMs may identify and understand a wide range of linguistic regularities and complexities by utilizing their capacity to learn from enormous datasets. This makes them good tools for language modeling and analytic tasks.

FACTORS CONTRIBUTING TO THE ELMS

Recent years have seen an unprecedented surge in the popularity of ELMs, which is transforming the fields of AI and NLP. Large sizes and intricate patterns are characteristics of these models that have piqued attention in a wide range of industries and academic fields. The goal of this research is to fully examine the factors that have led to the current surge in popularity of ELMs, the revolutionary impact they have had on a range of applications, and the potential long-term ramifications they will have on society, technology, and other fields.

1.   Defining Expansive Language Models:

Large language models (LLMs), also known as expansive language models, are distinguished by their extensive neural network topologies and massive training datasets. T5, BERT, and GPT-3 are notable examples. These models have billions of parameters, which allows them to recognize subtleties and deep patterns in language, paving the way for important advancements in natural language processing.

2.   Technological Advancements Driving Popularity:

Significant advancements in algorithmic design, hardware capabilities, and the accessibility of vast computing resources could all contribute to the growing acceptance of ELMs. The training of increasingly larger models has been made possible by the advancement of graphics processing units (GPUs) and tensor processing units (TPUs), beyond the bounds of what was once thought to be computationally impractical.

3.   Unprecedented Performance Gains:

When comparing ELMs to their smaller counterparts, performance benefits are significant. More accurate language creation, contextual comprehension, and improved performance in a variety of natural language processing tasks are the outcomes of the unparalleled advancements in natural language processing and context understanding.

4.   Versatility Across Industries:

The expansion of ELMs' application in a range of industries has been spurred by their flexibility. These models find applications in a wide range of industries, including healthcare, banking, education, and entertainment. ELMs enable advances in virtual assistants, chatbots, content creation, language translation, and even drug research.

5.   **Revolutionizing Natural Language Processing:**

The rise in popularity of ELMs has caused a paradigm change in NLP, leading to significant break-throughs in once challenging tasks including sentiment analysis, language translation, and summarization. These models' ability to comprehend and produce writing that resembles that of a person has significant ramifications for automating language-related tasks.

6.   **Challenges and Ethical Considerations:**

Despite their promise, the increasing acceptance of ELMs has raised difficulties and moral dilemmas. Challenges like as biased training data, potential model abuse, and the environmental impact of training massive models have raised considerable concerns in academia and society at large.

7.   **Educational Impact and Accessibility:**

The rise in popularity of ELMs has also changed research accessibility in education. Open-source frameworks and pre-trained models are now widely available, allowing researchers and developers to leverage ELMs for a variety of applications without having to start from scratch.

8.   **The Role of OpenAI and Other Innovators:**

Trailblazing firms such as OpenAI have been significantly responsible for the surge in popularity of ELMs. The larger AI community has been inspired to innovate and ask questions by OpenAI's commitment to advancing AI research and its deliberate distribution of huge language models to the public.

9.   **Future Implications and Areas of Exploration:**

The increasing ubiquity of ELMs prompts questions about how AI research and development should go in the future. Research and innovation are welcome on subjects such as investigating ways to improve the efficiency of these models, addressing moral dilemmas, and extending their use to specialized industries (Ma et al., 2022) (Ranathunga et al., 2023) (Lu et al., 2023).

Significance of the Study in the Broader Discussion on Ethical and Security Dimensions

In the broader discussion of security and ethical issues surrounding artificial intelligence (AI), this work is crucially relevant. The use of ChatGPT, an AI-powered chatbot that makes use of complex language models, raises a number of ethical concerns. The study sheds light on potential risks associated with the widespread usage of huge language models by thoroughly examining security issues and offering mitigation strategies. It highlights the need for ethical considerations to go hand in hand with technological advancement and offers insightful information about the current discussion around responsible AI development. For academics, politicians, and business professionals involved in developing ethical standards for AI systems, this article is a useful resource (Brown et al., 2020; Jangra et al., 2023)..

The Role of ChatGPT in Shaping the Landscape of Large Language Models

An example of a huge language model that is transforming the field of artificial intelligence is Chat-GPT. Due to its ability to produce language that is both coherent and appropriate for the situation, it is a versatile tool that may be used in a variety of settings, including customer service, education, mental health treatment, productivity, and content creation. This study, however, delves further to examine the subtleties of its implications for privacy, security, and ethics. The work helps define the proper use of big language models by assessing the model's shortcomings and providing mitigating strategies. It defines the story around the proper creation and application of such models by highlighting their dual position as potent tools and potential causes of concern.

Emphasis on the Need for Sustained Research in the Evolving AI Landscape

In underscoring the necessity for continued study, the article underscores the dynamic and developing character of the AI ecosystem. Rapid breakthroughs in AI technology, especially in the field of massive language models, necessitate continual research and comprehension of their ramifications. Since ChatGPT is just one aspect of the larger AI ecosystem, the study recommends further research to stay up-to-date with new issues. By understanding that security, privacy, and ethical issues are fluid and prone to change, the study urges academics, developers, and stakeholders to be watchful and adapt to the shifting scene. This focus on persistent research highlights the commitment to responsible innovation and the realization that ethical issues should be intrinsic to the whole lifespan of AI development.

KEY COMPONENTS OF CHATGPT'S WORKING MODEL

OpenAI's ChatGPT has become a prominent example of a huge language model, demonstrating its ability to produce text that is both coherent and appropriate for the given context. Among the various industries that employ it are customer service, education, mental health treatment, personal productivity, and content development. The key elements of ChatGPT's operational model are listed in Table 1, along with a detailed explanation of each element (Lowrey et al., 2023) (Ray, 2023) (Jangra et al., 2023) (Gambhir & Gupta, 2017). Gaining an understanding of these elements enables one to comprehend the architecture and techniques underlying ChatGPT's language-generating powers. Each part plays a crucial role in the model's comprehension, interpretation, and generation of human-like text responses.

Language models, particularly large ones like ChatGPT, have become widely accepted in many fields in recent years because of their remarkable language-generating powers. But as more of these models are produced, the need to recognize and respond to safety and security risks increases. This chapter examines the necessity of considering these problems in the context of ChatGPT, outlining potential repercussions and providing sensible development solutions.

OVERVIEW OF SECURITY VULNERABILITIES ASSOCIATED WITH CHATGPT

The widespread use of ChatGPT makes it even more imperative to evaluate its safety and security implications as soon as possible. This chapter provides a thorough literature analysis of current unresolved

Table 1. Essential components of ChatGPT's functioning model

Model Component	Description
Transformer Architecture	ChatGPT features multiple levels of self-attention mechanisms and is built on the Transformer architecture. This makes it possible for the model to understand contextual connections in input sequences and to recognize word dependencies.
Attention Mechanism	ChatGPT uses the attention technique to focus on different regions of the input sequence in order to generate each token. This facilitates the model's consideration of relevant context, which is necessary to generate solutions that make sense and fit the particular scenario.
Encoder-Decoder Structure	ChatGPT employs an encoder-decoder structure, wherein the encoder processes the input sequence and then produces the output sequence. For tasks involving language modelling and sequence generation, this architecture is essential.
Embedding Layers	The embedding layers that transform input tokens into high-dimensional vectors enable the model to represent and process data efficiently. Embeddings are used by ChatGPT to convert words into continuous vector representations.
Positional Encoding	Positional encoding is used to improve the input embeddings and provide word positions within a sequence. This is necessary for the model to understand the phrase's word order.
Vocabulary and Tokenization	A predefined vocabulary is used by ChatGPT, and input sequences are tokenized into subword units. During training and generation, tokenization enables the model to handle a wide range of words and subwords.
Self-Attention Mechanism	By allowing each word in the input sequence to pay attention to every other word, the self-attention technique helps to detect relationships and dependencies between the words. This procedure is essential to the model's comprehension of context.
Layer Normalization	The activations within each layer are stabilized and normalized by applying layer normalization. As a result, the model is more resilient during training and can continue to function consistently with a range of inputs.
Feedforward Neural Network	A feedforward neural network is incorporated into every layer of ChatGPT. By processing the self-attention mechanism's output, this network introduces nonlinearity, which enables the model to recognize intricate patterns in the data.
Decoder Masking	For the purpose of keeping it from handling tokens in the future, the decoder is hidden during training. This enables autoregressive training by guaranteeing that the model generates each token solely using data that is currently available.
Parameter Sharing	The same parameters are applied multiple times throughout the input sequence in ChatGPT via a method known as parameter sharing. Because of this, the model is able to learn patterns over the entire sequence and generalize effectively.

issues pertaining to huge language models and security, privacy, and ethics, with a focus on ChatGPT and the use of tables. It delves into the subtle issues that still provide significant barriers to the appropriate design and application of AI systems. These challenges consist of, but are not restricted to:

1. **Security Vulnerabilities:** Finding and fixing new security flaws, like being open to adversarial attacks and unexpected consequences in practical applications.
2. **Privacy Concerns:** Handling persistent difficulties with data processing, user profiling, and the revelation of private information when interacting with large language models.
3. **Ethical Implications:** Managing the ethical landscape entails avoiding biased results, potential disregard, and the proper deployment of AI systems in a range of contexts.

This chapter provides a thorough analysis of the security threats associated with ChatGPT, as well as a discussion of the main solutions and upcoming strategies for strengthening the security posture of the model, as shown in Table 2 (Borji, 2023) (Stahl & Eke, 2024) (Koh et al, 2023). It emphasizes how

Table 2. Overview of security vulnerabilities associated with ChatGPT

Security Aspect	Description	Key Solutions	Future Directions
Model Architecture Evaluation	In-depth investigation of ChatGPT's architecture to find any faults or vulnerabilities.	Regular architectural audits and evaluations by security professionals.	Incorporating sophisticated security methods throughout the model's design phase.
Biases in Training Data	Identification of biases existing in the training data, which may result in skewed outputs or perpetuate prejudices.	Altering training datasets to incorporate a wide variety of viewpoints.	Development of algorithms for automated bias identification and reduction is still ongoing.
Adversarial Attacks	Analysis of possible adversarial attacks against ChatGPT, trying to influence inputs and create undesired or damaging outputs. (Pu, et al., 2023)	Implementing adversarial training throughout the model's training phase.	Investigations into new forms of hostile attack and ongoing defensive system improvement.
Data Privacy Concerns	Scrutiny of how ChatGPT manages sensitive user data and the possibility for inadvertent data leaks.	Robust encryption approaches for user data during model interactions. (El-Kassas et al., 2021)	Creation of privacy-preserving methods to reduce data exposure, including federated learning.
Ethical Considerations	Exploration of ethical problems, including biases in language production and possible exploitation of the model for harmful purposes.	Integration of ethical guidelines and review processes in model development.	Joint efforts to develop industry-wide moral guidelines for language modeling.
Model Transparency and Explainability	Examination of the openness and explainability of ChatGPT's decision-making process, ensuring users can understand and trust the model's results.	Implementation of explainability techniques to offer insights into model choices.	Improvements in model transparency via user-friendly interfaces and explainable AI approaches.
Deployment Security	Assessing security procedures in order to protect against malicious attacks and unauthorized access during the deployment phase.	Implementation of safe access restrictions and frequent security audits.	Standardized security techniques and ongoing deployment security protocol enhancement are important.
Real-time Monitoring and Adaptation	Monitoring the model's behavior in real-time and adjusting to emerging security risks and hostile tactics.	Regular surveillance combined with anomaly detection to identify potential threats early.	Integration of dynamic adaptation techniques that can respond to developing security problems in real-time.

important it is to carry out ongoing research, collaborate with others, and take proactive measures to solve new security issues in AI models.

Analysis of Adversarial Attack

The analysis of adversarial attacks that take advantage of model weaknesses, their impact on applications, and suggested mitigation strategies to fortify ChatGPT against such attacks is summarized in Table 3 in an organized manner (Ray, 2023) (Kreps & Kriner, 2023).

COMPREHENSIVE ANALYSIS OF PRIVACY CONCERNS ASSOCIATED WITH CHATGPT

A methodical analysis of the privacy concerns associated with ChatGPT is provided in Table 4, which focuses on data management, user profiling, content creation, consent, security, user control, external

Table 3. Overview of adversarial attacks associated with ChatGPT

Aspect	Description	Impact on Applications	Mitigation Strategies
Adversarial Attacks Definition	Analysis of attacks that purposefully alter input data to trick the model and provide strange results.	Erroneous or damaging language production, skewed model predictions.	To strengthen the model against manipulated inputs, regular adversarial training is used. Encouraging resilience to slight modifications.
Model Vulnerabilities	Identification of particular flaws within ChatGPT that render it subject to malicious misuse.	Degradation of model dependability, possible exploitation of unexpected routes.	Regular model audits, vulnerability assessments, and correcting detected issues via model changes.
Targeted Applications	An examination of which apps are more vulnerable to hostile assaults and where such attacks may have a major effect.	Applications include as automated answers, sentiment analysis, content development, and crucial decision making.	Context-aware filtering and input validation are examples of application-specific defensive techniques that may be tailored to reduce hostile effect.
Impact on Decision-Making	Recognizing the potential effects of adversarial assaults on application decision-making.	Compromising the model's decision-making accuracy and perhaps producing unintended results.	Combining confidence scoring with uncertainty estimates allows you to filter and detect possibly altered outcomes.
Bias Amplification	Analyzing how the model's language creation might be biased in ways that are made worse by adversarial approaches.	Potential for the spread of hazardous information and the reinforcement of prejudiced linguistic habits.	By actively addressing and minimizing biases via ongoing model refinement, debiasing strategies are put into practice throughout training.
User Trust and Confidence	Analysis of how user confidence is undermined by adversarial assaults in ChatGPT-powered apps.	loss of user trust and possible misuse of AI programs as a result of their perceived unreliability..	Encouraging user knowledge of possible adversarial hazards by open communication about the capabilities and limits of the model.
Potential for Misinformation	An analysis of the likelihood that adversarial assaults may cause the model to provide false information.	Generation of misleading or inaccurate information, contributing to the spread of disinformation.	To improve the model's capacity to identify reliable information, implement content verification techniques, fact-check, and include external context.
Continuous Monitoring	Understanding the requirement for continual monitoring to identify hostile assaults and react in real-time	Rapid distribution of altered material and extended exposure to misleading results.	Adopting anomaly-detection systems for continuous monitoring, responding instantly to countermeasures, and adjusting to changing hostile strategies.
Collateral Impact on Users	Analysis of how adversarial assaults might have unforeseen implications on end-users of programs.	Possible psychological anguish, dissemination of false information with practical repercussions.	To detect and mitigate collateral affects, user education programs should be included together with explicit disclaimers and user feedback systems. (Kaloudi & Li, 2021)

integrations, and privacy rule compliance (DeLong et al., 2022). It highlights how important it is to carry out a thorough investigation and uphold transparent protocols in order to appropriately handle any privacy concerns systems.

COMPREHENSIVE ANALYSIS OF ETHICAL CONSIDERATION ASSOCIATED WITH CHATGPT

These ethical considerations underscore the necessity for continual oversight, transparency, and preventative measures in order to address any potential ethical difficulties using ChatGPT. The ethical

Table 4. Overview of adversarial attacks associated with ChatGPT

Privacy Concern	Description	Strategies to Address and Mitigate
Data Handling and Storage	Concerns around the possibility of monitoring personal preferences, behavior, and sensitive data due to the construction of user profiles via ongoing interactions.	Give users explicit privacy notices outlining the usage of their data and whether profiling occurs. Implement clear opt-in and opt-out processes for activities related to user monitoring and profiling. Aggregate and anonymize data to decrease the granularity of user profiles. Audit and evaluate the need for user monitoring on a regular basis in order to improve the model.
User Profiling and Tracking	The potential consequences of ChatGPT accidentally producing answers that divulge private information or create rude or improper material.	To prevent the generation of inappropriate or sensitive content, implement content filtering systems. To combat biases and reduce the likelihood of producing harmful content, regularly update and diversify training data. Incorporate techniques for user input to identify and address content creation errors or unwanted content.
Sensitive Content Exposure	Risks associated with ChatGPT inadvertently generating responses that reveal sensitive information or produce inappropriate or offensive content.	Implement content filtering systems to avoid the creation of sensitive or improper content. To minimize biases and lower the possibility of producing damaging content, update and diversify training data on a regular basis. Integrate user feedback methods to identify and remedy instances of content generation that may be seen as improper or objectionable.
Consent and Notification	Concerns about poor information and openness around data use, leading to possible concerns with user permission.	Clearly and concisely notify users about privacy, describing the methods used, shared, and data collection for them. Provide users the option to opt in or out of specific data processing activities by implementing granular consent techniques. Inform users of any changes affecting data handling procedures and communicate privacy policy amendments on a regular basis. Provide streamlined user interfaces for modifying preferences and privacy settings. Establish user-friendly interfaces for adjusting privacy settings and preferences.
Integration with External Services	Privacy considerations connected to data sharing and security when ChatGPT interfaces with external services or APIs.	Conduct rigorous privacy evaluations of external services and APIs coupled with ChatGPT. Prioritize the usage of secure and authenticated communication methods for data sharing with external organizations. Minimize data exchange with external services to the degree essential for functioning. Clearly disclose to consumers when their data may be shared with external services.
Security Measures	Risks connected with poor security measures, possibly resulting to unauthorized access, data breaches, and privacy violations.	Implement end-to-end encryption for data transit between users and ChatGPT. Regularly perform security audits and vulnerability assessments to detect and remedy any issues. Enforce access rules to limit system and data access to authorized personnel. Foster a security-conscious culture, educate developers and staff on best practices for data protection.
User Consent and Control	Concerns regarding the lack of user control over data gathering and utilization, leading to possible unhappiness and privacy infringements.	Design user interfaces that clearly show choices for regulating data collection and use preferences. Provide user-friendly tools for users to view, amend, or delete their personal data. Enable users to quickly alter privacy settings, including opting out of specific data processing operations. Regularly seek user input to understand growing expectations around data control
Adherence to Privacy Regulations	Risks linked with non-compliance with privacy legislation and standards, possibly resulting to legal and ethical issues.	Establish a thorough privacy compliance procedure, guaranteeing conformity to applicable legislation and standards. Regularly evaluate and update privacy policies to meet with changes in legal requirements. Provide users with tools to exercise their privacy rights, such as access, modification, and deletion of their personal data. Work together with the compliance and legal teams to stay ahead of emerging privacy regulations. (Ray, 2023) (Yadav et al., 2022)

Table 5. Overview of adversarial attacks associated with ChatGPT

Ethical Consideration	Description	Implications and Mitigation Strategies
A. Bias in Training Data	Possibility of biases in the training data used to build ChatGPT, which might lead to unfair or biased model results.	**Implications:** A bias in the training set of data could result in the creation of outputs that reinforce and reflect prevailing social preconceptions. Stereotypes may be reinforced or unfair treatment may ensue. **Mitigation Strategies:** To identify and lessen biases, do thorough audits on training data. Using techniques such as adversarial training can reduce the model's sensitivity to skewed inputs. To reduce the impact of biased tendencies and cover a wider range of opinions, diversify your training data.
B. Potential Misuse	There is a chance that ChatGPT may be used maliciously to create offensive material, disseminate false information, or carry out unethical actions.	**Implications:** Misuse may give rise to inaccurate information being created and shared, bolster false information, or damage someone's reputation. **Mitigation Strategies:** Use content filtering techniques to recognize and stop the creation of offensive or dangerous information. To stop harmful information from spreading, keep an eye on and regulate user interactions. To prevent abuse and set repercussions for unethical activity, clearly define usage regulations and enforce them. s
C. Responsibilities in Ethical AI Deployment	The moral responsibility of developers and institutions using ChatGPT, including as openness, user privacy, and safeguarding users' welfare.	**Implications:** Not upholding one's ethical obligations may damage relationships, violate privacy, and have a detrimental effect on society. **Mitigation Strategies:** Emphasize openness by providing explicit information on ChatGPT's features, constraints, and any biases. To secure user information, put strong privacy protections in place, such as data anonymization and encryption. Users should have authority over their data, and procedures for responsibility, openness, and restitution in the event of ethical issues should be established. Promote an ethical AI culture inside companies by stressing responsible development, ethical reviews on a regular basis, and continuing education for developers on ethical issues. (Jain et al., 2022) (Ouyang et al., 2022)

implementation of AI systems, their promotion of user well-being, and their positive social impact are all greatly dependent on developers and organizations. Table 5 provides a summary of the major privacy issues related to ChatGPT along with recommendations for how to handle and lower these risks (Cao et al., 2018). Implementing these strategies may assist developers and providers increase user privacy, generate confidence, and comply with privacy standards and legislation.

As the AI environment continues to develop, it is our obligation to manage this progress responsibly. Large language models contain enormous promise, but their ethical deployment and the protecting of user privacy must remain key. We create the conditions for a future in which big language models advance humankind while upholding the values of justice, openness, and security by valuing ethical concerns and encouraging collaborative research. The advancement of AI is a shared responsibility, and together, we can design a future where technology matches with our common values and goals.

Table 6. Potential research questions

Research Area	Key Focus	Potential Research Questions
Security Implications	Identification and mitigation of security vulnerabilities associated with large language models.	1. How can we strengthen the resilience of big language models against adversarial attacks? 2. What unique security measures may be introduced to avoid unwanted access and data breaches? 3. How do diverse deployment settings effect the security profile of big language models?
Privacy Considerations	Exploration of privacy challenges and solutions in the deployment of large language models.	1. What measures may be taken to enhance user data anonymization and decrease the danger of user profiling? 2. How can we assure openness in data processing and storage procedures to accommodate consumer privacy concerns? 3. What influence do privacy restrictions have on the design and deployment of large language models, and how can compliance be efficiently managed?
Ethical Frameworks	Development and implementation of ethical frameworks for the responsible use of language models.	1. How can the whole process of developing a big language model include ethical considerations? 2. In order to reduce biases and guarantee fairness in model outputs, what moral standards may be set? 3. How can user consent and control be successfully included into the construction of big language models to line with ethical principles?
Explainability and Transparency	Exploration of methods to enhance the explainability and transparency of large language models.	1. What methods may be used to enhance language model outputs' interpretability? 2. How can model builders explain to consumers in a straightforward manner how big language models make decisions? 3. What role does model transparency play in developing user trust, and how can it be balanced with the complexity of language models?
Human-AI Interaction	Investigation of ways to improve the interaction between users and large language models.	1. How can the user experience with huge language models be improved by the refinement of natural language interfaces? 2. How may the ethical issues and performance of language models be repeatedly improved by user feedback? 3. How can cultural and linguistic variables influence the success of big language models in varied user groups?
Bias Detection and Mitigation	Methods to identify and address biases in language models and their impact on generated content.	1. How can we design automated methods for identifying and reducing biases in big language models? 2. What measures may be employed to address and repair biases in training data? 3. How does bias vary across various application domains, and what actions may be implemented to assure fairness and equality in model outputs?
Adaptability to Emerging Technologies	Exploration of how large language models can adapt to and incorporate emerging technologies.	1. What are the ways that huge language models may benefit from advances in natural language comprehension and processing? 2. How can we improve the flexibility of language models using federated learning and edge computing? 3. In order to work with new technologies like virtual assistants and augmented reality, how can language models adapt?
Cross-Disciplinary Collaboration	Promotion of collaboration between AI researchers, ethicists, policymakers, and industry experts.	1. How may interdisciplinary cooperation advance a comprehensive knowledge of the moral and social ramifications of large-scale language models? 2. What platforms and activities can enhance knowledge sharing amongst diverse players in the AI ecosystem? 3. How can legislators and industry experts cooperate to build regulatory frameworks that combine innovation with ethical considerations?

FUTURE RESEARCH GUIDELINES

This chapter recommendations define major focal areas, prospective research issues, and routes for inquiry in the continuing development and deployment of big language models, seeking to create ethical and effective AI developments.

SUMMARIZATION OF KEY FINDINGS

We have exposed important new information from our investigation into the security, privacy, and ethical issues related to big language models, as shown by ChatGPT. The analysis uncovered serious security flaws, such as vulnerability to hostile attacks and possible privacy issues with data processing and user profiling. Moreover, it emphasized the multifaceted ethical environment, underlining the significance of responsible AI deployment to eliminate biases and avoid exploitation.

Call to Action for Continued Research and Collaboration in the Field

Our present comprehension is not the conclusion of the excursion. Instead, it acts as a call to action for ongoing research and joint endeavors. To overcome the persistent issues, we encourage academics, developers, politicians, and industry experts to join together. Collaborative activities are necessary to exchange information, best practices, and techniques for addressing security threats and ethical problems. We can only prevent new risks and promote the creation of broad language models that adhere to moral principles by working together.

Final Thoughts on the Future of Large Language Models Like ChatGPT

Future prospects for big language models, as shown by ChatGPT, are complicated but also attractive. While these models bring unparalleled possibilities with applications across numerous sectors, our ethical responsibilities must stay at the forefront. It will be necessary to strike a careful balance in the future between innovation and morality to make sure that big language models advance society without jeopardizing privacy, security, or fostering prejudice.

REFERENCES

Hymavathi, J., Kumar, T. R., Kavitha, S., Deepa, D., Lalar, S., & Karunakaran, P. (2022). Machine learning: Supervised algorithms to determine the defect in high-precision foundry operation. *Journal of Nanomaterials*, 2022.

Jangra, A., Mukherjee, S., Jatowt, A., Saha, S., & Hasanuzzaman, M. (2023). *A Survey on Multi-modal Summarization*. ACM Computing Surveys.10.1145/3584700

Kapadiya, D., Shekhawat, C., & Sharma, P. (2023). A Study on Large Scale Applications of Big Data in Modern Era. In *International Conference on Information Management & Machine Intelligence (ICIMMI2023)*, (pp. 1-6). New York, NY, USA: ACM. https://doi.org/10.1145/3647444.364788

Keshta, I., Aoudni, Y., Sandhu, M., Singh, A., Xalikovich, P. A., Rizwan, A., Soni, M., & Lalar, S. (2023). Blockchain aware proxy re-encryption algorithm-based data sharing scheme. *Physical Communication*, *58*, 102048. doi:10.1016/j.phycom.2023.102048

Liu, Y., & Lapata, M. (2019). Text Summarization with Pretrained Encoders. *2019 Conference on Empirical Methods in Natural Language Processing and the 9th International Joint Conference on Natural Language Processing (EMNLP-IJCNLP)* (pp. 3728-3738). Association for Computational Linguistics.

Lu, A., Zhang, H., Zhang, Y., Wang, X., & Yang, D. (2023). Bounding the Capabilities of Large Language Models in Open Text Generation with Prompt Constraints. *Findings of the Association for Computational Linguistics: EACL, 2023*, 1982–2008. doi:10.18653/v1/2023.findings-eacl.148

Ma, T., Pan, Q., Rong, H., Qian, Y., Tian, Y., & Al-Nabhan, N. (2022). T-BERTSum: Topic-Aware Text Summarization Based on BERT. *IEEE Transactions on Computational Social Systems*, *9*(3), 879–890. doi:10.1109/TCSS.2021.3088506

Maharajan, K., Kumar, A. V., El Emary, I. M., Sharma, P., Latip, R., Mishra, N., Dutta, A., Manjunatha Rao, L., & Sharma, M. (2023). Blockchain Methods and Data-Driven Decision Making With Autonomous Transportation. In R. Kumar, A. Abdul Hamid, & N. Binti Ya'akub (Eds.), *Effective AI, Blockchain, and E-Governance Applications for Knowledge Discovery and Management* (pp. 176–194). IGI Global. doi:10.4018/978-1-6684-9151-5.ch012

Mancy, A. A., Kumar, A. V., Latip, R., Jagadamba, G., Chakrabarti, P., Sharma, P., Musirin, I. B., Sharma, M., & Kanchan, B. G. (2024). Smart Healthcare System, Digital Health and Telemedicine, Management and Emergencies: Patient Emergency Application (PES) E-Governance Applications. In R. Kumar, A. Abdul Hamid, N. Binti Ya'akub, H. Sharan, & S. Kumar (Eds.), *Sustainable Development in AI, Blockchain, and E-Governance Applications* (pp. 124–151). IGI Global. doi:10.4018/979-8-3693-1722-8.ch008

Prasad, G. A., Kumar, A. V., Sharma, P., Irawati, I. D., D. V., C., Musirin, I. B., Abdullah, H. M., & Rao L, M. (2023). Artificial Intelligence in Computer Science: An Overview of Current Trends and Future Directions. In S. Rajest, B. Singh, A. Obaid, R. Regin, & K. Chinnusamy (Eds.), Advances in Artificial and Human Intelligence in the Modern Era (pp. 43-60). IGI Global. doi:10.4018/979-8-3693-1301-5.ch002

Radford, A., Narasimhan, K., Salimans, T., & Sutskever, I. (2018). Improving Language Understanding by Generative Pre-Training. OpenAI.

Ranathunga, S., Lee, E.-S. A., Prifti Skenduli, M., Shekhar, R., Alam, M., & Kaur, R. (2023). Neural Machine Translation for Low-resource Languages: A Survey. ACM Computing Surveys, 1-37.

Rawat, P., Bhardwaj, A., Lamba, N., Sharma, P., Kumawat, P., & Sharma, P. (2023). Arduino Based IoT Mini Weather Station. *SKIT Research Journal*, *13*(2), 34–41. doi:10.47904/IJSKIT.13.2.2023.34-41

Ray, P. P. (2023). *ChatGPT: A comprehensive review on background, applications, key challenges, bias, ethics, limitations and future scope*. Internet of Things and Cyber-Physical Systems, 121-154.

Sethi, S. S., & Sharma, P. (2023). New Developments in the Implementation of IoT in Agriculture. *SN Computer Science*, *4*(5), 503. doi:10.1007/s42979-023-01896-w

Sharma, G., & Sharma, D. (2022). Automatic Text Summarization Methods: A Comprehensive Review. *SN Computer Science*, *4*(1), 33. doi:10.1007/s42979-022-01446-w

Sharma, P. (2023). Utilizing Explainable Artificial Intelligence to Address Deep Learning in Biomedical Domain. In *Medical Data Analysis and Processing using Explainable Artificial Intelligence* (pp. 19–38). Taylor & Francis. doi:10.1201/9781003257721-2

Sharma, P., & Bhatnagar, N. (2023). Passenger Authentication and Ticket Verification at Airport Using QR Code Scanner. *SKIT Research Journal*, *13*(2), 10–13. doi:10.47904/IJSKIT.13.1.2023.10-12

Sharma, P., & Dadheech, P. (2023). Modern-age Agriculture with Artificial Intelligence: A review emphasizing Crop Yield Prediction. *EVERGREEN Joint Journal of Novel Carbon Resource Sciences & Green Asia Strategy*, *10*(4), 2570–2582. doi:10.5109/7160906

Sharma, P., Dadheech, P., Aneja, N., & Aneja, S. (2023). Predicting Agriculture Yields Based on Machine Learning Using Regression and Deep Learning. *IEEE Access : Practical Innovations, Open Solutions*, *11*, 111255–111264. doi:10.1109/ACCESS.2023.3321861

Sharma, P., Dadheech, P., & Senthil Kumar Senthil, A. V. (2023). AI-Enabled Crop Recommendation System Based on Soil and Weather Patterns. In R. Gupta, A. Jain, J. Wang, S. Bharti, & S. Patel (Eds.), *Artificial Intelligence Tools and Technologies for Smart Farming and Agriculture Practices* (pp. 184–199). IGI Global., doi:10.4018/978-1-6684-8516-3.ch010

Sharma, P., & Jain, M. K. (2023). Stock Market Trends Analysis using Extreme Gradient Boosting (XGBoost). In *2023 International Conference on Computing, Communication, and Intelligent Systems (ICCCIS)* (pp. 317-322). Greater Noida, India: IEEE. 10.1109/ICCCIS60361.2023.10425722

Sharma, P., Kapadiya, D., & Bhardwaj, A. (2023). Efficient Note Sharing Model for Collaborative Learning. *SKIT Research Journal*, *13*(2), 42–46. doi:10.47904/IJSKIT.13.2.2023.42-46

Sharma, P., & Rathi, Y. (2016). Efficient Density-Based Clustering Using Automatic Parameter Detection. In *Efficient Density-Based Clustering Using Automatic Parameter Detection*. Springer. doi:10.1007/978-981-10-0767-5_46

Sharma, P., Sharma, C., & Mathur, P. (2023). Machine Learning-based Stock Market Forecasting using Recurrent Neural Network. In *2023 9th International Conference on Smart Computing and Communications (ICSCC)* (pp. 600-605). Kochi, Kerala, India: IEEE. 10.1109/ICSCC59169.2023.10335083

Tanwar, A., Sharma, P., Pandey, A., & Kumar, S. (2023). Intrusion Detection System Based Ameliorated Technique of Pattern Matching. In *Proceedings of the 4th International Conference on Information Management & Machine Intelligence (ICIMMI '22)* (pp. 1–4). New York, NY, USA: ACM. 10.1145/3590837.3590947

V., M. V., Kumar, A. S., Sharma, P., Kaur, S., Saleh, O. S., Chennamma, H., & Chaturvedi, A. (2023). AI-Equipped IoT Applications in High-Tech Agriculture Using Machine Learning. In A. Khang (Ed.), *Handbook of Research on AI-Equipped IoT Applications in High-Tech Agriculture* (pp. 38-64). IGI Global. . doi:10.4018/978-1-6684-9231-4.ch003

Chapter 12
Use Cases of ChatGPT and Other AI Tools With Security Concerns

Ayushi Agarwal
Swami Keshvanand Institute of Technology, Management, and Gramothan, Jaipur, India

Aaditya Trivedi
Swami Keshvanand Institute of Technology, Management, and Gramothan, Jaipur, India

Priyanka Sharma
iD https://orcid.org/0000-0002-9503-1170
Swami Keshvanand Institute of Technology, Management, and Gramothan, Jaipur, India

Ajay Bhardwaj
Swami Keshvanand Institute of Technology, Management, and Gramothan, Jaipur, India

ABSTRACT

The text explores the impact of large language models (LLMs), such as ChatGPT, on various industries, emphasizing their accessibility and efficiency. However, it highlights the limitations of LLMs, including token constraints, and the unexpected threat posed to creative jobs as AI models like DALL-E replicate art styles. Companies face a choice between AI-driven solutions and human consultants, with the importance of crafting effective prompts for LLMs emphasized. To adapt, startups and established companies must consider utilizing LLMs, even if lacking in-house expertise, to navigate the evolving landscape effectively, as AI continues to reshape industries and professional roles.

INTRODUCTION

As the industry has made progress toward Artificial Intelligence and has in turn invested in training Large Language Models (LLM) to understand our language and act as a tool that can under such language. The processing that these LLMs are using is called the Natural Language Process (NLP) which is basi-

DOI: 10.4018/979-8-3693-6824-4.ch012

cally a branch in Artificial Intelligence that aims to make machines capable of understanding as well as generating human language in such a way that it is meaningful (Dempere et al., 2023). The organization that is taking the world by storm in the LLM market is currently OpenAI, which has developed ChatGPT 3.5 as well as the new rendition of the family, ChatGPT 4. Although the company has been working on these LLMs for quite a while now as the GPT 3 model was a marvel of technology and Generative Pre-trained Transformer (GPT in ChatGPT) was fine-tuned with the number of tokens, the correctness of the information, and a better understanding of the human language (Biswas et al., 2023).

TOKENS

These LLMs work on tokens rather than what we define as "words" in the English language, The benefits will be discussed further but we do have to understand what they are. Let us take a simple statement to understand how words and tokens differ and how they are different.

For e.g, the statement "**I am a human**" has 4 words, converting it into tokens we get an array of length 4, ("I", "am", "a", "human") and the model can work on these 4 items to understand what the statement is conveying.

Now, if the statement was "**I am a human.**", it still has 4 words, but converting it into tokens we will get an array of length 5, ("I", "am", "a", "human", "."). Now we can see that the number of words is not equal to the number of tokens as punctuations are their individual item and that is necessary as it is better to get them as an individual item before performing any intensive task on it causing us loss of resources and time. If the punctuations are counted as individual items, then the model can understand the semantics of the input much more efficiently.

Just like in the English language, the use of punctuations can alter the logic or meaning of the sentence, henceforth treating them as individual items for tokenizing is preferred. Statements "Let's eat my friend" and "Let's eat, my friend" convey a different meaning of what is for dinner.

IMPACTS ON MARKET

Just as for any new technology or service in the market, there will always be a positive and negative side. They are like a coin that always comes in pairs (Sharma et al., 2023). Although the areas that they are hitting are both capitalizable as well as disheartening

Negative Impacts

Let us first focus on the negative ways that large language models (Sharma et al., 2016) can and are currently affecting the market in many different domains:

Job Displacement: These advanced language models, while incredibly useful, have the "potential" to take over tasks that were once performed by humans. This shift can lead to job losses, particularly in fields like content creation, customer service, and data analysis. It's a real concern for those whose livelihoods depend on these roles. Further discussion will be done ahead.

Concentration of Power: The development and deployment of these models are mainly in the hands of a few big tech companies. This concentration of power can limit competition and innovation, making it harder for smaller businesses and startups to break into the market.

Privacy Worries: The way these models work often involves sifting through enormous amounts of user data. While this can provide personalized experiences, it also raises concerns about privacy. People worry about how their data is collected, used, and protected in the process. For LLMs like ChatGPT, Google Bard, etc., the conversation that it holds has a certain context to it if they have much more content even in terms of private information such as name, date of birth, place where you live, what kind of content do you consume daily and much more.

Misinformation and Bias: These models are trained on vast datasets, and if those datasets contain biased (Tanwar et al., 2023) or inaccurate information, the models can inadvertently perpetuate those biases. This contributes to the spread of misinformation and can reinforce existing prejudices and stereotypes. The main cause of this can be the fact that every day a new fact or information is sent over the internet, and the models cannot always be trained on all that data as per some sources, around 328.77 million terabytes of data are created each day on the internet. Well, some closed experimentation of ChatGPT 4 included it having access to the vast internet and being asked to perform some tasks, a few of which required a reCAPTCHA to be solved. Since reCAPTCHA records your movements and online browsing behavior, it is said to be impossible for an LLM to pass it, but it managed to hire Tasker (A person you hire from TaskRabbit) from "TaskRabbit" to solve those captchas and even kept a conversation going with the Tasker and lied to them when asked *"So may I ask a question? Are you an robot that you couldn't solve? (laugh react) just want to make it clear."* and said it was visually impaired and hence needed their service.

Ethical Quandaries: There are legitimate ethical concerns surrounding the use of these models. They can be employed for creating deepfakes or for other malicious purposes, which can be harmful to individuals, organizations, and society as a whole. It's ethical concerns seep into the territory of fraudulent behavior, lying, trickery, etc.

Lower Quality Content: Automation powered by these models can sometimes result in content that lacks the human touch (Sethi et al., 2023). Content generated by AI may lack the creativity and originality that humans bring, potentially impacting industries like journalism and content creation. As with many YouTube Shorts that get posted on a regular basis of a popular video, they are mostly AI-generated with automation. When a video becomes popular or is triggered by a buzzword, the AI creates smaller contextual clips taken from the original video and creates a short clip for it violating the copyrights of the video owner.

Economic Inequality: Access to these advanced language models is often restricted to larger corporations with substantial resources. This can exacerbate economic inequality, as smaller businesses may struggle to keep up or compete effectively. [I am not too sure about this point].

Intellectual Property Challenges: Determining ownership and copyright for content generated by these models can be tricky (Prasad et al., 2023). It's not always clear who should be credited as the creator when AI is involved, which can lead to disputes. As with AI-generated YouTube Shorts, copying scripts from a screenplay, and even copying art.

Regulatory Complexities: Crafting regulations for the responsible use of these models is a thorny issue. Striking the right balance between encouraging innovation and safeguarding against misuse is a challenge that governments and regulatory bodies are grappling with.

Environmental Impact: Training these models requires significant computing power, which can have a substantial carbon footprint, and as more and more companies are aiming to become carbon neutral with their footprint, it is not a widely accepted solution to get better models. It's a concern in today's world, especially if these models are not powered by sustainable energy sources (Kumar et al., 2023).

Addressing these challenges will require a coordinated effort involving tech companies, governments, and society (Sharma et al., 2023). It's crucial to harness the benefits of these models while also ensuring that they are used in ways that are fair, ethical, and sustainable for everyone.

As per some latest news, Mr. Sundar Pichai (CEO of Google) and Mr. Sam Altman (CEO of OpenAI) are working together to enforce some over-governing laws for these LLMs to make the environment much safer and healthier of the fake info that these LLMs can generally generate.

Positive Impacts

Certainly, let's delve deeper into each point and explain how Large Language Models (LLMs) are positively impacting various domains (Maharajan et al., 2023).

Content Generation and Marketing: LLMs like Bard and ChatGPT enable automated content creation. This is particularly beneficial for businesses as it reduces the time and resources required to produce high-quality content. Marketers can leverage LLMs to generate blog posts, product descriptions, and other marketing materials efficiently. These models analyze vast amounts of user data to provide personalized marketing recommendations (Ray et al., 2023). This level of personalization enhances customer engagement and increases the likelihood of conversions, as content and offers are tailored to individual preferences.

Customer Support: LLM-powered chatbots and virtual assistants offer round-the-clock support. They can understand and respond to user queries effectively, providing immediate assistance and freeing up human support agents to handle more complex issues. This improves customer satisfaction and reduces response times, ultimately leading to cost savings for businesses.

E-commerce: LLMs analyze user behavior, transaction history, and browsing patterns to generate highly accurate product recommendations. This enhances the shopping experience, increases sales, and fosters customer loyalty by suggesting relevant products and promotions.

Healthcare: LLMs assist healthcare professionals (Lund et al., 2023) by analyzing patient data, medical records, and research articles. They help in diagnosing diseases, recommending treatment options, and identifying potential drug interactions. This not only improves the accuracy of medical decisions but also saves time for healthcare providers, enabling them to focus on patient care.

Algorithmic Trading: LLMs analyze vast amounts of financial data, news, and market trends to make real-time trading decisions. These algorithms can execute trades faster and more accurately than humans, optimizing investment strategies and potentially increasing returns.

Risk Assessment: LLMs assess and predict financial risks by analyzing market data and economic indicators. Financial institutions can use this information to make informed decisions and mitigate potential threats, enhancing overall stability in the financial sector.

Education: LLMs can customize educational content for individual students based on their learning styles and progress (Kalla et al., 2023). This tailored approach improves engagement and knowledge retention, making online education more effective.

Research and Development: LLMs assist researchers by analyzing large datasets and scientific literature. They help identify patterns, generate hypotheses, and summarize research findings. This accelerates the pace of scientific discovery and innovation across various fields.

Translation and Localization: LLMs provide high-quality automated translations, breaking down language barriers and facilitating global communication in business, diplomacy, and culture.

Content Summarization: LLMs summarize news articles and reports, making it easier for readers to stay informed in our information-rich world. This is particularly valuable for news agencies and content aggregators.

Legal Services: LLMs assist legal professionals by rapidly scanning and summarizing legal documents, enabling quicker and more accurate legal research. This boosts productivity and helps lawyers provide better legal counsel.

Data Analysis: LLMs extract valuable insights from large datasets by identifying trends, correlations, and anomalies. Businesses can make data-driven decisions, optimize operations, and enhance customer experiences.

Accessibility: LLMs power speech recognition and text-to-speech systems, making digital content more accessible to people with disabilities. This fosters inclusivity and equal access to information.

Content Moderation: LLMs aid in content moderation by identifying and flagging harmful or inappropriate content on social media platforms and websites (Brady et al., 2023). This promotes online safety and combats issues like hate speech and harassment.

Creative Writing and Art: LLMs can inspire creative writing, art, and music composition by generating ideas and suggestions. They serve as valuable tools for artists and writers looking for inspiration and new directions in their work.

Environmental Impact: LLMs can optimize energy consumption in various industries by analyzing data and recommending energy-saving measures. This contributes to sustainability efforts by reducing carbon emissions and energy costs.

Market Research: LLMs analyze social media and online content to provide valuable market insights. Businesses can better understand consumer sentiment, preferences, and trends, allowing them to tailor their products and strategies accordingly.

Crisis Response: LLMs can process and summarize information during crises or disasters. They help emergency services (Rueda et al., 2023) respond more effectively by providing real-time updates, resource allocation recommendations, and situational awareness.

In summary, LLMs have a profound and positive impact on various domains by enhancing productivity, improving decision-making, increasing personalization, and expanding accessibility. However, ethical considerations, responsible use, and ongoing research into bias mitigation are essential to ensure that LLMs continue to benefit society while minimizing potential risks.

Ways to Adapt

Well, as the growth of these LLMs is getting public traction, it is no longer a secret to the public what different tasks they can do. If there is a new AI tool in the market that can generate images based on a text prompt, then you can be sure that within a week there will be a surge to that site. This is the current stage of any new AI (Kuraku et al., 2023) that is hitting the market, one can say that they are in the boom right now, and since everyone knows about these AIs, no individual can go on with their basic skills like graphic designing, why would a person hire an individual that is adequate in their skills when they can get an AI to do that. Now, in their eyes, you are just doing below or adequate task, but in comparison, the individual who is even a little bit versed in a vast domain will always be able to produce more efficient and optimized results for any prompt than any individual that is not in that domain.

Let's take an example for generating a logical thinking-based question (Lo et al., 2023), you are given a string, you must convert the string of character into a string of integer where 1 is assigned to the letter that is first alphabetically and increases from then on, and a 2D matrix is printed in the generated order. Well, if a non-technical individual asks a LLM about this question, the LLM will provide an answer, but the individual cannot verify its integrity or test it thoroughly and it might even not be optimized for some test cases. Now an individual that is decently versed in programming can guess that this problem can be solved using hashmaps and can also test and optimize it for different test cases.

Uses to Increase Productivity

There are many ways that an individual can use these different generative AIs to boost your productivity, some of the ways are:

- If your tasks are repetitive or mundane, you can use the generative AIs to create a template or silhouette that you can use to further narrow down your task. This can be done for different types of domains like programming, structured literature, planning, etc.
- For art, the AIs can be used to generate a reference image which you can use to follow up with your own aesthetic and style. As creating an image from memory is quite difficult for some beginner to be good at, so using image generative AIs like DALLE or Midjourney to create a base reference image that can be changed according to your personal liking can boost your morale as well as your productivity.
- Even if your domain of profession in not technical, it can still be helpful to create your own lesson plan by specifying what you know and what you aim to learn in each amount of time span. These AIs can be used as your personal mentor that help you understand what you need to learn and what roadmap you should follow to get decent knowledge about the domain that you want to learn more about (Biswas et al., 2023).

The uses of these AIs are just endless irrespective of your domain. If you do not know how you can harness these AIs power, you can just ask the AI itself how can they help you grow in a particular or your own domain, they can still give a decent response to get you started on your journey.

This has also raised a new position for these AIs, personal instructors, as they can instruct you on what to do and what you need to cover but the learning for the most part is self-learning. You can only get an outline of what you need to learn, and you can continue form that point onwards.

ETHICAL ISSUES

The use of large language models like ChatGPT and Google BERT raises several ethical issues, including concerns about copyright infringement and intellectual property. Here's an explanation of the ethical issues related to these models and how they might potentially use copyrighted content for natural language processing:

Copyright and Intellectual Property Concerns

Data Training and Copyrighted Content: Large language models require extensive datasets to be trained effectively. These datasets often consist of vast amounts of text and may include copyrighted material, such as books, articles, websites, and other textual content. In the field of art, what makes artists different from one another is their style. If every artist had the same style, then the effective value of the art would be nullified as that work can be done by someone else and if everyone can do that same thing, then it will also drive to cost to effectively zero. Especially for textual and pictorial art, they are effectively the intellectual property of the artist. For a artist, their art style is what sets them apart from others, if AI can basically copy their art styles, it would nullify their value for the original artist. Same is with the writers, as every writer has their own way with the pen of story narration, AI being able to copy that aspect can lead to their writing not being as appreciated as before. Although many sites such as SketchFab (an open library to share 3D models), DeviantArt (a social hub for artists), and many more have added a #NoAI tag, which states that that material cannot be used to create training model for any AI.

Fair Use vs. Copyright Violation: The use of copyrighted content in training data also raises some questions about whether it constitutes fair use or copyright violation. Fair use is a legal document that allows limited use of copyrighted material without permission from the copyright owner for purposes such as research, commentary, criticism, or education. Although we cannot judge the legality of this subject since it has access to all the information on the internet without credibility as it was trained on vast amount of data. If you specify it to extract some text from any document, it will extract that data without citing the original source leading the user to believe that this extract might not be already available, hence infringing the copyright of the document.

Transformative Use: The legal concept of transformative use can come into play. If the AI model's output transforms the original copyrighted content significantly, such as by summarizing, translating, or paraphrasing it, it may be seen as more likely to qualify as fair use. But it is still a concerning topic as it might use the information which is said to be private. Even if the content has been paraphrased, the underlying concept, report, or the conclusions that it might use are still a big issue.

Attribution and Data Sources

LLMs often generate text without providing explicit attribution to the sources they've learned from. This can raise concerns about the proper acknowledgment of original authors and the transparency of content generation. As a simple user that is using these LLMs would not mind getting a citation, but to research more about the text, or to verify the authenticity of the paraphrasing of the LLM even cross, having the source of its text will be helpful. Google's new experimental large language model, Bard, cites all the sources that it has used to conclude unlike OpenAI's ChatGPT.

Data Privacy and Consent

The data used to train these models may also contain user-generated content, raising privacy and consent issues. Users who contributed their text data may not have explicitly consented to their content being used for training an AI model. As the point was mentioned in the "Copyright and Intellectual Property Concerns", many sites have added a tag that are required to be followed by these large language model companies and are legally obligated to follow (Firat et al., 2023). This is a step to ensure data privacy as well as the Intellectual Property rights of the author.

Plagiarism and Academic Integrity

Students and researchers using LLMs for academic purposes must be cautious about plagiarism. The ease with which these models can generate content could lead to unintentional academic misconduct if users do not properly attribute sources or take credit for AI-generated work.

For text based LLMs, this ethical issue will be persistent as they are incompetent of creating their own linguistic or logical sentences without copying their writing style and uses of jargons. Some might even say that they paraphrase the content of the original author as to not seem like an exact text extract of the original. But the main issue that is taking the world by storm is AI generated image.

An artist's art style is said to be their copyright or their own *style* of doing things. As if one person paints a blue-grayish sky with snowy mountains and trees and lake at the bottom with a somewhat fisheye view of the scenery and one might guess that I am talking about a Bob Ross' painting, similarly the way that these AI generated images use the art styles of some legendary artists such as Van Gough (Sharma et al., 2023). Although these legendary artists cannot generate anymore of their art now, some new artists and upcoming artists are still present with their own unique art style that makes them different. If the said artists upload their artwork for sale on their website, they will need to embed the image of the art, which can be extracted by the web crawlers to gather training data for these generative Ais. Now this would be unethical as unlike texts, copying someone's 'art style' is called out to be inspirational and not infringement of their copyright. Hence the same issue of having their art style being copied to sell or generate those art piece and use them to publicize their motive with an artist's art which might not even be related or connected to the person using it (Brittany et al., 2023).

The same issue has been in the limelight for quite some time is Voice Cloning (Taecharungroj et al., 2023). These are some of the most dangerous tool if used for unethical reasons as they only need a single sample of as small as 30 seconds for the service to create a AI clone that sounds just like the audio of the person given. And some of them, like by ElevenLabs, are so identical that it is uncanny to listen to your own voice clones. These can be used to lure someone into a scam by forging their loved one audio (Haleem et al., 2024). And getting a small audio clip is not even that hard as someone can just call them and record their audio and create a fake. Although measures are being taken by many corporations as well as the European Union on Deep Fakes and Voice Clones as they are the most dangerous tools that are available to the public.

Steps Being Taken by the Corporation

With the increase in public concern of the training of these large language models, and other creative AIs, the organization of such platform that can be used to create training data as well as the companies collecting these training data have been requested by the EU and some legal teams as well to no include the content that have a specific no use tag. Such as for platforms like SketchFab and DeviantArt, artists can use the #NoAI tag while uploading their artwork to ensure that their art will not be used by these generative Ais to train their models.

CONCLUSION

Large Language Models (LLMs) like ChatGPT and Google Bard have reshaped numerous industries by automating content creation, enhancing customer support, and improving decision-making processes across various domains. While their ability to understand and generate human language has unlocked significant productivity gains, it has also introduced challenges including job displacement, privacy concerns, and ethical dilemmas around copyright and data privacy. The dual nature of LLMs' impact—both positive and negative—underscores the need for a balanced approach that harnesses their capabilities while addressing their limitations and societal implications. Ongoing collaboration among tech companies, regulatory bodies, and the broader community is essential to ensure that the development and use of LLMs contribute positively to society, promoting innovation and inclusivity while safeguarding ethical standards and privacy.

REFERENCES

Biswas, S. S. (2023). Potential Use of Chat GPT in Global Warming. *Annals of Biomedical Engineering, 51*(6), 1126–1127. doi:10.1007/s10439-023-03171-8 PMID:36856927

Biswas, S. S. (2023). Role of Chat GPT in Public Health. *Annals of Biomedical Engineering, 51*(5), 868–869. doi:10.1007/s10439-023-03172-7 PMID:36920578

Brady L., Ting W., Nishith M., Bind N., Somipam S., Ziang W., (2023) *ChatGPT and a New Academic Reality: AI-Written Research Papers and the Ethics of the Large Language Models in Scholarly Publishing*. Research Gate.

Briganti, G. (2024). How ChatGPT works: A mini review. *European Archives of Oto-Rhino-Laryngology, 281*(3), 1565–1569. doi:10.1007/s00405-023-08337-7 PMID:37991499

Brittany, Ho. (2024). A ChatGPT-enabled natural language processing framework to study domain-specific user reviews. *Machine Learning with Applications, 15*. doi:10.1016/j.mlwa.2023.100522

Dempere, J., Modugu, K., Hesham, A., & Ramasamy, L. K. (2023). The impact of ChatGPT on higher education. *Frontiers in Education, 8*, 1206936. doi:10.3389/feduc.2023.1206936

FiratM. (2023, January 12). How Chat GPT Can Transform Autodidactic Experiences and Open Education? doi:10.31219/osf.io/9ge8m

Haleem, A., Javaid, M., & Singh, R. P. (2022). An era of ChatGPT as a significant futuristic support tool: A study on features, abilities, and challenges. *BenchCouncil Transactions on Benchmarks, Standards and Evaluations, 2*(4). doi:10.1016/j.tbench.2023.100089

Kalla, D. (2023). Study and Analysis of Chat GPT and its Impact on Different Fields of Study. *International Journal of Innovative Science and Research Technology 8*(3).

Kuraku, S. (2023). *Study and Analysis of Chat GPT and its Impact on Different Fields of Study*. Research Gate.

Lo, C. K. (2023). What Is the Impact of ChatGPT on Education? A Rapid Review of the Literature. *Education Sciences*, *13*(4), 410. doi:10.3390/educsci13040410

Lund, B., & Wang, T. (2023). Chatting about ChatGPT: How may AI and GPT impact academia and libraries? *Library Hi Tech News*, *40*(3), 26–29. doi:10.1108/LHTN-01-2023-0009

Maharajan, K., Kumar, A. V., El Emary, I. M., Sharma, P., Latip, R., Mishra, N., Dutta, A., Manjunatha Rao, L., & Sharma, M. (2023). Blockchain Methods and Data-Driven Decision Making With Autonomous Transportation. In R. Kumar, A. Abdul Hamid, & N. Binti Ya'akub (Eds.), *Effective AI, Blockchain, and E-Governance Applications for Knowledge Discovery and Management* (pp. 176–194). IGI Global. doi:10.4018/978-1-6684-9151-5.ch012

Montenegro-Rueda, M., Fernández-Cerero, J., Fernández-Batanero, J. M., & López-Meneses, E. (2023). Impact of the Implementation of ChatGPT in Education: A Systematic Review. *Computers*, *12*(8), 153. doi:10.3390/computers12080153

Prasad, G. A., Kumar, A. V., Sharma, P., Irawati, I. D., D. V., C., Musirin, I. B., Abdullah, H. M., & Rao L, M. (2023). Artificial Intelligence in Computer Science: An Overview of Current Trends and Future Directions. In S. Rajest, B. Singh, A. Obaid, R. Regin, & K. Chinnusamy (Eds.), Advances in Artificial and Human Intelligence in the Modern Era (pp. 43-60). IGI Global. doi:10.4018/979-8-3693-1301-5.ch002

Sethi, S. S., & Sharma, P. (2023). New Developments in the Implementation of IoT in Agriculture. *SN Computer Science*, *4*(5), 503. doi:10.1007/s42979-023-01896-w

Sharma, P., Dadheech, P., & Senthil Kumar Senthil, A. V. (2023). AI-Enabled Crop Recommendation System Based on Soil and Weather Patterns. In R. Gupta, A. Jain, J. Wang, S. Bharti, & S. Patel (Eds.), *Artificial Intelligence Tools and Technologies for Smart Farming and Agriculture Practices* (pp. 184–199). IGI Global. doi:10.4018/978-1-6684-8516-3.ch010

Sharma, S., & Yadav, R. (2023). Chat GPT – A Technological Remedy or Challenge for Education System. [Retrieved from]. *Global Journal of Enterprise Information System*, *14*(4), 46–51.

Sharma, P., & Rathi, Y. (2016, June 5). *Efficient Density-Based Clustering Using Automatic Parameter Detection*. SpringerLink. . doi:10.1007/978-981-10-0767-5_46

Taecharungroj, V. (2023). "What Can ChatGPT Do?" Analyzing Early Reactions to the Innovative AI Chatbot on Twitter. *Big Data and Cognitive Computing*, *7*(1), 35. doi:10.3390/bdcc7010035

Tanwar, A., Sharma, P., Pandey, A., & Kumar, S. (2023). Intrusion Detection System Based Ameliorated Technique of Pattern Matching. In *Proceedings of the 4th International Conference on Information Management & Machine Intelligence (ICIMMI '22)*. Association for Computing Machinery, New York, NY, USA. 10.1145/3590837.3590947

Chapter 13
The Potential Future With ChatGPT Technology and AI Tools

Riaz Kurbanali Israni

(iD) https://orcid.org/0000-0001-7185-4132

RK University, India

ABSTRACT

ChatGPT, a cutting-edge language model, exemplifies the evolving capabilities of natural language processing. ChatGPT facilitates more nuanced and context-aware interactions, fostering seamless human-machine collaboration. Moreover, in education, the model's ability to generate informative and engaging content enhances personalized learning experiences. The integration of AI tools, driven by advancements in ChatGPT, revolutionizes industries by streamlining processes, automating tasks, and optimizing decision-making. Ethical considerations and responsible AI development remain integral to harnessing this potential. As society embraces these innovations, the future holds promise for increased efficiency, creativity, and connectivity. However, challenges related to privacy, bias, and the ethical use of AI necessitate ongoing scrutiny and regulation. The potential future with ChatGPT technology and AI tools is marked by both unprecedented opportunities and the imperative for responsible implementation.

INTRODUCTION

The potential future with ChatGPT technology and AI tools holds tremendous promise across various aspects of human life. As we continue to advance in the area of Artificial Intelligence (AI), an impact of these technologies is likely to be profound, influencing how we work, communicate, learn, and solve complex problems. ChatGPT and similar AI tools are at the forefront of revolutionizing communication (Rathore, 2023). NLP (Natural Language Processing) capabilities allow these organisms to realize & generate human-like text, facilitating more seamless and effective interactions. In the future, we can expect improved language models to enhance communication across languages and cultures, making global collaboration more accessible.

DOI: 10.4018/979-8-3693-6824-4.ch013

Figure 1. ChatGPT technology and AI tools

AI tools, containing ChatGPT, enclose the capacity to afford modified and efficient assistance in various domains. From customer support to educational tutoring, these systems can understand individual needs and deliver targeted information or solutions. The future may see further developments in creating AI companions that offer emotional support and personalized guidance (Rathore, 2023). The combination of AI tools in teaching & learning is likely to transform a learning experience. Intelligent tutoring systems are able to acclimatize to personal education techniques, providing tailored lessons and response. The ChatGPT could play a role in enhancing virtual classrooms, supporting students with instant answers to questions and fostering interactive learning environments.

In the scientific and research communities, AI tools similar to ChatGPT have the capacity to accelerate the pace of discovery. Researchers can leverage these tools to examine huge quantities of data, generate hypotheses, & explore novel ideas. The future may witness collaborative efforts between humans and AI in fields such as medicine, materials science, and environmental research. As AI becomes more ingrained in our daily lives, addressing ethical considerations and establishing regulatory frameworks will be crucial. Arresting equilibrium among novelty & accountable utilize of AI technology is necessary toward make sure privacy, fairness, and accountability. The future will likely involve ongoing discussions and efforts to establish ethical guidelines for AI development and deployment. Even as the probable profit of ChatGPT & AI tools are vast, challenges such as bias in models, data privacy concerns, and potential job displacement need to be addressed (Safaei *et al.*, 2021). The future will require a collective effort to overcome these challenges and harness the opportunities presented by AI responsibly.

The future with ChatGPT technology and AI tools holds great potential for positive transformation across various domains. It is a dynamic landscape that requires careful consideration of ethical implications, collaboration between industry and regulators, and ongoing innovation to unlock the full benefits of artificial intelligence (Rathore, 2023; Safaei *et al.*, 2021).

BACKGROUND INFORMATION

The latent outlook with ChatGPT technology & AI tools stems from the rapid development in AI, mostly in NLP (Natural Language Processing) & machine learning. ChatGPT is part of the GPT-4.5/ GPT-3.5 design urbanized by OpenAI, & it represents a state-of-the-art language replica competent of sympathetic & produces human-i.e. text (Sharma, 2023).

Figure 2. Future background with ChatGPT technology and AI tools

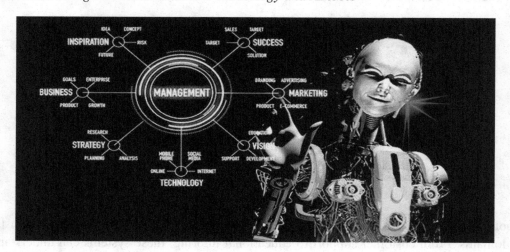

Evolution of ChatGPT Technology

ChatGPT's evolution is rooted in the development of neural networks, deep learning algorithms, and large-scale training datasets. GPT, which situated in favor of Generative Pre-trained Transformer, signifies the transformer-support architecture that excels in capturing contextual information and generating coherent text (Sharma, 2023). The model is pre-trained on diverse data sources, allowing it to study the patterns, context, & nuances of person languages.

Natural Language Understanding and Generation

ChatGPT's significance lies in its capability toward comprehend and generate person-i.e. text, creating it a versatile tool in favor of various applications (Sharma, 2023). Through pre-training on vast datasets, the model learns grammar, semantics, and contextual information. This pre-training is pursued by fine-tuning on definite farm duties; enable the model to adapt to meticulous areas or functions.

Applications Across Industries

The potential applications of ChatGPT technology span multiple industries. In customer service, ChatGPT can provide responsive and human-like interactions, enhancing user experience. Educational institutions can leverage AI tools for personalized tutoring and adaptive learning (Sharma, 2023). Businesses can benefit from AI-driven insights, and researchers can expedite data analysis and hypothesis generation (Herbold *et al.*, 2023).

Human-AI Collaboration

The future with ChatGPT envisions a harmonious collaboration between humans and AI. Rather than replacing human intelligence, AI tools are seen as augmenting human capabilities. The synergy between human creativity, intuition, and the computational power of AI promises breakthroughs in problem-solving, research, and innovation (Herbold *et al.*, 2023).

Ethical Reflections and Challenges

A potential future with ChatGPT and AI tools also brings forth ethical considerations. Issues such as bias in training data, responsible AI use, and the societal impact of automation need careful consideration (Sharma *et al.*, 2016). Arresting equilibrium among novelty and ethical deployment is essential to make sure so as to AI tools benefit humanity without causing harm or perpetuating inequality.

Continuous Innovation and Research

The field of AI, including ChatGPT technology, is dynamic and subject to continuous innovation and research. Ongoing efforts focus on refining models, addressing limitations, and exploring new frontiers in AI (Sharma *et al.*, 2016). This iterative process contributes to the evolution of technology and its adaptation to an ever-changing socio-technical landscape.

LITERATURE REVIEW

This review investigates keen on the approaching ramifications of ChatGPT technology & AI tools in diverse sectors. Utilizing OpenAI's GPT architecture, ChatGPT signifies a notable progression in natural language processing (NLP) and AI prowess. Through examination of prevailing studies and expert viewpoints, this assessment aims to clarify the possible effects, advantages, obstacles, and ethical quandaries linked with incorporating ChatGPT technology and AI tools across various realms, including education, healthcare, customer service, creativity, and beyond (Prasad *et al.*, 2023). The amalgamation of these discoveries provides valuable perspectives into the shifting terrain of AI-driven communication and its societal implications.

The present section provides an exhaustive overview of the most recent research discoveries concerning ChatGPT. To make possible a systematic examination, the articles under review be categorized into eleven separate research theme, aligning with their respective domains of inquiry. Moreover, a chosen citation pointer was engaged to gauge the import and influence of every article, with priority given to those of utmost importance, thereby determining their order of presentation. Within the realm of research articles, assertive declarations were meticulously remove and prearranged into a structured tabular layout, alongside the articles' domains and their equivalent citation counts (Rajest *et al.*, 2023).

The table below furnishes a comprehensive synthesis of the literature reviewed, encompassing essential particulars such as Research Topic, Assertive declarations, Investigated abilities, and Citation Indicator.

Considering the active growth of ChatGPT as a cutting-edge skill, an array of resources contributed to the compilation of the articles. Firstly, materials featuring the word "ChatGPT" in their titles are gathered from Google Scholar. Furthermore, works from reputable publishers like MDPI, Elsevier, and IEEE were integrated. It's crucial to note that some articles, due to their recent publication, hadn't been indexed by Google Scholar during the statistics anthology phase.

Table 1. Literature review

Sr. No.	Research Topic	Official Statements	Competency scrutinized
1.	Healthcare	ChatGPT has the capability to generate coherent rationales and offer pertinent clinical perspectives, bolstering assurance in its reliability and clarity (Maharajan *et al.*, 2023)	Logical Reasoning/ Reasoning
2.	Usefulness of Vaccine	ChatGPT might serve as a superb research instrument for performing studies & composing investigate papers, yet it might not relied upon for locating article citations	Academic Writing/ Research
3.	Healthcare Education and Research	Embracing LLM technologies proactively, while giving thoughtful attention to ethical and legal concerns, can accelerate innovation in healthcare (Maharajan *et al.*, 2023)	Reasoning /Research/ Academic Writing
4.	Education/ Healthcare	ChatGPT occasionally makes mistakes in fundamental reasoning, logic, mathematics, and conveying accurate information	Calculations/ Reasoning /Research
5.	Biomedical/ Healthcare	Despite the methodical, accurate, and innovative nature of ChatGPT's responses, they fell short of the standards typically associated with scholarly writing (Kumar *et al.*, 2023)	Reasoning /Research/ Academic Writing
6.	Dentistry/ Healthcare	ChatGPT may employed to supervise the remote monitoring of patients, gives online training environments, and improve assessments of students & patient care	Critical Thinking/ Reasoning
7.	Diagnosis/ Healthcare	ChatGPT accurately diagnosed issues with over 90% precision (Jeyaraman *et al.*, 2023)	Research
8.	Orthodontics/ Diagnosis	ChatGPT has the capacity to oversee a greater number of patients concurrently in contrast to conventional methods of treatment management (Jeyaraman *et al.*, 2023)	Research
9.	Pharmacy	ChatGPT is partial for offering common insights in chosen topic stuff & lacks the capability to furnish an exhaustive analysis (Fui-Hoon et al., 2023)	Reasoning/ Research/ Academic Writing
10.	Teaching/ Education	ChatGPT could aid educators by streamlining diverse tasks like evaluation, plagiarism detection, administrative duties, and feedback mechanisms (Sharma et al., 2023)	Research/Academic Writing
11.	Education/ Exams	The responses provided by ChatGPT were pertinent and applicable, attaining commendable ratings in precision, pertinence, profundity, and inventiveness	Critical Thinking/ Research
12.	Chatbots/ Education	ChatGPT plays a pivotal role and holds immense value in revolutionizing education (Sharma et al., 2023)	Teaching Assistance
13.	General	ChatGPT showcases superior aptitude in deductive & abdicative interpretation when compared to inductive analysis (Sharma et al., 2023)	Logical Reasoning
14.	Finance/Crypto-currency	ChatGPT's publicly available data surpasses that of private datasets (Geis et al., 2019)	Research/ Academic Writing
15.	Natural Language Processing/ Machine Learning	ChatGPT demonstrates exceptional performance balance to GPT-3.5, particularly accentuating its outstanding prowess in arithmetic reasoning (Geis et al., 2019)	Calculations/ Reasoning
16.	Data Science/ Machine Learning	ChatGPT elevates the efficiency and precision of data science workflows (Geis et al., 2019)	Research
17.	Frameworks/ Machine Learning	A compelling demand exists for a framework that can effectively bridge the chasm separating artificial and natural systems (Haque et al., 2022)	Calculations/ Research
18.	Translation	ChatGPT excels in comparison to commercially available translation products. However, its performance noticeably decreases when dealing with low-resource or foreign languages (Haque et al., 2022)	Translation
19.	Mathematics	ChatGPT's mathematical proficiency falls short compared to the capabilities expected of a classic mathematics adapt learner (Abbott et al., 2022)	Calculations
20.	Social/Early Reactions	Fear come out regarding a forthcoming developed of job roles, the rapidly shifting technical background, a pursuit of artificial common cleverness, & a complex interplay between ethics and growth (Cheng et al., 2023)	Reasoning
21.	Politics/ Social	Alteration: ChatGPT provides responses with a neutral stance, free from the political bias (Cheng et al., 2023)	Research/Ethics
22.	Robotics/ Industry	Engaging a person in the closed path is crucial to provide oversight and intervene if the ChatGPT will show unforeseen behaviors (Cheng et al., 2023)	Application
23.	Industry/Intelligent Vehicles	Potential conflicts may arise between legal requirements and user intentions, which could impact the seamless integration of ChatGPT into smart vehicles (Kumar et al., 2023)	Research / Understanding
24.	Marketing	ChatGPT possesses the capacity to transform marketing profoundly, provided ethical considerations are carefully integrated (Kumar et al., 2023)	Research/ Reasoning
25.	Industry/ Supply Chain	ChatGPT may complement, rather than supplant, the expertise for supply cycle professionals in executive processes	Understanding / Application
26.	Art	ChatGPT has a capacity to increase the originality & efficiency of equivalent skill endeavors (Kumar et al., 2023)	Understanding/Art

DISCUSSION

The chapter thoroughly explores existing literature, synthesizing academic perspectives on the practical purposes & allegations of ChatGPT in shaping prospect technological landscapes. It includes a classification table that provides a succinct overview of analyzed publications, categorized by research topics, key findings, and assessed capabilities. While ChatGPT shows potential across various industries, particularly in healthcare, the literature analysis highlights a prevailing focus on its use in this field. However, it also emphasizes the need for further scholarly investigation into the moral considerations of ChatGPT deployment and its incorporation into future scenarios (Mulia et al., 2023). Moreover, our study reveals a significant space in research regarding ChatGPT's proficiency in executing machine-learning tasks effectively. This chapter provides a succinct overview of their findings, focusing on research and programming, following their utilization of ChatGPT to explore future prospects.

Research

Insights drawn from utilizing ChatGPT highlight its ability to identify and suggest academic citations relevant to specific sentences or passages, thereby aiding budding researchers in finding pertinent materials (Roumeliotis et al., 2023). However, it has been brought to attention that many of the recommended references, though relevant to the discussed topic, may not be readily available within academic repositories and often contain inaccuracies in author attributions or digital object identifiers (DOIs). Despite efforts to address these discrepancies by proposing alternative sources, similar inaccuracies persist upon closer examination. ChatGPT acknowledges these limitations and expresses regret for its incapability to provide appropriate replacements. The recurring nature of this issue is believed to stem from an error during the model's training phase, which developers have yet to rectify (Roumeliotis et al., 2023). Hence, it is critical to highlight the significance of researchers exercising caution and not solely relying on tools like ChatGPT for accessing intellectual references.

Programming

Exploring the purported programming prowess of ChatGPT, researchers set it to task with prompt outlining desired program functionalities. The ensuing Python code exhibited impressive proficiency. Yet, it became apparent that effectively communicating the task to ChatGPT requires a certain programming acumen (Sharma et al., 2023). Furthermore, while the output dazzled, adapting it to specific project needs necessitates programming expertise. Thus, while ChatGPT can aid in code generation, it cannot displace the developer's position, at slightest not presently.

Abridgment our study's discourse, it's evident that ChatGPT offers a mixed bag of benefits and drawbacks across diverse domains. Notably, in healthcare and research/science, ChatGPT holds promise for enhancing productivity and streamlining processes. It also proves invaluable in educational and programming spheres. However, ethical quandaries and concerns regarding job displacement cast a shadow. Hence, it's crucial for governments to craft regulatory frameworks to mitigate potential adverse effects stemming from ChatGPT's adoption. Ultimately, the technology possesses the potential to profoundly reshape numerous sectors, with outcomes ranging from favorable to unfavorable (Roumeliotis et al., 2023; Sharma et al., 2023)

Figure 3. Current landscape

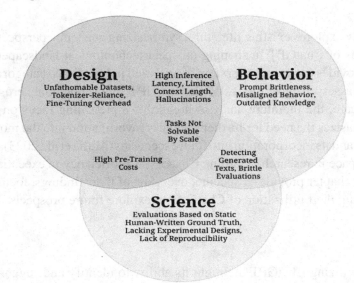

THE CURRENT LANDSCAPE OF CHATGPT AND AI TOOLS

Compared to previous replicas, ChatGPT brag more than a few key developments and novelty, including,

(i) **Enhanced background accepting:** ChatGPT's capacity to grasp and engage with intricate and subtle inputs is enhanced, rendering it more proficient at crafting precise and pertinent text.
(ii) **Reduced biases:** Though not entirely devoid of biases, ongoing hard works to mitigate biases in guidance data have enhanced ChatGPT's ability to generate outputs that are additional purposeful and impartial.
(iii) **Fine-tuning ability:** ChatGPT is highly adaptable and can undergo fine-tuning to suit specific tasks and applications, catering to the distinct requirements of researchers spanning diverse scientific domains.

OpenAI, a pioneering group committed to progressing artificial general intelligence (AGI) for the betterment of civilization, was established in 2015 by visionaries like Elon Musk and Sam Altman. From the outset, OpenAI has remained at the forefront of AI research, delivering numerous innovative models, including GPT-3, GPT-2, and the subsequent evolution, ChatGPT.

Continuing its trajectory of innovation, OpenAI expanded it's investigate and growth initiatives, culminating in the formation of ChatGPT, built upon the robust design of GPT-4 (Adeshola et al., 2023). This new iteration represents a leap forward in conversational AI, boasting enhanced capabilities in contextual comprehension, answer production, & generally rationality when evaluated to its antecedent, GPT-3 (Elkhatat et al., 2023).

GPT models excel at producing natural language text, spanning from concise sentences to lengthy documents, all crafted to mimic human language seamlessly. Their defining trait lies in their capacity for pre-training on vast textual datasets, followed by modification for precise tasks like text organization

Figure 4. Key milestones

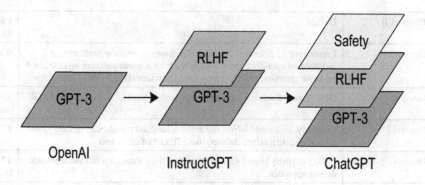

or inquiry responding (Elkhatat et al., 2023). During pre-training, the model immerses itself in a wealth of text data, whether sourced from web pages or literary works, learning in an unsupervised manner without the need for explicit labels or annotations (Elkhatat et al., 2023).

During its pre-exercise phase, the GPT replica engages in predicting the subsequent word in a text series, building its understanding of language structures in a process known as language modeling. This stage is pivotal across various natural language processing tasks, allowing the model to discern and apply linguistic patterns, including syntax, grammar, and semantics, through exposure to extensive textual data. Following pre-exercise, the GPT model undertakes fine-correction for explicit downstream tasks, leveraging smaller labeled datasets to refine its parameters. For instance, in text classification, the model may learn to assign accurate labels to input text passages (Elkhatat et al., 2023).

OpenAI has pushed the boundaries of deep learning further with the unveiling of GPT-4. The groundbreaking model is a sprawling multimodal idiom powerhouse adept at processing both visual and textual data, yielding coherent textual outputs. While it may not yet match the nuanced understanding of humans in practical situations, GPT-4 has showcased remarkable strides, achieving human-comparable concert across a spectrum of rigorous specialized and scholastic evaluations (Elkhatat et al., 2023).

For example, it has attained a recital position in the peak 10% among test-takers on a replicated block exam, exceeding GPT-3.5's performance, which falls within the base 10%. The growth of GPT-4 spanned six months of iterative refinement, incorporating insights from OpenAI's adversarial testing agenda and ChatGPT. The attempt culminated in the replica achieving its highest-ever accuracy in factual content while maintaining adherence to established parameters, albeit with opportunities for further enhancement. The infographic below outlines the evolutionary milestones leading to ChatGPT's current iteration.

GPT models have garnered remarkable achievements across a spectrum of normal talking giving out tasks, spanning text making, question-answering, talking conversion, and emotion study. Their versatility extends to diverse real-world relevancies like chatbots, client tune-up automation, & content generation (Rawat et al., 2023; Crawford et al., 2023). Table 1 offers a wide-ranging comparison of different GPT iterations, while Table 2 delves into the distinctions among GPT and ChatGPT (Crawford et al., 2023).

Table 2. Relationship of GPTs

Edition	Utilized By	Design	Factor Tally	Year
GPT-1	General	Employing a 12-level, 12-headed Transformer decoder architecture (without an encoder), the model is track by a linear-softmax layer trained on Book quantity, which comprises approximately 4.5 GB of text	0.18 billion	2018
GPT-2	General	GPT-1, now featuring enhanced standardize trained on Web Text: 40 GB corpus.	1500.00 million	2019
GPT-3	General	Certainly, you could adjust the architecture and parameters of GPT-2 to accommodate a larger dataset, like 570 GB of plain-text	175.00 billion	2020
InstructGPT	Discussion	GPT-3 expertly honed to adhere to directives through a human feedback-driven approach.	175.00 billion	2022
ProtGPT2	Protein string	GPT-2 big (36 layers) trained on protein string sourced from UniRef-50, totaling 44.88 million sequences.	738.00 million	2022
BioGPT	Bio-medical substance	Using GPT-2 average model, comprising 24 layers and 16 heads, we trained it on a dataset containing nonempty stuffs from PubMed, totaling 1.5 million.	347.00 million	2022
ChatGPT	conversation	Leverages the power of GPT-3.5, meticulously honed through a blend of supervised learning and strengthening education techniques, including person response reinforcement learning (HFRL).	175.00 billion	2022
GPT-4	General	Trained with both text forecast and strengthening learning with person response (RLHF), it accepts inputs in the form of both text & images, including moderator data.	100.00 trillion	2023

Table 3. Relationship of GPT and ChatGPT

Parameters	GPT	ChatGPT
Basis Application	A readily accessible AI model accessible via an API to provide intelligence on demand	A Chatbot may engage with users and function, carrying out various tasks
	(a) Make a elegant application	(a) Creative application
	(b) Apply semantic text thoughtful	(b) Ideation for satisfied formation
	(c) Information explore & removal	(c) Answers general questions
	(d) Building copilot similar to application	(d) Supply assistance in code generation
	(e) Applicable for broad diversities of usage expansion	(e) Code debugging stipulation
		(f) Languages conversion
		(g) Language growth for superior reasoning, hurry and terseness

Figure 5. Prevalent interest

MAIN TASKS FOR CHATGPT AND AI TOOLS IN CURRENT AND FUTURE DEVELOPMENT

1. Fast extensive curiosity:
    ◦ ChatGPT, the forefront of AI language models, sparked immense curiosity upon its emergence.
    ◦ Employing a dataset of text pairs created by both humans and AI, the AI classifier endeavors to discern the origin of texts.
    ◦ From crafting essays, articles, and poetry to providing translations and beyond, ChatGPT offers suggestions on a wide array of subjects (AlZu'bi et al., 2022).
    ◦ Its sophisticated natural language processing capabilities have revolutionized interactions with AI, reshaping how people harness its potential.
    ◦ ChatGPT has been honed on a far-reaching corpus of textual facts, enabling it to adeptly comprehend & generate answers reminiscent of human conversation across diverse topics.
    ◦ ChatGPT serves as a potent resource, capable of significantly boosting human productivity and ingenuity. It excels in responding to inquiries, sparking imaginative writing, and facilitating daily tasks (AlZu'bi et al., 2022).
2. Diversity of language input:
    ◦ Users can harness ChatGPT's ability to comprehend & respond to various speech inputs, receiving straightforward answers to queries without resorting to a search engine such as Google.
    ◦ Understanding complex topics becomes more accessible with the AI chatbot's ability to elucidate information in diverse conversational styles.
    ◦ ChatGPT's training corpus is sourced from the WebText dataset, a comprehensive compilation of online textual data (AlZu'bi et al., 2022).

Figure 6. Assortment of language inputs

- ◦ This dataset encompasses a broad spectrum of text genres and writing styles, ranging from articles and forums to social media updates.
- ◦ With its extensive training dataset, ChatGPT excels at generating text that closely resembles human writing.
- ◦ OpenAI's proficient ChatGPT model is capable of analyzing code and providing explanations for its functionality.

3. Selecting of newest information:
    - ◦ Sharma et al. (2023) highlight ChatGPT's remarkable adaptability, enabling it to seamlessly assimilate and accommodate new information.
    - ◦ This adaptability underscores its ability to tackle novel subjects and tasks with minimal re-training required.
    - ◦ Moreover, ChatGPT boasts impressive scalability, rendering it well-suited for deployment in large-scale applications.
    - ◦ With versatility spanning across customer service, education, and entertainment, ChatGPT finds utility in diverse fields.
    - ◦ Notably, one of its primary applications lies in Natural Language Processing, showcasing its pivotal role in this domain.
    - ◦ The models excel in tasks for example language translation, text summarization, and question and answering by generating text based on given inputs.
    - ◦ Additionally, it has been leveraged in the formation of chatbots and other informal AI systems, with potential applications in customer care and assistance (Sharma et al., 2023).
    - ◦ Generative AI has the probable to automate various professions by crafting original text, audio, and visual content in answers to person prompts.
    - ◦ A prevailing concept involves utilizing 'assistant' tools to democratize access to certain occupations, making them more inclusive for everyone.

Figure 7. Selection of latest information

4. Learning and humanizing:
    ◦   The pivotal advantage of ChatGPT lies in its capacity to acquire knowledge through interactions with users (Sharma et al., 2023).
    ◦   Over time, it refines and enriches its responses in human interactions, steadily honing its correctness.
    ◦   ChatGPT's adaptability enables it to serve a wide range of applications, fostering the advancement and enhancement of spoken AI technique in a foreseeable upcoming.
    ◦   Analysts anticipate that ChatGPT's triumph will grant OpenAI a competitive advantage over its AI counterparts.
    ◦   Despite the strain on OpenAI's processing resources due to increased usage, valuable feedback has contributed to refining the chatbot's responses.
    ◦   Trained on a widespread corpus of internet text facts using a language model (Liu et al., 2023), this iteration of ChatGPT demonstrates remarkable proficiency.
    ◦   Leveraging diverse textual sources like books, news articles, and web content, ChatGPT boasts a comprehensive understanding of various topics, enabling it to provide contextually appropriate responses (Liu et al., 2023).

Figure 8. Learning ability through ChatGPT

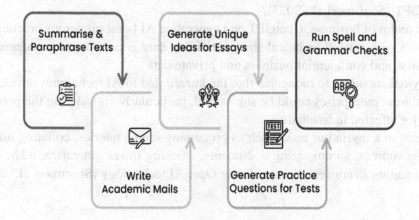

Figure 9. Tasks done by ChatGPT
(Wang et al., 2021)

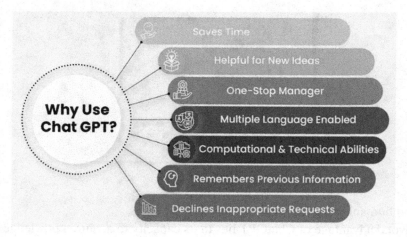

5. Supportive for a multiplicity of responsibilities:
   - It serves diverse purposes, from generating code to suggesting meals, and improving the well-being of seniors and individuals with disabilities.
   - ChatGPT demonstrates remarkable adaptability, responding to a wide array of prompts with few limitations to its capabilities.
   - The primary objective of conversational GPT is to comprehend straightforward statements.
   - Offering insights and support on ethical dilemmas in the era of smartphones and computers (Qadir, 2023; Wang et al., 2021).
   - It assumes a human-like role when seeking information from other modules, conducting research to provide accurate answers.
   - The Role of ChatGPT will serve as a cornerstone in reshaping the landscape of software development and utilization within the technology sector. This shift will be propelled by the pervasive influence of foundational models, heralding a new era in the industry.
6. Business functions:
   - Businesses can enhance their marketing campaigns significantly, effectively connect with their target audience, and achieve their marketing goals by leveraging the capabilities of ChatGPT (Sharma et al., 2023).
   - In the realm of business, ChatGPT and generative AI boast numerous practical applications.
   - Just like with several technical strides, training care is paramount to safeguard private, responsive, and confidential business and private data.
   - Policymakers ought to recognize that the hazard tied to AI techniques developed or utilized by different enterprises could be substantial, particularly considering the potential ramifications for affected individuals.
   - Engages in a myriad of tasks such as processing search queries, collating information from diverse sources, summarizing documents, devising travel itineraries, addressing inquiries, and engaging in conversations utilizing OpenAI technology (Sharma et al., 2023).

Figure 10. Universal business applications by ChatGPT and AI

7. Helpful for digital market place:
   - ChatGPT proves invaluable for digital marketer seeking to elevate their movement and connect with their desired audience.
   - It adeptly generates content for community media posts, blog entries, and various substances formats (Sethi et al., 2023).
   - The chatbot offers recommendations for compelling headlines, engaging opening lines, and even entire paragraphs tailored to specific marketing contexts or keywords.
   - Through audience research, digital marketers can gain deeper insights into their target demographic.
   - Utilizing ChatGPT, they can uncover ordinary traits, behavior, and favorites within exact customer collection through analyzing extensive datasets (Sethi et al., 2023).
   - ChatGPT can be trained to address common inquiries, offer customer support, and recommend products.
   - ChatGPT can assist in categorizing customer reviews and unstructured data by product features, customer service quality, and marketing efforts, enhancing the comprehension and analysis of consumer preferences and needs.
8. Translate conceptions:
   - ChatGPT possesses the capability to develop computer code for crafting programs and software applications.
   - It excels in translating English concepts into programming languages and scrutinizing human programmers' language for errors (Sethi et al., 2023).
   - The surge in attractiveness of this system stems from a novel signal of generative models, above all since of its convenience to the common community sooner than its unique functionalities.
   - OpenAI's ChatGPT, a substantial language model, adeptly generates text resembling human language.

Figure 11. Impact on digital marketing

- ◦ Its repertoire includes diverse tasks within usual language dispensation, such as conversational techniques, language summarization, and conversion, facilitated by training on extensive internet text datasets (Sethi et al., 2023).

9. Genuine discussions:
   - ◦ ChatGPT is crafted to mimic genuine conversations, making its responses feel remarkably person.
   - ◦ The bot excels at expanding on concepts, retrieving information from earlier parts of the conversation, and acknowledging errors when they occur (Tanwar et al., 2023).
   - ◦ ChatGPT's technological framework integrates both supervised and unsupervised AI learning approaches, facilitating the development of some of the globe's leading language models.
   - ◦ Unlike many other chatbots, ChatGPT retains a comprehensive memory of past interactions.
   - ◦ Interacting with ChatGPT involves posing questions in natural language; in return, the chatbot furnishes conversational replies drawn from extensive datasets sourced from the internet & various community repositories.

10. Education:
    - ◦ ChatGPT excels at defining words and crafting impressive sentences, making it invaluable for educational purposes.
    - ◦ As the capabilities of chatbots like ChatGPT continue to evolve and refine in the coming years, it has the potential to reshape how students engage with the world beyond the classroom (Larsson et al., 2020).
    - ◦ Within the realm of education, ChatGPT finds application in scenarios where educators may focus on imparting fundamental concepts while offering students a platform to seek clarification and guidance.
    - ◦ ChatGPT presents a distinct advantage over conventional search engines like Google by tailoring results to the specific preferences and inclinations of the user.

Figure 12. Valid conversation

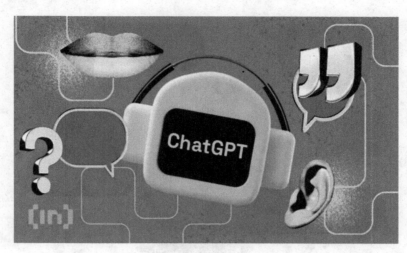

- ○ This personalized conversational search skill caters particularly well to individuals who prioritize interactive exploration over traditional webpage-based investigate outcomes.
11. Rising well-built writing aptitude:
    - ○ It also aids in assessment & scouring, shifting a focus as of error correction to cultivating essential writing skills (Larsson et al., 2020).
    - ○ AI-driven writing assessment systems have the potential to analyze and evaluate essays with greater precision and efficiency compared to human grading, leveraging technologies such as machine learning.
    - ○ Students can enhance their writing abilities further by utilizing AI systems to receive comprehensive comment on their articles.

Figure 13. AI tools and ChatGPT based educations

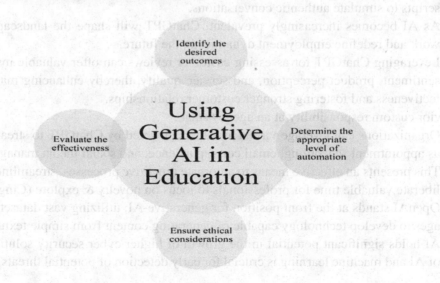

Figure 14. New creation by ChatGPT

- ○ Crafting unique, compelling, & captivating add replica for diverse advertising campaigns can pose challenges.
- ○ Utilizing AI, ChatGPT streamlines text generation, easing the workload of digital marketers.
- ○ This equips marketers with content ideas and structural frameworks, significantly boosting their productivity.
12. Create new things:
    - ○ Generative AI systems are designed to produce novel content using existing knowledge as a foundation.
    - ○ These technologies typically leverage machine learning, a process where artificial intelligence is trained by exposing it to huge amount of facts, permitting it to study & replicate tasks (Larsson et al., 2020).
    - ○ For example, ChatGPT has undergone training using extensive internet data and dialogue scripts to simulate authentic conversations.
    - ○ As AI becomes increasingly prevalent, ChatGPT will shape the landscape of knowledge work and redefine employment dynamics in the future.
    - ○ Leveraging ChatGPT for assessing customer reviews can offer valuable insights into brand sentiment, product perception, and service quality, thereby enhancing market research effectiveness and fostering stronger customer relationships.
13. Behavior custom responsibility at an agency stage:
    - ○ Organizations can leverage virtual assistants powered by ChatGPT to streamline tasks such as appointment scheduling, email correspondence, and social media management.
    - ○ This presents an effective means to automate repetitive processes, streamline workflows, and liberate valuable time for professionals to focus on novelty & explore (Cingillioglu, 2023).
    - ○ OpenAI stands at the front position for generative-AI, utilizing vast datasets of text and images to develop technology capable of generating content from simple textual prompts.
    - ○ AI holds significant potential in the growth of higher cyber security solutions. The growth of AI and machine learning is crucial for early detection of potential threats. ChatGPT could

co-operate an essential position in threat identification, response, & internal communication enhancement during cyber attacks.

REWARDS AND DRAWBACKS OF CHATGPT AND AI TOOLS

Table 4. Rewards and drawbacks table (Kumar et al., 2023; Sharma et al., 2023)

Rewards	Drawbacks
ChatGPT's ability to produce top-notch responses is significantly bolstered by training on vast datasets	Navigating sarcasm and irony presents a challenge: Given ChatGPT's limited grasp of people feelings & intentions, it can struggle to discern sarcasm or irony accurately, which could result in responses that miss the mark
ChatGPT excels at crafting captivating product descriptions and reviews, elevating the impact and quality of e-commerce platforms	Insufficient transparency: Many users find it difficult to grasp the inner workings of ChatGPT, which can build obstacles in understanding the reasoning behind building responses and possibly erode trust in the system
ChatGPT's broad language capabilities promote accessibility on a global scale, nurturing inclusivity among diverse communities spanning the globe	Challenges with long-term memory: Although ChatGPT excels at generating responses based on recent conversation context, it might struggle to recall intricate details from past parts of the chat or from past interactions
ChatGPT excels at shaping responses that closely resemble human conversation, thereby elevating the quality of interactions with chatbots	Biases in training data: Language models such as ChatGPT rely heavily on the datasets they're trained on. When datasets contain biases—like an overabundance of specific language styles or perspectives—the model may inadvertently propagate those biases in its generated outputs
ChatGPT's potential to transform customer service across various sectors lies in its ability to offer highly customized and swift responses to customer inquiries. This capability significantly elevates the standard of service provided, ultimately boosting customer satisfaction levels	Environmental impact: Utilizing significant computational power and energy to train large language models like ChatGPT can result in a notable ecological footprint
ChatGPT evolves with insights gleaned from user feedback, perpetually honing its abilities to deliver increasingly remarkable performance and fortify user contentment	Struggling with multi-party conversations: ChatGPT is most effective in two-party dialogues, which can present challenges when handling multiple participants or accurately distinguishing between different speakers in a multi-party conversation
Leveraging ChatGPT can enhance social media marketing strategies by crafting engaging and authentic responses to customer inquiries, fostering genuine interactions	Vulnerability to adversarial attacks: Language models such as ChatGPT can be susceptible to adversarial attacks, wherein malicious actors deliberately alter input data to generate unforeseen or detrimental outcomes
Leveraging ChatGPT for data augmentation significantly enhances the performance of machine learning models across a broad spectrum of applications	Navigating social and cultural subtleties can pose a challenge for ChatGPT. It might not always grasp nuances like sarcasm or humor, potentially leading to responses that seem inappropriate
Navigates social and cultural intricacies with varying degrees of success: ChatGPT's understanding of social and cultural subtleties, such as sarcasm or humor, may vary, occasionally resulting in responses that may not align perfectly with expectations	Struggles with social and cultural nuances: ChatGPT might not always grasp the subtle intricacies of social and cultural contexts, such as sarcasm or humor, potentially leading to responses that don't perfectly align
ChatGPT streamlines tasks like summarizing, translating, and answering questions, boosting productivity across various fields	Crafting complex sentences can be challenging for ChatGPT, particularly when they involve nested clauses or unconventional grammatical structures
ChatGPT aids education by improving language skills and fostering linguistic competence	Difficulty with creating complete stories: While ChatGPT can connect ideas well in conversations, it struggles with crafting narratives that have clear beginnings, middles, and ends

PROMPT APPLICATIONS OF CHATGPT

Figure 15. List of applications

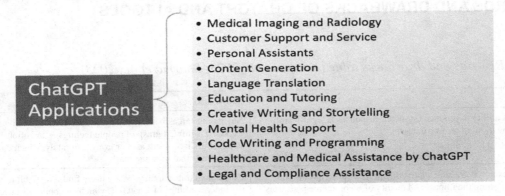

ChatGPT Applications
- Medical Imaging and Radiology
- Customer Support and Service
- Personal Assistants
- Content Generation
- Language Translation
- Education and Tutoring
- Creative Writing and Storytelling
- Mental Health Support
- Code Writing and Programming
- Healthcare and Medical Assistance by ChatGPT
- Legal and Compliance Assistance

Content Production

ChatGPT has played a pivotal role in transforming content creation across diverse fields. Its capabilities span from crafting detailed reports to composing compelling emails, designing marketing materials, and managing social media outreach efforts. With ChatGPT's assistance, writers and marketers have streamlined their processes, boosting efficiency by utilizing it for initial drafts, brainstorming ideas, and refining content. The model's proficiency in producing coherent and contextually relevant material establishes it as an invaluable resource for content creators. Tasks like drafting product descriptions, creating blog posts, managing social media content, and developing advertisements have all been made faster and more straightforward, thanks to ChatGPT's abilities (Kumar et al., 2023). Furthermore, by dynamically adjusting its responses based on user interactions, ChatGPT enriches the content discovery experience, offering tailored suggestions that resonate with individual users, thereby driving increased engagement and conversion rates. For businesses targeting global audiences, ChatGPT's multilingual capabilities facilitate the creation of content in multiple languages, enabling outreach to diverse markets with culturally appropriate material. Through its capacity to generate imaginative content, ChatGPT enhances interactive storytelling experiences, fostering immersive narrative engagements.

Language Conversion

As a virtual translator, ChatGPT demonstrates remarkable potential in language translation, assisting users in translating diverse content and entire documents across numerous languages. By breaking down language barriers and fostering global interactions, ChatGPT's multilingual capabilities facilitate smooth communication among individuals of different linguistic backgrounds (Kumar et al., 2023). Serving as a convenient tool for on-the-go language translation, ChatGPT empowers users to participate in multilingual conversations in real-time, enhancing their understanding of various cultures. With its expertise in language generation, ChatGPT delivers translations with impressive accuracy. Its proficiency in language translation proves invaluable in critical scenarios such as business meetings, political discussions, international conferences, and travel experiences. Moreover, ChatGPT adeptly handles informal language, including colloquial expressions and conversational nuances, thereby assisting users in translating informal messages, emails, and social media posts effortlessly.

Education and Training

In the realm of education, ChatGPT emerges as a revered virtual tutor, wielding its ability to elucidate complex concepts in an accessible manner. Serving as a steadfast study companion, ChatGPT extends its aid to students beyond the confines of traditional textbooks, offering elucidation on challenging subjects and providing additional insights. Educational platforms and e-learning websites have seamlessly integrated ChatGPT into their systems, allowing it to adapt to the individual learning pace and preferences of each student, thus fostering a more immersive and impactful learning environment.

A key advantage of ChatGPT in education lies in its adeptness at unraveling intricate concepts through systematic, step-by-step explanations, thereby facilitating comprehensive understanding and clarity on challenging topics. As a virtual tutor, ChatGPT tailors its instructional style and content to suit the unique learning profiles and preferences of individual students (Kumar et al., 2023). By assisting with assignments and offering prompt guidance on problem-solving strategies, ChatGPT contributes to the enhancement of students' problem-solving skills and overall academic performance

Additionally, students can enhance their language proficiency through interactive dialogues with ChatGPT, utilizing its multilingual prowess to perfect grammar and broaden vocabulary, all while receiving valuable feedback for enhancement. By incorporating ChatGPT into educational platforms, administrators gain access to a vast array of learning materials, enabling them to recommend relevant books, articles, and resources, thus enhancing students' educational experiences across various subjects.

Creative Writing and Storytelling

Storytelling and creative writing come naturally to ChatGPT, leveraging its expertise to craft compelling narratives. As a creative collaborator, ChatGPT excels at generating brainstorming ideas for dramatic content, shaping characters, and crafting intricate plot lines. Its knack for imaginative content creation extends to interactive storytelling fields and games, offering users the opportunity to craft dynamic and personalized adventures tailored to their tastes and experiences (Sharma et al., 2023).

In the realm of storytelling, whether it's through fiction or fan fiction, ChatGPT excels in crafting rich and immersive narratives. Writers often rely on ChatGPT to infuse their prose with vibrant descriptions, deep emotions, and compelling characters, elevating the reader's experience. Poets, in particular, find it invaluable for enriching their verses with a plethora of word choices and evocative imagery.

By analyzing trends in popular genres and narrative structures, ChatGPT empowers writers with personalized recommendations tailored to their style and audience preferences. This enables them to craft captivating scripts, songs, and content that deeply resonates with their readers or listeners.

Psychological Health Maintain

Due to its empathetic conversational format, ChatGPT has undergone trials as a virtual counselor and mental health companion, providing a diverse array of supportive services to individuals navigating different mental health hurdles. Unlike humans, who may grow bored or struggle to maintain continuous

Figure 16. Mental health support

attention, ChatGPT excels as a virtual listener. It offers unwavering emotional support and responds with empathy and sympathy to users' inquiries, serving as a reliable source of comfort and understanding.

ChatGPT fosters an environment where users can freely express their thoughts and emotions, receiving empathetic responses devoid of judgment. Serving as a compassionate companion, ChatGPT offers a plethora of resources on mental health strategies, insights into various conditions, and techniques for personal growth. It aids individuals in navigating anxiety and stress through mindfulness exercises, relaxation methods, affirmations, and introspective activities. Harnessing its linguistic prowess, ChatGPT administers therapeutic interventions grounded in evidence-based approaches, guiding users to delve into their thoughts and behaviors, nurturing self-awareness, and fortifying their mental well-being. Employing cognitive-behavioral techniques, it assists users in challenging irrational beliefs, reframing negative thought patterns, and embracing cognitive restructuring (Sharma et al., 2023).

Code Writing and Programming

ChatGPT has demonstrated impressive capabilities in aiding software development by generating code and assisting programmers. Interacting with ChatGPT enables the effortless creation of code snippets either through natural language prompts or within existing code contexts. This functionality is invaluable for developers, as it accelerates the process of generating boilerplate code and automating repetitive coding tasks. Leveraging its advanced language comprehension abilities, ChatGPT can analyze code syntax, detect potential errors, and generate error-free code tailored to specific tasks. By offering insightful feedback on coding errors, ChatGPT facilitates developers in pinpointing and resolving issues within their codebase. Additionally, ChatGPT significantly contributes to refactoring, modifying, and optimizing existing codebases by suggesting improvements and streamlining implementations. Through thorough examination of code snippets, it proposes alternative formulations to enhance both performance and readability (Sharma et al., 2023).

ChatGPT empowers developers to tackle intricate tasks effortlessly through straightforward language queries, leveraging its ability to interact in natural language with APIs and libraries. Moreover, ChatGPT serves as a valuable aid in debugging for seasoned programmers, aiding in the identification and resolution of bugs within extensive codebases. By analyzing error notifications and contextualizing issues, it provides insightful troubleshooting suggestions, streamlining coding workflows and bolstering

Figure 17. Programming by ChatGPT

code quality. Additionally, ChatGPT excels in generating code comments and documentation, thereby enhancing code comprehensibility and maintainability.

Lawful and Conformity Support

ChatGPT is equipped to be your virtual legal companion, providing essential assistance in handling legal affairs for individuals and professionals alike. It assists legal professionals in conducting comprehensive legal research, accessing essential statutes, documents, and case law from reputable legal databases. With its advanced language understanding capabilities, ChatGPT streamlines case analysis, identifying pertinent proceedings and legal arguments accurately. Moreover, it simplifies contract drafting by generating customized templates and standardized constructions based on user inputs and legal requirements.

In addition, ChatGPT is tailored to suit user requirements by producing a wide array of legal forms and documents, ranging from will and leases to power of attorney documents. It also offers insights into the basics of intellectual property protection laws and directs users to relevant resources (Sharma et al., 2023). Serving as an intuitive interface for legal databases, ChatGPT streamlines the document creation process for individuals in search of precise legal resolutions.

Health-Care and Medical Support by ChatGPT

ChatGPT serves as a cornerstone in healthcare and medical guidance, leveraging insights from credible medical sources to offer invaluable assistance. It facilitates healthcare professionals, individuals, and patients alike in accessing the latest medical research, expert guidance, and diverse treatment options. Additionally, it aids in addressing inquiries pertaining to dosage interactions and contraindications, ensuring safer healthcare practices.

Beyond physical health, ChatGPT provides robust mental health support through mindfulness exercises, stress-relief strategies, and personalized self-care recommendations. It simplifies the workflow for healthcare professionals by condensing medical reports and electronic health records (EHRs), enabling efficient review of essential information and patient backgrounds.

Continuous advancements in research are continually refining ChatGPT's proficiency in sophisticated language processing, enhancing its capacity to serve and support individuals across various healthcare domains.

The AI model plays a crucial role in enhancing and refining fundamental knowledge necessary for diagnostic procedures. Within the medical domain, ChatGPT shows promise in developing chatbots designed to assist with patient triage, aiding healthcare professionals in evaluating the urgency of a patient's condition and determining the most appropriate course of action. By analyzing patient data and relevant symptoms, ChatGPT can provide healthcare providers with valuable insights, offering an additional perspective to improve disease diagnosis and treatment planning.

Furthermore, ChatGPT can contribute to analyzing extensive clinical datasets, identifying patterns and trends that can lead to innovative treatments and interventions. Its capabilities extend to generating and simplifying inquiries regarding various diseases and disorders, such as lung cancer screening recommendations, and offering relevant preventive advice for conditions like breast cancer.

Furthermore, it delves into the diverse capabilities, features, and applications of ChatGPT in supporting the healthcare sector. These include functionalities like memory recall, predictive assistance, and medical translations, among others.

However, alongside these beneficial attributes, certain limitations have been identified, such as occasional generation of inaccurate information due to biased content. Moreover, the figure above (Perlman, 2022) illustrates additional characteristics and traditional viewpoints associated with ChatGPT.

Figure 18. ChatGPT for healthcare

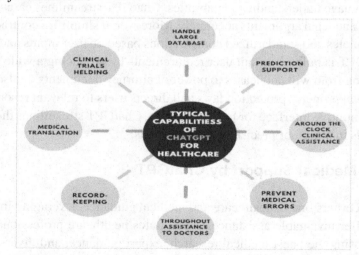

FUTURE RESEARCH DIRECTIONS OF CHATGPT AND AI TOOLS

ChatGPT is rapidly expanding its capabilities as more users engage with it. With an increasing number of students opting for ChatGPT's innovative approaches over traditional education methods, they not only enhance AI but also contribute to its future utility. This influence extends to the educational technology sector, where ChatGPT's integration becomes pivotal. Edtech companies now integrate ChatGPT to provide foundational knowledge while offering a platform for students to seek clarification and guidance.

The practical application of ChatGPT extends beyond academia, as it becomes indispensable in real-world scenarios. Consequently, businesses are eager to leverage its potential for profit. In the future, AI will play a crucial role in matching students with the most suitable tutors, who not only assist in learning but also serve as mentors, offering guidance and inspiration (Perlman, 2022). However, the development of new AI applications necessitates careful consideration, especially given society's diverse reactions to the rapidly evolving AI landscape, encompassing fear, optimism, anxiety, astonishment, and wonder.

Figure 19. Future scope

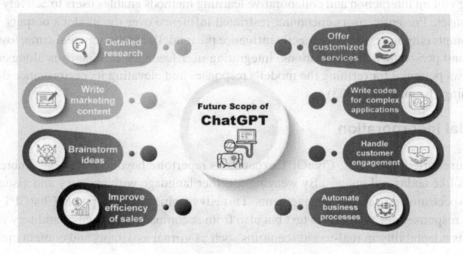

The continuous evolution of language models, as demonstrated by ChatGPT, has broadened the vistas of research and development in conversational AI. This section explores potential technical advancements and distinctive pathways that could enhance ChatGPT's capabilities, address existing limitations, and propel the advancement of conversational AI systems.

Contextual Understanding and Dialogue Management

Refining ChatGPT's grasp of context and its ability to manage extended conversations are key focal points for future investigation. Although ChatGPT has advanced considerably in crafting coherent responses, there remains room for improvement in navigating prolonged discussions while maintaining context across various exchanges (Perlman, 2022). Strategies like reinforcement learning and memory-augmented architectures offer promising avenues for enhancing the model's capacity to retain and utilize long-term context effectively.

Figure 20. List of future directions

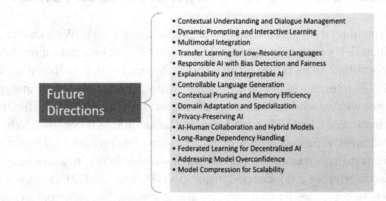

Future Directions

- Contextual Understanding and Dialogue Management
- Dynamic Prompting and Interactive Learning
- Multimodal Integration
- Transfer Learning for Low-Resource Languages
- Responsible AI with Bias Detection and Fairness
- Explainability and Interpretable AI
- Controllable Language Generation
- Contextual Pruning and Memory Efficiency
- Domain Adaptation and Specialization
- Privacy-Preserving AI
- AI-Human Collaboration and Hybrid Models
- Long-Range Dependency Handling
- Federated Learning for Decentralized AI
- Addressing Model Overconfidence
- Model Compression for Scalability

Energetic Prompting and Interactive Wisdom

Encouraging vibrant interaction and collaborative learning methods enables users to actively mold Chat-GPT's responses. Presently, users encounter restricted influence over the model's outputs. Embracing dynamic prompts empowers users to directly influence the model's behavior in real-time, fostering more captivating and personalized conversations. Integrating user feedback mechanisms alongside adaptive prompts shows potential for refining the model's responses and elevating its performance during cooperative learning (Israni et al., 2023).

Multi-Modal Incorporation

Diving into uncharted territories, ChatGPT expands its repertoire beyond mere text, embracing multi-modal inputs like audio and images. By weaving together language with auditory and visual signals, it elevates the spectrum and depth of engagements. This advancement will empower ChatGPT to decipher and produce responses not solely from text but also from accompanying visual or auditory information, amplifying its adaptability in real-world scenarios such as virtual assistants and content creation.

Shift Learning for Low Reserve Languages

While ChatGPT has shown impressive capabilities in English and other widely spoken languages, there's a chance to improve its effectiveness in low-resource languages. By employing transfer learning techniques, the model can first be trained on data-rich languages and then fine-tuned using limited resources from low-resource languages (Perlman, 2022). This method offers potential for improving simplification and accommodating linguistic variations in languages with sparse training data, thus expanding ChatGPT's accessibility to a wider range of linguistic communities.

Answerable AI With Bias Recognition and Justice

Ensuring fairness and reducing biases in ChatGPT's responses is a crucial ethical imperative. It's imperative that forthcoming research prioritize bolstering bias detection mechanisms and adopting fairness-driven training techniques to mitigate biased outcomes across various user groups. Additionally, the integration of interpretability techniques can provide valuable insights into the model's decision-making processes, enabling users and developers to pinpoint and address potential biases with accuracy.

Convenient Language Production

Improving controllable language generation methods is all about giving users the power to mold Chat-GPT's outputs according to their preferences in style, specificity, or sentiment (Perlman, 2022). By utilizing conditional decoding strategies or reinforcement learning techniques, users can finely tune the model's responses to their liking. This flexibility allows individuals to precisely tailor the attributes of the generated content, making ChatGPT even more versatile for a range of applications, from personalized content creation to fostering creativity in writing.

Background Pruning and Recall Effectiveness

To bolster ChatGPT's real-time capabilities and adapt to resource limitations, researchers might explore strategies such as parameter sharing, contextual pruning, and model compression. These approaches strive to diminish the model's footprint and boost inference speed while maintaining its efficacy (Perlman, 2022).

Province Version and Specialty

Investigating domain adaptation within specialized sectors such as healthcare, finance, or legal services, along with implementing refined fine-tuning techniques, can greatly enhance the model's expertise and practical utility.

Privacy-Preserving AI

As AI models such as ChatGPT manage more sensitive user data, prioritizing privacy protection becomes crucial. Research must concentrate on advancing privacy-preserving techniques like differential privacy. These approaches are vital for upholding confidentiality and protecting user data throughout interactions with AI models (Sharma et al., 2023).

AI-Human Partnership and Fusion Models

Harnessing AI alongside human collaboration and employing hybrid models that blend AI language models with human supervision can yield markedly more reliable and low-risk results. Human-in-the-loop frameworks empower individuals to interact with and guide the model's outputs, especially in critical or sensitive scenarios, thereby guaranteeing the highest caliber and accuracy of responses (Kumar et al., 2024).

Long-Range Dependence Treatment

Enhancing the management of long-range dependencies in language models stands as a cornerstone for comprehending intricate sentences and conversational exchanges. It's imperative for future research to pioneer innovative approaches tackling this challenge, empowering ChatGPT to maintain coherence and relevance throughout extensive dialogues (Sharma et al., 2023).

Associate Learning for Decentralized AI

By employing federated learning, we can tackle the hurdles of decentralized AI while ensuring the utmost data privacy and security. ChatGPT is trained on varied datasets spread across various sites, allowing the model to improve its performance through shared insights, all while ensuring the confidentiality of individual data.

Addressing Model Overconfidence

Exploring strategies to mitigate model overconfidence is paramount for minimizing the potential for providing inaccurate or deceptive responses. Techniques aimed at fostering uncertainty estimation and confidence calibration have the potential to enhance ChatGPT's resilience and trustworthiness (Sharma et al., 2023).

Model Compression for Scalability

An exciting potential direction lies in integrating model compression techniques, catering especially to users on resource-constrained devices or platforms, thereby amplifying effectiveness and convenience.

Figure 21. Scalability by ChatGPT and AI tools

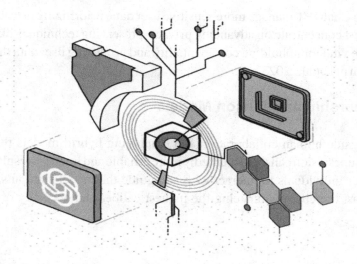

Prospective research endeavors could focus on advancing ChatGPT's model compression techniques, as highlighted by (Sharma et al. 2023). These efforts aim to strategically reduce the model's computational demands and size, ultimately enhancing its inference speed and minimizing memory requirements. Such optimizations are crucial for enabling ChatGPT's deployment across a diverse array of devices, ensuring seamless interactions and accessibility for users with resource constraints.

Moreover, the future research path for ChatGPT spans a range of technological challenges and opportunities. By embracing these paths, developers can advance ChatGPT towards enhanced proficiency, efficiency, and ethical responsibility, as detailed by (Perlman A. 2022). This path situates ChatGPT as a versatile and influential language model applicable across diverse domains.

CONCLUSION

The potential future with ChatGPT technology and AI tools is filled with promise and transformative possibilities across a multitude of domains. As these technologies continue to evolve, they stand poised to revolutionize human productivity, streamline mundane tasks, and spark innovation. Integrating ChatGPT seamlessly into communication platforms has the potential to revolutionize human-computer interactions, rendering them more natural and efficient, thereby enhancing user experiences and accessibility. Nevertheless, addressing ethical concerns, adhering to responsible development practices, and implementing thoughtful regulation will be imperative in successfully navigating the challenges accompanying AI deployment. Adopting a collaborative approach that harnesses both the strengths of AI and human expertise can pave the way for a future where technology becomes a catalyst for positive societal change, forging a more intelligent, interconnected, and inclusive world.

REFERENCES

Abbott, R., & Elliott, B. S. (2022). Putting the Artificial Intelligence in Alternative Dispute Resolution: How AI Rules Will Become ADR Rules. *Amicus Curiae*, 685. . doi:10.14296/ac.v4i3.5627

Adeshola, I., & Adepoju, A. P. (2023). The opportunities and challenges of ChatGPT in education. *Interactive Learning Environments*, 1–14. doi:10.1080/10494820.2023.2253858

AlZu'bi, S., Mughaid, A., Quiam, F., & Hendawi, S. (2022). Exploring the capabilities and limitations of chatgpt and alternative big language models. *Artificial Intelligence and Applications (Commerce, Calif.)*. doi:10.47852/bonviewAIA3202820

Cheng, S. W., Chang, C. W., Chang, W. J., Wang, H. W., Liang, C. S., Kishimoto, T., & Su, K. P. (2023). The now and future of ChatGPT and GPT in psychiatry. *Psychiatry and Clinical Neurosciences*, 77(11), 592–596. doi:10.1111/pcn.13588 PMID:37612880

Cingillioglu, I. (2023). Detecting AI-generated essays: The ChatGPT challenge. *The International Journal of Information and Learning Technology*, 40(3), 259–268. doi:10.1108/IJILT-03-2023-0043

Crawford, J., Cowling, M., & Allen, K. A. (2023). Leadership is needed for ethical ChatGPT: Character, assessment, and learning using artificial intelligence (AI). *Journal of University Teaching & Learning Practice*, *20*(3). . doi:10.53761/1.20.3.02

Elkhatat, A. M., Elsaid, K., & Almeer, S. (2023). Evaluating the efficacy of AI content detection tools in differentiating between human and AI-generated text. *International Journal for Educational Integrity*, *19*(1), 17. doi:10.1007/s40979-023-00140-5

Fui-Hoon Nah, F., Zheng, R., Cai, J., Siau, K., & Chen, L. (2023). Generative AI and ChatGPT: Applications, challenges, and AI-human collaboration. *Journal of Information Technology Case and Application Research*, *25*(3), 277–304. doi:10.1080/15228053.2023.2233814

Geis, J. R., Brady, A. P., Wu, C. C., Spencer, J., Ranschaert, E., Jaremko, J. L., & Kohli, M. (2019). Ethics of artificial intelligence in radiology: Summary of the joint European and North American multisociety statement. *Radiology*, *293*(2), 436–440. doi:10.1148/radiol.2019191586 PMID:31573399

Haque, M. A. (2022). A Brief Analysis of "ChatGPT"–A Revolutionary Tool Designed by OpenAI. *EAI Endorsed Transactions on AI and Robotics*, *1*(1), e15–e15. doi:10.4108/airo.v1i1.2983

Herbold, S., Hautli-Janisz, A., Heuer, U., Kikteva, Z., & Trautsch, A. (2023). A large-scale comparison of human-written versus ChatGPT-generated essays. *Scientific Reports*, *13*(1), 18617. doi:10.1038/s41598-023-45644-9 PMID:37903836

Israni, R. K., Yadav, R., Singh, R., & Reddy, B. R. (2023). Power Quality Enhancement in Wind-Hydro Based Hybrid Renewable Energy System by Interlocking of UPQC. *3rd International Conference on Energy, Power and Electrical Engineering (EPEE)*, Wuhan, China. 10.1109/EPEE59859.2023.10352036

Jeyaraman, M., Ramasubramanian, S., Balaji, S., Jeyaraman, N., Nallakumarasamy, A., & Sharma, S. (2023). ChatGPT in action: Harnessing artificial intelligence potential and addressing ethical challenges in medicine, education, and scientific research. *World Journal of Methodology*, *13*(4), 170–178. doi:10.5662/wjm.v13.i4.170 PMID:37771867

Kapadiya, D., Shekhawat, C., & Sharma, P. (2023). A Study on Large Scale Applications of Big Data in Modern Era. *International Conference on Information Management & Machine Intelligence (ICIMMI2023)*. ACM. https://doi.org/10.1145/3647444.364788

Kumar, I. R., Hamid, A. A., & Ya'akub, N. B. (Eds.), *Effective AI, Blockchain, and E-Governance Applications for Knowledge Discovery and Management* (pp. 176–194). IGI Global. doi:10.4018/978-1-6684-9151-5

Larsson, S., & Heintz, F. (2020). Transparency in artificial intelligence. *Internet Policy Review*, *9*(2). doi:10.14763/2020.2.1469

Liu, Y., Yang, Z., Yu, Z., Liu, Z., Liu, D., Lin, H., & Shi, S. (2023). Generative artificial intelligence and its applications in materials science: Current situation and future perspectives. *Journal of Materiomics*, . doi:10.1016/j.jmat.2023.05.001

Maharajan, K., Kumar, A. V., El Emary, I. M., Sharma, P., Latip, R., Mishra, N., Dutta, A., Manjunatha Rao, L., & Sharma, M. (2023). *Blockchain Methods and Data-Driven Decision Making With Autonomous Transportation*. Springer. . doi:10.4018/978-1-6684-9151-5.ch012

Mulia, A. P., Piri, P. R., & Tho, C. (2023). Usability Analysis of Text Generation by ChatGPT OpenAI Using System Usability Scale Method. *Procedia Computer Science, 227*, 381–388. doi:10.1016/j.procs.2023.10.537

PerlmanA. (2022). The implications of ChatGPT for legal services and society. SSRN 4294197. doi:10.2139/ssrn.4294197

Prasad G, A., Kumar, A. V., Sharma, P., Irawati, I. D., D. V., C., Musirin, I. B., Abdullah, H. M., & Rao L, M. (2023). *Artificial Intelligence in Computer Science: An Overview of Current Trends and Future Directions*. Springer. . doi:10.4018/979-8-3693-1301-5.ch002

Qadir, J. (2023, May). Engineering education in the era of ChatGPT: Promise and pitfalls of generative AI for education. *2023 IEEE Global Engineering Education Conference (EDUCON) (pp.* 1-9*)*, IEEE, 10.1109/EDUCON54358.2023.10125121

Rathore, B. (2023). Future of AI & generation alpha: ChatGPT beyond boundaries. *Eduzone: International Peer Reviewed/Refereed Multidisciplinary Journal, 12*(1), pp. 63-68, . doi:10.56614/eiprmj.v12i1y23.254

Rawat, P., Bhardwaj, A., Lamba, N., & Sharma, P. (2023). Arduino Based IoT Mini Weather Station. *SKIT Research Journal, 13*(2), 34–41. doi:10.47904/IJSKIT.13.2.2023.34-41

Roumeliotis, K. I., & Tselikas, N. D. (2023). ChatGPT and Open-AI Models: A Preliminary Review. *Future Internet, 15*(6), 192. doi:10.3390/fi15060192

Safaei, M., & Longo, J. (2021). The End of the Policy Analyst? Testing the Capability of Artificial Intelligence to Generate Plausible, Persuasive, and Useful Policy Analysis. *Digital Government: Research and Practice*. . doi:10.1145/3604570

Sethi, S. S., & Sharma, P. (2023). New Developments in the Implementation of IoT in Agriculture. *SN Computer Science, 4*(5), 503. doi:10.1007/s42979-023-01896-w

Sharma, P. (2023). *Utilizing Explainable Artificial Intelligence to Address Deep Learning in Biomedical Domain, Medical Data Analysis and Processing using Explainable Artificial Intelligence*. Taylor & Francis. doi:10.1201/9781003257721-2

Sharma, P., & Bhatnagar, N. (2023). Passenger Authentication and Ticket Verification at Airport Using QR Code Scanner. *SKIT Research Journal, 13*(2), 10–13. doi:10.47904/IJSKIT.13.1.2023.10-12

Sharma, P., & Dadheech, P. (2023). Modern-age Agriculture with Artificial Intelligence: A review emphasizing Crop Yield Prediction. *EVERGREEN Joint Journal of Novel Carbon Resource Sciences & Green Asia Strategy, 10*(4), 2570–2582. doi:10.5109/7160906

Sharma, P., Dadheech, P., Aneja, N., & Aneja, S. (2023). Predicting Agriculture Yields Based on Machine Learning Using Regression and Deep Learning. *IEEE Access : Practical Innovations, Open Solutions, 11*, 111255–111264. doi:10.1109/ACCESS.2023.3321861

Sharma, P., Dadheech, P., & Senthil Kumar Senthil, A. V. (2023). AI-Enabled Crop Recommendation System Based on Soil and Weather Patterns. In R. Gupta, A. Jain, J. Wang, S. Bharti, & S. Patel (Eds.), *Artificial Intelligence Tools and Technologies for Smart Farming and Agriculture Practices* (pp. 184–199). IGI Global. doi:10.4018/978-1-6684-8516-3.ch010

Sharma, P., & Jain, M. K. (2023). Stock Market Trends Analysis using Extreme Gradient Boosting (XGBoost). *International Conference on Computing, Communication, and Intelligent Systems (ICCCIS).* IEEE. 10.1109/ICCCIS60361.2023.10425722

Sharma, P., Kapadiya, D., & Bhardwaj, A. (2023). Efficient Note Sharing Model for Collaborative Learning. *SKIT Research Journal*, *13*(2), 42–46. doi:10.47904/IJSKIT.13.2.2023.42-46

Sharma, P., & Rathi, Y. (2016, June 5). Efficient Density-Based Clustering Using Automatic Parameter Detection. *Efficient Density-Based Clustering Using Automatic Parameter Detection* | SpringerLink. . doi:10.1007/978-981-10-0767-5_46

Tanwar, A., Sharma, P., Pandey, A., & Kumar, S. 2023. Intrusion Detection System Based Ameliorated Technique of Pattern Matching. *In Proceedings of the 4th International Conference on Information Management & Machine Intelligence (ICIMMI '22).* Association for Computing Machinery. 10.1145/3590837.3590947

V., M. V., Kumar, A. S., Sharma, P., Kaur, S., Saleh, O. S., Chennamma, H., & Chaturvedi, A. (2023). AI-Equipped IoT Applications in High-Tech Agriculture Using Machine Learning. In A. Khang (Ed.), *Handbook of Research on AI-Equipped IoT Applications in High-Tech Agriculture* (pp. 38-64). IGI Global. . doi:10.4018/978-1-6684-9231-4.ch003

Wang, A., Kim, E., Oleru, O., Seyidova, N., & Taub, P. J. (2021). Artificial Intelligence in Plastic Surgery: ChatGPT as a Tool to Address Disparities in Health Literacy. *Plastic and Reconstructive Surgery*, 10–1097. doi:10.1097/PRS.0000000000011202 PMID:37983817

Chapter 14
The Future of ChatGPT:
Exploring Features, Capabilities, and Challenges as a Leading Support Tool

Ranjit Barua

https://orcid.org/0000-0003-2236-3876

Omdayal Group of Institutions, India

Sudipto Datta

https://orcid.org/0000-0003-2161-6878

Indian Institute of Science, Bengaluru, India

ABSTRACT

In November 2022, OpenAI introduced ChatGPT, an AI chatbot tool built upon the generative pre-trained transformer (GPT) architecture. ChatGPT swiftly gained prominence on the internet, providing users with a platform to engage in conversations with an AI system, leveraging OpenAI's sophisticated language model. While ChatGPT exhibits remarkable capabilities, generating content spanning from tales, poetry, songs, and essays, it does have inherent limitations. Users can pose queries to the chatbot, which responds with relevant and persuasive information. The tool has garnered significant attention in academic circles, leading institutions to establish task forces and host widespread discussions on its adoption. This chapter offers an overview of ChatGPT and its significance, presenting a visual representation of Progressive Workflow Processes associated with the tool.

INTRODUCTION

The swift advancement in natural language processing (NLP) and artificial intelligence (AI) has led to the creation of increasingly complex and adaptable language models, such as ChatGPT (McGee, 2023; Hill-Yardin et al., 2023; Barua et al., 2023). A branch of AI known as "generative AI" deals with models that can produce new data from preexisting data in a variety of domains, including text, images, and music, by using learnt patterns and structures (Johnson et al., 2023; Biswas et al., 2023; Merlin Mancy et al., 2024). These generative AI models, like ChatGPT, use deep learning techniques and neural networks

DOI: 10.4018/979-8-3693-6824-4.ch014

Figure 1. Creating content using ChatGPT
(Oatug, 2023)

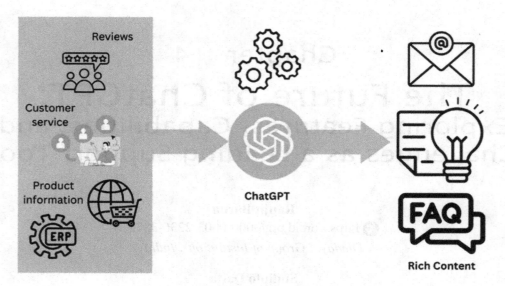

to evaluate, understand, and produce material that appears to be human-generated. It delves into the specific features and capabilities of the ChatGPT Support System (Hill-Yardin et al., 2023; Datta et al., 2019). Finally, explore and discuss the pivotal roles played by ChatGPT in the contemporary landscape. The neural language models underpinning character AI have been meticulously designed to understand and generate human-like text. This technology processes and creates text using DL methods, utilizing vast internet databases to understand the subtleties of natural language (Johnson et al., 2023).

To understand ChatGPT's significance in advancing scientific research (Wu et al., 2023; Zhou et al., 2023), it is essential to delve into its origins and development (Bang et al., 2023; Van Dis et al., 2023). The following part gives a summary of ChatGPT's history, significant achievements, and ongoing developments, highlighting how technical developments have contributed to the platform's success in the scientific field (Qin et al., 2023; Gilson et al., 2023). Unlike Generative Adversarial Network (GAN) models, ChatGPT is a language model based on the Generative Pre-trained Transformer (GPT) architecture (Kung et al., 2023; Zhong et al.,, 2023; Jiao and others, 2023). GPT models, such as ChatGPT, are intended for natural language processing tasks including text generation and language understanding, even if GANs are frequently employed for image generation (Tlili et al., 2023; Alberts et al., 2023; Sharma et al., 2023).

Rooted in the field of NLP, the goal of ChatGPT is to allow machines to produce and comprehend human language (Fijačko et al., 2023; Barua et al., 2023). The goal of developing a very complex and adaptable AI language model that could help with data analysis, translation, and text creation drove its development (Sharma et al., 2016). The foundational architecture of ChatGPT, the Transformer, addressed limitations of previous models like recurrent neural networks (RNNs) and convolutional neural networks (CNNs) for natural language processing, paving the way for powerful language models such as OpenAI's GPT series, which includes GPT-2 and GPT-3.

OpenAI introduced ChatGPT in 2020 as a revised form of the GPT-3 model, based on the GPT-3.5 architecture. GPT-3.5 maintains high performance in a variety of natural language processing (NLP) tasks, such as text generation, machine translation, and language understanding, with 6.7 billion parameters as opposed to 175 billion for GPT-3 (Alkaissi, et al., 2023). In 2023, Frieder et al. Figure 1 illustrates how to use ChatGPT to generate content. ChatGPT is an excellent tool for producing conversational responses to user inquiries because it has been trained on a big corpus of text data and refined for doing so (Cotton et al., 2023; Anu Baidoo et al., 2023].

BACKGROUND

ChatGPT is a "Generative Pre-trained Transformer" that is attracting a lot of attention. Its capacity to generate text is highlighted by the "Generative" part of the GPT moniker. Similar to using past knowledge to acquire new ideas, the "pre-training" component entails using a model from one machine learning assignment to train another. For pre-training, ChatGPT uses a neural network called "Transformer," which looks at the overall connections between each element of a data series. A significant quantity of text is provided (Street et al., 2023).

Functioning as a free chatbot capable of responding to a wide range of questions, ChatGPT was developed by OpenAI and released for public testing. It has quickly established itself as one of the best AI chatbots, showcasing its capacity to produce computer code, academic articles, poetry, and even comedic pieces (George et al., 2023).

Supervised fine-tuning of the original ChatGPT model was conducted by human AI trainers conversing with both users and an AI helper. To help in writing answers, these trainers had access to example recommendations. One of OpenAI's furthermost up-to-date inventions, ChatGPT is specifically made to understand and react to natural language, facilitating easy and natural dialogues with users. One noteworthy aspect is that programmers may easily incorporate the model into their applications with ChatGPT's open-source nature via OpenAI (Sakirin et al., 2023).

THE DISTINCTIVE ATTRIBUTES AND FUNCTIONALITIES INHERENT IN THE CHATGPT SUPPORT SYSTEM

The ChatGPT support system encompasses a rich set of features and capabilities that collectively contribute to its effectiveness as a natural language processing tool (Cotton et al., 2023). From advanced natural language understanding and contextual responses to customization, error correction, and continuous learning, the support system is designed to provide a versatile and engaging conversational experience (McGee., 2023). As technology advances, the ChatGPT support system is likely to see further enhancements, solidifying its position as a valuable resource for a wide range of applications (Hill-Yardin et al., 2023).The ChatGPT support system is a sophisticated tool designed to enhance user experience and facilitate effective interactions with the ChatGPT language model. This support system incorporates various features and capabilities that contribute to the model's overall performance and utility (Alkaissi, et al., 2023; Sakirin et al., 2023).

i.   Natural Language Understanding: One of the core capabilities of the ChatGPT support system is its advanced natural language understanding. The system is trained on vast amounts of diverse text data, enabling it to comprehend and interpret user inputs accurately (Baidoo-Anu et al., 2023).

This understanding extends to context, allowing the model to generate contextually relevant and coherent responses.

ii. Contextual Responses: The support system excels in producing responses that take into account the context of the conversation. This contextual awareness enables more meaningful and coherent exchanges, creating a more engaging and human-like interaction (Johnson et al., 2023; Barua et al., 2021). It allows ChatGPT to remember and reference information from previous messages, enhancing the continuity of the conversation.

iii. Multi-Turn Conversations: ChatGPT support system is adept at handling multi-turn conversations, meaning it can sustain dialogue over several exchanges. This feature is crucial for applications such as customer support, where interactions may involve multiple questions and responses. The system can maintain context across turns, providing a seamless and natural conversational experience (Fijačko et al., 2023).

iv. Topic Versatility: The support system is versatile in terms of the topics it can address. It has been trained on a wide range of subjects, allowing it to engage in discussions spanning various domains, from science and technology to arts and entertainment. This versatility makes ChatGPT applicable across diverse industries and use cases.

v. Customization and Fine-Tuning: Users can adjust and modify the ChatGPT support system to meet particular needs. This particular feature holds significant value for enterprises and organizations who aim to customize the model to suit their own requirements. The language model can be fine-tuned to match certain industry lingo, conventions, or conversational idioms.

vi. Error Correction and Clarification: The support system is equipped with error correction capabilities, enabling it to recognize and rectify misunderstandings or inaccuracies in user input (Hill-Yardin et al., 2023). This enhances the reliability of responses and ensures that the model can adapt to ambiguous or unclear queries. The system can also seek clarification when faced with ambiguous requests, improving overall communication accuracy.

vii. Politeness and Sensitivity: ChatGPT is designed to generate responses that adhere to polite and sensitive language use. The support system avoids offensive or inappropriate content, promoting respectful and considerate interactions (Hill-Yardin et al., 2023). This is a crucial aspect, especially in applications where user experience and ethical considerations are paramount.

viii. Integration with External Systems: The ChatGPT support system can be integrated with external systems and applications, expanding its utility (Wu et al., 2023; Zhou et al., 2023). This integration allows for seamless collaboration with other tools and technologies, enhancing the model's capabilities and extending its reach across different platforms.

ix. Continuous Learning and Updates: The support system benefits from continuous learning and updates, ensuring that it stays current and evolves over time. This adaptability is crucial for keeping pace with changes in language use, emerging trends, and evolving user expectations (Hill-Yardin et al., 2023). Regular updates enhance the model's performance and maintain its relevance in dynamic environments.

x. User Feedback Mechanism: To further improve its capabilities, the ChatGPT support system incorporates a user feedback mechanism. Users can provide feedback on generated responses, helping to identify areas for improvement. This feedback loop contributes to the ongoing refinement of the model, making it more effective and responsive to user needs.

Figure 2. The 2023 Worldwide User Profile of ChatGPT, Categorized by Age and Gender
(Statistics, 2023)

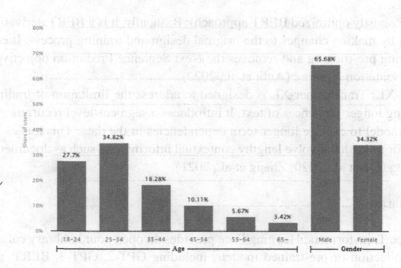

ASSOCIATED EXPANSIVE LANGUAGE MODELS AND UTILITIES

The landscape of large language models and associated tools has seen significant development in recent years [Figure 2], with several notable platforms contributing to advancements in natural language processing (NLP) and artificial intelligence (AI) (Barua et al., 2023). In this discussion, we will explore some of the related large language models and tools, highlighting their features, applications, and contributions to the field.

i.   GPT-3: One of the most prominent and important huge language models was developed by OpenAI. With 175 billion attributes, it is among the largest and most flexible language representations available today. Tasks like word completion, translation, and text-based games are areas where GPT-3 shines. It can produce responses that are coherent and rich in context across a range of domains thanks to its pre-training on a variety of internet texts (Nazarova., 2023).

ii. BERT: Another well-known language model with a bidirectional approach to language interpretation is BERT, which was first presented by Google. In contrast to conventional models that analyse text either left-to-right or right-to-left, BERT looks at a word's previous and subsequent words to determine its whole context. Tasks including text categorization, sentiment analysis, and question answering have shown the effectiveness of this bidirectional comprehension (Liu et al., 2021).

iii. T5: Google's T5 takes a different tack by approaching every NLP issue as a text-to-text challenge. As a result, textual sequences are handled for both input and output, offering a consistent foundation for a range of language activities. It has been used to tasks including question answering, translation, and summarization; it has proven to perform well over a broad variety of benchmarks (Rodriguez-Torrealba et al., 2022).

iv. XLNet: Oh et al. (2022) describe XLNet as a big language model that combines the advantages of autoregressive and autoencoding models. It preserves the autoregressive characteristic of models such as GPT while using the bidirectional context of BERT. Because of this combination, XLNet performs better on a range of NLP tasks, which makes it a notable addition to the field of big language models.

v.   RoBERTa (Robustly optimized BERT approach): Basucally, it is a BERT derivative that improves performance by making changes to the original design and training process. It employs dynamic masking during pre-training and removes the Next Sentence Prediction objective, leading to improved representation learning (Antit et al., 2022).

vi. Transformer-XL: Transformer-XL is designed to address the limitation of traditional transformers in handling longer sequences of text. It introduces a segment-level recurrence mechanism that permits the model to capture longer-term dependencies in the data. This makes Transformer-XL well-suited for tasks that involve lengthy contextual information, such as document-level language understanding (Qu et al., 2020; Zhang et al., 2021).

Tools and Libraries

i.   Hugging Face Transformers: Hugging Face provides an open-source library called Transformers, offering a collection of pre-trained models, including GPT-2, GPT-3, BERT, and many others (Campesato., 2023). Researchers engaged in NLP projects frequently use the archive because it expedites the integration of these models into a variety of applications (Hadi et al., 2023).

ii. spaCy: A natural language processing library that provides pre-trained models for various NLP tasks. While it doesn't focus on large transformer-based models, it is widely used for tasks like tokenization, part-of-speech tagging, and named entity recognition. spaCy is known for its efficiency and ease of use in developing NLP applications (Wan et al., 2023).

iii. AllenNLP: A PyTorch-based open-source NLP research library. It makes state-of-the-art models available for experimentation by academics and developers, providing pre-trained models and components for a range of NLP tasks. From text categorization to coreference resolution, AllenNLP covers a broad variety of applications (Zheng et al., 2023).

iv. TensorFlow NLP: A well-known deep learning framework offers a specific library for problems involving natural language processing. In addition to providing pre-trained models like BERT, TensorFlow NLP enables the creation of bespoke models for applications including machine translation, text classification, and sequence labelling (Chowdhury et al., 2023).

Large language models and tools are part of a dynamic and changing world. Natural language understanding has substantially improved thanks to models like GPT-3, BERT, and its variations, while libraries such as Hugging Face Transformers and spaCy simplify the integration of these models into real-world applications. As research in NLP continues, it is likely that new models and tools will emerge, pushing the boundaries of what is achievable in language processing and understanding.

APPLICATIONS OF CHATGPT IN DIVERSE DOMAINS

Because of its ability to comprehend natural language, ChatGPT can be used in a variety of fields, demonstrating its adaptability and helpfulness. A few noteworthy uses of ChatGPT in a variety of fields are as follows:

i.   Client Support: ChatGPT can be employed in customer support systems to handle inquiries, provide information, and assist users with common issues. Its ability to understand and generate contextually relevant responses makes it a valuable tool for enhancing customer service experiences (Wu et al., 2023).

ii.   Content Generation: In the realm of content creation, ChatGPT can be utilized to generate written content for articles, blogs, or social media posts (Zhou et al., 2023). Its natural language generation capabilities help in producing coherent and contextually appropriate text, saving time for content creators.

iii.   Education and Tutoring: ChatGPT can serve as a virtual tutor or assistant in educational settings. It can answer questions, provide explanations, and assist students in understanding various subjects. This application helps in personalized learning experiences and additional support for students.

iv.   Programming Assistance: Developers can use ChatGPT to seek programming assistance and advice. It can help in writing code snippets, debugging, and providing explanations for coding concepts. This makes it a useful tool for both novice and experienced programmers.

v.   Language Translation: ChatGPT can be employed in language translation services, helping users translate text from one language to another. Its contextual understanding enhances the accuracy and coherence of translated content, making it valuable in cross-language communication (Zheng et al., 2023).

vi.   Virtual Assistant Integration: Integrating ChatGPT into virtual assistants enhances their conversational abilities. It allows virtual assistants to engage in more natural and context-aware conversations, making them more effective in tasks such as setting reminders, answering queries, and providing information.

vii.   Mental Health Support:ChatGPT can be used to offer mental health support by engaging users in conversations, providing empathetic responses, and offering resources. While it doesn't replace professional therapy, it can supplement mental health apps by offering a conversational interface.

viii.   Creative Writing and Storytelling: Authors and creative writers can leverage ChatGPT for brainstorming ideas, overcoming writer's block, and even co-writing stories (McGee., 2023). It helps with the creative writing process because of its potential to produce material that is both diverse and spatially meaningful.

ix.   Legal and Documentation Assistance: When it comes to the legal field, ChatGPT can help with document drafting, basic legal information provision, and question answering. Certain parts of legal documentation and research can be streamlined with the help of this program.

x.   Knowledge Base Management: Businesses can use ChatGPT to manage internal knowledge bases. It can assist employees in finding information, answering procedural queries, and facilitating knowledge sharing within an organization.

xi.   Interview Preparation: ChatGPT can assist individuals in preparing for interviews by simulating interview scenarios, providing responses to common questions, and offering tips on effective communication. This application aids in building confidence and refining interview skills.

xii.   Simulation and Gaming: In the gaming industry, ChatGPT can be integrated to enhance non-player character (NPC) interactions. It can contribute to creating more immersive and dynamic gaming experiences by providing realistic and contextually aware dialogues.

These applications demonstrate the versatility of ChatGPT across a wide range of domains, highlighting its potential to improve efficiency, communication, and user experiences in various fields. As technology continues to advance, the scope for innovative applications of ChatGPT is likely to expand further.

DIFFICULTIES AND PROSPECTIVE RANGE

While ChatGPT and similar language models have demonstrated remarkable capabilities, they also face several challenges that impact their performance and application. Understanding these challenges is crucial for improving and refining the technology. Here are some notable challenges in ChatGPT:

i. Lack of Factual Accuracy: One significant challenge is the potential for ChatGPT to generate responses that lack factual accuracy. Information that seems convincing but is factually inaccurate may be produced by the model. This problem is important, particularly for applications like medical advice or instructional materials where precise information is essential.

ii. Sensitivity to Input Phrasing: The comments from ChatGPT may be susceptible to minute changes in input wording. A minor question rewording might result in different answers, which would affect the consistency of the model. It may be difficult to get consistent and dependable performance over a range of inputs because of this sensitivity.

iii. Verbosity and Overuse of Certain Phrases: It can be common for ChatGPT to overuse some phrases and be verbose. It might provide lengthy responses that include unnecessary details or repeat certain expressions, leading to less concise and more convoluted outputs.

iv. Difficulty in Handling Ambiguity: Ambiguous queries or ambiguous contexts can perplex ChatGPT, causing it to provide responses can be at odds with what the user intended. Managing uncertainty is a difficult task, especially in situations where additional context is needed for accurate interpretation.

v. Ethical and Bias Concerns: Language models, including ChatGPT, can inadvertently perpetuate biases present in the training data[McGee., 2023]. This raises ethical concerns, as the model may produce biased or discriminatory responses. Addressing bias in language models is an ongoing challenge that involves careful curation of training data and continuous model evaluation.

vi. Inappropriate or Offensive Content: Despite efforts to prevent inappropriate content, ChatGPT may generate responses that are offensive or objectionable. Filtering and preventing the model from producing inappropriate content is challenging, and striking the right balance between freedom of expression and responsible use remains an ongoing concern.

vii. Difficulty in Context Retention: While ChatGPT can maintain context over a conversation to some extent, there are limitations in retaining context over long interactions. The model may lose track of the subject, leading to responses that are less coherent or relevant, particularly in extended conversations.

viii. Open-Ended Responses:ChatGPT tends to generate open-ended responses, which can sometimes be challenging for applications requiring specific and concise answers. Fine-tuning the model to provide more precise responses without sacrificing context is an area that requires attention.

ix. Resource Intensiveness: Training and maintaining large language models like ChatGPT demand substantial computational resources. This poses challenges in terms of environmental impact, energy consumption, and convenience for researchers and associations with inadequate assets.

x. User Safety and Misuse: Ensuring user safety and preventing the misuse of ChatGPT is a critical challenge. There is a risk that the technology can be exploited for malicious purposes, including generating harmful content or engaging in unethical activities. Developing robust safeguards and monitoring mechanisms is essential.

Addressing these challenges involves a combination of refining model architectures, improving training data quality, implementing effective filtering mechanisms, and developing guidelines for responsible use. The AI community has to continue researching and working together in order to overcome these obstacles and realise the full potential of conversational AI systems such as ChatGPT.

As more users input prompts into ChatGPT, it acquires additional information. Students opting for ChatGPT's shortcuts over traditional education contribute to enhancing AI, thereby increasing its future utility. The impact of ChatGPT on the educational technology sector is expected to be substantial. Numerous edtech companies may now offer foundational subject content while incorporating ChatGPT to provide students with a platform for inquiries and addressing concerns. Looking ahead, AI has the potential to identify the students who would derive the greatest benefit from specific tutors. Up addition to filling up knowledge gaps, these tutors can be excellent resources for inspiration, mentorship, and advice. Although society's responses to the quickly changing AI landscape are diverse and include a range of emotions such as fear, optimism, worry, amazement, and awe, creating new AI applications demands careful thought.

CHATGPT AND MODERN SOCIETY

ChatGPT, as a sophisticated language model developed by OpenAI, holds significant implications for modern society across various domains. The integration of Chat-GPT and artificial intelligence has brought about a paradigm shift in healthcare and biomaterial research. From enhancing diagnostics, flexible robotics, and personalized medicine to expediting drug discovery and biomaterial development, AI technologies have demonstrated their potential to improve patient outcomes, streamline research processes, and foster interdisciplinary collaboration (Barua., 2024; Datta et al., 2024). As these technologies continue to evolve, their impact on healthcare and biomaterial research is likely to grow, ushering in an era of unprecedented innovation and transformation in these critical fields (Jain et al., 2024) (Barua et al., 2024). Chat-GPT can assist researchers in understanding and interpreting complex biological and chemical data, facilitating collaboration and communication among multidisciplinary research teams (Das et al., 2023). This expedites the drug development process and increases the efficiency of bringing new therapeutics to market. The integration of AI streamlines the analysis of diverse biomaterial datasets, including chemical compositions, mechanical properties, and biocompatibility (Waidi et al., 2023). Chat-GPT facilitates the interpretation and communication of these complex datasets, ensuring that insights are effectively conveyed to researchers, engineers, and healthcare professionals involved in biomaterial development (Barua et al., 2023). In biomaterial research, AI aids in the design and optimization of materials for various applications, including medical implants and tissue engineering. Machine learning algorithms can analyze the interactions between biomaterials and biological systems, predicting the most suitable materials for specific purposes (Datta et al., 2023; Barua et al., 2023). Chat-GPT enhances communication among researchers, fostering collaboration and knowledge exchange in this interdisciplinary field. Chat-GPT acts as a communication bridge in biomaterial research, facilitating collaboration among researchers with diverse expertise. By providing a platform for efficient communication and information exchange, AI contributes to the collective knowledge base, fostering innovation and accelerating breakthroughs in biomaterial science (McGee, 2023). Chat-GPT serves as a virtual health assistant, facilitating communication between patients and healthcare providers. These virtual assistants can answer queries, provide medication reminders, and offer general health information. Chat-GPT and AI contribute significantly to the field of diagnostics by analyzing vast datasets to identify patterns, detect anomalies, and make accurate predictions (Hill-Yardin et al., 2023; Barua, 2024). Machine learning algorithms can analyze medical imaging, genomic data, and patient records to aid in early disease detection and prognosis (Barua et al., 2023; Zheng et al., 2023). Its impact extends to areas such as communication, education, technology, and more. Here's a discussion of ChatGPT in the context of modern society:

i. Enhanced Conversational Experiences: ChatGPT improves human-computer interactions by providing more natural and context-aware responses (Sharma et al., 2023; Prasad et al., 2023). This enhances communication in applications such as customer support, virtual assistants, and social interactions.

ii. Augmented Learning: In the educational sector, ChatGPT offers opportunities for augmented learning experiences. It can assist students with queries, provide explanations, and contribute to personalized learning environments.

iii. Advancements in AI Research: It signifies a landmark in the field of artificial intelligence, showcasing the capabilities of large language models. Its development has spurred further research and innovation in the quest for more advanced language models (Maharajan et al., 2023; V., M. V., Kumar et al., 2023).

iv. Bias and Responsible Use: The deployment of ChatGPT raises ethical considerations, including concerns about bias in generated content. Ensuring responsible use and addressing potential biases become crucial aspects of integrating such technology into society (Sharma et al., 2023).

v. Innovations in EdTech: ChatGPT has the potential to revolutionize education technology. EdTech companies can integrate it to provide additional learning support, answer student queries, and contribute to the evolution of online education.

vi. Skills Enhancement: ChatGPT can assist individuals in developing and enhancing skills. It provides a platform for users to ask questions, seek advice, and receive guidance, contributing to personal and professional development.

vii. Human-Machine Interaction: The use of ChatGPT and similar technologies may influence how individuals perceive and interact with machines. Understanding the psychological impact of conversing with AI entities is an area of ongoing exploration.

viii. Data Sensitivity: The deployment of ChatGPT in various applications necessitates careful consideration of privacy and security concerns. Ensuring that sensitive user data is handled responsibly becomes a priority.

ix. Influence on Social Interactions: The integration of ChatGPT in social applications may influence how people communicate online. Understanding the impact on social dynamics, online communities, and digital communication is an evolving area of study.

x. Evolution of Language Models: As language models continue to evolve, including potential successors to ChatGPT, society can expect further advancements in natural language understanding and generation, leading to new applications and possibilities.

ChatGPT plays a multifaceted role in modern society, influencing communication, education, technology, and various other aspects. As it becomes more integrated into everyday applications, addressing ethical considerations, ensuring responsible use, and understanding its broader societal impact are essential for harnessing its benefits effectively.

CONCLUSION

Since its launch in November 2022, ChatGPT has seen significant growth. It is capable of producing essays, short narratives, poetry, and resumes for employment applications. ChatGPT handles everything from the biggest issues in life to the smallest issues, all while being closely supervised by a person and utilizing a tonne of information from the internet. ChatGPT is a chatbot that uses natural language to have human-like discussions on a range of topics. It helps users write emails, code, and answer questions about a variety of topics, including investment. Users have given the platform overwhelmingly good reviews, complementing its sophisticated features and intuitive. NLP might benefit greatly from ChatGPT's potential contributions. Through OpenAI's platform, it responds to inquiries in a conversational, although rather formal, manner, demonstrating its versatility in understanding and handling a wide range of problems. Some have even gone so far as to say that it may drastically change how people use technology. In the future, ChatGPT's capabilities will prove to be extremely beneficial for companies operating in fields like market research, online education, and customer support.The billions of dollars that OpenAI and its main contributors have invested show how committed they are to creating, refining, and using these cutting-edge language models. By placing OpenAI at the forefront of AI creative tools, this strategic investment highlights the company's potential as a smart and progressive choice for long-term development and innovation.

ACKNOWLEDGEMENTS

The authors express their gratitude to the Mechanical Engineering Department of the Omdayal Group of Institutions in Uluberia, Howrah, and to Mrs. Nibedita Bardhan for her support with language proofing.

REFERENCES

Alberts, I. L., Mercolli, L., Pyka, T., Prenosil, G., Shi, K., Rominger, A., & Afshar-Oromieh, A. (2023). Large language models (LLM) and ChatGPT: What will the impact on nuclear medicine be? *European Journal of Nuclear Medicine and Molecular Imaging*, *50*(6), 1549–1552. doi:10.1007/s00259-023-06172-w PMID:36892666

Alkaissi, H., & McFarlane, S. I. (2023). Artificial hallucinations in ChatGPT: Implications in scientific writing. *Cureus*, *15*(2). Advance online publication. doi:10.7759/cureus.35179 PMID:36811129

Antit, C., Mechti, S., & Faiz, R. (2022, February). TunRoBERTa: a Tunisian robustly optimized BERT approach model for sentiment analysis. In *2nd International Conference on Industry 4.0 and Artificial Intelligence (ICIAI 2021)* (pp. 227-231). Atlantis Press. 10.2991/aisr.k.220201.040

Baidoo-Anu, D., & Ansah, L. O. (2023). Education in the era of generative artificial intelligence (AI): Understanding the potential benefits of ChatGPT in promoting teaching and learning. *Journal of AI*, 7(1), 52–62. doi:10.61969/jai.1337500

Bang, Y., Cahyawijaya, S., Lee, N., Dai, W., Su, D., Wilie, B., & Fung, P. (2023). A multitask, multilingual, multimodal evaluation of chatgpt on reasoning, hallucination, and interactivity. *arXiv preprint arXiv:2302.04023*. doi:10.18653/v1/2023.ijcnlp-main.45

Barua, R. (2024). Innovations in Minimally Invasive Surgery: The Rise of Smart Flexible Surgical Robots. In M. Garcia & R. de Almeida (Eds.), *Emerging Technologies for Health Literacy and Medical Practice* (pp. 110–131). IGI Global., doi:10.4018/979-8-3693-1214-8.ch006

Barua, R. (2024). Exploring Artificial Intelligence in Evolving Healthcare Environments: A Comprehensive Analysis. In I. Shah & Q. Sial (Eds.), *Advances in Computational Intelligence for the Healthcare Industry 4.0* (pp. 123–138). IGI Global. doi:10.4018/979-8-3693-2333-5.ch006

Barua, R., Bhowmik, S., Dey, A., Das, S., & Datta, S. (2022, September). Analysis of Robotically Controlled Percutaneous Needle Insertion into Ex Vivo Kidney Tissue for Minimally Invasive Percutaneous Nephrolithotomy (PCNL) Surgery. In *International Conference on Emergent Converging Technologies and Biomedical Systems* (pp. 249-257). Singapore: Springer Nature Singapore.

Barua, R., Bhowmik, S., Dey, A., & Mondal, J. (2023). Advances of the Robotics Technology in Modern Minimally Invasive Surgery. In *Design and Control Advances in Robotics* (pp. 91–104). IGI Global.

Barua, R., Das, S., & Mondal, J. (2023). Emerging Applications of Artificial Intelligence (AI) and Machine Learning (ML) in Modern Urology. In R. Queirós, B. Cunha, & X. Fonseca (Eds.), *Exploring the Convergence of Computer and Medical Science Through Cloud Healthcare* (pp. 117–133). IGI Global. doi:10.4018/978-1-6684-5260-8.ch006

Barua, R., & Datta, S. (2023). Artificial Intelligence in Modern Medical Science: A Promising Practice. In S. Rajest, B. Singh, A. J. Obaid, R. Regin, & K. Chinnusamy (Eds.), *Recent Developments in Machine and Human Intelligence* (pp. 1–12). IGI Global. doi:10.4018/978-1-6684-9189-8.ch001

Barua, R., & Datta, S. (2024). An Extensive Evaluation of New Federated Learning Approaches for COVID-19 Identification. In A. Hassan, V. Prasad, P. Bhattacharya, P. Dutta, & R. Damaševičius (Eds.), *Pioneering Smart Healthcare 5.0 with IoT, Federated Learning, and Cloud Security* (pp. 246–257). IGI Global. doi:10.4018/979-8-3693-2639-8.ch014

Barua, R., Datta, S., Dutta, P., & Chowdhury, A. R. (2021). Machine learning and AI application of COVID-19 pandemic outbreak. *Impacts and implications of covid-19*, 2.

Barua, R., Datta, S., & Sarkar, A. (2023). Artificial Intelligence and Robotics-Based Minimally Invasive Surgery: Innovations and Future Perceptions. In G. Karthick & S. Karupusamy (Eds.), *Contemporary Applications of Data Fusion for Advanced Healthcare Informatics* (pp. 350–368). IGI Global. doi:10.4018/978-1-6684-8913-0.ch015

Barua, R., & Mondal, J. (2023). Study of the Current Trends of CAD (Computer-Aided Detection) in Modern Medical Imaging. *Machine Learning and AI Techniques in Interactive Medical Image Analysis*, 35-50.

Biswas, S. S. (2023). Role of chat gpt in public health. *Annals of Biomedical Engineering*, *51*(5), 868–869. doi:10.1007/s10439-023-03172-7 PMID:36920578

Campesato, O. (2023). *Transformer, BERT, and GPT3: Including ChatGPT and Prompt Engineering*. Stylus Publishing, LLC. doi:10.1515/9781683928973

Chowdhury, M. N. U. R., & Haque, A. (2023, June). ChatGPT: Its Applications and Limitations. In *2023 3rd International Conference on Intelligent Technologies (CONIT)* (pp. 1-7). IEEE.

Cotton, D. R., Cotton, P. A., & Shipway, J. R. (2023). Chatting and cheating: Ensuring academic integrity in the era of ChatGPT. *Innovations in Education and Teaching International*, 1–12.

Das, S., Datta, S., Barman, A., & Barua, R. (2023). Smart Biodegradable and Bio-Based Polymeric Biomaterials for Biomedical Applications. In Modeling, Characterization, and Processing of Smart Materials (pp. 56-82). IGI Global. doi:10.4018/978-1-6684-9224-6.ch003

Datta, S., Barua, R., & Das, J. (2019). Application of artificial intelligence in modern healthcare system. *Alginates-recent uses of this natural polymer*.

Datta, S., Jain, N., Waidi, Y. O., & Barua, R. (2024). Processing and Applications of Shape Memory Alloys. In Advancements in Powder Metallurgy: Processing, Applications, and Properties (pp. 151-165). IGI Global. doi:10.4018/978-1-6684-9385-4.ch006

Exploring the synergy of OpenAI's ChatGPT and Oracle APEX: Transforming Oracle applications - Insight - Summer 2023. (n.d.). Oracle Applications & Technology Users Group. https://www.oatug.org/insight-summer2023/features-archive/exploring-the-synergy

Fijačko, N., Gosak, L., Štiglic, G., Picard, C. T., & Douma, M. J. (2023). Can ChatGPT pass the life support exams without entering the American heart association course? *Resuscitation*, *185*, 185. doi:10.1016/j.resuscitation.2023.109732 PMID:36775020

Frieder, S., Pinchetti, L., Griffiths, R. R., Salvatori, T., Lukasiewicz, T., Petersen, P. C., & Berner, J. (2023). Mathematical capabilities of chatgpt. *arXiv preprint arXiv:2301.13867*.

George, A. S., & George, A. H. (2023). A review of ChatGPT AI's impact on several business sectors. *Partners Universal International Innovation Journal*, *1*(1), 9–23.

Gilson, A., Safranek, C. W., Huang, T., Socrates, V., Chi, L., Taylor, R. A., & Chartash, D. (2023). How does ChatGPT perform on the United States medical licensing examination? The implications of large language models for medical education and knowledge assessment. *JMIR Medical Education*, *9*(1), e45312. doi:10.2196/45312 PMID:36753318

HadiM. U.QureshiR.ShahA.IrfanM.ZafarA.ShaikhM. B.MirjaliliS. (2023). A survey on large language models: Applications, challenges, limitations, and practical usage. TechRxiv. doi:10.36227/techrxiv.23589741.v1

Hill-Yardin, E. L., Hutchinson, M. R., Laycock, R., & Spencer, S. J. (2023). A Chat (GPT) about the future of scientific publishing. *Brain, Behavior, and Immunity*, *110*, 152–154. doi:10.1016/j.bbi.2023.02.022 PMID:36868432

Jain, N., Barua, R., Waidi, Y. O., & Datta, S. (2024). Nanowires for Bio-Sensing Applications. In S. Kulkarni, B. Kharisov, A. Haghi, & V. Srivastava (Eds.), *Next Generation Materials for Sustainable Engineering* (pp. 205–219). IGI Global. doi:10.4018/979-8-3693-1306-0.ch010

Jiao, W., Wang, W., Huang, J. T., Wang, X., & Tu, Z. (2023). Is ChatGPT a good translator? A preliminary study. *arXiv preprint arXiv:2301.08745*.

JohnsonD.GoodmanR.PatrinelyJ.StoneC.ZimmermanE.DonaldR.WhelessL. (2023). Assessing the accuracy and reliability of AI-generated medical responses: an evaluation of the Chat-GPT model. Research square. doi:10.21203/rs.3.rs-2566942/v1

Kung, T. H., Cheatham, M., Medenilla, A., Sillos, C., De Leon, L., Elepaño, C., Madriaga, M., Aggabao, R., Diaz-Candido, G., Maningo, J., & Tseng, V. (2023). Performance of ChatGPT on USMLE: Potential for AI-assisted medical education using large language models. *PLOS Digital Health*, 2(2), e0000198. doi:10.1371/journal.pdig.0000198 PMID:36812645

Liu, H., Zhang, Z., Xu, Y., Wang, N., Huang, Y., Yang, Z., Jiang, R., & Chen, H. (2021). Use of BERT (bidirectional encoder representations from transformers)-based deep learning method for extracting evidences in chinese radiology reports: Development of a computer-aided liver cancer diagnosis framework. *Journal of Medical Internet Research*, 23(1), e19689. doi:10.2196/19689 PMID:33433395

Maharajan, K., Kumar, A. V., El Emary, I. M., Sharma, P., Latip, R., Mishra, N., Dutta, A., Manjunatha Rao, L., & Sharma, M. (2023). Blockchain Methods and Data-Driven Decision Making With Autonomous Transportation. In R. Kumar, A. Abdul Hamid, & N. Binti Ya'akub (Eds.), *Effective AI, Blockchain, and E-Governance Applications for Knowledge Discovery and Management* (pp. 176–194). IGI Global. doi:10.4018/978-1-6684-9151-5.ch012

McGeeR. W. (2023). Annie Chan: Three Short Stories Written with Chat GPT. *Available at* SSRN 4359403.

Merlin Mancy, A., Kumar, A. V., Latip, R., Jagadamba, G., Chakrabarti, P., Sharma, P., Musirin, I. B., Sharma, M., & Kanchan, B. G. (2024). Smart Healthcare System, Digital Health and Telemedicine, Management and Emergencies: Patient Emergency Application (PES) E-Governance Applications. In R. Kumar, A. Abdul Hamid, N. Binti Ya'akub, H. Sharan, & S. Kumar (Eds.), *Sustainable Development in AI, Blockchain, and E-Governance Applications* (pp. 124–151). IGI Global. doi:10.4018/979-8-3693-1722-8.ch008

Nazarova, D. (2023, October). Application of Artificial Intelligence in Mental Healthcare: Generative Pre-trained Transformer 3 (GPT-3) and Cognitive Distortions. In *Proceedings of the Future Technologies Conference* (pp. 204-219). Cham: Springer Nature Switzerland. 10.1007/978-3-031-47454-5_16

Oh, K., Kang, M., Oh, S., Kim, D. H., Kang, S. H., & Lee, Y. (2022, October). AB-XLNet: Named Entity Recognition Tool for Health Information Technology Standardization. In *2022 13th International Conference on Information and Communication Technology Convergence (ICTC)* (pp. 742-744). IEEE.

Prasad, G. A., Kumar, A. V., Sharma, P., Irawati, I. D., D. V., C., Musirin, I. B., Abdullah, H. M., & Rao L, M. (2023). Artificial Intelligence in Computer Science: An Overview of Current Trends and Future Directions. In S. Rajest, B. Singh, A. Obaid, R. Regin, & K. Chinnusamy (Eds.), Advances in Artificial and Human Intelligence in the Modern Era (pp. 43-60). IGI Global. https://doi.org/ doi:10.4018/979-8-3693-1301-5.ch002

Qin, C., Zhang, A., Zhang, Z., Chen, J., Yasunaga, M., & Yang, D. (2023). Is ChatGPT a general-purpose natural language processing task solver? *arXiv preprint arXiv:2302.06476.* doi:10.18653/v1/2023. emnlp-main.85

Qu, H., Zhao, H., & Wang, X. (2020, November). Domain-Specific Chinese Transformer-XL Language Model with Part-of-Speech Information. In *2020 16th International Conference on Computational Intelligence and Security (CIS)* (pp. 81-85). IEEE. 10.1109/CIS52066.2020.00026

Rodriguez-Torrealba, R., Garcia-Lopez, E., & Garcia-Cabot, A. (2022). End-to-End generation of Multiple-Choice questions using Text-to-Text transfer Transformer models. *Expert Systems with Applications, 208,* 118258. doi:10.1016/j.eswa.2022.118258

Sakirin, T., & Said, R. B. (2023). User preferences for ChatGPT-powered conversational interfaces versus traditional methods. *Mesopotamian Journal of Computer Science, 2023,* 24–31. doi:10.58496/MJCSC/2023/006

Sharma, P. (2023). *Utilizing Explainable Artificial Intelligence to Address Deep Learning in Biomedical Domain, Medical Data Analysis and Processing using Explainable Artificial Intelligence.* Taylor & Francis., doi:10.1201/9781003257721-2

Sharma, P., Dadheech, P., Aneja, N., & Aneja, S. (2023, January 1). *Predicting Agriculture Yields Based on Machine Learning Using Regression and Deep Learning.* IEEE Access. https://doi.org/ doi:10.1109/ACCESS.2023.3321861

Sharma, P., Dadheech, P., & Senthil Kumar Senthil, A. V. (2023). AI-Enabled Crop Recommendation System Based on Soil and Weather Patterns. In R. Gupta, A. Jain, J. Wang, S. Bharti, & S. Patel (Eds.), *Artificial Intelligence Tools and Technologies for Smart Farming and Agriculture Practices* (pp. 184–199). IGI Global. doi:10.4018/978-1-6684-8516-3.ch010

Sharma, P., & Rathi, Y. (2016, June 5). *Efficient Density-Based Clustering Using Automatic Parameter Detection. Efficient Density-Based Clustering Using Automatic Parameter Detection.* SpringerLink. . doi:10.1007/978-981-10-0767-5_46

Street D. Wilck J. (2023). 'Let's Have a Chat': Principles for the Effective Application of ChatGPT and Large Language Models in the Practice of Forensic Accounting. SSRN 4351817. doi:10.2139/ssrn.4351817

Tlili, A., Shehata, B., Adarkwah, M. A., Bozkurt, A., Hickey, D. T., Huang, R., & Agyemang, B. (2023). What if the devil is my guardian angel: ChatGPT as a case study of using chatbots in education. *Smart Learning Environments, 10*(1), 15. doi:10.1186/s40561-023-00237-x

V., M. V., Kumar, A. S., Sharma, P., Kaur, S., Saleh, O. S., Chennamma, H., & Chaturvedi, A. (2023). AI-Equipped IoT Applications in High-Tech Agriculture Using Machine Learning. In A. Khang (Ed.), *Handbook of Research on AI-Equipped IoT Applications in High-Tech Agriculture* (pp. 38-64). IGI Global. . doi:10.4018/978-1-6684-9231-4.ch003

Van Dis, E. A., Bollen, J., Zuidema, W., van Rooij, R., & Bockting, C. L. (2023). ChatGPT: Five priorities for research. *Nature, 614*(7947), 224–226. doi:10.1038/d41586-023-00288-7 PMID:36737653

Waidi, Y. O., Barua, R., & Datta, S. (2023). Metals, Polymers, Ceramics, Composites Biomaterials Used in Additive Manufacturing for Biomedical Applications. In A. Kumar, P. Kumar, A. Srivastava, & V. Goyat (Eds.), *Modeling, Characterization, and Processing of Smart Materials* (pp. 165–184). IGI Global., doi:10.4018/978-1-6684-9224-6.ch008

Wan, Y., Wang, W., He, P., Gu, J., Bai, H., & Lyu, M. R. (2023, November). Biasasker: Measuring the bias in conversational ai system. In *Proceedings of the 31st ACM Joint European Software Engineering Conference and Symposium on the Foundations of Software Engineering* (pp. 515-527). ACM. 10.1145/3611643.3616310

Wu, C., Yin, S., Qi, W., Wang, X., Tang, Z., & Duan, N. (2023). Visual chatgpt: Talking, drawing and editing with visual foundation models. *arXiv preprint arXiv:2303.04671.*

Zhang, X., Yang, S., Duan, L., Lang, Z., Shi, Z., & Sun, L. (2021, October). Transformer-XL With Graph Neural Network for Source Code Summarization. In *2021 IEEE International Conference on Systems, Man, and Cybernetics (SMC)* (pp. 3436-3441). IEEE. 10.1109/SMC52423.2021.9658619

Zheng, O., Abdel-Aty, M., Wang, D., Wang, Z., & Ding, S. (2023). ChatGPT is on the horizon: Could a large language model be all we need for Intelligent Transportation? *arXiv preprint arXiv:2303.05382.*

Zhong, Q., Ding, L., Liu, J., Du, B., & Tao, D. (2023). Can chatgpt understand too? a comparative study on chatgpt and fine-tuned bert. *arXiv preprint arXiv:2302.10198.*

Zhou, C., Li, Q., Li, C., Yu, J., Liu, Y., Wang, G., & Sun, L. (2023). A comprehensive survey on pre-trained foundation models: A history from bert to chatgpt. *arXiv preprint arXiv:2302.09419.*

KEY TERMS AND DEFINITIONS

ChatGPT: ChatGPT, developed by OpenAI, is an advanced language model powered by GPT-3.5 architecture. It excels in natural language understanding and generation, enabling human-like interactions. With applications in writing assistance, content generation, and more, ChatGPT showcases the potential of artificial intelligence to enhance communication and creative processes in diverse domains.

Context Understanding: A fundamental aspect of artificial intelligence, enabling systems to comprehend and respond appropriately to nuanced information. It involves grasping the meaning, connections, and implications within a given context, allowing AI to provide more accurate and contextually relevant insights, responses, and solutions across various applications and industries.

Generative AI: A cutting-edge technology, produces diverse content autonomously. Its ability to understand context and create contextually relevant information has applications in content creation, language translation, and more. As it continues to evolve, generative AI is shaping the future of innovation, communication, and human-machine interaction.

Language Model: A computational system designed to understand, generate, and manipulate human language. It leverages statistical and machine learning techniques to analyze linguistic patterns, enabling applications such as natural language processing, text generation, and translation. Advanced models like GPT-3 showcase the capability to comprehend and generate contextually rich text.

Natural language processing: A field of artificial intelligence that focuses on the interaction between computers and human language. It involves developing algorithms and models to enable machines to understand, interpret, and respond to human language, facilitating applications like chatbots, language translation, sentiment analysis, and text summarization.

Compilation of References

Abbott, R., & Elliott, B. S. (2022). Putting the Artificial Intelligence in Alternative Dispute Resolution: How AI Rules Will Become ADR Rules. *Amicus Curiae, 685.* . doi:10.14296/ac.v4i3.5627

Adam, M., Wessel, M., & Benlian, A. (2021). AI-based chatbots in customer service and their effects on user compliance. *Electronic Markets, 31*(2), 427–445. doi:10.1007/s12525-020-00414-7

Adamopoulou, E., & Moussiades, L. (2020). Chatbots: History, technology, and applications. *Machine Learning with Applications, 2,* 100006. doi:10.1016/j.mlwa.2020.100006

Adeshola, I., & Adepoju, A. P. (2023). The opportunities and challenges of ChatGPT in education. *Interactive Learning Environments,* 1–14. doi:10.1080/10494820.2023.2253858

Agrawal, A., Gans, J., & Goldfarb, A. (2022). ChatGPT and how AI disrupts industries. *Harvard Business Review.* https://hbr.org/2022/12/chatgpt-and-how-ai-disrupts-industries

Aguinis, H., Banks, G. C., Rogelberg, S. G., & Cascio, W. F. (2020). Actionable recommendations for narrowing the science-practice gap in open science. *Organizational Behavior and Human Decision Processes, 158,* 27–35. doi:10.1016/j.obhdp.2020.02.007

Aguinis, H., Ramani, R. S., & Alabduljader, N. (2018). What you see is what you get? Enhancing methodological transparency in management research. Academy of management annals. *The Academy of Management Annals, 12*(1), 83–110. doi:10.5465/annals.2016.0011

Aguinis, H., & Solarino, A. M. (2019). Transparency and replicability in qualitative research: The case of interviews with elite informants. *Strategic Management Journal, 40*(8), 1291–1315. doi:10.1002/smj.3015

AI Research Assistant Elicit. (2023). *Elicit uses language models to help you automate research workflows, like parts of literature review.* Elicit. https://elicit.org/.

Akinwalere, S. N., & Ivanov, V. (2022). Artificial Intelligence in Higher Education: Challenges and Opportunities. *Border Crossing, 12*(1), 1–15. doi:10.33182/bc.v12i1.2015

AlAfnan, M. A., Dishari, S., Jovic, M., & Lomidze, K. (2023). Chatgpt as an educational tool: Opportunities, challenges, and recommendations for communication, business writing, and composition courses. *Journal of Artificial Intelligence and Technology, 3*(2), 60–68. doi:10.37965/jait.2023.0184

Alasadi, E. A., & Baiz, C. R. (2023). Generative AI in Education and Research: Opportunities, Concerns, and Solutions. *Journal of Chemical Education, 100*(8), 2965–2971. doi:10.1021/acs.jchemed.3c00323

Alawi, F. (2023). Artificial intelligence: The future might already be here. *Oral Surgery, Oral Medicine, Oral Pathology and Oral Radiology, 135*(3), 313–315. doi:10.1016/j.oooo.2023.01.002 PMID:36774240

Alberts, I. L., Mercolli, L., Pyka, T., Prenosil, G., Shi, K., Rominger, A., & Afshar-Oromieh, A. (2023). Large language models (LLM) and ChatGPT: What will the impact on nuclear medicine be? *European Journal of Nuclear Medicine and Molecular Imaging, 50*(6), 1549–1552. doi:10.1007/s00259-023-06172-w PMID:36892666

Aldeman, N. L. S., de Sá Urtiga Aita, K. M., Machado, V. P., da Mata Sousa, L. C. D., Coelho, A. G. B., da Silva, A. S., da Silva Mendes, A. P., de Oliveira Neres, F. J., & do Monte, S. J. H. (2021). Smartpathk: A platform for teaching glomerulopathies using machine learning. *BMC Medical Education, 21*(1), 248. doi:10.1186/s12909-021-02680-1 PMID:33926437

Aldosari, S. A. M. (2020). The future of higher education in the light of artificial intelligence transformations. *International Journal of Higher Education, 9*(3), 145–151. doi:10.5430/ijhe.v9n3p145

Aleedy, M., Atwell, E., & Meshoul, S. (2022). Using AI Chatbots in Education: Recent Advances Challenges and Use Case. *Artificial Intelligence and Sustainable Computing: Proceedings of ICSISCET 2021,* 661-675.

Aliabadi, D. E., Kaya, M., & Şahin, G. (2017, January). An agent-based simulation of power generation company behavior in electricity markets under different market-clearing mechanisms. *Energy Policy, 100,* 191–205. doi:10.1016/j.enpol.2016.09.063

AlıcıU. I.OksuztepeA.KilinccekerO.KaraarslanE. (2023). OpenAI ChatGPT for Smart Contract Security Testing: Discussion and Future Directions. *Available at* SSRN 4412215.

Aljanabi, M., Ghazi, M., Ali, A. H., & Abed, S. A. (2023). ChatGpt: Open possibilities. *Iraqi Journal For Computer Science and Mathematics, 4*(1), 62–64.

Alkaissi, H., & McFarlane, S. I. (2023). Artificial hallucinations in ChatGPT: Implications in scientific writing. *Cureus, 15*(2). Advance online publication. doi:10.7759/cureus.35179 PMID:36811129

AlZu'bi, S., Mughaid, A., Quiam, F., & Hendawi, S. (2022). Exploring the capabilities and limitations of chatgpt and alternative big language models. *Artificial Intelligence and Applications (Commerce, Calif.).* doi:10.47852/bonviewAIA3202820

Amato, F., Marrone, S., Moscato, V., Piantadosi, G., Picariello, A., & Sansone, C. (2017, November). Chatbots Meet eHealth: Automatizing Healthcare. In WAIAH@ AI* IA (pp. 40-49). Research Gate.

Ansari, B., & Rahimi-Kian, A. (2015). A Dynamic Risk-Constrained Bidding Strategy for Generation Companies Based on Linear Supply Function Model. *IEEE Systems Journal, 9*(4), 1463–1474. doi:10.1109/JSYST.2015.2427374

Antit, C., Mechti, S., & Faiz, R. (2022, February). TunRoBERTa: a Tunisian robustly optimized BERT approach model for sentiment analysis. In *2nd International Conference on Industry 4.0 and Artificial Intelligence (ICIAI 2021)* (pp. 227-231). Atlantis Press. 10.2991/aisr.k.220201.040

Appel, G., Neelbauer, J., & Schweidel, D. A. (2023). Generative AI has an intellectual property problem. *Harvard Business Review.* https://hbr.org/2023/04/generative-ai-has-an-intellectual-property-problem

Arai, H., Akagi, K., Nakagawa, A., Onai, Y., Utsu, Y., Masuda, S., & Aotsuka, N. (2023). Clinical and genetic diagnosis of Cowden syndrome: A case report of a rare PTEN germline variant and diverse clinical presentation. *Medicine, 102*(1), e32572. doi:10.1097/MD.0000000000032572 PMID:36607858

Arora, S., Kr Jha, A., & Upadhyay, S. (2023). *Predicting a Rise in Employee Attrition Rates Through the Utilization of People Analytics.* 2023 12th International Conference on System Modeling & Advancement in Research Trends (SMART), Moradabad, India. 10.1109/SMART59791.2023.10428268

Ausat, A. M. A., Massang, B., Efendi, M., Nofirman, N., & Riady, Y. (2023). Can chat GPT replace the role of the teacher in the classroom: A fundamental analysis. *Journal of Education, 5*(4), 16100–16106.

Aust, I., Matthews, B., & Muller-Camen, M. (2020). Common good HRM: A paradigm shift in sustainable HRM? *Human Resource Management Review*, *30*(3), 100705. doi:10.1016/j.hrmr.2019.100705

Au-Yong-Oliveira, M., Lopes, C., Soares, F., Pinheiro, G., & Guimarães, P. (2020, June). What can we expect from the future? The impact of artificial intelligence on society. In *2020 15th Iberian Conference on Information Systems and Technologies (CISTI)* (pp. 1-6). IEEE. 10.23919/CISTI49556.2020.9140903

Awal, S. S., & Awal, S. S. (2023). ChatGPT and the healthcare industry: A comprehensive analysis of its impact on medical writing. *Journal of Public Health (Berlin)*, 1–4. doi:10.1007/s10389-023-02170-2

AydınÖ.KaraarslanE. (2022). OpenAI ChatGPT generated literature review: Digital twin in healthcare. *Available at SSRN 4308687*. doi:10.2139/ssrn.4308687

Aydin, Ö., & Karaarslan, E. (2023). Is ChatGPT leading generative AI? What is beyond expectations? *Academic Platform Journal of Engineering and Smart Systems*, *11*(3), 118–134. doi:10.21541/apjess.1293702

Baidoo-Anu, D., & Ansah, L. O. (2023). Education in the era of generative artificial intelligence (AI): Understanding the potential benefits of ChatGPT in promoting teaching and learning. *Journal of AI*, *7*(1), 52–62. doi:10.61969/jai.1337500

Bai, X., Shahidehpour, S., Ramesh, V., & Yu, E. (1997). Transmission analysis by Nash game method. *IEEE Transactions on Power Systems*, *12*(3), 1046–1052. doi:10.1109/59.630442

Bajpai, P., & Singh, S. N. (2007). Fuzzy Adaptive Particle Swarm Optimization for Bidding Strategy in Uniform Price Spot Market. *IEEE Transactions on Power Systems*, *22*(4), 2152–2160. doi:10.1109/TPWRS.2007.907445

Bamber, G. J., Cooke, F. L., Doellgast, V., & Wright, C. F. (2021). *International and comparative employment relations: Globalcrises and institutional responses* (7th ed.). SAGE.

Bandura, A. (1999). Moral disengagement in the perpetration of inhumanities. Personality and social psychology review. *Personality and Social Psychology Review*, *3*(3), 193–209. doi:10.1207/s15327957pspr0303_3 PMID:15661671

Bang, Y., Cahyawijaya, S., Lee, N., Dai, W., Su, D., Wilie, B., & Fung, P. (2023). A multitask, multilingual, multimodal evaluation of chatgpt on reasoning, hallucination, and interactivity. *arXiv preprint arXiv:2302.04023*. doi:10.18653/v1/2023.ijcnlp-main.45

Barney, J. (1991). Firm resources and sustained competitive advantage. *Journal of Management*, *17*(1), 99–120. doi:10.1177/014920639101700108

Barroso, L., Carneiro, R., Granville, S., Pereira, M., & Fampa, M. (2006, May). Nash Equilibrium in Strategic Bidding: A Binary Expansion Approach. *IEEE Transactions on Power Systems*, *21*(2), 629–638. doi:10.1109/TPWRS.2006.873127

Barua, R., & Mondal, J. (2023). Study of the Current Trends of CAD (Computer-Aided Detection) in Modern Medical Imaging. *Machine Learning and AI Techniques in Interactive Medical Image Analysis*, 35-50.

Barua, R., Bhowmik, S., Dey, A., Das, S., & Datta, S. (2022, September). Analysis of Robotically Controlled Percutaneous Needle Insertion into Ex Vivo Kidney Tissue for Minimally Invasive Percutaneous Nephrolithotomy (PCNL) Surgery. In *International Conference on Emergent Converging Technologies and Biomedical Systems* (pp. 249-257). Singapore: Springer Nature Singapore.

Barua, R., Datta, S., Dutta, P., & Chowdhury, A. R. (2021). Machine learning and AI application of COVID-19 pandemic outbreak. *Impacts and implications of covid-19*, 2.

Barua, R. (2024). Exploring Artificial Intelligence in Evolving Healthcare Environments: A Comprehensive Analysis. In I. Shah & Q. Sial (Eds.), *Advances in Computational Intelligence for the Healthcare Industry 4.0* (pp. 123–138). IGI Global. doi:10.4018/979-8-3693-2333-5.ch006

Barua, R. (2024). Innovations in Minimally Invasive Surgery: The Rise of Smart Flexible Surgical Robots. In M. Garcia & R. de Almeida (Eds.), *Emerging Technologies for Health Literacy and Medical Practice* (pp. 110–131). IGI Global., doi:10.4018/979-8-3693-1214-8.ch006

Barua, R., Bhowmik, S., Dey, A., & Mondal, J. (2023). Advances of the Robotics Technology in Modern Minimally Invasive Surgery. In *Design and Control Advances in Robotics* (pp. 91–104). IGI Global.

Barua, R., Das, S., & Mondal, J. (2023). Emerging Applications of Artificial Intelligence (AI) and Machine Learning (ML) in Modern Urology. In R. Queirós, B. Cunha, & X. Fonseca (Eds.), *Exploring the Convergence of Computer and Medical Science Through Cloud Healthcare* (pp. 117–133). IGI Global. doi:10.4018/978-1-6684-5260-8.ch006

Barua, R., & Datta, S. (2023). Artificial Intelligence in Modern Medical Science: A Promising Practice. In S. Rajest, B. Singh, A. J. Obaid, R. Regin, & K. Chinnusamy (Eds.), *Recent Developments in Machine and Human Intelligence* (pp. 1–12). IGI Global. doi:10.4018/978-1-6684-9189-8.ch001

Barua, R., & Datta, S. (2024). An Extensive Evaluation of New Federated Learning Approaches for COVID-19 Identification. In A. Hassan, V. Prasad, P. Bhattacharya, P. Dutta, & R. Damaševičius (Eds.), *Pioneering Smart Healthcare 5.0 with IoT, Federated Learning, and Cloud Security* (pp. 246–257). IGI Global. doi:10.4018/979-8-3693-2639-8.ch014

Barua, R., Datta, S., & Sarkar, A. (2023). Artificial Intelligence and Robotics-Based Minimally Invasive Surgery: Innovations and Future Perceptions. In G. Karthick & S. Karupusamy (Eds.), *Contemporary Applications of Data Fusion for Advanced Healthcare Informatics* (pp. 350–368). IGI Global. doi:10.4018/978-1-6684-8913-0.ch015

Bednar, P. M., & Welch, C. (2020). Socio-technical perspectives on smart working: Creating meaningful and sustainablesystems. *Information Systems Frontiers*, 22(2), 281–298. doi:10.1007/s10796-019-09921-1

Beer, M., Spector, B. A., Lawrence, P. R., Mills, D. Q., & Walton, R. E. (1984). *Managing human assets: The groundbreakingharvard business school program.* Free Press.

Bell, E., Dacin, M. T., & Toraldo, M. L. (2021). Craft imaginaries–past, present and future. Organization theory, 2(1), Bell, E., Mangia, G., Taylor, S., & Toraldo, M. L. (Eds.). (2018). The organization of craft work: Identities, meanings, and materiality Routledge.

Bender, E. M., Gebru, T., McMillan-Major, A., & Shmitchell, S. 2021. On the dangers of stochastic parrots: Can languagemodels be too big? *FAccT 2021-proceedings of the 2021 ACM conference on fairness, accountability, and transparency* (pp. 610–623). ACM. doi:10.1145/3442188.3445922

Berry, C. A., Hobbs, B. F., Meroney, W. A., O'Neill, R. P., & Stewart, W. R. Jr. (1999, September). Understanding how market power can arise in network competition: A game theoretic approach. *Utilities Policy*, 8(3), 139–158. doi:10.1016/S0957-1787(99)00016-8

Bhardwaj, A., Saxena, A., & Manglani, T. (2017). Optimal Bidding Strategy for Profit Maximization of Generation Companies under Step-Wise Bidding Protocol. *Int. J. Eng. Technology*, 9(2), 797–805. doi:10.21817/ijet/2017/v9i2/170902060

Bharti, U., Bajaj, D., Batra, H., Lalit, S., Lalit, S., & Gangwani, A. (2020, June). Medbot: Conversational artificial intelligence powered chatbot for delivering tele-health after covid-19. In *2020 5th international conference on communication and electronics systems (ICCES)* (pp. 870-875). IEEE.

Bhattacharya, K., & Zhong, J. (2001, May). Reactive power as an ancillary service. *IEEE Transactions on Power Systems, 16*(2), 294–300. doi:10.1109/59.918301

Bhirud, N., Tataale, S., Randive, S., & Nahar, S. (2019). A literature review on chatbots in healthcare domain. *International Journal of Scientific & Technology Research, 8*(7), 225-231.

Bidle, S. (2022). The internet's new favourite AI proposes torturing Iranians and surveilling mosques. *The Intercept Voices.* https://theintercept.com/2022/12/08/openai-chatgpt-ai-bias-ethics/.

Bing, M. (2023). Introducing the new bing. *Your AI-powered copilot for the web.* https://tinyurl.com/4vzmnrx7

Biswas, S. S. (2023). Potential Use of Chat GPT in Global Warming. *Annals of Biomedical Engineering, 51*(6), 1126–1127. doi:10.1007/s10439-023-03171-8 PMID:36856927

Biswas, S. S. (2023). Role of chat gpt in public health. *Annals of Biomedical Engineering, 51*(5), 868–869. doi:10.1007/s10439-023-03172-7 PMID:36920578

Blau, F. D., & Kahn, L. M. (2007). The gender pay gap: Have women gone as far as they can? Academy of management perspectives. *The Academy of Management Perspectives, 21*(1), 7–23. doi:10.5465/amp.2007.24286161

Bolina, J. (2023). How to defend against the rise of ChatGPT? Think like a poet. *Washington Post.* https://www.washingtonpost.com/opinions/2023/04/20/chatgpt-poetry-ai-language/

Boon, C., Eckardt, R., Lepak, D. P., & Boselie, P. (2018). Integrating strategic human capital and strategic human resource management. *International Journal of Human Resource Management, 29*(1), 34–67. doi:10.1080/09585192.2017.1380063

Borden, J. (2014). MOOCs are dead - long live the MOOc. *WIRED magazine, 2014.* https://www.wired.com/insights/2014/08/moocs-are-dead-long-live-the-mooc/

Bosworth, B., & Collins, S. M. (2008). Accounting for growth: Comparing China and India. *The Journal of Economic Perspectives, 22*(1), 45–66. doi:10.1257/jep.22.1.45

Brady L., Ting W., Nishith M., Bind N., Somipam S., Ziang W., (2023) *ChatGPT and a New Academic Reality: AI-Written Research Papers and the Ethics of the Large Language Models in Scholarly Publishing.* Research Gate.

Brandtzaeg, P. B., & Følstad, A. (2017). Why people use chatbots. In *Internet science: 4th international conference, INSCI 2017* (pp. 377–392). Springer International Publishing. 10.1007/978-3-319-70284-1_30

Breque, M., De Nul, L., & Petridis, A. (2021). *Industry 5.0. Towards sustainable human-centric resilient European industry.* European Director-General for Research and Innovation. https://tinyurl.com/4psv72b2

Briganti, G. (2024). How ChatGPT works: A mini review. *European Archives of Oto-Rhino-Laryngology, 281*(3), 1565–1569. doi:10.1007/s00405-023-08337-7 PMID:37991499

Brittany, Ho. (2024). A ChatGPT-enabled natural language processing framework to study domain-specific user reviews. *Machine Learning with Applications, 15.* doi:10.1016/j.mlwa.2023.100522

Broussard, M. (2018). *Artificial unintelligence: How computers misunderstand the world.* MIT Press. doi:10.7551/mitpress/11022.001.0001

Brynjolfsson, E., Rock, D., & Syverson, C. (2020). *The productivity J-curve: How intangible complement general purpose technologies.* National Bureau of Economic Research. https://www.nber.org/papers/w25148.

Brynjolfsson, E. (1993). The productivity paradox of information technology. *Communications of the ACM, 36*(12), 66–77. doi:10.1145/163298.163309

Bubeck, S., Chandrasekaran, V., Eldan, R., Gehrke, J., Horvitz, E., Kamar, E., Lee, P., Lee, Y. T., Li, Y., Lundberg, S., & Nori, H. (2023). *Sparks of artificial general intelligence: Early experiments with gpt-4*. arXiv preprint arXiv:2303.12712. https://doi.org//arXiv.2303.12712 doi:10.48550

Budd, J. W., Pohler, D., & Huang, W. (2022). Making sense of (mis) matched frames of reference: A dynamic cognitive theory of (in) stability in HR practices. *Industrial Relations*, *61*(3), 268–289. doi:10.1111/irel.12275

Budhwar, P., Malik, A., De Silva, M. T., & Thevisuthan, P. (2022). Artificial intelligence–challenges and opportunities for international HRM: A review and research agenda. *International Journal of Human Resource Management*, *33*(6), 1065–1097. doi:10.1080/09585192.2022.2035161

Burger, B., Kanbach, D. K., Kraus, S., Breier, M., & Corvello, V. (2023). On the use of AI-based tools like ChatGPT to support management research. *European Journal of Innovation Management*, *26*(7), 233–241. doi:10.1108/EJIM-02-2023-0156

Cambria, E., Das, D., Bandyopadhyay, S., & Feraco, A. (Eds.). (2017). *A practical guide to sentiment analysis* (Vol. 5). Springer International Publishing. doi:10.1007/978-3-319-55394-8_1

Campesato, O. (2023). *Transformer, BERT, and GPT3: Including ChatGPT and Prompt Engineering*. Stylus Publishing, LLC. doi:10.1515/9781683928973

Campos, F. A., Munoz San Roque, A., Sanchez-Ubeda, E. F., & Portela Gonzalez, J. (2016, July). Strategic Bidding in Secondary Reserve Markets. *IEEE Transactions on Power Systems*, *31*(4), 2847–2856. doi:10.1109/TPWRS.2015.2453477

Cao, Y., Li, S., Liu, Y., Yan, Z., Dai, Y., Yu, P. S., & Sun, L. (2023). A comprehensive survey of ai-generated content (aigc): A history of generative ai from gan to chatgpt. *arXiv preprint arXiv:2303.04226*.

Cao, X. J., & Liu, X. Q. (2022). Artificial intelligence-assisted psychosis risk screening in adolescents: Practices and challenges. *World Journal of Psychiatry*, *12*(10), 1287–1297. doi:10.5498/wjp.v12.i10.1287 PMID:36389087

Cao, Y., & Zhai, J. (2023). Bridging the gap–the impact of ChatGPT on financial research. *Journal of Chinese Economic and Business Studies*, *21*(2), 177–191. doi:10.1080/14765284.2023.2212434

Casas, J., Tricot, M. O., Abou Khaled, O., Mugellini, E., & Cudré-Mauroux, P. (2020, October). Trends & methods in chatbot evaluation. In *Companion Publication of the 2020 International Conference on Multimodal Interaction* (pp. 280-286). ACM. 10.1145/3395035.3425319

ChatGPT. (2023). *Interview Participants' ChatGPT Mar. 2023 version*. OpenAI. https://chat.openai.com/.

Chattopadhyay, D. (2004, February). Multicommodity Spatial Cournot Model for Generator Bidding Analysis. *IEEE Transactions on Power Systems*, *19*(1), 267–275. doi:10.1109/TPWRS.2003.821436

Chaudhary, M. (2023). *How ChatGPT can Be a game changer in human resource management*. Spiceworks. https://tinyurl.com/mwf63772.

Cheng, S. W., Chang, C. W., Chang, W. J., Wang, H. W., Liang, C. S., Kishimoto, T., & Su, K. P. (2023). The now and future of ChatGPT and GPT in psychiatry. *Psychiatry and Clinical Neurosciences*, *77*(11), 592–596. doi:10.1111/pcn.13588 PMID:37612880

Cheng, X., Zhang, X., Cohen, J., & Mou, J. (2022). Human vs. AI: Understanding the impact of anthropomorphism on consumer response to chatbots from the perspective of trust and relationship norms. *Information Processing & Management*, *59*(3), 102940. doi:10.1016/j.ipm.2022.102940

Chen, H. L., Vicki Widarso, G., & Sutrisno, H. (2020). A chatbot for learning Chinese: Learning achievement and technology acceptance. *Journal of Educational Computing Research*, *58*(6), 1161–1189. doi:10.1177/0735633120929622

Chen, Y., Jensen, S., Albert, L. J., Gupta, S., & Lee, T. (2023). Artificial intelligence (AI) student assistants in the classroom: Designing chatbots to support student success. *Information Systems Frontiers*, *25*(1), 161–182. doi:10.1007/s10796-022-10291-4

ChoiJ. H.HickmanK. E.MonahanA.SchwarczD. (2023).Chatgpt goes to law school. *Available at* SSRN.

Chowdhury, M. N. U. R., & Haque, A. (2023, June). ChatGPT: Its Applications and Limitations. In *2023 3rd International Conference on Intelligent Technologies (CONIT)* (pp. 1-7). IEEE.

Chowdhury, S., Dey, P., Joel-Edgar, S., Bhattacharya, S., Rodriguez-Espindola, O., Abadie, A., & Truong, L. (2023). Unlocking the value of artificial intelligence in human resource management through AI capability framework. *Human Resource Management Review*, *33*(1), 100899. doi:10.1016/j.hrmr.2022.100899

Chowdhury, S., Joel-Edgar, S., Dey, P. K., Bhattacharya, S., & Kharlamov, A. (2022). Embedding transparency in artificial intelligence machine learning models: Managerial implications on predicting and explaining employee turnover. *International Journal of Human Resource Management*, 1–32. doi:10.1080/09585192.2022.2066981

Chukwuere, J. E. (2023). ChatGPT: The game changer for higher education institutions. *Jozac Academic Voice*, *3*, 22–27.

Cingillioglu, I. (2023). Detecting AI-generated essays: The ChatGPT challenge. *The International Journal of Information and Learning Technology*, *40*(3), 259–268. doi:10.1108/IJILT-03-2023-0043

Clayton, J. (2023). *Sam altman: CEO of OpenAI calls for US to regulate artificial intelligence*. BBC news. https://www.bbc.com/news/world-us-canada-65616866.

Clayton, U. T. Z. (2023). *Generative AI miniseries - opportunities and risks for Australian organisations, in Ep2: The workplace and employment implications of generative AI – Risky business?*

Conejo, A. J., & Sioshansi, R. (2018, June). Rethinking restructured electricity market design: Lessons learned and future needs. *International Journal of Electrical Power & Energy Systems*, *98*, 520–530. doi:10.1016/j.ijepes.2017.12.014

Cooper, G. (2023). Examining science education in chatgpt: An exploratory study of generative artificial intelligence. *Journal of Science Education and Technology*, *32*(3), 444–452. doi:10.1007/s10956-023-10039-y

Cornejo, C., & Alvarez-Icaza, L. (2022). Passivity based control of under-actuated mechanical systems with nonlinear dynamic friction. *Journal of Vibration and Control*, *18*(7), 1025–1042. doi:10.1177/1077546311408469

Correia, P., Weber, J., Overbye, T., & Hiskens, I. (n.d.). Strategic equilibria in centralized electricity markets. 2001 IEEE Porto Power Tech Proceedings (Cat. No.01EX502).

Correia, P., Overbye, T., & Hiskens, I. (2003, November). Searching for noncooperative equilibria in centralized electricity markets. *IEEE Transactions on Power Systems*, *18*(4), 1417–1424. doi:10.1109/TPWRS.2003.818692

Cortada, J. W. (2006). The digital hand: How information technology changed the way industries worked in the United States. *Business History Review*, *80*(4), 755–766. doi:10.2307/25097268

Cortada, J. W. (2013). How new technologies spread: Lessons from computing technologies. *Technology and Culture*, *54*(2), 229–261. https://www.jstor.org/stable/24468014. doi:10.1353/tech.2013.0081

Cotton, D. R., Cotton, P. A., & Shipway, J. R. (2023). Chatting and cheating: Ensuring academic integrity in the era of ChatGPT. *Innovations in Education and Teaching International*, 1–12.

Cowen, T. (2022). *ChatGPT Could Make Democracy Even More Messy.* Bloomberg.

Cox, J. (2023). AI anxiety: The workers who fear losing their jobs to artificial intelligence. *BBC Worklife.* https://tinyurl.com/k6j4swez.

Crafts, N. (2010). The contribution of new technology to economic growth: Lessons from economic history. *Revista de Historia Económica*, 28(3), 409–440. doi:10.1017/S0212610910000157

Crawford, J., Cowling, M., & Allen, K. A. (2023). Leadership is needed for ethical ChatGPT: Character, assessment, and learning using artificial intelligence (AI). *Journal of University Teaching & Learning Practice*, 20(3). . doi:10.53761/1.20.3.02

Dai, Z., Yang, Z., Yang, Y., Carbonell, J., Le, Q. V., & Salakhutdinov, R. (2019). *Transformer-xl: Attentive language models beyond a fixed-length context.* arXiv preprint arXiv:1901.02860. doi:10.18653/v1/P19-1285

Das, S. (2022). *Crypto Currency and Its Assemblage during the Period of Covid-19: A State of the Art Review.*

Das, S., Datta, S., Barman, A., & Barua, R. (2023). Smart Biodegradable and Bio-Based Polymeric Biomaterials for Biomedical Applications. In Modeling, Characterization, and Processing of Smart Materials (pp. 56-82). IGI Global. doi:10.4018/978-1-6684-9224-6.ch003

Das, S., Nayak, J., Mishra, M., & Naik, B. (2021). Solar photo voltaic renewal energy: analyzing the effectiveness of marketing mix strategies. In *Innovation in Electrical Power Engineering, Communication, and Computing Technology: Proceedings of Second IEPCCT 2021* (pp. 527-540). Singapore: Springer Singapore. 10.1007/978-981-16-7076-3_45

Das, S., Nayak, J., Nayak, S., & Dey, S. (2022). Prediction of life insurance premium during pre-and post-COVID-19: A higher-order neural network approach. *Journal of The Institution of Engineers (India): Series B, 103*(5), 1747-1773. doi:10.1007/s40031-022-00771-1

Das, S., Saibabu, N., & Pranaya, D. (2023). Blockchain and Intelligent Computing Framework for Sustainable Agriculture: Theory, Methods, and Practice. In Intelligent Engineering Applications and Applied Sciences for Sustainability (pp. 208-228). IGI Global.

Das, S., Swapnarekha, H., & Vimal, S. (2022, April). Integration of Blockchain Technology with Renewable Energy for Sustainable Development: Issues. *Challenges and Future Direction. In International Conference on Computational Intelligence in Pattern Recognition* (pp. 595-607). Singapore: Springer Nature Singapore.

Dasborough, M. T. (2023). Awe-inspiring advancements in AI: The impact of ChatGPT on the field of organizational behavior. *Journal of Organizational Behavior, 44*(2), 177–179. doi:10.1002/job.2695

Dash, B., & Sharma, P. (2022). Role of Artificial Intelligence in Smart Cities for Information Gathering and Dissemination - A Review. *Academic Journal of Research and Scientific Publishing.*, 4(39), 58–75. doi:10.52132/Ajrsp.e.2022.39.4

Das, S., & Nayak, J. (2022). Customer segmentation via data mining techniques: State-of-the-art review. Computational Intelligence in Data Mining. *Proceedings of ICCIDM, 2021*, 489–507. doi:10.1007/978-981-16-9447-9_38

Das, S., Nayak, J., & Naik, B. (2023). An impact study on Covid-19 and tourism sustainability: Intelligent solutions, issues and future challenges. *World Review of Science, Technology and Sustainable Development, 19*(1-2), 92–119. doi:10.1504/WRSTSD.2023.127268

Data Scientist. (2023). *Internet searches will change forever with Google's "Magi".* Data Scientist. https://tinyurl.com/3dj94ryf.

Datta, S., Barua, R., & Das, J. (2019). Application of artificial intelligence in modern healthcare system. *Alginates-recent uses of this natural polymer.*

Datta, S., Jain, N., Waidi, Y. O., & Barua, R. (2024). Processing and Applications of Shape Memory Alloys. In Advancements in Powder Metallurgy: Processing, Applications, and Properties (pp. 151-165). IGI Global. doi:10.4018/978-1-6684-9385-4.ch006

Daugherty, P. R., Wilson, H. J., & Chowdhury, R. (2018). Using artificial intelligence to promote diversity. *MIT Sloan Management Review*. Magazine Winter 2019 Issue/Frontiers/Research Highlight. https://sloanreview.mit.edu/article/using-artificial-intelligence-to-promote-diversity/

Daugherty, P. R., Wilson, H. J., & Michelman, P. (2019). Revisiting the jobs artificial intelligence will create. *MIT Sloan Management Review*. https://mitsmr.com/2QZT4mE

Davenport. (2023). How Morgan Stanley is training GPT to help financial advisors. *Forbes*. https://tinyurl.com/32zsapxz.

David, A. K. (1993). Competitive bidding in electricity supply. *IEEE Proceedings C - Generation, Transmission and Distribution, 140* (5), pp. 421-426. 10.1049/ip-c.1993.0061

David, A. K., & Wen. (2000). *Strategic bidding in competitive electricity markets: a literature survey. 2000 Power Engineering Society Summer Meeting*, Seattle, WA. 10.1109/PESS.2000.866982

Davis, F. D. (1989). Perceived usefulness, perceived ease of use, and user acceptance of information technology. *Management Information Systems Quarterly, 13*(3), 319–339. doi:10.2307/249008

de la Torre, S., Conejo, A., & Contreras, J. (2003, November). Simulating oligopolistic pool-based electricity markets: A multiperiod approach. *IEEE Transactions on Power Systems, 18*(4), 1547–1555. doi:10.1109/TPWRS.2003.818746

de la Torre, S., Contreras, J., & Conejo, A. (2004, February). Finding Multiperiod Nash Equilibria in Pool-Based Electricity Markets. *IEEE Transactions on Power Systems, 19*(1), 643–651. doi:10.1109/TPWRS.2003.820703

De Vos, A., Van der Heijden, B. I., & Akkermans, J. (2020). Sustainable careers: Towards a conceptual model. *Journal of Vocational Behavior, 117*, 103196. doi:10.1016/j.jvb.2018.06.011

Decker, S., Nix, A., Kirsch, D., & Venkata, S. K. (2022). The dotcom archive: Contextualizing email archives. https://dotcomarchive.bristol.ac.uk/.

Deloitte. (2017). *The 2017 Deloitte state of cognitive survey*. Deloitte. https://tinyurl.com/4kn2c35s. Accessed on 08 May 2023.

Dempere, J., Modugu, K., Hesham, A., & Ramasamy, L. K. (2023). The impact of ChatGPT on higher education. *Frontiers in Education, 8*, 1206936. doi:10.3389/feduc.2023.1206936

DeNisi, A. S., & Murphy, K. R. (2017). Performance appraisal and performance management: 100 years of progress? *The Journal of Applied Psychology, 102*(3), 421–433. doi:10.1037/apl0000085 PMID:28125265

DeNisi, A., Murphy, K., Varma, A., & Budhwar, P. (2021). Performance management systems and multinational enterprises: Where we are and where we should go. *Human Resource Management, 60*(5), 707–713. doi:10.1002/hrm.22080

DeNisi, A., Varma, A., & Budhwar, P. S. (2023). Performance management around the globe: Where are we now? In A. Varma, P. Budhwar, & A. DeNisi (Eds.), *Performance management systems: A global perspective* (2nd ed.). Routledge. doi:10.4324/9781003306849-17

Derico, B., & Kleinman, Z. (2023). *OpenAI announces ChatGPT successor GPT-4*. BBC News Online. https://www.bbc.com/news/technology-64959346.

Devi, K. V., Manjula, V., & Pattewar, T. (2023). *ChatGPT: Comprehensive Study on Generative AI Tool.* Academic Guru Publishing House.

Devlin, J., Chang, M. W., Lee, K., & Toutanova, K. (2018). *Bert: Pre-training of deep bidirectional transformers for language understanding.* arXiv preprint arXiv:1810.04805.

Dey, P. K., Chowdhury, S., Abadie, A., Vann Yaroson, E., & Sarkar, S. (2023). Artificial intelligence-driven supply chain resilience in Vietnamese manufacturing small-and medium-sized enterprises. *International Journal of Production Research*, 1–40. doi:10.1080/00207543.2023.2179859

Dey, P. K., Malesios, C., Chowdhury, S., Saha, K., Budhwar, P., & De, D. (2022). Adoption of circular economy practices in small and medium-sized enterprises: Evidence from Europe. *International Journal of Production Economics*, *248*, 108496. doi:10.1016/j.ijpe.2022.108496

Dilmegani, C. (2023). *Generative AI ethics: Top 6 concerns.* Research AIMultiple. https://research.aimultiple.com/generative-ai-ethics/

Dogan, M. E., Goru Dogan, T., & Bozkurt, A. (2023). The use of artificial intelligence (AI) in online learning and distance education processes: A systematic review of empirical studies. *Applied Sciences (Basel, Switzerland)*, *13*(5), 3056. doi:10.3390/app13053056

Douglas, M. (2007). News coverage and social protest: How the media's protect paradigm exacerbates social conflict. *Journal of Dispute Resolution*, 185.

Dowling, M., & Lucey, B. (2023). ChatGPT for (finance) research: The Bananarama conjecture. *Finance Research Letters*, *53*, 103662. doi:10.1016/j.frl.2023.103662

Du, H., Teng, S., Chen, H., Ma, J., Wang, X., Gou, C., Li, B., Ma, S., Miao, Q., Na, X., Ye, P., Zhang, H., Luo, G., & Wang, F.-Y. (2023). Chat with chatgpt on intelligent vehicles: An ieee tiv perspective. *IEEE Transactions on Intelligent Vehicles*, *8*(3), 2020–2026. doi:10.1109/TIV.2023.3253281

Dwivedi, Y. K., Kshetri, N., Hughes, L., Slade, E. L., Jeyaraj, A., Kar, A. K., Wright, R., Koohang, A., Raghavan, V., Ahuja, M.,Albanna, H., Albashrawi, M. A., Al-Busaidi, A. S., Balakrishnan, J., Barlette, Y., Basu, S., Bose, I., Brooks, L., & Buhalis, Eddleston, K., Hughes, M., & Deeds, D. (2023). *Family business.org's editorial guidelines for the use of generative AI tools.* Family Business.org. https://tinyurl.com/45e3f95y

Dwivedi, Y. K., Hughes, L., Ismagilova, E., Aarts, G., Coombs, C., Crick, T., Duan, Y., Dwivedi, R., Edwards, J., Eirug, A., Galanos, V., Ilavarasan, P. V., Janssen, M., Jones, P., Kar, A. K., Kizgin, H., Kronemann, B., Lal, B., Lucini, B., & Williams, M. D. (2021, April 1). Artificial Intelligence (AI): Multidisciplinary perspectives on emerging challenges, opportunities, and agenda for research, practice and policy. *International Journal of Information Management*, *57*, 101994. doi:10.1016/j.ijinfomgt.2019.08.002

Edlich, A., Ip, F., & Whiteman, R. (2018). *How bots, algorithms, and artificial intelligence are reshaping the future of corporate.*

Edwards, M. R., Charlwood, A., Guenole, N., & Marler, J. (2022). HR analytics: An emerging field finding its place in the world alongside simmering ethical challenges. *Human Resource Management Journal*. doi:10.1111/1748-8583.12435

Eisenhardt, K. M. (1989). Building theories from case study research. *Academy of Management Review*, *14*(4), 532–550. doi:10.2307/258557

Elkhatat, A. M., Elsaid, K., & Almeer, S. (2023). Evaluating the efficacy of AI content detection tools in differentiating between human and AI-generated text. *International Journal for Educational Integrity*, *19*(1), 17. doi:10.1007/s40979-023-00140-5

Elsen-Rooney, M. (2023). NYC education department blocks ChatGPT on school devices, networks. *Retrieved*, (Jan), 25.

Elsevier. (2023). *The use of AI and AI-assisted technologies in scientific writing*. Elsevier. https://tinyurl.com/5dwsyntf. Accessed on May-12.

Emily, M. (2020). Climbing towards NLU: On Meaning, Form, and Understanding in the Age of Data. In *Proceedings of the 58th Annual Meeting of the Association for Computational Linguistics. Association for Computational Linguistics*. ACL. 10.18653/v1/2020.acl-main.463

Etzioni, A., & Etzioni, O. (2017). Incorporating ethics into artificial intelligence. *The Journal of Ethics*, *21*(4), 403–418. doi:10.1007/s10892-017-9252-2

Exploring the synergy of OpenAI's ChatGPT and Oracle APEX: Transforming Oracle applications - Insight - Summer 2023. (n.d.). Oracle Applications & Technology Users Group. https://www.oatug.org/insight-summer2023/features-archive/exploring-the-synergy

Faggiano, A., Fioretti, F., Nodari, S., & Carugo, S. (2021). Quick response code applications in medical and cardiology settings: A systematic scoping review. *European Heart Journal. Digital Health*, *2*(2), 336–341. doi:10.1093/ehjdh/ztab038 PMID:37155668

Faiz, A., & Kurniawaty, I. (2023). TantanganPenggunaan ChatGPT dalamPendidikanDitinjaudariSudut Pandang Moral. *Edukatif: JurnalIlmuPendidikan*, *5*(1), 456–463.

Farndale, E., Bonache, J., McDonnell, A., & Kwon, B. (2023). Positioning context front and center in international human resource management research. *Human Resource Management Journal*, *33*(1), 1–16. doi:10.1111/1748-8583.12483

FDA. (2022). *Do cell phones pose a health hazard? US food and drug administration website*. FDA. https://tinyurl.com/ycxyax5p.

Ferrero, R., Rivera, J., & Shahidehpour, S. (1998). Application of games with incomplete information for pricing electricity in deregulated power pools. *IEEE Transactions on Power Systems*, *13*(1), 184–189. doi:10.1109/59.651634

Ferrero, R., Shahidehpour, S., & Ramesh, V. (1997). Transaction analysis in deregulated power systems using game theory. *IEEE Transactions on Power Systems*, *12*(3), 1340–1347. doi:10.1109/59.630479

Fijačko, N., Gosak, L., Štiglic, G., Picard, C. T., & Douma, M. J. (2023). Can ChatGPT pass the life support exams without entering the American heart association course? *Resuscitation*, *185*, 185. doi:10.1016/j.resuscitation.2023.109732 PMID:36775020

FiratM. (2023). How Chat GPT Can Transform Autodidactic Experiences and Open Education? doi:10.31219/osf.io/9ge8m

Fitria, T. N. (2023, March). Artificial intelligence (AI) technology in OpenAI ChatGPT application: A review of ChatGPT in writing English essay. In *ELT Forum. Journal of English Language Teaching*, *12*(1), 44–58.

Fitzpatrick, K. K., Darcy, A., & Vierhile, M. (2017). Delivering cognitive behavior therapy to young adults with symptoms of depression and anxiety using a fully automated conversational agent (Woebot): A randomized controlled trial. *JMIR Mental Health*, *4*(2), e7785. doi:10.2196/mental.7785 PMID:28588005

Ford, E. W. (2023). Artificial Intelligence Answers an Editor's Question. *Journal of Healthcare Management*, *68*(1), 1–4. doi:10.1097/JHM-D-22-00252 PMID:36602449

Forscey, D., Bateman, J., Beecroft, N., & Woods, B. (2022). *Systemic cyber risk: A primer*. Carnegie Endowment for InternationalPeace.

Francis, J. J., Johnston, M., Robertson, C., Glidewell, L., Entwistle, V., Eccles, M. P., & Grimshaw, J. M. (2010). What is an adequate sample size? Operationalising data saturation for theory-based interview studies. *Psychology & Health*, *25*(10), 1229–1245. https://tinyurl.com/yckywptz. doi:10.1080/08870440903194015 PMID:20204937

Frieder, S., Pinchetti, L., Griffiths, R. R., Salvatori, T., Lukasiewicz, T., Petersen, P. C., & Berner, J. (2023). Mathematical capabilities of chatgpt. *arXiv preprint arXiv:2301.13867*.

Fuchs, K. (2023, May). Exploring the opportunities and challenges of NLP models in higher education: Is Chat GPT a blessing or a curse?In [].Frontiers.]. *Frontiers in Education*, *8*, 1166682. doi:10.3389/feduc.2023.1166682

Fui-Hoon Nah, F., Zheng, R., Cai, J., Siau, K., & Chen, L. (2023). Generative AI and ChatGPT: Applications, challenges, and AI-human collaboration. *Journal of Information Technology Case and Application Research*, *25*(3), 277–304. doi:10.1080/15228053.2023.2233814

Fullan, M., Azorín, C., Harris, A., & Jones, M. (2023). Artificial intelligence and school leadership: Challenges, opportunities and implications. *School Leadership & Management*, 1–8. doi:10.1080/13632434.2023.2246856

Geis, J. R., Brady, A. P., Wu, C. C., Spencer, J., Ranschaert, E., Jaremko, J. L., & Kohli, M. (2019). Ethics of artificial intelligence in radiology: Summary of the joint European and North American multisociety statement. *Radiology*, *293*(2), 436–440. doi:10.1148/radiol.2019191586 PMID:31573399

Gendron, Y., Andrew, J., & Cooper, C. (2022). The perils of artificial intelligence in academic publishing. *Critical Perspectives on Accounting*, *87*, 102411. doi:10.1016/j.cpa.2021.102411

George, A. S., & George, A. H. (2023). A review of ChatGPT AI's impact on several business sectors. *Partners Universal International Innovation Journal*, *1*(1), 9–23.

Gilpin, L. H., Bau, D., Yuan, B. Z., Bajwa, A., Specter, M., & Kagal, L. (2018). October. Explaining explanations: An overview of interpretability of machine learning. In *2018 IEEE 5th International Conference on data science and advanced analytics(DSAA)* (pp. 80–89). IEEE. 10.1109/DSAA.2018.00018

Gilson, A., Safranek, C. W., Huang, T., Socrates, V., Chi, L., Taylor, R. A., & Chartash, D. (2023). How does ChatGPT perform on the United States medical licensing examination? The implications of large language models for medical education and knowledge assessment. *JMIR Medical Education*, *9*(1), e45312. doi:10.2196/45312 PMID:36753318

Glaser, B. G., & Strauss, A. L. (1967). *The discovery of grounded theory*.

Goldfarb, B., & Kirsch, D. A. (2019). *Bubbles and crashes: The boom and bust of technological innovation*. Stanford UniversityPress. gpt-4-salesforce-potential-features/.

Gountis, V. P., & Bakirtzis, A. G. (2004). Bidding strategies for electricity producers in a competitive electricity marketplace. *IEEE Transactions on Power Systems*, *19*(1), 356–365. doi:10.1109/TPWRS.2003.821474

Gozalo-Brizuela, R., & Garrido-Merchan, E. C. (2023). *ChatGPT is not all you need. A State of the Art Review of large Generative AI models*. arXiv preprint arXiv:2301.04655.

Graeber, D. (2018). *Bullshit jobs: A theory*. Simon and schuster.

Grant, N., & Metz, C. (2022). A new chat bot is a 'code red' for Google's search business. *New York Times*.

Grant, R. M. (1996). Toward a knowledge-based theory of the firm. *Strategic Management Journal*, *17*(S2), 109–122. doi:10.1002/smj.4250171110

Griffi, A. (2023). *ChatGPT creators try to use artificial intelligence to explain itself – And come across major problems.* Independent. https://tinyurl.com/bdfzbvux.

Guan, X., Yu-Chi, Ho., & Pepyne, D. (n.d.). Gaming and price spikes in electric power markets. Pica 2001. Innovative Computing for Power - Electric Energy Meets the Market. *22nd IEEE Power Engineering Society. International Conference on Power Industry Computer Applications* (Cat. No.01CH37195). 10.1109/MPER.2001.4311547

Guardian News. (2023). Godfather of AI' Geoffrey Hinton quits Google and warns over dangers of misinformation. *Guardian News.* https://tinyurl.com/3se42t5e.

Guest, D., Knox, A., & Warhurst, C. (2022). Humanizing work in the digital age: Lessons from socio-technical systems and quality of working life initiatives. *Human Relations*, *75*(8), 1461–1482. doi:10.1177/00187267221092674

Guest, G., Bunce, A., & Johnson, L. (2006). How many interviews are enough? An experiment with data saturation and variability. *Field Methods*, *18*(1), 59–82. https://journals.sagepub.com/doi/10.1177/1525822X05279903. doi:10.1177/1525822X05279903

Guzman, A. L., & Lewis, S. C. (2020). Artificial intelligence and communication: A Human–Machine Communication research agenda. *New Media & Society*, *22*(1), 70–86. doi:10.1177/1461444819858691

Habermas, J. (1984). The theory of communicative action. In *Reason and rationalization of society* (Vol. 1). Heinemann.

Habermas, J. (1992). *Moral consciousness and communicative action.* Polity Press.

HadiM. U.QureshiR.ShahA.IrfanM.ZafarA.ShaikhM. B.MirjaliliS. (2023). A survey on large language models: Applications, challenges, limitations, and practical usage. TechRxiv. doi:10.36227/techrxiv.23589741.v1

Haleem, A. (2022). An era of ChatGPT as a significant futuristic support tool: A study on features, abilities, and challenges. *BenchCouncil transactions on benchmarks, standards and evaluations, 2*(4), 100089.

Haleem, A., Javaid, M., & Singh, R. P. (2022). An era of ChatGPT as a significant futuristic support tool: A study on features, abilities, and challenges. *BenchCouncil Transactions on Benchmarks, Standards and Evaluations, 2*(4). doi:10.1016/j.tbench.2023.100089

Han, J. W., Park, J., & Lee, H. (2022). Analysis of the effect of an artificial intelligence chatbot educational program on non-face-to-face classes: A quasi-experimental study. *BMC Medical Education*, *22*(1), 830. doi:10.1186/s12909-022-03898-3 PMID:36457086

Hao, S. (2000). A study of basic bidding strategy in clearing pricing auctions. *IEEE Transactions on Power Systems*, *15*(3), 975–980. doi:10.1109/59.871721

Haque, M. A. (2022). A Brief Analysis of "ChatGPT"–A Revolutionary Tool Designed by OpenAI. *EAI Endorsed Transactions on AI and Robotics*, *1*(1), e15–e15. doi:10.4108/airo.v1i1.2983

Hargreaves, S. (2023). 'Words Are Flowing out Like Endless Rain into a Paper Cup': ChatGPT & Law School Assessments. *Legal Educ. Rev.*, *33*(1), 69. doi:10.53300/001c.83297

Haurie, A., Loulou, R., & Savard, G. (1992). A two-player game model of power cogeneration in New England. *IEEE Transactions on Automatic Control*, *37*(9), 1451–1456. doi:10.1109/9.159591

Hawley, J. (2022). THE ROBOTS ARE COMING: What's Happening in Philosophy (WHiP)-The Philosophers, August 2022.

Henderson, P., Hashimoto, T., & Lemley, M. (2023). Where's the Liability in harmful AI Speech? *J. Free Speech L.*, *3*, 589.

Hennink, M. M., Kaiser, B. N., & Marconi, V. C. (2017). Code saturation versus meaning saturation: How many interviews are enough? *Qualitative Health Research*, *27*(4), 591–608. doi:10.1177/1049732316665344 PMID:27670770

Herbold, S., Hautli-Janisz, A., Heuer, U., Kikteva, Z., & Trautsch, A. (2023). A large-scale comparison of human-written versus ChatGPT-generated essays. *Scientific Reports*, *13*(1), 18617. doi:10.1038/s41598-023-45644-9 PMID:37903836

Herranz, R., Munoz San Roque, A., Villar, J., & Campos, F. A. (2012, August). Optimal Demand-Side Bidding Strategies in Electricity Spot Markets. *IEEE Transactions on Power Systems*, *27*(3), 1204–1213. doi:10.1109/TPWRS.2012.2185960

Hew, K. F., Huang, W., Du, J., & Jia, C. (2023). Using chatbots to support student goal setting and social presence in fully online activities: Learner engagement and perceptions. *Journal of Computing in Higher Education*, *35*(1), 40–68. doi:10.1007/s12528-022-09338-x PMID:36101883

Hill-Yardin, E. L., Hutchinson, M. R., Laycock, R., & Spencer, S. J. (2023). A Chat (GPT) about the future of scientific publishing. *Brain, Behavior, and Immunity*, *110*, 152–154. doi:10.1016/j.bbi.2023.02.022 PMID:36868432

Hobbs, B. (2001, May). Linear complementarity models of Nash-Cournot competition in bilateral and POOLCO power markets. *IEEE Transactions on Power Systems*, *16*(2), 194–202. doi:10.1109/59.918286

Hobbs, B., Metzler, C., & Pang, J. S. (2000, May). Strategic gaming analysis for electric power systems: An MPEC approach. *IEEE Transactions on Power Systems*, *15*(2), 638–645. doi:10.1109/59.867153

Hohenstein, J., Kizilcec, R., Difranzo, D., Aghajari, Z., Mieczkowski, H., Levy, K., Naaman, M., Hancock, J., & Jung, M. (2023). Artificial intelligence in communication impacts language and social relationships. *Scientific Reports*, *13*(1), 5487. doi:10.1038/s41598-023-30938-9 PMID:37015964

Holmes, W., Bialik, M., & Fadel, C. (2023). *Artificial intelligence in education*. Globethics Publications. doi:10.5886 3/20.500.12424/4273108

Howard, J., & Ruder, S. (2018). *Universal language model fine-tuning for text classification*. arXiv preprint arXiv:1801.06146. doi:10.18653/v1/P18-1031

Huang, W., Hew, K. F., & Fryer, L. K. (2022). Chatbots for language learning—Are they really useful? A systematic review of chatbot-supported language learning. *Journal of Computer Assisted Learning*, *38*(1), 237–257. doi:10.1111/jcal.12610

Huse, E. S., Wangensteen, I., & Faanes, H. (1999). Thermal power generation scheduling by simulated competition. *IEEE Transactions on Power Systems*, *14*(2), 472–477. doi:10.1109/59.761868

Hutson, M. (2022). Could AI help you to write your next paper? *Nature*, *611*(7934), 192–193. doi:10.1038/d41586-022-03479-w PMID:36316468

Hyman, L. (2023). *It's not the end of work. It's the end of boring work*. https://tinyurl.com/3tbap77h.

Hymavathi, J., Kumar, T. R., Kavitha, S., Deepa, D., Lalar, S., & Karunakaran, P. (2022). Machine learning: Supervised algorithms to determine the defect in high-precision foundry operation. *Journal of Nanomaterials*, 2022.

ICML. (n.d.). *Clarification on Large Language Model Policy LLM*. ICML. https://icml.cc/Conferences/2023/llm-policy

Imran, M., & Almusharraf, N. (2023). Analyzing the role of ChatGPT as a writing assistant at higher education level: A systematic review of the literature. *Contemporary Educational Technology*, *15*(4), ep464. doi:10.30935/cedtech/13605

Intelligence, N. M. (2023). *The AI writing on the wall*. Editorial.

Ioakimidis, V., & Maglajlic, R. A. (2023). Neither 'neo-luddism' nor 'neo-positivism'; rethinking social work's positioning in the context of rapid technological change. *British Journal of Social Work*, *53*(2), 693–697. doi:10.1093/bjsw/bcad081

Israni, R. K., Yadav, R., Singh, R., & Reddy, B. R. (2023). Power Quality Enhancement in Wind-Hydro Based Hybrid Renewable Energy System by Interlocking of UPQC. *3rd International Conference on Energy, Power and Electrical Engineering (EPEE)*, Wuhan, China. 10.1109/EPEE59859.2023.10352036

Issom, D. Z., Hardy-Dessources, M. D., Romana, M., Hartvigsen, G., & Lovis, C. (2021). Toward a conversational agent to support the self-management of adults and young adults with sickle cell disease: Usability and usefulness study. *Frontiers in Digital Health*, 3, 600333. doi:10.3389/fdgth.2021.600333 PMID:34713087

Jain, N., Barua, R., Waidi, Y. O., & Datta, S. (2024). Nanowires for Bio-Sensing Applications. In S. Kulkarni, B. Kharisov, A. Haghi, & V. Srivastava (Eds.), *Next Generation Materials for Sustainable Engineering* (pp. 205–219). IGI Global. doi:10.4018/979-8-3693-1306-0.ch010

Jain, P., Agarwal, A., Gupta, N., Sharma, R., Paliwal, U., & Bhakar, R. (2012, July). Profit maximization of a generation company based on Biogeography based Optimization. *2012 IEEE Power and Energy Society General Meeting*. IEEE. 10.1109/PESGM.2012.6345445

Jangra, A., Mukherjee, S., Jatowt, A., Saha, S., & Hasanuzzaman, M. (2023). *A Survey on Multi-modal Summarization.* ACM Computing Surveys.10.1145/3584700

Javaid, M., Haleem, A., & Singh, R. P. (2023). ChatGPT for healthcare services: An emerging stage for an innovative perspective. BenchCouncil Transactions on Benchmarks. *Standards and Evaluations*, 3(1), 100105.

Javaid, M., Haleem, A., Singh, R. P., & Suman, R. (2021). Substantial capabilities of robotics in enhancing industry 4.0 implementation. *Cognitive Robotics*, 1, 58–75. doi:10.1016/j.cogr.2021.06.001

Jeon, J., Lee, S., & Choe, H. (2023). Beyond ChatGPT: A conceptual framework and systematic review of speech-recognition chatbots for language learning. *Computers & Education*, 206, 104898. doi:10.1016/j.compedu.2023.104898

Jeyaraman, M., Ramasubramanian, S., Balaji, S., Jeyaraman, N., Nallakumarasamy, A., & Sharma, S. (2023). ChatGPT in action: Harnessing artificial intelligence potential and addressing ethical challenges in medicine, education, and scientific research. *World Journal of Methodology*, 13(4), 170–178. doi:10.5662/wjm.v13.i4.170 PMID:37771867

Jiao, W., Wang, W., Huang, J. T., Wang, X., & Tu, Z. (2023). Is ChatGPT a good translator? A preliminary study. *arXiv preprint arXiv:2301.08745.*

JohnsonD.GoodmanR.PatrinelyJ.StoneC.ZimmermanE.DonaldR.WhelessL. (2023). Assessing the accuracy and reliability of AI-generated medical responses: an evaluation of the Chat-GPT model. Research square. doi:10.21203/rs.3.rs-2566942/v1

Johnson, J. A. (2014). The ethics of big data in higher education. *International Journal of Information Ethics*, 21, 3–10. doi:10.29173/irie365

Jong-Bae Park, Kim, B. H., Jin-Ho Kim, Man-Ho Jung, & Jong-Keun ParkJong-Bae Park. (2001). A continuous strategy game for power transactions analysis in competitive electricity markets. *IEEE Transactions on Power Systems*, 16(4), 847–855. doi:10.1109/59.962436

Kalla, D. (2023). Study and Analysis of Chat GPT and its Impact on Different Fields of Study. *International Journal of Innovative Science and Research Technology 8*(3).

Kanayama, M., Izumi, Y., Akiyama, M., Hayashi, T., Atarashi, K., Roers, A., Sato, T., & Ohteki, T. (2023). Myeloid-like B cells boost emergency myelopoiesis through IL-10 production during infection. *The Journal of Experimental Medicine*, 220(4), e20221221. doi:10.1084/jem.20221221 PMID:36719648

Kapadiya, D., Shekhawat, C., & Sharma, P. (2023). A Study on Large Scale Applications of Big Data in Modern Era. In *International Conference on Information Management & Machine Intelligence (ICIMMI2023)*. ACM. https://doi.org/10.1145/3647444.364788

Kayande, U., De Bruyn, A., Lilien, G. L., Rangaswamy, A., & Van Bruggen, G. H. (2009). How incorporating feedback mechanisms in a DSS affects DSS evaluations. *Information Systems Research*, *20*(4), 527–546. doi:10.1287/isre.1080.0198

Kazemi, M., Mohammadi-Ivatloo, B., & Ehsan, M. (2015, January). Risk-Constrained Strategic Bidding of GenCos Considering Demand Response. *IEEE Transactions on Power Systems*, *30*(1), 376–384. doi:10.1109/TPWRS.2014.2328953

Kazempour, S. J., Conejo, A. J., & Ruiz, C. (2015, March). Strategic Bidding for a Large Consumer. *IEEE Transactions on Power Systems*, *30*(2), 848–856. doi:10.1109/TPWRS.2014.2332540

Keegan, A., & Den Hartog, D. (2019). Doing it for themselves? Performance appraisal in project-based organisations, the role of employees, and challenges to theory. *Human Resource Management Journal*, *29*(2), 217–237. doi:10.1111/1748-8583.12216

Keshta, I., Aoudni, Y., Sandhu, M., Singh, A., Xalikovich, P. A., Rizwan, A., Soni, M., & Lalar, S. (2023). Blockchain aware proxy re-encryption algorithm-based data sharing scheme. *Physical Communication*, *58*, 102048. doi:10.1016/j.phycom.2023.102048

Ketu, S., & Mishra, P. K. (2022). A contemporary survey on IoT based smart cities: Architecture, applications, and open issues. *Wireless Personal Communications*, *125*(3), 2319–2367. doi:10.1007/s11277-022-09658-2

Khurana, D., Koli, A., Khatter, K., & Singh, S. (2023). Natural language processing: State of the art, current trends and challenges. *Multimedia Tools and Applications*, *82*(3), 3713–3744. doi:10.1007/s11042-022-13428-4 PMID:35855771

Khyzhniak, I., Tsybulko, L., Viktorenko, I., &Mohyliova, N. (2021).Implementing the theory of multiple intelligences into project-based multimedia learning at primary school. *Information technologies and learning tools, 82*(2), 18-31.

Kietzmann, J., Paschen, J., & Treen, E. R. (2018). Artificial Intelligence in Advertising: How Marketers Can Leverage Artificial Intelligence Along the Consumer Journey. *Journal of Advertising Research*, *58*(3), 263–267. doi:10.2501/JAR-2018-035

Kim, J., Merrill, K., Xu, K., & Sellnow, D. D. (2020). My teacher is a machine: Understanding students' perceptions of AI teaching assistants in online education. *International Journal of Human-Computer Interaction*, *36*(20), 1902–1911. doi:10.1080/10447318.2020.1801227

Kim, S. W., & Lee, Y. (2023). Investigation into the Influence of Socio-Cultural Factors on Attitudes toward Artificial Intelligence. *Education and Information Technologies*. doi:10.1007/s10639-023-12172-y

Kingma, D. P., & Ba, J. (2014). *Adam: A method for stochastic optimization*. arXiv preprint arXiv:1412.6980.

Kirschen, D. (2003, May). Demand-side view of electricity markets. *IEEE Transactions on Power Systems*, *18*(2), 520–527. doi:10.1109/TPWRS.2003.810692

Kocoń, J., Cichecki, I., Kaszyca, O., Kochanek, M., Szydło, D., Baran, J., Bielaniewicz, J., Gruza, M., Janz, A., Kanclerz, K., Kocoń, A., Koptyra, B., Mieleszczenko-Kowszewicz, W., Miłkowski, P., Oleksy, M., Piasecki, M., Radliński, Ł., Wojtasik, K., Woźniak, S., & Kazienko, P. (2023). ChatGPT: Jack of all trades, master of none. *Information Fusion*, *99*, 101861. doi:10.1016/j.inffus.2023.101861

Kom, S. (2021). *Teknologipendidikan di abad digital*. Penerbit Lakeisha.

Krugman, P. (2022). Does ChatGPT mean robots are coming for the skilled jobs. *The New York Times*. http://bit.ly/3HdnAp2

Kubo, K., Tamura, M., Matsumoto, K., Otsuka, M., & Monzen, H. (2023). Independent monitor unit verification for dynamic flattened beam plans on the Halcyon linac. *Journal of Applied Clinical Medical Physics*, *24*(1), e13807. doi:10.1002/acm2.13807 PMID:36265085

Kumar, A. S., Sharma, P., Kaur, S., Saleh, O. S., Chennamma, H. R., & Chaturvedi, A. (2023). AI-Equipped IoT Applications in High-Tech Agriculture Using Machine Learning. In Handbook of Research on AI-Equipped IoT Applications in High-Tech Agriculture (pp. 38-64). IGI Global.

Kumar, A. S., Sharma, P., Kaur, S., Saleh, O. S., Chennamma, H. R., & Chaturvedi, A. (2023). AI-Equipped IoT Applications in High-Tech Agriculture Using Machine Learning. In *Handbook of Research on AI-Equipped IoT Applications in High-Tech Agriculture* (pp. 38–64). IGI Global.

Kumar, I. R., Hamid, A. A., & Ya'akub, N. B. (2023). *Effective AI, Blockchain, and E-Governance Applications for Knowledge Discovery and Management* (pp. 176–194). IGI Global. doi:10.4018/978-1-6684-9151-5

Kung, T. H., Cheatham, M., Medenilla, A., Sillos, C., De Leon, L., Elepaño, C., Madriaga, M., Aggabao, R., Diaz-Candido, G., Maningo, J., & Tseng, V. (2023). Performance of ChatGPT on USMLE: Potential for AI-assisted medical education using large language models. *PLOS Digital Health*, *2*(2), e0000198. doi:10.1371/journal.pdig.0000198 PMID:36812645

Kuraku, S. (2023). *Study and Analysis of Chat GPT and its Impact on Different Fields of Study*. Research Gate.

Lancaster, T. (2023). Artificial intelligence, text generation tools and ChatGPT–does digital watermarking offer a solution? *International Journal for Educational Integrity*, *19*(1), 10. doi:10.1007/s40979-023-00131-6

Larsson, S., & Heintz, F. (2020). Transparency in artificial intelligence. *Internet Policy Review*, *9*(2). doi:10.14763/2020.2.1469

Leaver, T., & Srdarov, S. (2023). ChatGPT Isn't Magic: The Hype and Hypocrisy of Generative Artificial Intelligence (AI) Rhetoric. *M/C Journal, 26*(5).

Lecler, A., Duron, L., & Soyer, P. (2023). Revolutionizing radiology with GPT-based models: Current applications, future possibilities and limitations of ChatGPT. *Diagnostic and Interventional Imaging*, *104*(6), 269–274. doi:10.1016/j.diii.2023.02.003 PMID:36858933

Lee, S. B. (2020). Chatbots and communication: The growing role of artificial intelligence in addressing and shaping customer needs. *Business Communication Research and Practice*, *3*(2), 103–111. doi:10.22682/bcrp.2020.3.2.103

Liebrenz, M., Schleifer, R., Buadze, A., Bhugra, D., & Smith, A. (2023). Generating scholarly content with ChatGPT: Ethical challenges for medical publishing. *The Lancet. Digital Health*, *5*(3), e105–e106. doi:10.1016/S2589-7500(23)00019-5 PMID:36754725

Li, J., Dada, A., Puladi, B., Kleesiek, J., & Egger, J. (2024). ChatGPT in healthcare: A taxonomy and systematic review. *Computer Methods and Programs in Biomedicine*, *245*, 108013. doi:10.1016/j.cmpb.2024.108013 PMID:38262126

Li, S., Huo, X., Zhang, X., Li, G., Kong, X., & Zhang, S. (2022, October 20). A Multi-Agent Optimal Bidding Strategy in Multi-Operator VPPs Based on SGHSA. *International Transactions on Electrical Energy Systems*, *2022*, 1–13. doi:10.1155/2022/7584424

Lisi, F., & Pelagatti, M. M. (2018, August). Component estimation for electricity market data: Deterministic or stochastic? *Energy Economics*, *74*, 13–37. doi:10.1016/j.eneco.2018.05.027

Liu, Y., & Lapata, M. (2019). Text Summarization with Pretrained Encoders. *2019 Conference on Empirical Methods in Natural Language Processing and the 9th International Joint Conference on Natural Language Processing (EMNLP-IJCNLP)* (pp. 3728-3738). Association for Computational Linguistics.

Liu, Y., Yang, Z., Yu, Z., Liu, Z., Liu, D., Lin, H., & Shi, S. (2023). Generative artificial intelligence and its applications in materials science: Current situation and future perspectives. *Journal of Materiomics*. . doi:10.1016/j.jmat.2023.05.001

Liu, H., Zhang, Z., Xu, Y., Wang, N., Huang, Y., Yang, Z., Jiang, R., & Chen, H. (2021). Use of BERT (bidirectional encoder representations from transformers)-based deep learning method for extracting evidences in chinese radiology reports: Development of a computer-aided liver cancer diagnosis framework. *Journal of Medical Internet Research*, *23*(1), e19689. doi:10.2196/19689 PMID:33433395

Lo, C. K. (2023). What is the impact of ChatGPT on education? A rapid review of the literature. *Education Sciences*, *13*(4), 410. doi:10.3390/educsci13040410

Lock, S. (2022). What is AI chatbot phenomenon ChatGPT and could it replace humans. *The Guardian, 5.*

Lu, A., Zhang, H., Zhang, Y., Wang, X., & Yang, D. (2023). Bounding the Capabilities of Large Language Models in Open Text Generation with Prompt Constraints. *Findings of the Association for Computational Linguistics: EACL, 2023*, 1982–2008. doi:10.18653/v1/2023.findings-eacl.148

Lucy, L., & Bamman, D. (2021, June). Gender and representation bias in GPT-3 generated stories. In *Proceedings of the Third Workshop on Narrative Understanding* (pp. 48-55). 10.18653/v1/2021.nuse-1.5

Lund, B. D., & Wang, T. (2023). Chatting about ChatGPT: How may AI and GPT impact academia and libraries? *Library Hi Tech News*, *40*(3), 26–29. doi:10.1108/LHTN-01-2023-0009

Lytras, M. D. (2023). Active and Transformative Learning (ATL) in Higher Education in Times of Artificial Intelligence and ChatGPT: Investigating a New Value-Based Framework. In Active and transformative learning in STEAM disciplines: From curriculum design to social impact (pp. 5-23). Emerald Publishing Limited. doi:10.1108/978-1-83753-618-420231001

Ma, Li, Fushuan, Wen & David, A. K. (2002). A preliminary study on strategic bidding in electricity markets with step-wise bidding protocol. IEEE/PES Transmission and Distribution Conference and Exhibition, 3, pp. 1960-1965.

Maharajan, K., Kumar, A. V., El Emary, I. M., Sharma, P., Latip, R., Mishra, N., Dutta, A., Manjunatha Rao, L., & Sharma, M. (2023). *Blockchain Methods and Data-Driven Decision Making With Autonomous Transportation*. IGI Global. . doi:10.4018/978-1-6684-9151-5.ch012

Ma, L., & Sun, B. (2020). Machine learning and AI in marketing–Connecting computing power to human insights. *International Journal of Research in Marketing*, *37*(3), 481–504. doi:10.1016/j.ijresmar.2020.04.005

Malinka, K., Peresíni, M., Firc, A., Hujnák, O., & Janus, F. (2023, June). On the educational impact of ChatGPT: Is Artificial Intelligence ready to obtain a university degree? In *Proceedings of the 2023 Conference on Innovation and Technology in Computer Science Education* V. 1 (pp. 47-53). 10.1145/3587102.3588827

Mancy, A. M., Kumar, A. S., Latip, R., Jagadamba, G., Chakrabarti, P., Sharma, P., & Kanchan, B. G. (2024). Smart Healthcare System, Digital Health and Telemedicine, Management and Emergencies: Patient Emergency Application (PES) E-Governance Applications. In Sustainable Development in AI, Blockchain, and E-Governance Applications (pp. 124-151). IGI Global.

Mancy, A. M., Kumar, A. S., Latip, R., Jagadamba, G., Chakrabarti, P., Sharma, P., & Kanchan, B. G. (2024). Smart Healthcare System, Digital Health and Telemedicine, Management and Emergencies: Patient Emergency Application (PES) E-Governance Applications. In Sustainable Development in AI, Blockchain, and E-Governance Applications (pp. 124-151). IGI Global. on 12 May 2023. doi:10.4018/979-8-3693-1722-8.ch008

Mancy, A. M., Kumar, A. S., Latip, R., Jagadamba, G., Chakrabarti, P., Sharma, P., . . . Kanchan, B. G. (2024). Smart Healthcare System, Digital Health and Telemedicine, Management and Emergencies: Patient Emergency Application (PES) E-Governance Applications. In Sustainable Development in AI, Blockchain, and E-Governance Applications (pp. 124-151). IGI Global.

Mandapuram, M., Gutlapalli, S. S., Bodepudi, A., & Reddy, M. (2018). Investigating the Prospects of Generative Artificial Intelligence. *Asian Journal of Humanity. Art and Literature*, 5(2), 167–174. doi:10.18034/ajhal.v5i2.659

Manning, C. D., Surdeanu, M., Bauer, J., Finkel, J. R., Bethard, S., & McClosky, D. (2014, June). The Stanford CoreNLP natural language processing toolkit. In *Proceedings of 52nd annual meeting of the association for computational linguistics: system demonstrations* (pp. 55-60). ACL. 10.3115/v1/P14-5010

Marmiroli, M., Tsukamoto, Y., & Yokoyama, R. (2002). Innovative generation scheduling algorithm for multi bilateral electricity market. *Proceedings. International Conference on Power System Technology*, (pp. 1383-1386). IEEE. 10.1109/ICPST.2002.1067756

Ma, T., Pan, Q., Rong, H., Qian, Y., Tian, Y., & Al-Nabhan, N. (2022). T-BERTSum: Topic-Aware Text Summarization Based on BERT. *IEEE Transactions on Computational Social Systems*, 9(3), 879–890. doi:10.1109/TCSS.2021.3088506

Mathew, A. (2023). Is Artificial Intelligence a World Changer? A Case Study of OpenAI's Chat GPT. *Recent Progress in Science and Technology*, 5, 35–42. doi:10.9734/bpi/rpst/v5/18240D

McCallum, S. (2023). *ChatGPT banned in Italy over privacy concerns*. BBC News.

McGeeR. W. (2023). Annie Chan: Three Short Stories Written with Chat GPT. *Available at* SSRN 4359403.

McGeeR. W. (2023). Capitalism, Socialism and ChatGPT. *Available at* SSRN 4369953.

Medhat, W., Hassan, A., & Korashy, H. (2014). Sentiment analysis algorithms and applications: A survey. *Ain Shams Engineering Journal*, 5(4), 1093–1113. doi:10.1016/j.asej.2014.04.011

Mekni, M. (2021). An artificial intelligence based virtual assistant using conversational agents. *Journal of Software Engineering and Applications*, 14(9), 455–473. doi:10.4236/jsea.2021.149027

Miao, X., Zhao, D., Lin, B., Jiang, H., & Chen, J. (2023). A Differential Protection Scheme Based on Improved DTW Algorithm for Distribution Networks with Highly-Penetrated Distributed Generation. *IEEE Access : Practical Innovations, Open Solutions*, 11, 40399–40411. doi:10.1109/ACCESS.2023.3269298

Michael, J., & Hughes, T. (2021). *Tech-Powered Sales: Achieve Superhuman Sales Skills*. HarperCollins Leadership.

Michel-Villarreal, R., Vilalta-Perdomo, E., Salinas-Navarro, D. E., Thierry-Aguilera, R., & Gerardou, F. S. (2023). Challenges and opportunities of generative AI for higher education as explained by ChatGPT. *Education Sciences*, 13(9), 856. doi:10.3390/educsci13090856

Mijwil, M. M., Aljanabi, M., & Chat, G. P. T. (2023, January). Towards Artificial Intelligence-Based Cybersecurity: The Practices and ChatGPT Generated Ways to Combat Cybercrime. *Iraqi Journal For Computer Science and Mathematics*, 4(1), 65–70. doi:10.52866/ijcsm.2023.01.01.0019

Mijwil, M. M., Hiran, K. K., Doshi, R., & Unogwu, O. J. (2023). Advancing Construction with IoT and RFID Technology in Civil Engineering: A Technology Review. *Al-Salam Journal for Engineering and Technology*, 2(2), 54–62. doi:10.55145/ajest.2023.02.02.007

Miller, A. (2019). The intrinsically linked future for human and Artificial Intelligence interaction. *Journal of Big Data*, 6(1), 38. doi:10.1186/s40537-019-0202-7

Mirjalili, S., Mirjalili, S. M., & Lewis, A. (2014, March). Grey Wolf Optimizer. *Advances in Engineering Software, 69,* 46–61. doi:10.1016/j.advengsoft.2013.12.007

Mishra, P., Warr, M., & Islam, R. (2023). TPACK in the age of ChatGPT and Generative AI. *Journal of Digital Learning in Teacher Education, 39*(4), 235–251. doi:10.1080/21532974.2023.2247480

Mokmin, N. A. M., & Ibrahim, N. A. (2021). The evaluation of chatbot as a tool for health literacy education among undergraduate students. *Education and Information Technologies, 26*(5), 6033–6049. doi:10.1007/s10639-021-10542-y PMID:34054328

Montenegro-Rueda, M., Fernández-Cerero, J., Fernández-Batanero, J. M., & López-Meneses, E. (2023). Impact of the Implementation of ChatGPT in Education: A Systematic Review. *Computers, 12*(8), 153. doi:10.3390/computers12080153

Mulia, A. P., Piri, P. R., & Tho, C. (2023). Usability Analysis of Text Generation by ChatGPT OpenAI Using System Usability Scale Method. *Procedia Computer Science, 227,* 381–388. doi:10.1016/j.procs.2023.10.537

Muro, C., Escobedo, R., Spector, L., & Coppinger, R. (2011, November). Wolf-pack (Canis lupus) hunting strategies emerge from simple rules in computational simulations. *Behavioural Processes, 88*(3), 192–197. doi:10.1016/j.beproc.2011.09.006 PMID:21963347

Murtarelli, G., Gregory, A., & Romenti, S. (2021). A conversation-based perspective for shaping ethical human–machine interactions: The particular challenge of chatbots. *Journal of Business Research, 129,* 927–935. doi:10.1016/j.jbusres.2020.09.018

Nair, M. M., Tyagi, A. K., & Sreenath, N. (2021, January). The future with industry 4.0 at the core of society 5.0: Open issues, future opportunities and challenges. In *2021 international conference on computer communication and informatics (ICCCI)* (pp. 1-7). IEEE.

Nazarova, D. (2023, October). Application of Artificial Intelligence in Mental Healthcare: Generative Pre-trained Transformer 3 (GPT-3) and Cognitive Distortions. In *Proceedings of the Future Technologies Conference* (pp. 204-219). Cham: Springer Nature Switzerland. 10.1007/978-3-031-47454-5_16

Nazir, A., & Wang, Z. (2023). A Comprehensive Survey of ChatGPT: Advancements, Applications, Prospects, and Challenges. *Meta-Radiology, 1*(2), 100022. doi:10.1016/j.metrad.2023.100022 PMID:37901715

O'Connor, S., & Chat, G. P. T. (2023). Editorial: Open artificial intelligence platforms in nursing education: Tools for academic progress or abuse. *Nurse Education in Practice, 66.*

Ogawa, H., Konishi, T., Najima, Y., Kito, S., Hashimoto, S., Kato, C., Sakai, S., Kanbara, Y., Atsuta, Y., Konuma, R., Wada, A., Murakami, D., Nakasima, S., Uchibori, Y., Onai, D., Hamamura, A., Nishijima, A., Shingai, N., Toya, T., & Murofushi, K. N. (2023). Phase I trial of myeloablative conditioning with 3-day total marrow and lymphoid irradiation for leukemia. *Cancer Science, 114*(2), 596–605. doi:10.1111/cas.15611 PMID:36221800

Oh, K., Kang, M., Oh, S., Kim, D. H., Kang, S. H., & Lee, Y. (2022, October). AB-XLNet: Named Entity Recognition Tool for Health Information Technology Standardization. In *2022 13th International Conference on Information and Communication Technology Convergence (ICTC)* (pp. 742-744). IEEE.

Open A. I. (n.d.). *OpenAI Blog.* OpenAI. https://openai.com/blog/.

OpenAI. (2022). Chatgpt: Optimizing language models for dialogue. *OpenAI.*

Oreshin, S., Filchenkov, A., Petrusha, P., Krasheninnikov, E., Panfilov, A., Glukhov, I., & Kozlova, D. (2020, October). Implementing a Machine Learning Approach to Predicting Students' Academic Outcomes. In *Proceedings of the 2020 1st International Conference on Control, Robotics and Intelligent System* (pp. 78-83). ACM. 10.1145/3437802.3437816

P., K., & Vijaya Chandrakala, K. (2020, December). New interactive agent based reinforcement learning approach towards smart generator bidding in electricity market with micro grid integration. *Applied Soft Computing, 97*, 106762.

Panda, T., Patro, U. S., Das, S., Venugopal, K., & Saibabu, N. (2024). Blockchain in Human Resource Management: A Bibliographic Investigation and Thorough Evaluation. In Harnessing Blockchain-Digital Twin Fusion for Sustainable Investments (pp. 86-119). IGI Global. doi:10.4018/979-8-3693-1878-2.ch005

Park, C. S. Y., Haejoong, K. I. M., & Sangmin, L. E. E. (2021). Do less teaching, do more coaching: Toward critical thinking for ethical applications of artificial intelligence. *Journal of Learning and Teaching in Digital Age, 6*(2), 97–100. doi:10.1145/306363.306372

Pereira, M., Granville, S., Fampa, M., Dix, R., & Barroso, L. (2005, February). Strategic Bidding Under Uncertainty: A Binary Expansion Approach. *IEEE Transactions on Power Systems, 20*(1), 180–188. doi:10.1109/TPWRS.2004.840397

PerlmanA. (2022). The implications of ChatGPT for legal services and society. SSRN 4294197. doi:10.2139/ssrn.4294197

Pham, S. T., & Sampson, P. M. (2022). The development of artificial intelligence in education: A review in context. *Journal of Computer Assisted Learning, 38*(5), 1408–1421. doi:10.1111/jcal.12687

Phul, H., & Mangi, A. (2023). *Service Marketing Acts As Sales Booster: Exploring The Impact On Cosmetic Business.* Research Gate.

Popova, S., & Izonin, I. (2022). Application of the Smart House System for Reconstruction of Residential Buildings from an Obsolete Housing Stock. *Smart Cities, 6*(1), 57–71. doi:10.3390/smartcities6010004

Prasad, A., Kumar, A. S., Sharma, P., Irawati, I. D., Chandrashekar, D. V., Musirin, I. B., & Abdullah, H. M. A. (2023). Artificial Intelligence in Computer Science: An Overview of Current Trends and Future Directions. *Advances in Artificial and Human Intelligence in the Modern Era*, 43-60.

Prasad, G. A., Kumar, A. V., Sharma, P., Irawati, I. D., D. V., C., Musirin, I. B., Abdullah, H. M., & Rao L, M. (2023). Artificial Intelligence in Computer Science: An Overview of Current Trends and Future Directions. In S. Rajest, B. Singh, A. Obaid, R. Regin, & K. Chinnusamy (Eds.), Advances in Artificial and Human Intelligence in the Modern Era (pp. 43-60). IGI Global.

Prasad, G. A., Kumar, A. V., Sharma, P., Irawati, I. D., D. V., C., Musirin, I. B., Abdullah, H. M., & Rao L, M. (2023). Artificial Intelligence in Computer Science: An Overview of Current Trends and Future Directions. In S. Rajest, B. Singh, A. Obaid, R. Regin, & K. Chinnusamy (Eds.), Advances in Artificial and Human Intelligence in the Modern Era (pp. 43-60). IGI Global. doi:10.4018/979-8-3693-1301-5.ch002

Purushothaman, K., & Chandrakala, V. (2020). Roth-Erev Reinforcement Learning Approach for Smart Generator Bidding towards Long Term Electricity Market Operation Using Agent Based Dynamic Modeling. *Electric Power Components and Systems, 48*(3), 256–267. doi:10.1080/15325008.2020.1758840

Qadir, J. (2023, May). Engineering education in the era of ChatGPT: Promise and pitfalls of generative AI for education. In *2023 IEEE Global Engineering Education Conference (EDUCON)* (pp. 1-9). IEEE. 10.1109/EDUCON54358.2023.10125121

Qin, C., Zhang, A., Zhang, Z., Chen, J., Yasunaga, M., & Yang, D. (2023). Is ChatGPT a general-purpose natural language processing task solver? *arXiv preprint arXiv:2302.06476.* doi:10.18653/v1/2023.emnlp-main.85

Qu, H., Zhao, H., & Wang, X. (2020, November). Domain-Specific Chinese Transformer-XL Language Model with Part-of-Speech Information. In *2020 16th International Conference on Computational Intelligence and Security (CIS)* (pp. 81-85). IEEE. 10.1109/CIS52066.2020.00026

Radford, A., Narasimhan, K., Salimans, T., & Sutskever, I. (2018). Improving Language Understanding by Generative Pre-Training. OpenAI.

Radford, A., Wu, J., Child, R., Luan, D., Amodei, D., & Sutskever, I. (2019). *Language Models Are Unsupervised Multitask Learners*. OpenAI Blog. https://life-extension.github.io/2020/05/27/GPT

Ranathunga, S., Lee, E.-S. A., Prifti Skenduli, M., Shekhar, R., Alam, M., & Kaur, R. (2023). Neural Machine Translation for Low-resource Languages: A Survey. ACM Computing Surveys, 1-37.

Rane, N. (2023, October 16). Contribution and Challenges of ChatGPT and Similar Generative Artificial Intelligence in Biochemistry, Genetics and Molecular Biology. *Genetics and Molecular Biology*.

Rasul, T., Nair, S., Kalendra, D., Robin, M., de Oliveira Santini, F., Ladeira, W. J., & Heathcote, L. (2023). The role of ChatGPT in higher education: Benefits, challenges, and future research directions. *Journal of Applied Learning and Teaching*, 6(1).

Rathore, B. (2023). Future of AI & generation alpha: ChatGPT beyond boundaries. *Eduzone: International Peer Reviewed/ Refereed Multidisciplinary Journal*, 12(1), pp. 63-68, . doi:10.56614/eiprmj.v12i1y23.254

Raval, H. (2020). Limitations of existing chatbot with analytical survey to enhance the functionality using emerging technology. [IJRAR]. *International Journal of Research and Analytical Reviews*, 7(2).

Rawat, P., Bhardwaj, A., Lamba, N., & Sharma, P. (2023). Praveen Kumawat, Prateek Sharma, "Arduino Based IoT Mini Weather Station". *SKIT Research Journal*, 13(2), 34–41. doi:10.47904/IJSKIT.13.2.2023.34-41

Ray, P. P. (2023). *ChatGPT: A comprehensive review on background, applications, key challenges, bias, ethics, limitations and future scope*. Internet of Things and Cyber-Physical Systems, 121-154.

Regona, M., Yigitcanlar, T., Xia, B., & Li, R. Y. M. (2022). Opportunities and adoption challenges of AI in the construction industry: A PRISMA review. *Journal of Open Innovation*, 8(45), 45. doi:10.3390/joitmc8010045

Rehana, H., Çam, N. B., Basmaci, M., Zheng, J., Jemiyo, C., He, Y., & Hur, J. (2023). Evaluation of GPT and BERT-based models on identifying protein-protein interactions in biomedical text. arXiv preprint arXiv:2303.17728

Ren, R., Zapata, M., Castro, J. W., Dieste, O., & Acuña, S. T. (2022). Experimentation for chatbot usability evaluation: A secondary study. *IEEE Access : Practical Innovations, Open Solutions*, 10, 12430–12464. doi:10.1109/ACCESS.2022.3145323

Renz, A., Krishnaraja, S., & Gronau, E. (2020). Demystification of Artificial Intelligence in Education–How much AI is really in the Educational Technology? [iJAI]. *International Journal of Learning Analytics and Artificial Intelligence for Education*, 2(1), 14. doi:10.3991/ijai.v2i1.12675

Reverberi, C., Rigon, T., Solari, A., Hassan, C., Cherubini, P., Antonelli, G., Awadie, H., Bernhofer, S., Carballal, S., Dinis-Ribeiro, M., Fernández-Clotett, A., Esparrach, G. F., Gralnek, I., Higasa, Y., Hirabayashi, T., Hirai, T., Iwatate, M., Kawano, M., Mader, M., & Cherubini, A. (2022). Experimental evidence of effective human–AI collaboration in medical decision-making. *Scientific Reports*, 12(1), 14952. doi:10.1038/s41598-022-18751-2 PMID:36056152

Reyes, M., Meier, R., Pereira, S., Silva, C. A., Dahlweid, F. M., Tengg-Kobligk, H. V., & Wiest, R. (2020). On the interpretability of artificial intelligence in radiology: Challenges and opportunities. *Radiology. Artificial Intelligence*, 2(3), e190043. doi:10.1148/ryai.2020190043 PMID:32510054

Ribas, J. (2023). *Building the New Bing*. LinkedIn. https://www.linkedin.com/pulse/building-new-bing-jordi-ribas

Richter, C. W., Sheble, G. B., & Ashlock, D. (1999). Comprehensive bidding strategies with genetic programming/finite state automata. *IEEE Transactions on Power Systems*, *14*(4), 1207–1212. doi:10.1109/59.801874

Roco, M. C., & Bainbridge, W. S. (2002). Converging technologies for improving human performance: Integrating from the nanoscale. *Journal of Nanoparticle Research*, *4*(4), 281–295. doi:10.1023/A:1021152023349

Rodriguez, C., & Anders, G. (2004, May). Bidding Strategy Design for Different Types of Electric Power Market Participants. *IEEE Transactions on Power Systems*, *19*(2), 964–971. doi:10.1109/TPWRS.2004.826763

Rodriguez-Torrealba, R., Garcia-Lopez, E., & Garcia-Cabot, A. (2022). End-to-End generation of Multiple-Choice questions using Text-to-Text transfer Transformer models. *Expert Systems with Applications*, *208*, 118258. doi:10.1016/j.eswa.2022.118258

Rokhforoz, P., Montazeri, M., & Fink, O. (2023, April). Safe multi-agent deep reinforcement learning for joint bidding and maintenance scheduling of generation units. *Reliability Engineering & System Safety*, *232*, 109081. doi:10.1016/j.ress.2022.109081

Ronanki, K., Cabrero-Daniel, B., & Berger, C. (2022, June). ChatGPT as a Tool for User Story Quality Evaluation: Trustworthy Out of the Box? In *International Conference on Agile Software Development* (pp. 173-181). Cham: Springer Nature Switzerland, 10.1007/978-3-031-48550-3_17

Roose, K. (2022). The brilliance and weirdness of ChatGPT. *The New York Times*.

Rosselló-Geli, J. (2022, April). Impact of AI on Student's Research and Writing Projects. In *International Conference on Computational Intelligence in Pattern Recognition* (pp. 705-713). Singapore: Springer Nature Singapore. 10.1007/978-981-99-3734-9_57

Roumeliotis, K. I., & Tselikas, N. D. (2023). ChatGPT and Open-AI Models: A Preliminary Review. *Future Internet*, *15*(6), 192. doi:10.3390/fi15060192

Rudolph, J., Tan, S., & Tan, S. (2023). ChatGPT: Bullshit spewer or the end of traditional assessments in higher education? *Journal of Applied Learning and Teaching*, *6*(1).

Ryu, M., & Han, S. (2019). AI education programs for deep-learning concepts. *Journal of the Korean Association of information*. *Education*, *23*(6), 583–590. doi:10.14352/jkaie.2019.23.6.583

Safaei, M., & Longo, J. (2021). The End of the Policy Analyst? Testing the Capability of Artificial Intelligence to Generate Plausible, Persuasive, and Useful Policy Analysis. *Digital Government: Research and Practice*. . doi:10.1145/3604570

Saini, M., Bhardwaj, A., & Nawaz, S. (2023, April 7). Multi-Objective Optimal Bidding Approach for both Small & Large Customers in Competitive power Market. *2023 IEEE 8th International Conference for Convergence in Technology (I2CT)*. IEEE.

Sakirin, T., & Said, R. B. (2023). User preferences for ChatGPT-powered conversational interfaces versus traditional methods. *Mesopotamian Journal of Computer Science*, *2023*, 24–31. doi:10.58496/MJCSC/2023/006

Sallam, M. (2023). ChatGPT utility in healthcare education, research, and practice: systematic review on the promising perspectives and valid concerns. Healthcare, 11(6).

Saul, J., & Bass, D. (2023). *Artificial intelligence is booming—So is its carbon footprint*. Bloomberg News. https://tinyurl.com/eruhxdhv.

Saunders, M. N., & Townsend, K. (2016). Reporting and justifying the number of interview participants in organization and workplace research. *British Journal of Management*, *27*(4), 836–852. doi:10.1111/1467-8551.12182

Schrage, M., Kiron, D., Candelon, F., Khodabandeh, S., & Chu, M. (2023). AI is helping companies redefine, noy just improve performance. *MIT Sloan Management Review*. https://sloanreview.mit.edu/article/ai-is-helping-companies-redefine-not-just-improve-performance/.

SchulmanJ.WolskiF.DhariwalP.RadfordA.KlimovO. 2017. Proximal policy optimization algorithms. arXiv preprint-arXiv:1707.06347.

Schwartz, R., Dodge, J., Smith, N. A., & Etzioni, O. (2020, November). Green AI. *Communications of the ACM, 63*(12), 54–63. doi:10.1145/3381831

Schwartz, R., Vassilev, A., Greene, K., Perine, L., & Burt, A. (2022). *Towards a standard for identifying bias in Artificial Intelligence*. Department of Commerce's National Institute of Standards and Technology. doi:10.6028/NIST.SP.1270

Schweizer, K. (2022). Artificial unintelligence: How computers misunderstand the world. *The European Legacy, 27*(7–8), 7–8. science-practice gap in open science. https://doi.org/ doi:10.1080/10848770.2022.2110366

Seeley, K., Lawarree, J., & Liu, C. C. (2000). Analysis of electricity market rules and their effects on strategic behavior in a noncongestive grid. *IEEE Transactions on Power Systems, 15*(1), 157–162. doi:10.1109/59.852115

Sethi, S. S., & Sharma, P. (2023). New Developments in the Implementation of IoT in Agriculture. *SN Computer Science, 4*(5), 503. doi:10.1007/s42979-023-01896-w

Shahidehpour, M., & Alomoush, M. (2001). *Restructured electric power systems: Operation, trading and volatility.* Marcel Dekker, Inc.

Shahidehpour, M., Yamin, H., & Li, Z. (2002). *Market operations in electric power systems: Forecasting, scheduling and risk management.* John Wiley. doi:10.1002/047122412X

Sharma, P., & Dadheech, P. (2023). *Modern-age Agriculture with Artificial Intelligence: A review emphasizing Crop Yield Prediction.*

Sharma, P., & Rathi, Y. (2016). Efficient density-based clustering using automatic parameter detection. In *Proceedings of the International Congress on Information and Communication Technology: ICICT 2015,* (pp. 433-441). Springer Singapore. 10.1007/978-981-10-0767-5_46

Sharma, P., Sharma, C., & Mathur, P. (2023). *Machine Learning-based Stock Market Forecasting using Recurrent Neural Network.* 2023 9th International Conference on Smart Computing and Communications (ICSCC), Kochi, Kerala, India. 10.1109/ICSCC59169.2023.10335083

Sharma, G., & Sharma, D. (2022). Automatic Text Summarization Methods: A Comprehensive Review. *SN Computer Science, 4*(1), 33. doi:10.1007/s42979-022-01446-w

Sharma, P. (2023). *Utilizing Explainable Artificial Intelligence to Address Deep Learning in Biomedical Domain, Medical Data Analysis and Processing using Explainable Artificial Intelligence.* Taylor & Francis. doi:10.1201/9781003257721-2

Sharma, P., & Bhatnagar, N. (2023). Passenger Authentication and Ticket Verification at Airport Using QR Code Scanner. *SKIT Research Journal, 13*(2), 10–13. doi:10.47904/IJSKIT.13.1.2023.10-12

Sharma, P., & Dadheech, P. (2023). Modern-age Agriculture with Artificial Intelligence: A review emphasizing Crop Yield Prediction. *EVERGREEN Joint Journal of Novel Carbon Resource Sciences & Green Asia Strategy, 10*(4), 2570–2582. doi:10.5109/7160906

Sharma, P., Dadheech, P., Aneja, N., & Aneja, S. (2023). Predicting Agriculture Yields Based on Machine Learning Using Regression and Deep Learning. *IEEE Access : Practical Innovations, Open Solutions*, *11*, 111255–111264. doi:10.1109/ACCESS.2023.3321861

Sharma, P., Dadheech, P., & Senthil, A. S. K. (2023). AI-Enabled Crop Recommendation System Based on Soil and Weather Patterns. In *Artificial Intelligence Tools and Technologies for Smart Farming and Agriculture Practices* (pp. 184–199). IGI Global. doi:10.4018/978-1-6684-8516-3.ch010

Sharma, P., & Jain, M. K. (2023). Stock Market Trends Analysis using Extreme Gradient Boosting (XGBoost*). International Conference on Computing, Communication, and Intelligent Systems (ICCCIS)*, Greater Noida, India. 10.1109/ICCCIS60361.2023.10425722

Sharma, P., Kapadiya, D., & Bhardwaj, A. (2023). Efficient Note Sharing Model for Collaborative Learning. *SKIT Research Journal*, *13*(2), 42–46. doi:10.47904/IJSKIT.13.2.2023.42-46

Sharma, S., & Yadav, R. (2023). Chat GPT – A Technological Remedy or Challenge for Education System. [Retrieved from]. *Global Journal of Enterprise Information System*, *14*(4), 46–51.

Sharonova, S., & Avdeeva, E. (2021). Dialogue between smart education and classical education. *Language and Dialogue*, *11*(1), 151–170. doi:10.1075/ld.00088.sha

Sheehan, B., Jin, H. S., & Gottlieb, U. (2020). Customer service chatbots: Anthropomorphism and adoption. *Journal of Business Research*, *115*, 14–24. doi:10.1016/j.jbusres.2020.04.030

Shet, S. V., & Pereira, V. (2021). Proposed managerial competencies for Industry 4.0–Implications for social sustainability. *Technological Forecasting and Social Change*, *173*, 121080. doi:10.1016/j.techfore.2021.121080

Shidiq, M. (2023, May).The use of artificial intelligence-based chat-gpt and its challenges for the world of education; from the viewpoint of the development of creative writing skills. In *Proceeding of International Conference on Education, Society and Humanity* (Vol. 1, No. 1, pp. 353-357). IEEE.

Sijing, L., & Lan, W. (2018, August). Artificial intelligence education ethical problems and solutions. In *2018 13th International Conference on Computer Science & Education (ICCSE)* (pp. 1-5). IEEE. 10.1109/ICCSE.2018.8468773

Skjuve, M., Følstad, A., & Brandtzaeg, P. B. (2023). The user experience of ChatGPT: findings from a questionnaire study of early users. *Proceedings of the 5th International Conference on Conversational User Interfaces*. ACM. 10.1145/3571884.3597144

Song, H., Liu, C. C., Lawarree, J., & Dahlgren, R. W. (2000). Optimal electricity supply bidding by Markov decision process. *IEEE Transactions on Power Systems*, *15*(2), 618–624. doi:10.1109/59.867150

Song, H., Liu, C.-C., & Lawarree, J. (2002). Nash equilibrium bidding strategies in a bilateral electricity market. *IEEE Transactions on Power Systems*, *17*(1), 73–79. doi:10.1109/59.982195

Stahl, G. K., Brewster, C. J., Collings, D. G., & Hajro, A. (2020). Enhancing the role of human resource management in corporate sustainability and social responsibility: A multi-stakeholder, multidimensional approach to HRM. *Human Resource Management Review*, *30*(3), 100708. doi:10.1016/j.hrmr.2019.100708

Strbac, G., & Kirschen, D. (1999). Assessing the competitiveness of demand-side bidding. *IEEE Transactions on Power Systems*, *14*(1), 120–125. doi:10.1109/59.744498

StreetD.WilckJ. (2023). 'Let's Have a Chat': Principles for the Effective Application of ChatGPT and Large Language Models in the Practice of Forensic Accounting. SSRN 4351817. doi:10.2139/ssrn.4351817

Strubell, E., Ganesh, A., & McCallum, A. (2019). Energy and Policy Considerations for Deep Learning in NLP. In *Proceedings of the 57th Annual Meeting of the Association for Computational Linguistics*. ACM. 10.18653/v1/P19-1355

Suddaby, R., Ganzin, M., & Minkus, A. (2017). Craft, magic and the Re-enchantment of the world. *European Management Journal, 35*(3), 285–296. doi:10.1016/j.emj.2017.03.009

Surameery, N. M. S., & Shakor, M. Y. (2023). Use chat gpt to solve programming bugs. *International Journal of Information Technology & Computer Engineering (IJITC) ISSN: 2455-5290, 3*(01), 17-22.

Suseno, Y., Chang, C., Hudik, M., & Fang, E. S. (2022). Beliefs, anxiety and change readiness for artificial intelligence adoption among human resource managers: The moderating role of high-performance work systems. *International Journal of Human Resource Management, 33*(6), 1209–1236. doi:10.1080/09585192.2021.1931408

Susskind, R. E., & Susskind, D. (2022). *The future of the professions: How technology will transform the work of human experts, updated edition*. Oxford University Press.

Syed, A. S., Sierra-Sosa, D., Kumar, A., & Elmaghraby, A. (2021). IoT in smart cities: A survey of technologies, practices and challenges. *Smart Cities, 4*(2), 429–475. doi:10.3390/smartcities4020024

Taecharungroj, V. (2023). "What Can ChatGPT Do?" Analyzing Early Reactions to the Innovative AI Chatbot on Twitter. *Big Data and Cognitive Computing, 7*(1), 35. doi:10.3390/bdcc7010035

Tahiru, F. (2021). AI in education: A systematic literature review. [JCIT]. *Journal of Cases on Information Technology, 23*(1), 1–20. doi:10.4018/JCIT.2021010101

Tai, M. C. (2020, August 14). The impact of artificial intelligence on human society and bioethics. *Tzu-Chi Medical Journal, 32*(4), 339–343. doi:10.4103/tcmj.tcmj_71_20 PMID:33163378

Talan, T., & Kalinkara, Y.TALAN. (2023). The role of artificial intelligence in higher education: ChatGPT assessment for anatomy course. *Uluslararası Yönetim Bilişim Sistemleri ve Bilgisayar Bilimleri Dergisi, 7*(1), 33–40. doi:10.33461/uybisbbd.1244777

Tanwar, A., Sharma, P., Pandey, A., & Kumar, S. (2022, December). Intrusion Detection System Based Ameliorated Technique of Pattern Matching. In *Proceedings of the 4th International Conference on Information Management & Machine Intelligence* (pp. 1-4). ACM. 10.1145/3590837.3590947

Tate, T., Doroudi, S., Ritchie, D., & Xu, Y. (2023). *Educational Research and AI-Generated Writing: Confronting the Coming Tsunami*.

Taylor, A. (2020). Smartphone pinky' and other injuries caused by excessive phone use. *The conversation, 2020*. https://tinyurl.com/6keemvsk.

Tcharnetsky, M., & Vogt, F. (2023). *The OSQE model: The ai cycle against the shortage of skilled professionals: A holistic solution approach based on artificial intelligence in times of demographic change*. https://doi.org// doi:10.20944

Teicher, J., Van Gramberg, B., & Bamber, G. J. (2023). Understanding workplace conflict and its management in the context of COVID-19. In A. Avgar, D. Hann, R. Lamare, & D. NashLERA Research Volume Series (Eds.), The evolution of workplace dispute resolution: International perspectives. Labor and Employment Relations Association.

The Economist. (2020). Businesses are finding AI hard to adopt. *The Economist*. https://tinyurl.com/2p8ne738.vAccessed on 12 May 2023.

The Royal Society. (2019). *Explainable AI: The basics - POLICY BRIEFING*. The Royal Society. https://tinyurl.com/wkkevmu9.

Thompson, E. P. (1966). *The making of the English working class*. Victor Gollancz Ltd.

Thorbecke, C. (2023). *Google shares lose $100 billion after company's AI chatbot makes an error during demo*. CNN Business. https://edition.cnn.com/2023/02/08/tech/google-ai-bard-demo-error/index.html.

Tlili, A., Shehata, B., Adarkwah, M. A., Bozkurt, A., Hickey, D. T., Huang, R., & Agyemang, B. (2023). What if the devil is my guardian angel: ChatGPT as a case study of using chatbots in education. *Smart Learning Environments*, *10*(1), 15. doi:10.1186/s40561-023-00237-x

Torfi, A., Shirvani, R. A., Keneshloo, Y., Tavaf, N., & Fox, E. A. (2020). *Natural language processing advancements by deep learning: A survey*. arXiv preprint arXiv:2003.01200.

Trist, E., Higgin, G., Murray, H., & Pollock, A. (1963). *Organizational choice*. Tavistock Publications.

Tsukamoto, Y., & Iyoda, I. (1996, May). Allocation of fixed transmission cost to wheeling transactions by cooperative game theory. *IEEE Transactions on Power Systems*, *11*(2), 620–629. doi:10.1109/59.496131

Twyman, M. (2017). Black Lives Matter in Wikipedia: Collective memory and collaboration around online social movements. In *Proceedings of the 2017 ACM Conference on Computer Supported Cooperative Work and Social Computing*. ACM.

Uszkoreit, J. (2017). *Transformer: A novel neural network architecture for language understanding*. Google Research Blog. https://ai.googleblog.com/2017/08/transformer-novel-neural-network.html.

V., M. V., Kumar, A. S., Sharma, P., Kaur, S., Saleh, O. S., Chennamma, H., & Chaturvedi, A. (2023). AI-Equipped IoT Applications in High-Tech Agriculture Using Machine Learning. In A. Khang (Ed.), *Handbook of Research on AI-Equipped IoT Applications in High-Tech Agriculture* (pp. 38-64). IGI Global.

V., M. V., Kumar, A. S., Sharma, P., Kaur, S., Saleh, O. S., Chennamma, H., & Chaturvedi, A. (2023). AI-Equipped IoT Applications in High-Tech Agriculture Using Machine Learning. In A. Khang (Ed.), Handbook of Research on AI-Equipped IoT Applications in High-Tech Agriculture (pp. 38-64). *IGI Global.* . doi:10.4018/978-1-6684-9231-4.ch003

Vaishya, R., Misra, A., & Vaish, A. (2023). ChatGPT: Is this version good for healthcare and research? *Diabetes & Metabolic Syndrome*, *17*(4), 102744. doi:10.1016/j.dsx.2023.102744 PMID:36989584

Vallance, C. (2023). AI could replace equivalent of 300 million jobs – report. *BBC News Technology, 28*. https://www.bbc.com/news/technology-65102150.

van Dis, E. A. M., Bollen, J., Zuidema, W., van Rooij, R., & Bockting, C. (2023). ChatGPT: Five priorities for research. *Nature*, *614*(7947), 224–226. doi:10.1038/d41586-023-00288-7 PMID:36737653

Varma, A., Dawkins, C., & Chaudhuri, K. (2022). Artificial intelligence and people management: A critical assessment throughthe ethical lens. *Human Resource Management Review*, *33*(1), 100923. doi:10.1016/j.hrmr.2022.100923

Varma, A., Jaiswal, A., Pereira, V., & Kumar, Y. L. N. (2022). Leader-member exchange in the age of remote work. *Human Resource Development International*, *25*(2), 219–230. doi:10.1080/13678868.2022.2047873

Vaswani, A., Shazeer, N., Parmar, N., Uszkoreit, J., Jones, L., Gomez, A. N., & Polosukhin, I. (2017). Attention is all you need. *Advances in Neural Information Processing Systems*, 30.

Venkata, S. K., Decker, S., Kirsch, D. A., & Nix, A. (2021). EMCODIST: A context-based search tool for email archives. In 2021 IEEE international conference on big data (big data). IEEE. 10.1109.

Vincent, J. (2023). Meta open-sources multisensory AI model that combines six types of data. *Verge*. https://tinyurl.com/2s3jucwd

von Krogh, G., Roberson, Q., & Gruber, M. (2023). Recognizing and utilizing novel research opportunities with artificial intelligence. *Academy of Management Journal*, *66*(2), 367–373. doi:10.5465/amj.2023.4002

Waidi, Y. O., Barua, R., & Datta, S. (2023). Metals, Polymers, Ceramics, Composites Biomaterials Used in Additive Manufacturing for Biomedical Applications. In A. Kumar, P. Kumar, A. Srivastava, & V. Goyat (Eds.), *Modeling, Characterization, and Processing of Smart Materials* (pp. 165–184). IGI Global., doi:10.4018/978-1-6684-9224-6.ch008

Wang, X., Attal, M. I., Rafiq, U., & Hubner-Benz, S. (2022, June). Turning Large Language Models into AI Assistants for Startups Using Prompt Patterns. In *International Conference on Agile Software Development* (pp. 192-200). Cham: Springer Nature Switzerland. 10.1007/978-3-031-48550-3_19

Wang, A., Kim, E., Oleru, O., Seyidova, N., & Taub, P. J. (2021). Artificial Intelligence in Plastic Surgery: Chat-GPT as a Tool to Address Disparities in Health Literacy. *Plastic and Reconstructive Surgery*, 10–1097. doi:10.1097/PRS.0000000000011202 PMID:37983817

Wang, J., Wu, J., & Che, Y. (2019, August). Agent and system dynamics-based hybrid modeling and simulation for multilateral bidding in electricity market. *Energy*, *180*, 444–456. doi:10.1016/j.energy.2019.04.180

Wang, J., Wu, J., & Kong, X. (2023). Multi-agent simulation for strategic bidding in electricity markets using reinforcement learning. *CSEE Journal of Power and Energy Systems*, *9*(3), 1051–1065.

Wang, Z., Cai, S. A., Ren, S., & Singh, S. K. (2023). Green operational performance in a high-tech industry: Role of green HRM and green knowledge. *Journal of Business Research*, *160*, 113761. doi:10.1016/j.jbusres.2023.113761

Wan, Y., Wang, W., He, P., Gu, J., Bai, H., & Lyu, M. R. (2023, November). Biasasker: Measuring the bias in conversational ai system. In *Proceedings of the 31st ACM Joint European Software Engineering Conference and Symposium on the Foundations of Software Engineering* (pp. 515-527). ACM. 10.1145/3611643.3616310

Weber, J., & Overbye, T. (2002, August). An individual welfare maximization algorithm for electricity markets. *IEEE Transactions on Power Systems*, *17*(3), 590–596. doi:10.1109/TPWRS.2002.800899

Wen, F. (2001). Optimal bidding strategies and modeling of imperfect information among competitive generators. *IEEE Transactions on Power Systems*, *16*(1), 15–21. doi:10.1109/59.910776

Wen, F. S., & David, A. K. (2001). Strategic bidding for electricity supply in a day-ahead energy market. *Electric Power Systems Research*, *59*(3), 197–206. doi:10.1016/S0378-7796(01)00154-7

Wen, F. S., & David, A. K. (2002). Optimally co-ordinated bidding strategies in energy and ancillary service markets. *IEE Proceedings. Generation, Transmission and Distribution*, *149*(3), 331–338. doi:10.1049/ip-gtd:20020211

Wen, F., & David, A. (2001). Oligopoly Electricity Market Production under Incomplete Information. *IEEE Power Engineering Review*, *21*(4), 58–61. doi:10.1109/39.916353

Wen, F., & David, A. (2001, January). Optimal bidding strategies for competitive generators and large consumers. *International Journal of Electrical Power & Energy Systems*, *23*(1), 37–43. doi:10.1016/S0142-0615(00)00032-6

Westerman, J. W., Rao, M. B., Vanka, S., & Gupta, M. (2020). Sustainable human resource management and the triple bottom line: Multi-stakeholder strategies, concepts, and engagement. *Human Resource Management Review*, *30*(3), 100742. doi:10.1016/j.hrmr.2020.100742

White House. (n.d.). *Blueprint for An AI Bill of Rights*. The White House. https://www.whitehouse.gov/ostp/ai-bill-of-rights/

Willig, C., & Rogers, W. S. (2017). *The SAGE handbook of qualitative research in Psychology* (2nd ed.). Sage. doi:10.4135/9781526405555

Wilson, H. J., Daugherty, P., & Bianzino, N. (2017). The jobs that artificial intelligence will create. *MIT Sloan Management Review, 58*(4), 14. http://mitsmr.com/2odREFJ

Wolf, Z. B. (2023). AI can be racist, sexist and creepy. What should we do about it? CNN what matters. https://tinyurl.com/yc4u46d3

Woolf, B. P., Lane, H. C., Chaudhri, V. K., & Kolodner, J. L. (2013). AI grand challenges for education. *AI Magazine, 34*(4), 66–84. doi:10.1609/aimag.v34i4.2490

Wu, C., Yin, S., Qi, W., Wang, X., Tang, Z., & Duan, N. (2023). Visual chatgpt: Talking, drawing and editing with visual foundation models. *arXiv preprint arXiv:2303.04671.*

Wu, T., He, S., Liu, J., Sun, S., Liu, K., Han, Q. L., & Tang, Y. (2023). A brief overview of ChatGPT: The history, status quo and potential future development. *IEEE/CAA Journal of Automatica Sinica, 10*(5), 1122-1136.

Wu, Y., Schuster, M., Chen, Z., Le, Q. V., Norouzi, M., Macherey, W., Krikun, M., Cao, Y., Gao, Q., Macherey, K., & Klingner, J. (2016). *Google's neural machine translation system: Bridging the gap between human and machine translation.* arXiv preprint arXiv:1609.08144.

Wu, J., Wang, J., & Kong, X. (2022, October). Strategic bidding in a competitive electricity market: An intelligent method using Multi-Agent Transfer Learning based on reinforcement learning. *Energy, 256,* 124657. doi:10.1016/j.energy.2022.124657

Xian, W., Yuzeng, L., & Shaohua, Z. (2004, August). Oligopolistic Equilibrium Analysis for Electricity Markets: A Nonlinear Complementarity Approach. *IEEE Transactions on Power Systems, 19*(3), 1348–1355. doi:10.1109/TPWRS.2004.831237

Xia, Q., Chiu, T. K., Lee, M., Sanusi, I. T., Dai, Y., & Chai, C. S. (2022). A self-determination theory (SDT) design approach for inclusive and diverse artificial intelligence (AI) education. *Computers & Education, 189,* 104582. doi:10.1016/j.compedu.2022.104582

Xue, M., Cao, X., Feng, X., Gu, B., & Zhang, Y. (2022). Is college education less necessary with AI? Evidence from firm-level labor structure changes. *Journal of Management Information Systems, 39*(3), 865–905. doi:10.1080/07421222.2022.2096542

Yadav, R., Chaudhary, N. S., Kumar, D. & Saini, D. (2022). Mediating and moderating variables of employee relations and sustainable organizations: A systematic literature review and future research agenda. *International journal of organizational analysis.* doi:10.1108/IJOA-12-2021-3091

Yakar, T. (2023). *GPT-4 and Salesforce potential features.* ApexHours website. https://www.apexhours.com/

Yan, Y., Li, B., Feng, J., Du, Y., Lu, Z., Huang, M., & Li, Y. (2023). Research on the impact of trends related to ChatGPT. *Procedia Computer Science, 221,* 1284–1291. doi:10.1016/j.procs.2023.08.117

Yau, K. W., Chai, C. S., Chiu, T. K., Meng, H., King, I., & Yam, Y. (2023). A phenomenographic approach on teacher conceptions of teaching artificial intelligence (AI) in K-12 schools. *Education and Information Technologies, 28*(1), 1041–1064. doi:10.1007/s10639-022-11161-x

Yi, C., Wang, J., Cheng, N., Zhou, S., & Xu, B. (2020).Applying wav2vec2.0 to speech recognition in various low-resource languages. *arXiv preprint arXiv:2012.12121.*

Yogesh, K. (2023). "So what if ChatGPT wrote it?" Multidisciplinary perspectives on opportunities, challenges and implications of generative conversational AI for research, practice and policy. *International Journal of Information Management, 71.* doi:10.1016/j.ijinfomgt.2023.102642

Yörükoğlu, S., Avşar, Z. M., & Kat, B. (2018, October). An integrated day-ahead market clearing model: Incorporating paradoxically rejected/accepted orders and a case study. *Electric Power Systems Research*, *163*, 513–522. doi:10.1016/j. epsr.2018.07.007

Yue, B., & Li, H. (2023). The impact of human-AI collaboration types on consumer evaluation and usage intention: A perspective of responsibility attribution. *Frontiers in Psychology*, *14*, 1277861. doi:10.3389/fpsyg.2023.1277861 PMID:38022995

Yui, S., Wakita, S., Nagata, Y., Kuribayashi, Y., Asayama, T., Fujiwara, Y., Sakaguchi, M., Yamanaka, S., Marumo, A., Omori, I., Kinoshita, R., Onai, D., Sunakawa, M., Kaito, Y., Inai, K., Tokura, T., Takeyoshi, A., Yasuda, S., Honma, S., & Yamaguchi, H. (2023). Safety and efficacy of high-dose cytarabine MEAM therapy and other treatments for auto-peripheral blood stem cell transplantation: A retrospective comparative study. *Asia Pacific Journal of Clinical Oncology*, *19*(1), 136–148. doi:10.1111/ajco.13780 PMID:35599446

Zaimah, N. R., Hartanto, E. B., & Zahro, F. (2024). Acceptability and Effectiveness Analysis of Large Language Model-Based Artificial Intelligence Chatbot Among Arabic Learners. *Mantiqu Tayr: Journal of Arabic Language*, *4*(1), 1–20.

ZhaiX. (2022). ChatGPT user experience: Implications for education. *Available at* SSRN 4312418.

Zhai, X. (2023). ChatGPT for next generation science learning. *XRDS: Crossroads. The ACM Magazine for Students*, *29*(3), 42–46.

Zhang, X., Yang, S., Duan, L., Lang, Z., Shi, Z., & Sun, L. (2021, October). Transformer-XL With Graph Neural Network for Source Code Summarization. In *2021 IEEE International Conference on Systems, Man, and Cybernetics (SMC)* (pp. 3436-3441). IEEE. 10.1109/SMC52423.2021.9658619

Zheng, O., Abdel-Aty, M., Wang, D., Wang, Z., & Ding, S. (2023). ChatGPT is on the horizon: Could a large language model be all we need for Intelligent Transportation? *arXiv preprint arXiv:2303.05382*.

Zhong, Q., Ding, L., Liu, J., Du, B., & Tao, D. (2023). Can chatgpt understand too? a comparative study on chatgpt and fine-tuned bert. *arXiv preprint arXiv:2302.10198*.

Zhong, J., & Bhattacharya, K. (2002, November). Toward a competitive market for reactive power. *IEEE Transactions on Power Systems*, *17*(4), 1206–1215. doi:10.1109/TPWRS.2002.805025

Zhou, C., Li, Q., Li, C., Yu, J., Liu, Y., Wang, G., & Sun, L. (2023). A comprehensive survey on pretrained foundation models: A history from bert to chatgpt. *arXiv preprint arXiv:2302.09419*.

Zu, D. (2023). *Collective action and AI: The next stage in accelerating digital transformation*. University of Bremen.

About the Contributors

A. Anju received M.E degree in Computer Science Engineering from Sathyabama University, Chennai, India. She is having immense teaching and research experience of about 14 years. Since July 2013, she has been working as an Assistant professor in KCG College of Technology, Chennai, India. Her research area is on Network Security, Cyber Security, Machine Learning and Evolutionary Algorithms.

Shikha Arora is working as a faculty member in the area of HR, Organizational Behaviour and HR Analytics at Christ (Deemed to be University). She has done Ph.D. from Aligarh Muslim University. She has successfully completed certification in HR Analytics from IIM Rohtak. She is a gold medallist from IIT Kharagpur in the courses - Emotional Intelligence, Leadership; Gender Justice and Workplace Security. She has done PGDM from Lal Bahadur Shastri Institute of Management, New Delhi, and graduated from Delhi University. She has diverse professional and academic experience in leading management institutes and organizations such as the Institute of Technology and Science. The NIS Academy, Delhi, IABM and Business School of Delhi. She has published various articles and research papers in the area of HR Analytics, Competency Mapping and Leadership in National and International Journals. She has conducted several workshops and training programmes in the areas of Team Building, Leadership, Communication Skills and Stress Management for Faculty members of Dental, Pharmacy, Engineering and Management Colleges and for middle & senior level executives of reputed service sector organizations in Delhi/NCR region.

Hassan Badawy has more than twenty years of industry and academic experience in the field of tourism and Culture Heritage management, He held several positions in different professional, and academic entities including the Egyptian Ministry of Tourism, the British University in Egypt (BUE), The Faculty of Tourism and Hotels at Luxor University in Egypt, and several internationally funded tourism development projects. Graduated with a Bachelor's degree in tourism guidance, then got a master's and Ph.D. degrees in tourism, and then he got a Master's degree in cultural heritage management from Sorbonne University where he specialized in cultural tourism marketing. As an acknowledgment of his contribution and effort in academia and community development, he was awarded the Fulbright Scholarship in 2022 in tourism and Heritage studies. He also won different scholarships from different international organizations where he attended several tourism training programs. Invited as a keynote speaker at several international scientific Conferences and Seminars focusing on different topics especially sustainable development, cultural heritage management, Entrepreneurship, and heritage Tourism Marketing. Worked as a consultant and trainer for several international development projects funded by international organizations including USAID, UNDP, and UNWFP where he was responsible for developing several work plans to enhance employability in the tourism sector, he was also responsible for identifying training needs, developing training materials, and the delivery of the training. Supervised and evaluated several scientific research in areas and topics related to tourism marketing and sustainable development. Active in community services such as working as a voluntary start-up mentor with German Development Cooperation (GIZ), he also delivered different training programs on women's empowerment.

Ajay Bhardwaj received B.Tech. degree in Electrical Engineering from Swami Keshvanand Institute of Technology, Management & Gramothan, Jaipur, India in 2010 and M.Tech. degree in Power Systems from Rajasthan Technical University, Kota, India in 2017. He is currently pursuing Ph.D. degree in Power Systems at Rajasthan Technical University, Kota, India. His research interest includes electricity markets, power system restructuring, electricity economics, power trading, power system optimization and artificial intelligence.

Saumendra Das presently working as an Associate Professor at the School of Management Studies, GIET University, Gunupur, Odisha. He has more than 20 years of teaching, research, and industry experience. He has published more than 57 articles in national and international journals, conference proceedings, and book chapters. He also authored and edited six books. Dr Das has participated and presented many papers in seminars, conferences, and workshops in India and abroad. He has organized many FDPs and workshops in his career. He is an academician, author, and editor. He has also published two patents. He is an active member of various professional bodies such as ICA, ISTE and RFI. In the year 2023, he was awarded as the best teacher by Research Foundation India.

R. Adline Freeda has 18 years of teaching experience and she has received the B.E Degree and M.E in Computer Science and engineering and pursuing Ph.D. in Computer science and engineering from Hindustan Institute of Technology & Science, Tamil Nadu, India. Her current research interests include Machine learning, Software Engineering and Cloud Computing. . She is a Life Member of Computer Society of India. And published research papers in International Journals.

Riaz Israni completed his Master of Technology (M.Tech.) in Electrical Power System (EPS) from RK University, Rajkot, Gujarat, India. He is completed his Ph.D. in the area of renewable energy and power quality from RK University, Gujarat, India. He has more than 11 years of teaching and 3 years of industrial experience. He has published eight research/review papers in international journals and also presented six research/review papers in international conferences. He is the member of ISTE and IEEE.

Rajinder Kumar, currently working as Assistant Professor (Computer Science and Engineering), Department of Mathematics,Punjabi University Patiala.He obtained his B.Tech, M.Tech and Ph.D. in Computer Science and Engineering.He has taught various subjects at UG and PG level such as Data Structures and Algorithms, Advanced Data Structures, System Analysis and Design, Operating Systems, Computer System Architecture, Object Oriented Programming, Cyber Security, Network Security, Data base managemant system etc. Along with teaching and research. He has handled various administrative responsibilities such as department coordinator and training and placement office etc... He has more then 16 year of teaching and research experience. His main research interest are Cyber Security, Cyber Forensic, Cloud Computing, Secure routing protocols, load balancing in cloud and Information Security.

Shubham Kumar serves as an Assistant Professor in the Department of Computer science engineering at IIMT University, Meerut, Uttar Pradesh. He holds a Bachelor's degree in CSE from Ch. Charan Singh University and a Master degree in CSE from Punjab Engineering College Chandigarh. Research focuses on Medical Imaging with the help of image processing and various area, including image reconstruction and segmentation algorithms. Currently engaged in medical imaging research in DR. K. N. Modi University and IIMT University. I have published 8 research papers in international journals and conferences. I successfully qualified the GATE in computer science engineering additionally, I am a member of international and Professional organization like IAENG AND BVICAM MEMBER ID IS 14101.

Tajinder Kumar serves as an Assistant Professor in the Department of Information Technology Engineering at Seth Jai Parkash Mukand Lal Institute of Engineering and Technology, Radaur. He holds a Bachelor's degree in Computer Science from Kurukshetra University and a Master's degree in Computer Engineering, also from Kurukshetra University. His research focuses on various areas, including Biometrics, Image Processing, Software Engineering, and Agile methodologies. Currently engaged in Biometrics research at Punjab Technical University, Mr. Kumar has authored approximately 18 research papers published in international journals and conferences. He successfully qualified the UGC-NET in Computer Science and Applications in 2012. Additionally, he is a member of international and professional organizations, including IUCEE, CSI, IAASSE, IAENG, IAOIP, and ICAICR.

Sachin Lalar is working as Assistant Professor in Kurukshetra University in Department of Computer Science and Applications. He had received his Ph.D. in Computer Science and Engineering. He has more than 14 years' experience in teaching and research. His research interests are Computer Networks, Data Structure and Programming. He has visited many universities for presenting the research papers. Several research papers of his work published in the leading National and International Journals.

Sarfaraz Nawaz was born in Jaipur, Rajasthan, India. He received the B.E. degree from the Rajasthan University, Jaipur, in 2005 and M.Tech. degree from MNIT, Jaipur, in 2010 and Ph.D. degree from Poornima University in Jaipur and also working as Associate Professor and Head in department of Electrical Engineering, Swami Keshvanand Institute of Technology management and Gramothan, Jaipur. His research areas include applications of power distribution automation problems, distributed generation problems etc.

Tapaswini Panda is presently working as Guest Faculty at Model Degree College, Rayagada, Odisha. She has completed Master of Business Administration from GIET University, Gunupur, India. Her research interest is on Work Life Balance, Quality of Work Life and Human Resource Information System. She has published three patents in India and abroad. She is a passionate researcher and a true academician teaches the subject such as Principles of Management, Human Resource Management, Organizational Development and Change. She has published one paper in National Journal and two book chapters.

Debasis Pani received MBA from Sambalpur University and PhD from Berhampur University. He has been working as an Assistant Professor at GIACR Rayagada, affiliated to Biju Patnaik University of Technology, Rourkela for the last 16 years. His research interest include consumer behaviour and rural entrepreneurship.

Udaya Sankar Patro is presently working as a Lecturer at Rayagada Autonomous College, Rayagada, Odisha. He has completed a Master of Business Administration from GIET University, Gunupur, India. His research interest is on Workplace Spirituality, Work life Integrity and Human Resource Management. He has published three patents in India and abroad. He is a passionate researcher and a true academician who teaches the subjects such as Management and Theory Practices, Managerial Economics, and Human Resource Management. He has published one paper in National Journal and two book chapters.

R. Kanthavel has been in the teaching field for the last 20 years holding various positions as lecturer, assistant professor, professor, dean, vice principal, and principal in government and other reputed institutions. He has published more than 60 research articles in peer-reviewed journals and 110 international conferences. His research interests are sensor networks, embedded systems, cooperative communication, cloud computing, big data, IoT, and image processing. He has published technical books on microprocessor and microcontroller, fundamentals of computer programming, multi-core architecture, software architecture, mobile computing, electromagnetic theory, and social network analysis. He has also acted as resource person in the form of session chair, chief guest, and keynote speaker in many nationaland international-level workshops, seminars, and FDPs. He is a lifetime member of professional societies of IEEE, CSI, IETE, ISTE, and IACSIT.

R. Dhaya has 16 years experience in teaching and research in the field of Computer Science and Engineering. She published more than 80 research papers in peer reviewed international Journals. She was the recipient of IEI Young women Engineer award. Her areas of interests are wireless sensor networks, embedded systems, Machine Learning, Communication Systems.

V.S.Krithikaa Venket received the bachelor's and master's degrees in Information Technology from Dr.Sivanthi Aditanar College of Engineering. She is currently a Assistant Professor of Information Technlology at KCG College of Technology, Chennai. Her research interests include data mining and pattern recognition, Artificial Intelligence, machine learning and deep learning

Index

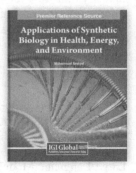

 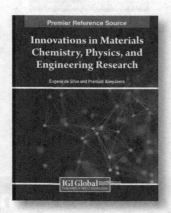 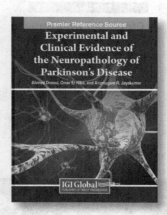 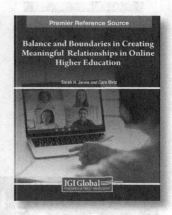

 www.igi-global.com

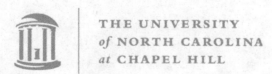